An Updated Edition

WOMEN & ALCOHOL IN A HIGHLAND MAYA TOWN

Water of Hope, Water of Sorrow

CHRISTINE EBER

University of Texas Press, Austin

Requests for permission to reproduce material from this work should be sent to
Permissions, University of Texas, Box 7819, Austin, TX 78713-7819.

♾ The paper used in this publication meets the minimum requirements of
American National Standard for Information Sciences—Permanence of Paper
for Printed Library Materials, ANSI Z39.48-1984.

Library of Congress Cataloging-in-Publication Data
Eber, Christine Engla.
    Women and alcohol in a highland Maya town : water of hope, water of
sorrow / Christine Eber. — rev. ed.
        p.   cm.
    Includes bibliographical references and index.
    ISBN: 978-0-292-72104-3
    1. Tzotzil women—Alcohol use.   2. Tzotzil women—Social conditions.
3. Tzotzil women—Religion.   4. Abused women—Mexico—Chenalhó.   5. Social
structure—Mexico—Chenalhó.   6. Feminist anthropology—Mexico—Chenalhó.
7. Chenalhó (Mexico)—Social conditions.   I. Title.
F1221.T9E24   1995
305.42′0972′75—dc20   94-31546

I have something to say to you,
something that passed before my eyes,
entered my heart,
one hour, one day, one year . . .
about God's gift of rum,
how his children use it and abuse it,
how they work together to control it,
to keep it beneath his flowery hands,
his flowery feet.

May these words enter your heart.
May they honor the people of Chenalhó.

Contents

List of Major Characters

Major characters are listed in order of appearance; members of their households or extended families, grouped under them, do not always enter the scene when they do. I have changed names and some circumstantial details in my narrative to protect anonymity.

Antonia, the woman I lived with my first year

> Domingo, her husband
> María, her mother
> Hilario, her father
> Felipe, her first son
> Sebastián, her second son
> baby, her one-year-old son
> Anita, her younger sister
> Marcela, her youngest sister
> Orlando, her older brother
> Francisco, her oldest brother
> Andrés, Anita's husband
> Moisés, Marcela's husband

Angélika, woman leader of the Feast of St. Peter

> Victorio, her husband
> Reina, her eldest daughter
> Pancha, her second eldest daughter
> Josefina, her youngest daughter
> Alejandro, her eldest son
> Enrique, her youngest son
> Daniel, Reina's baby
> Rafaela, Reina's daughter

Verónica, Protestant woman
> Ernesto, her husband
> Carmela, her daughter

Pascuala, woman I met through my survey
> Mariano, her husband
> Javier, her son

Otelia, shaman
> Bartolo, her husband
> Bernabé, her son
> Mónica, Bernabé's wife

Magdalena, shaman

Manuela, shaman

Juana, shaman
> Rogelio, her son
> Rosa, her daughter
> Rosita, her sister
> Salvador, Rosita's husband

Hilario, Otelia, and Juana have passed away since I conducted research for this book.

Acknowledgments

No change comes unequivocally.
ROBERT K. DENTAN

On December 6, 1988, around five A.M. I woke with a start in my hotel room in Mexico City. I was on my way home after fieldwork in San Pedro Chenalhó, highland Chiapas, Mexico. I lay in bed smiling because I had had a dream that made me feel content. I didn't get up and write it down in my journal because it was engraved in my mind and heart.

In my dream I was looking up to a tall figure that had come to give me something. The figure didn't seem to be on my plane, but to have come from somewhere above me. He or she bent down to me and put a book in my hands. The book was upside down but I could see that the words weren't in English. It seemed that they were either Tzotzil or Spanish.

It didn't seem to matter in my dream whether the figure was a man or a woman, but afterward I thought of it as a woman. She had long, light brown hair and a light colored face. She was wearing a long robe. The color seemed light, too. She smiled as she held the book out to me. It was a big, solid thing with gold letters on the cover. Matter of factly she said, "This is your *cargo*, the way you will serve your people."

Unlike Pedranos who receive callings to be shamans or leaders in dreams, I didn't have the sense to be afraid. In the pleasure of waking up to having had the sort of dream Pedranos have, I didn't think about the soul searching and long, lonely hours of writing that it would take for me to fulfill my cargo.

Seven years after that morning in Mexico City the first edition of this book was published. Although I had fulfilled my cargo dream, I had yet to learn my most important lessons about service and responsibility. While this book was in press the Zapatista uprising occurred. Several years later on December 22, 1997, 45 Pedranos were massacred by a paramilitary group. In 1998 the Mexican government stepped up repression of domestic and foreign research, increasing the risks of participating in research projects for both indigenous people and researchers. During the course of these tumultuous years my relationships with Pedrano friends and colleagues have taken on special value, and my debt of gratitude keeps mounting.

In Mexico I owe my greatest debt to the people of San Pedro Chenalhó, who befriended me and taught me about their traditions. I am especially grateful to my compadres, Antonia and Domingo, and to their children. Antonia, more than anyone, is responsible for helping me develop the understandings I offer in the epilogue to this book. I am also grateful to assistance from members of two women's cooperatives—Mujeres Marginadas (Marginalized Women), a Zapatista baking cooperative; and Tsobol Antzetik (Women United), a weaving cooperative. I am also indebted to the women shamans, Manuela, Margarita "La Meca," Margarita of Chenalhó, Catarina of Las Limas, and Catarina of Chenalhó, who shared their ritual knowledge and healing power with me and my people. Since this book was published, La Meca and Catarina of Las Limas passed away. So did Pablo, Antonia's father, and Joe, my American friend for whom I asked La Meca to pray. They are sorely missed. Other Pedranos generously shared with me their experiences of daily life. I would like to thank Francisco, Juana, María, Marta, Miguel, Rosa, Rosita, Angélika and Pablo, Anita and Antonio, Antonio and Petra, Lucía and Cristóbal, María and Manuel, Pancha and Bernabé, and Anita and Sebastián for being especially helpful to me.*

At home I owe my greatest debt to Robert Dentan and Elizabeth Kennedy. As my advisor in the Anthropology Department at the State University of New York at Buffalo, Bob made immeasurable contributions to the dissertation on which this book is based. From improving my writing to supporting me through the trials of graduate school and fieldwork, Bob has been a consummate advisor and friend. Liz went far beyond her role as a member of my thesis committee, spending long hours critiquing my work and helping me merge feminist and anthropological perspectives.

Many researchers and practitioners in several fields, including Anthropology, Alcohol Studies, Women's Studies, Religious Studies, and Latin American Studies, laid important foundations for my research. I am especially grateful to Nancy Modiano. Nancy introduced me to Chenalhó and my compadres, welcomed me into her family of friends, and gave generously of her advice and encouragement at every stage of my research and writing. Nancy died while I was finishing this book. I join with her many

* Other than here I use pseudonyms for Pedranos, except for Antonia and Domingo, whose real names I do not use here.

friends from Maya hamlets to U.S. cities in grieving the loss of a dear friend.

I am also grateful to June Nash for encouraging me to focus on local meanings and experiences, while helping me see how these fit into regional and historical trends. June's and others' contributions to a volume on drinking in highland Chiapas in the 1960s, edited by Henning Siverts, impressed me with the pivotal role drinking plays in relations between people and between people and their gods.

I also owe a great debt to Cuban anthropologist Calixta Guiteras-Holmes and to respected elder Manuel Arias for the book that resulted from interviews Guiteras-Holmes conducted with Arias in the 1950s. Arias' stories, analyses, and responses to Guiteras-Holmes' questions were rich sources of data for me. Arias and Guiteras-Holmes both died during my fieldwork. Jacinto Arias, Manuel's son, attended graduate school in the United States and wrote a thesis about Pedrano spirituality. Both Jacinto's thesis and book about Chenalhó have been a great help to me in writing this book.

I learned from many other people during the course of my research. Assistance from the following people was particularly helpful to me: Tomás Arias, Warren Barbour, Juan Blasco, Pete Brown, Bárbara Cárdenas, Geraldine Casey, Michel Chanteau, Ruth Chojnacki, José Vicente Comate, Graciela Freyermuth Enciso, Gary Gossen, Sigurd Gramstad, Dwight Heath, Angelika and Charlie Keil, Robert Laughlin, Ann McElroy, Carol-Jean McGreevy Morales, Brenda Miller, Heidi Moksnes, Guillermo Monteforte, Victor Montejo, Walter F. Morris, Rocio Palacio, Elias Pérez Pérez, Donna Platner, Robin O'Brian, José Vicente Resino, Susan Rippberger, Susanna Rostas, Diane and Jan Rus, Edward Starr, Carla and Vern Sterk, Phillips Stevens, Barbara Tedlock, Carter Wilson, Isabel Zambrano, and Guili Zobelein. This list would not be complete without Brenda Rosenbaum, who has been like a godmother to this book. Comparing my research in Chenalhó with hers in San Juan Chamula has taught me the importance of friendship.

For invaluable translation help both in Mexico and in the United States I thank Xalik Gusmán Lopes, Miguel Pérez Moreno, Agustín Nichim, Anita Ortiz Pérez, Antonio Pérez Pérez, Flor de Margarita Pérez Pérez, Victoria Quiroz-Becerra, Hileen Salas, and Agustín Ruíz Sánchez. Transcriptions and translations of the three prayers in this book represent the endpoint of an especially arduous process. I am indebted to Agustín for undertaking this work. I am also grateful to Robert Laughlin for correcting the final translations.

While preparing my ideas for inclusion in the epilogue to this updated edition I received helpful feedback from many colleagues. I would especially like to thank Jennifer Abbassi, Lisa Bond-Maupin, Graciela Freyermuth Enciso, Neil Harvey, Aída Hernández, Christine Kovic, Mac Marshall, Shannan Mattiace, Heidi Moksnes, Diane and Jan Rus, Heather Sinclair, Paul Spicer, Isabel Zambrano, the editorial collective at Latin American Perspectives, and colleagues in the panel "Alcohol and Drug Studies at the Millennium," organized by Linda Bennett for the 1998 International Union of Anthropological and Ethnological Sciences Congress.

While I wrote the first drafts of this book Sue Aki, Norma Kassirer, Shirley Lin, Laura McClusky, Michael Sticht, Donna Wyszomierski, and Zoe Zacharek gave generously of their feedback and emotional support. Reviewers for the University of Texas Press made many insightful comments. Theresa May of the University of Texas Press deserves my deepest gratitude for her abiding interest in my book and for her guidance in preparing a revised edition. I owe a special thanks to Sofia Bilgrami, Mike O'Malley, Tony Webster, and Rebecca Rodriguez for their editorial assistance. Students at Central Connecticut State University and New Mexico State University offered many insights that helped clarify key points I present in this book. I am especially grateful to graduate students in an advanced religion course at NMSU in fall 1999 for their feedback and support.

Several institutions and organizations provided the means for me to research, write, and speak about Pedranos' lives. I thank the National Institute on Alcohol Abuse and Alcoholism for funding the research on which this book is based. Additional funds for conducting research since the Zapatista uprising were provided by a New Mexico State University Mini Grant, an NMSU University Summer Research Grant, and an NMSU Mexico Small Grants Program grant.

Since I began my research in Chenalhó my family and friends have given me abundant expressions of love and support which I can never repay. I am especially grateful to my parents, Linnea and Woodrow Eber, to my husband, Michael O'Malley, and to my sister, Linda Laughlin. I'm also grateful to my stepchildren, Gabe and Krish, and my grandson, T. J., for encouraging me to draw as well as write. Among my Mexican friends, Violeta Malpica and Martha Rivera deserve my deepest thanks for befriending me when I stayed in San Cristóbal de Las Casas. Lastly, I thank Lisa Bond-Maupin, Gerrie Casey, Elaine Chamberlain, Shirley Chan, Carol Charnley, Filomena Critelli, Bobbie Grimm, Mary Hollifield, Maxine Insera, Joan Jacobs, Mary Kerwin, Weldon Lamb, Kathy Mang-Haag, Beth O'Leary, Amy Paylor, Tom Potts, Sylvia de Rosas, Hileen Salas, and Aileen Zarea for the generous and constant support they have given me and my Pedrano friends.

On Translations and Aids to Reading This Book

Writing this book I faced many translation and representation problems. The biggest problem was using written words to represent a people who consider talking the best way to analyze important issues. Although this contradiction is nothing new for anthropologists, each time we transform our field experiences into written works we rehash old issues and discover new ones.

Translating involved paying native Tzotzil speakers, bilingual in Spanish, to transcribe interviews for me as well as help me translate interviews into Spanish. Then I translated Spanish translations into English. In my first translations I tried to represent Pedranos' speech as dramatic events, preserving as much as possible particularities of Pedrano speech. However, reading these literal translations it seemed to me that what Pedranos were trying to say got lost in the maze of words on the page. Pedranos whom I knew to be astute commentators on events around them came off as either quaint poets or primitive, confused people. Since my priority is to convey to you as honestly as I can what I think Pedranos were saying to me and would want me to tell you, I decided that I would have to edit heavily and contextualize Pedranos' words within my narratives. If I have taken too many liberties, I hope that those Pedranos quoted will understand that my goal has been to represent them as the intelligent and generous people they are. (See Eber 1991: 58, 59 and 437, 438 to compare a lightly edited transcription of a story-telling event with a heavily edited version.)*

Translating Pedranas' prayers presented some unique problems. Agustín Ruíz Sánchez spent many months transcribing and translating the prayers that are excerpted in Chapter 8. I regret that space does not

---

* Translations not otherwise identified are my own.

permit me to reproduce these prayers in their entirety, nor in Tzotzil. I refer readers to my thesis (ibid.: 266–301, 485–526) for longer versions of each prayer and the full version of Juana's prayer in Tzotzil, Spanish, and English.

To refer to Indigenous women in Chenalhó I use *Pedrana/as*; *Pedrano/os* either refers to Indigenous men or to both Indigenous men and women, depending on the context. I use "Indigenous people" or "Native people" instead of "Indians" and "Spanish invasion" rather than "Conquest" in order to facilitate a view of contemporary Mayas as proud bearers of ancient and ever changing traditions, not abject, conquered peoples. I am grateful to Mayas who are writing about their own history for bringing the connotations of "Indian" and "Conquest" to my attention.

Orthography

To pronounce Mayan languages one follows many conventions of modern Spanish and some that colonial friars adopted when they transcribed these languages into Spanish. The Tzotzil pronunciation guide which follows incorporates standardizations of Tzotzil into a pronunciation model of Mayan languages found in Schele and Miller (1986: 7).

In Tzotzil, vowels are independent syllables, except when "u" precedes a, e, i, or o. In these cases "u" is pronounced like the English "v." Otherwise one pronounces vowels as in Spanish: a is like "a" in "car," e is like "e" in "hey," i is like the double "e" in "see," o is like the "o" in "broken," u is like the double "o" in "too."

Tzotzil has both plain and glottalized consonants. Glottalized consonants appear with an apostrophe after the letter. They include: p', t', tz', ch', k', and b. English speakers make a glottal stop, i.e., stopping the air between two consonants or syllables by closing the voice box, when they say "u'uh" to mean "no." To Tzotzil speakers glottal stops distinguish vastly different words. For example, *takin* = "dry," while *tak'in* = "money."

Indigenous writers in Highland Chiapas have been working with linguists and anthropologists to devise ways to write Tzotzil phonemes more simply. I have standardized the orthography in this book in accordance with the system used by *Sna Jtz'ibajom* (House of the Writer), Escritores Indígenas (Indigenous Writers), INEA/Instituto Nacional de Educación para Adultos (The National Institute for Adult Education), and INAREMAC/ Instituto de Asesoría Antropológica para la Región Maya, A.C. (Maya Region Applied Anthropology Institute). The new orthography recognizes the following phonemes: a, i, e, o, u, p, t, tz, ch, k, p', t', tz', ch', k', b (occluded glottalized sonorous consonant), v, s, x (a silent alveopalatal fricative like English "sh"), h, j, m, n, l, r, and y. Glottalized consonants include: p', t', tz', ch', k' , and b. The new orthography represents glottal stops between vowels, e.g., "chi'iltak" ("friends"), with " ' " .

Whereas in the past linguists and anthropologists differed over whether to use "c" and "k" for the "k" phoneme, the new orthography uses "k." The new orthography also uses "k'" in place of "q'u." Other replacements include "tz" for "ts" and "j" for "h".

Author's Note: Throughout this book, in place of "Catholic Action" readers should substitute "The Word of God." This is the phrase Pedranos use for "The Preferential Option for the Poor," the progressive movement of the Catholic Church in Chiapas under the direction of Bishop Samuel Ruiz García (1960–1999). Catholic Action predated The Preferential Option for the Poor, which the Conference of Latin American Bishops (CELAM) officially embraced in 1968 in Medellín, Colombia. The Option for the Poor is one facet of a "theology of liberation" being articulated by Catholic theologians in response to poverty and social inequality throughout Latin America.

Since the first edition of this book was published, many Catholics struggling for social justice in Chiapas have been persecuted. The Mexican government has expelled several priests known for their defense of human rights. In 1997 Michel Chanteau (Padre Miguel), the priest in Chenalhó for thirty-two years, was deported to his native France.

Preface

Reina

Reina,
baby on her back,
small child pasted to her side,
ladles a bowl of cane liquor
from her plastic bucket.

Every Sunday in a small town
she ladles for pesos.

Good Indian girls,
backs bent under sacks of corn,
step aside on trails.
Pass uncle, they say
and the man passes.

Women
like Reina
sell chicha on the trails to town
and there's no stepping aside.
Enter uncle, they say
and the man enters.

At twenty-five
she has birthed two bastard babies,
mashed mountains of sugar cane
and hoed her father's fields

and every Sunday she ladles for pesos.

I knew her from the night her first son
dropped into candlelight.
Clutching the bed, instead of a husband,
she was silent.
I nearly died,
she told me later.

I brought her tamales
a hat for the baby
and news from outside.

But the biggest news was Reina.

Did you hear the news about Reina?
Did you hear the news?
Did you hear?

It was the last day of a sacred fiesta.
Reina came outside with her children
to see the dusty saints squint in bright sun
and drink in incensed air.

How the mortals whispered
behind their woven shawls
and bowls of cane liquor.

Good Catechists
not wanting to cast the first stone
skipped little pebbles instead,

Did you hear the news about Reina?
Did you hear about Reina?
Did you hear?
Did you hear?
Did you?

Breasts swathing infant head
skirt sheltering her young child,
Reina heard only the saints,

It's time to change
It's time to change
dear Reina

It's time.

She buys a big metal pot,
12,000 pesos.
She will make a hot rice drink instead.
It's better, Reina tells me.

Now Reina
ladles up sweet rice
lulling the whispers within
and without her

every Sunday
in a small town.

I wrote "Reina" shortly after returning home from thirteen months of fieldwork in southern Mexico. I came back to a house full of reminders of a chapter in my life that preceded graduate school. There were all the drawings, stories, and an occasional poem that I had stuffed into closets and drawers while studying to be an anthropologist. In San Pedro Chenalhó, the Highland Chiapas township where I conducted fieldwork, the artist in me surfaced again, and I learned from this perspective as well as from a social science one.

"Reina" speaks specifically to my efforts to understand the contradiction between Indigenous women's strengths and their subservient position, a subject I turn to at many points in this book. Women's status, like drinking, provoked many conflicting feelings in myself and others with whom I have shared my research and writing. In Mexico one doesn't have to look hard to see how Indigenous men and *Ladinos* (non-Indigenous Mexicans) dominate Indigenous women. But over the year and a half I lived in Highland Chiapas I also witnessed how women's adherence to their people's collective traditions rewards them and helps them survive with dignity in difficult times. I saw this watching Reina's mother serve her community as the leader of a traditional fiesta. I also saw it living with Antonia, a young woman who has been organizing her kinswomen into weaving cooperatives.

Antonia, with whom I lived during my first year, understood that I had come to learn her language and how her people see drinking. She had ventured outside her culture enough to know that Ladinos and *Gringos* (light-skinned people from foreign countries) have different relations to their families and communities. Her keen mind enabled her to see her people through outsiders' eyes. Sometimes this other vision of her people made her self-conscious, but generally she was proud to live in a hamlet and follow her ancestors' ways. It was different with Reina. As a single woman with children living on the fringes of Ladino society, Reina had little to lose by her association with me. Reina didn't hold back, from the day we met wrapping steamed corn in leaves for the patron saint fiesta until we said goodbye in a restaurant in San Cristóbal de Las Casas, the urban center of Highland Chiapas. Reina and I each saw in the other someone who did not fit prescribed roles. Reina must have thought I would understand her situation when she asked me to be with her the night her second child was born.

Reina was in the last month of her pregnancy when we met. I had come to observe and participate in preparations for the patron saint fiesta in which Reina's parents were the leading religious celebrants. Early on the second day of the fiesta I went with Reina and her two younger sisters to cut weeds for her aunt's bulls. I watched with admiration as Reina wielded the machete. In the afternoon she asked me to come with her to visit a "friend." The friend was a midwife, and after examining Reina she said her baby would be born that night. On the way to find a room in which to have the baby Reina cried, and told me that this would be her second child. She would now have two children by two different men, and neither wanted to marry her. She said that her father and older brother wanted to kill her, and her mother had too many responsibilities to help her now. She asked me to stay with her that night. I stayed with Reina and tried to support her; but it was the first time I had seen a baby born. My awe and the speed with which everything happened left me feeling helpless. Fortunately, the midwife knew her work. Reina delivered her baby girl into candlelight onto a piece of plastic where she knelt, fully clothed, gripping the side of a bed.

As I learned about Reina and her family I was reminded of victims of abuse and children of alcoholics in the United States. Like American women in abusive situations, Reina and her mother and sisters have suffered emotionally and physically. Like them they often deny the extent of their pain and rationalize their own and others' actions. But in other important ways they are different. While abused women in my society frequently have nowhere to go, Pedranas have strong families and traditions through

which they find meaning and fulfill important work for their people. Angélika, Reina's mother, serves her people and their Gods in communal duties
called *cargos*. Pedranos say that this work is as important as the work they do
to feed and clothe their families. Along with her daughters Angélika cares for
her grandchildren, while Reina supports her children through selling *chicha*,
a fermented sugar cane drink, and *atole*, a hot rice drink. The women laugh
and joke in the fields, in the marketplace, and around the fire at home. I
never heard them blame themselves, as abused women often do in my society, although I discovered that they felt isolated and ashamed at times.

In 1987, inspired by feminist scholars, I went into the Highlands of
Chiapas determined to engage with Indigenous women, to offer them a forum to speak. I found that women's shyness, Pedranos' reserve in front of
strangers, the patriarchal structures of Pedrano society, and my own discomfort about intruding in people's lives, made it difficult to collaborate
with women in this way. I also discovered that one needs many years to
develop facility in other languages, to build trust and reciprocity and to
understand another society. That I was able to make progress toward these
goals with a few people in the year and a half I was in Chenalhó attests
to Pedranos' generosity and courage and my willingness to let Pedranos
teach me about humility.

Since my first year of fieldwork I've been in varying states of anguish
and fear about my responsibility to the Pedranos with whom I began a relationship in 1987. In Chenalhó I saw how power relations affect people's
lives. Children cried from hunger. Friends died in the prime of their lives.
Listening to the sorrow women expressed in their drunk songs haunted
me. I couldn't be ironic and detached.

Back home, faced with the task of conveying my own and Pedranos'
experiences of power and powerlessness, I experimented with various
writing styles. My models were the works of feminist anthropologists as well
as ethnographies using interpretive or reflexive methods. Through these approaches anthropologists have been exploring their presence in the communities they study and how this shapes their findings. Until quite recently
anthropologists wrote their ethnographies as if they were standing off at a
distance, casting a critical eye on some "exotic other" (e.g., Malinowski 1961;
Evans-Pritchard 1940). The strongest deterrent from including subjective experiences in these earlier reports was the received social science wisdom that
feelings are not valid, i.e., they are not falsifiable data. Consequently, allusions to an ethnographer's feelings or relationships with the people he or she
studied appeared in footnotes, an afterword, an appendix, or a memoir.

While I was inspired by the attention to ethnographers' experiences
and representational issues in recent ethnographies, many of these works

failed to help me better understand the people studied. Others did not make connections between power relations in the field and the ongoing effects of imperialism. By portraying fieldwork as a painful or "unruly dialogical encounter" (di Leonardo 1989), still others seemed to background the voices of the people being studied, to slight the struggles in which women and non-Western people are engaged to define their experiences in their own terms. As Antonia once told me, "Books don't matter to us. We don't have time to read. What matters to us is that our children are sick and die, that they don't have food to eat, clothes to wear." Although my representational approach combines both reflexive and feminist perspectives, I have found the political grounding of feminist perspectives most useful to confront issues of power and to foreground Pedranos' voices.[1]

In order to preserve the power of Pedrano beliefs and analyses and to show how I came to understand these, I have woven them into the story that follows. The storytelling medium seems close to the communal values Pedranos shared with me and offers a means to integrate subjective experiences with objective data. I believe that it also preserves the holistic perspective so important in anthropological research, while still allowing readers to make cross-cultural comparisons.

The story which follows begins by placing Pedranos' experiences within the literature about drinking and gender cross-culturally, and the history of Ladino/Native relations in Highland Chiapas (Chapters 1 and 2). Then it moves to a point in our separate and shared histories when Pedranos were experiencing tremendous social change and I was estranged from everything familiar. You will come to know Antonia and Reina, and several other women and men who befriended me and taught me about how their people regard drinking and gender relations. Focusing on my relationships with specific women and their families, I try to show how these women express differences between themselves, between themselves and their kinsmen, and between each of them and me. I explore the differences that matter to them and ways they are trying to resolve personal and collective conflicts. As the story evolves, I treat changes in my understanding of problem drinking and social relations in Chenalhó and in my own society.

On one level this is a universal tale of fieldwork. On another level it is an account of my relationships with a handful of people in a particular time and place. I hope that this story, born as it was in a community of story tellers and listeners, will inspire you to tell it again.

Women and Alcohol in a Highland Maya Town

1 Frameworks and Methods

Compulsive drinking and its consequences are social problems every-where. Although research on this subject has been increasing in recent years, researchers have only begun to consider alcohol's effects on women and their families. I chose to study women's relation to alcohol use and compulsive drinking because it is a topic relevant to women's lives cross-culturally and to my own experiences. In my marriage to a recovering alcoholic I have come to understand problems alcoholics and their families in my society face. As an anthropologist I am interested in how people's experiences with alcohol differ historically and cross-culturally. My review of the literature about alcoholism available in the mid-1980s indicated that scholars have given little attention to the diversity of women's experiences with alcohol and how these change over time. A preliminary trip to High-land Chiapas in 1985 confirmed that alcohol is an important issue to In-digenous women there.

The major questions that guided my research of women's experiences with ritual and problem drinking in San Pedro Chenalhó were: How is women's relationship to alcohol changing in Chenalhó, and how are Pe-dranas handling their own and others' drinking problems?

Several conceptual frameworks inevitably collide in efforts to study women's experiences and connections between gender and drinking in colonized communities. Perspectives include the colonizers' points of view, documented in reports from missionaries, government officials, settlers, and early travel writers; the perspectives of anthropologists and other scholars documented in ethnographies and reports; the perspective which the researcher has chosen; and the varied points of view of men and women in the communities studied. While colonial and anthropological perspectives are relevant to this study, I have tried to make Pedranos' perspectives paramount. Combining contemporary feminist and reflexive frameworks in anthropology enabled me to focus on Pedranos' ideas, while intermeshing them with my own and those of other anthropologists.

Conceptual Frameworks on Gender

The Spanish colonizers who came to Mexico in the early 1500s frequently feared and hated Indigenous people. They recognized, but condemned, their egalitarian attitudes and were shocked by the independence of women. Ethnohistorical studies of Indigenous women in North, Central, and South America (e.g., Burkhart 1992; Hellbom 1967; Nash 1978, 1980; Silverblatt 1987) indicate the important economic and social roles women filled before the Spanish invasion.

Early ethnographers studying peasants, like Pedranos, depicted women as passive victims. What they saw appeared congruent with Western conceptions of family, economics, and politics, i.e., men controlled public offices and women did low status child care and housework. Their preoccupation with male forms of power led them to see women's exclusion from the political realm as evidence of their insignificance. It follows that they did not consider men's lack of access to the women's world significant.[1]

Feminist researchers try to avoid research strategies which lead us to generalize from data about men to communities at large. Following their lead, I have studied drinking from women's points of view in order to balance the ethnographic record on drinking in Highland Chiapas.

In their fieldwork experiences feminist scholars frequently find their mindsets and concepts inadequate to understand gender relations in diverse cultural contexts. For example, a mindset based on rationality and prediction does not help one understand life in communities, like Chenalhó, where people do not draw strong lines between visible and invisible realms of experience. Similarly, the domestic/public dichotomy and the idea of the nuclear family as the natural nurturing unit do not necessarily fit non-Western gender systems. Gender, itself, is a concept that anthropologists are continually reworking to illuminate its connection to other ways people differentiate themselves, including race, class, caste, and ethnicity. My research contributes to these aims by shedding new light on Western concepts about gender and drinking, including: "self," "family," "community," "power," and "dependency."

Attempting a women-centered study, I build on the groundwork laid by women anthropologists studying sex-role variability in the 1930s and 1940s, e.g., Kaberry 1939, Mead 1949, and Underhill 1936. Since these pioneering studies and the spread of the women's liberation movement in the United States, cross-disciplinary and cross-cultural dialogue on women and gender has increased greatly. Contemporary feminist anthropologists draw on the rich legacy of their foremothers as well as insights that women from diverse cultural backgrounds offer, to refine several theoretical approaches to studying women and gender. In this study I rely on two major frameworks—symbolic and materialist. I also draw to a lesser extent from psychological perspectives.[2]

Feminists who study gender from the point of view of symbolic systems and the socialization of gender, interpret gender constructions as expressions of cultural values that maintain a cultural system (e.g., Rosaldo 1974, 1980; Collier and Rosaldo 1981; Ortner and Whitehead 1981; Rosaldo and Lamphere, eds. 1974; MacCormack and Strathern 1980). These scholars suggest that gender asymmetry and male dominance may be universal.

Feminists informed by a historical materialist perspective explain changes in gender relations on the basis of economic systems. They argue that gender asymmetry and male dominance are not universal, but the products of changing material conditions (e.g., Leacock 1972, 1983; Leacock and Nash 1977; Nash 1980).

Feminist researchers taking a psychological perspective study how different groups engender and reproduce ideas about relations between the sexes. They take child rearing and family relations as their data (e.g., Bunzel 1940; Chodorow 1974; Dinnerstein 1975). Comparing alcoholism in two Maya communities, Chamula and Chichicastenango, Ruth Bunzel (ibid.) applied psychoanalytic interpretations.

In the anthropological literature about Latin America, scholars are beginning to integrate gender issues into their studies and to treat more seriously how people construct their past and present histories (di Leonardo 1991: 29). In this book I try to address the social constructionist perspective by presenting Pedranos as actors who shape the social relations in which they are involved. Specifically, I have used Pedranas' life histories to elucidate collective traditions and one community's responses to change.[3]

Conceptual Frameworks on Drinking

Conceptual frameworks also collide in research about drinking. Perhaps the most important contribution anthropologists have made to alcohol research is the discovery that people learn how to act when they are drunk. People everywhere expect drunken people to act differently from sober ones, but drunken comportments are diverse (MacAndrew and

Edgerton 1969). As feminist anthropologists are doing for gender, anthropologists studying drinking are examining how culture, politics, and economic factors interact to shape drinking in specific times and places.

Indigenous people throughout the Americas have had a similar relationship to colonial powers, but a different relationship to alcohol. While Indigenous peoples in Mesoamerica had integrated fermented drinks into the fabric of their lives long before Spaniards invaded their lands, few Indigenous groups in North America used fermented drinks; those that did were mostly in the southwestern United States, and limited their drinking to specific rituals (MacAndrew and Edgerton 1969: 100).

During the colonial era Indigenous people soon learned the not-so-divine qualities of distilled spirits. They also learned new drunken comportment from colonists and internalized at least some of these outsider's views of them when they became drunk. Colonists who plied Indigenous people with liquor, whether they were Canadian trappers or Ladino plantation owners, either saw them as pitiful sots who could not hold their liquor or as dangerous crazies.[4]

As the wounds of colonialism festered and the pain of separation from their families, their lands, and their traditions deepened, Indigenous people turned more and more to drinking. Many Native people continued to drink in out-of-control ways, and almost everyone concluded that "Indians can't hold their liquor." Native communities most devastated by alcohol lost the collective knowledge of how to show respect and tenderness toward each other and their gods (Shkilnyk 1985). Tragically, stereotypes of "drunken Indians" who neglect their children persist today in the minds of many Native and non-Native Americans. But historical research indicates that before Europeans arrived, Indigenous people throughout the Americas kept their drinking under strict control; ethnographic studies indicate the high value traditional cultures placed on tender and respectful bonds between children and adults. In the 1990s many Native American communities are models to the world of effective community solutions to problem drinking.[5]

In contrast to Native societies before the European invasion, Western peoples have learned that alcohol is incapacitating, morally and physically. In heterogeneous Western societies people lack clear and consistent teaching about limits and sanctions on drinking. Variable behavior is predictable and in fact occurs (MacAndrew and Edgerton 1969).

Anthropologists find a "time-out" attitude about drinking across cultures. Perhaps because the physiological effects of alcohol are obvious and easily monitored, it makes a good vehicle for "time-out" (Marshall 1979; Bunzel 1940).

As feminists are doing for gender, anthropologists studying drinking are also reconstructing Western concepts and definitions of "alcoholism." Alcohol researchers and practitioners in the treatment field subscribe to a definition of alcoholism which views it as a homogeneous, progressive, irreversible, permanent, and incurable "biopsychosocial disease" (Heath 1988: 353). The definition incorporates several characteristics, including withdrawal symptoms, loss of control, severe damage to the body, and social, emotional, and behavioral problems (Chalfant and Roper 1980).

Counselors in treatment facilities in the United States also distinguish between "alcohol abusers" and "alcohol dependent" people (American Psychiatric Association 1987). In the first category they include people who have problems associated with their drinking, but who do not necessarily fulfill dependency criteria. Counselors determine dependency when a person has at least three out of a list of nine symptoms (ibid.: 167–168).

Anthropologists often find the disease framework of alcoholism limiting, due to a lack of fit between the focus on individual "pathologies" centered on loss of control (Room 1984), and the ethnographic record which indicates that loss of control is not intrinsic to drunken comportment (MacAndrew and Edgerton 1969). Ethnographic evidence suggests that many peoples do not view alcohol as problematic, and that few think of it as a major factor in the etiology of a debilitating disease. Ethnographic studies have suggested that drinking is integrative and functional for most of the world's people (Heath 1981). This observation has led ethnographers to apply their theories to patterns and trends of alcohol use and the functions that drinking or drunkenness seem to serve in particular environments at specific times (see Heath 1988: 359–396 for an overview of theoretical frameworks).

Ethnographic studies indicate that brewing alcoholic beverages is often the women's domain in much of the developing world (Kennedy 1978; Colson and Scudder 1988), and when ritual drinking is an important part of communal obligations, women often participate on a par with men (Allen 1988; Kennedy 1978). Although women participate extensively in producing, distributing, and consuming alcoholic beverages cross-culturally, studies indicate that women tend to drink less in amount, less often, and in less varied circumstances than do men (Heath 1991: 177).

References to drinking in Highland Chiapas a generation ago by Native scholars, anthropologists, and their students (Arias 1973; Cancian 1965; Collier 1968; Gossen 1974; Guiteras-Holmes 1961; Laughlin 1963, 1976; Linn 1976; Nash 1973, 1985; Navarette-Pellicer 1988; Siskel 1974; Vogt 1969; and Wilson 1973) demonstrate that drinking in Indigenous communities was woven into the social and sacred fabric of life. But studies also reveal that it brought suffering (Collier 1973; Haviland 1977; Lacy 1976; Pozas 1959, 1962; Wali 1974; and Wilson 1966).

Scholars in other fields, however, criticize anthropologists for deemphasizing problems (Room 1984). Anticipating this critique, some ethnographers have undertaken longterm studies of drinking. For example, Colson and Scudder (1988) state that if they had written on drinking among the Gwembe Tonga of Zambia in the 1950s, they would have described it as socially integrated. However, after thirty years of studying changes in gender roles, the arrival of new technology, and the penetration of a cash economy, they report that traditional controls can no longer keep heavy drinking from destroying much of Gwembe Tonga social life. Reevaluating his research on drinking in Truk, Federated States of Micronesia, Marshall (1991) states that changes in Truk and in himself forced him to revise his earlier position that men's drinking was unproblematic. Marshall attributes these changes to Trukese women finding their voices in a prohibition movement, and his attention to what they were saying (Marshall 1991; Marshall and Marshall 1990).

Based on recent studies (e.g., Menéndez 1992), anthropologists would do well to take the "problem deflation" critique and women's analyses of drinking seriously. A recent National Health Survey of the prevalence of alcohol use and concerns it causes families, in 54,000 rural and urban households in Mexico, indicates high use of alcohol among young people under eighteen and "worrisome drinking habits" among one-fourth of men between 30 and 49 years of age (Solache-Alcaraz et al. 1990). Listening to Pedranas tell me about problem drinking and then later analyzing what they told me, I came to believe that drinking has probably always been more problematic in most societies, particularly during stressful times, than seems apparent from the ethnohistorical record. Staying only one year in a community and talking mostly to men, anthropologists are not able to get much past normative drinking, which in most societies isn't problematic for most of the population. To learn about deviations from norms it takes time, and talking with people of all ages and groups.

Recent studies focusing on women's drinking in Western societies indicate that women's and men's drinking differ and that women problem drinkers face greater risks and barriers to treatment than men who drink (NIAAA 1990). Findings include: (1) among women drinkers in the United States, those who drink the most equal or surpass men in the numbers of problems resulting from drinking (Wilsnack, Wilsnack, and Klassen 1984); (2) controlling for body weight and height and given equal quantities of ingested alcohol, a woman's blood alcohol level rises faster than a man's (Jones and Jones 1976); (3) the detrimental effects of alcohol on the liver are more severe for women than for men; and (4) women alcoholics have death rates 50% to 100% higher than those of men alcoholics (Van Den Berg 1991).

Feminist scholars studying alcohol stress the negative effects on diverse groups of men and women of the competitive and hierarchical conditions capitalism and patriarchy engender (e.g., ibid.). Some scholars indicate that powerful groups selectively define the uses and effects of alcohol to benefit their interests (Morgan 1987: 129; Kilbourne 1991). For example, men have applied the disinhibitory effects of alcohol negatively to women's alcohol use, stating that when women drink compulsively they either neglect their nurturing roles or "act out" sexually. While the former attitude defines women's societal roles on a narrowly domestic basis, the latter masks the fact that women's public drunkenness is likely to put them at risk for rape (Gomberg 1982: 21).

Feminists working with problem drinkers in the United States criticize a tendency to overmedicalize and individualize problems, to develop treatment based on gender stereotypes, and to slight societal and historical processes contributing to alcohol use (e.g., Marsh, Colten, and Tucker 1982). While they note a broadening dialogue on these issues, they argue that the prevailing disease model of "family dysfunction" obscures unequal power relations within families and attributes a range of emotional and social problems to a family disease treatable through a path of prescriptive behaviors (Haaken 1993). Even when the various twelve-step programs, such as Alcoholics Anonymous, affirm women's outrage over their legacy as caregivers and assert women's right to self-determination, they fail to account for the range of women's experiences within families, and the extra-familial networks of support women create when poverty, sexism, and racism undermine their capacities to provide for themselves and their children (ibid.: 341). Mutual or self-help programs tend to perpetuate the status quo by taking the middle class family as the primary social unit and by applying the disease label to women's real conflicts and the strategies they have devised to deal with these conflicts (ibid.).

Based on numerous studies which reveal that women with drinking problems are much more likely to have experienced sexual abuse as children or to have experienced severe family violence than non-alcoholic women (e.g., Research Institute on Alcoholism 1991), feminists urge placing alcohol problems within the context of other women's issues, such as violence, incest, and sexual abuse. In their treatment proposals they stress respect for women's relationships and understanding cultural contexts of drinking and culturally different notions of power and dependence.[6] For example, Pedranos who value interdependence between people, and between humans and the gods, appear dependent and unhealthy measured against a formulaic program of individual spiritual recovery. Yet, Pedranos' ongoing commitment to rebuilding their wounded communities, at the same time as they treat their wounded selves, may be both more humane and workable than treatment philosophies which fail to address the limited possibilities within American society for healing (Haaken 1993).

Through addressing historical processes and integrating gender as a central construct in the etiology and treatment of problem drinking, feminist researchers are bridging a gap between studies in Western societies, largely problem and treatment oriented, and studies of non-Western societies, usually ethnographic and relativistic. Feminist researchers try to see the people and communities they study as both bearers of particular cultures and needing support for specific problems, often stemming from legacies of economic and social inequality.

A central task of my research was to understand ideas of power and social relations in Pedrano society. Although I asked questions relevant to any society (e.g., who wields power, how does one acquire power, who has the power to define problems, and who has the power to say how one can heal), I extended these questions beyond social contexts to the articulation between cosmic and transcendental phenomena. Based on their studies of non-Western societies, feminist anthropologists argue that although different in form, women's power arrangements are as significant as men's (e.g., Weiner 1976 on Trobriand women; Bell 1983 on Australian aboriginal women). In Highland Chiapas, while women do not hold political offices, they obtain power through the highly charged relationships they forge with their deities or ancestors during communal rituals (Rosenbaum 1993). In these rituals they interweave social and cosmic realms and control powerful symbolic substances, such as alcohol.

Pedranos' Perspectives on Drinking and Gender

Pedranos differ in the ways they relate to alcohol and other important aspects of social life. This study attempts to sort out their differences and discuss the contradictions which rise from them.

Pedranos now divide themselves into Traditionalists; members of various Protestant groups; and followers of Catholic Action, the Liberation Theology movement in Highland Chiapas. "Do you have religion?" was one of the first questions almost every Pedrano asked me. I discovered that "having religion" means listening to pastors and catechists (lay leaders) read passages from the Bible, or reading these oneself if one can read, and then using these words as guides in place of the oral traditions of the ancestors.

When someone asked me if I had religion I would tell them the truth, that I was raised Presbyterian, but now I respect all religions and want to learn about them.[7] No one accepted this explanation, except perhaps Antonia and Domingo, with whom I had time to discuss at length how variations of Protestants and Catholics in my country differ from those in Chenalhó. Except for Antonia and Domingo, most Pedranos seemed to be saying that if I didn't take a side, I didn't stand for anything, and that was truly pitiful. By the time I left Chenalhó my heart was somewhere between the Traditionalist camp and Catholic Action.

Traditionalists maintain an intimate relationship with Maya dieties and Catholic saints, which they have worshipped side by side in their communities since the Spanish invasion. Traditionalists generally say that alcohol is integral to the welding of the two symbolic systems and to forging reciprocal and complementary relations between people. They say that drinking makes their hearts happy and pleases the Gods. They also say it brings problems. When they recognize a drinking problem Traditionalists treat it as they do all physical and emotional problems, through prayer and dreams.

Members of Catholic Action stand midway between Traditionalists and Protestants. Catholic Action followers share with Traditionalists a respect for traditional fiestas and cargos. With Protestants they share a commitment to Bible study. Catholic Action members may or may not maintain a close relationship with Maya traditions, and say that it is acceptable to the saints to offer soft drinks in place of rum at fiestas and other rituals. Some Catholics favor abstinence, while others favor moderation. In contrast to Traditionalists, these people are more likely to see drinking as problematic and to seek care from doctors, but often while under a shaman's care as well.

Protestant groups are by no means homogeneous, even though most Pedranos use "Evangélicos" ("Evangelicals") to cover all Protestants. Protestant groups in Chenalhó in 1988 included: (1) Presbyterians, the first to arrive and the largest group; (2) Baptists; (3) The Church of Christ; (4) Jehovah's Witnesses; (5) Pentecostals; (6) Seventh Day Adventists; and (7) Mormons, the smallest group. Pedranos spoke of going to see Spiritists, but to my knowledge no Spiritists had organized a group in Chenalhó by 1988.

Conversion to Protestant sects in Chenalhó is increasing rapidly. Protestants estimate their numbers at a third of the township population of roughly 25,000. Protestants do not worship Maya deities nor Catholic saints, whom they consider idols. They link rum drinking in fiestas with worshiping idols and wasteful, wanton behavior. Protestants promote abstinence and private capital accumulation, and reject shamanic cures, preferring the care of Ladino doctors.

Knowing that Traditionalists suspect that strangers who associate with Protestants are missionaries who think drinking is sinful, I decided to leave my interviews with Protestants until later in my research. I regret that I was not able to spend the same amount of time and effort to identify with Protestants, as I did with Traditionalists and Catholic Action followers.

Methods

I geared my methods toward establishing a dialogue between Pedranos and myself while I was in the field; since returning home I have tried to sustain that dialogue. A necessary task toward this end was to become conversant in Tzotzil, the major Maya language of Highland Chiapas. Tzotzil was important for my study because most Pedranas over thirty are monolingual in Tzotzil. I usually recorded interviews that I conducted in Tzotzil, so that I could go over them with helpers and catch parts I had missed or misunderstood.

Although I tried to work on many levels, I focused on household relations. Several questions guided my study of family life and drinking (Heath 1981: 10): What do Pedranos learn about meanings and uses of alcohol? Who learns which meanings and uses, and how do they learn these? What are the effects of such knowledge on drinking and the results of drinking? How are meanings and uses changing?

My primary method was participant-observation, the cornerstone of anthropological research. Living in one household off and on for thirteen months and dividing my time between several others for another six months, I observed how families deal with power, intimacy, and boundaries, with and without alcohol. I noted how each individual related to herself or himself, alcohol, other people, and spiritual entities. By living in the societies they study, ethnographers actually see what people do, which is often different from what they say they do. Sustained observation and participation also has the advantage of revealing behavior and ideas about which people may feel ambivalent or confused (Heath 1988: 375). For example, violence associated with drinking is a world-wide concern; however it is not something of which most people are proud. Not surprisingly, it wasn't until I returned to Chenalhó for a second time that I realized the importance of this problem for Pedranas.

To find out how Pedranos define kinds of drinkers and drinking and how they distinguish between routinized and extraordinary problems I used the following techniques: observing and recording drinking events; in-depth interviews with Pedranos about their own and others' drinking; a household survey of forty-five households in one hamlet; recording Traditionalists, Catechists, and Protestants talking about their neighbors' drinking; and asking some literate Pedranos and nurses in rural clinics to write descriptions of women they knew who were problem drinkers or who had come to them for help with health problems related to drinking. I also collected folklore, and listened to gossip about drinkers and gender relations. As Haviland (1977) discovered in his study of gossip in Zinacantán, gossip is one of the best sources of information about what is important to people. Of themes in the corpus of gossip stories Haviland (ibid.: 207) collected, which include divorce, kin disputes, illicit sexual relations, and wealth and poverty, drinking is the one which most frequently occurs. Drinking is also a recurring theme in court cases in Chenalhó (Sigurd Gramstad, personal communication).

I also used drawing as a way to record my impressions of life in Chenalhó and to find out what children learn about drinking and gender relations. My own drawings as well as several children's drawings illustrate this book.[8]

While men seemed ambivalent about many aspects of drinking, women's clear analyses of problem drinking impressed me from the first days I was in Chenalhó. In societies such as Chenalhó, where men and women are clear about norms and roles, women speak out when deviations, like problem drinking, disrupt household and communal relations. With conviction and courage, they state what has gone wrong and who is to blame. As I analyzed my data and compared my study with others, I realized that while problem drinking may not be the norm in most societies, where it exists women bear the brunt of its damaging effects. Eventually, I understood Pedranas' roles in helping their people find solutions to problem drinking while still holding on to valued traditions.

My study has convinced me that Western scholars and treatment professionals would do well to focus on the strengths of non-Western and marginalized peoples and less on what these peoples lack in order to fit into Western culture. Since invading Highland Chiapas in 1528, Ladinos have continued to impose their beliefs and traditions on Pedranos. But Pedranos have not been powerless victims in this process. They have retained their connection to personal and collective power through prayers, dreams, song, and service to their people and their Gods.

In this study I try to celebrate what Pedranos do well, especially how competently women are dealing with their own and others' drinking problems. Traditional Pedranos seem to learn from birth some basic understandings about self and community which members of programs such as Alcoholics Anonymous and Alanon, a group for families of alcoholics, must learn later in their lives. (At various points in this book I discuss these shared understandings.)

I do not want to praise Pedranos uncritically, however, for like my people they do not do everything well. But I am convinced Americans have a lot to learn from Pedranos. Last week in the big city near my small town a mother and her baby died in the crossfire between two teenage drug dealers. A comparable incident in Chenalhó would signify a catastrophic imbalance in the universe. All religious and political leaders would assemble immediately, and go without food and sleep until they found a way to restore balance. In Hartford business went on as usual the next day.

2 *The Time of Suffering* [1]
Pedranos, Ladinos, and Rum

Well, about rum, it has its story. It's a little bad. According to the stories that I've heard, before Jesus Christ decided to make chicha there was only water. He didn't like that. So he made chicha. This was his idea. Jesus Christ was the one who made chicha and it belonged to him. He sowed the sugar cane and made chicha. This was all that Jesus Christ made. Jesus Christ made an apparatus that was moved by two people that extracts the honey from the sugar cane. With that he made drinks for putting on his fiestas. And they got a little drunk with the chicha.

Well, now the Devil had another idea. The Devil thought about how he could transform chicha to conquer Our Father. The Devil got together with his demons and they transformed chicha into vile rum. Since the Devil is more clever, he made an apparatus that is moved by two horses to extract the syrup of the sugar cane and with that he made rum. That was how he made the true rum. When he made it this Devil got good and drunk.

But then he went and deceived Our Father Jesus Christ. The Devil said to Jesus Christ,

"That's your drink, but it's no good," said the Devil. "This is mine; it's better. Mine gets us drunk really well," he said.

"Could it be true?" said Our Father.

"Yes, it's true. Try it," said the Devil.

Then Our Father drank it and he got drunk.

Then Jesus Christ said to the Devil,

"Well, here is your rum."

In the end the Devil tricked Our Father Jesus Christ. That's why now rum is the Devil's, according to what we've heard from our ancestors.

But, then it didn't set right with Our Father that rum wasn't blessed. That's why he blessed it. But he didn't bless it with his right hand. He blessed it with his left, because he didn't want to bless it with his whole heart. He had already tried it and rum was a little bad. But nevertheless, he blessed it. Well, then, that's how he gave rum power.

Hilario Pérez Guzman, respected Pedrano elder

Pedrano elders haven't forgotten that Jesus Christ blessed rum reluctantly. But bless it he did, and being the devout people they are, Pedranos treat rum respectfully. Over the centuries since the Spanish invasion Pedranos have struggled to come to terms with rum, Ladinos, the Christian God, and the Devil. Ladinos and Gringos have written about this struggle from many perspectives (Rus 1989). Time is well past due to put Indigenous people's memories and perspectives into the written record. The historical sketch which follows explores the complex dialectic between rum/the Devil/things Ladino and bad, and chicha/wild tobacco/God's son/things Pedrano and good, which Pedranos have created over centuries of economic and religious oppression.

Before the Spanish Invasion

The struggle Ladinos and Indigenous people are waging in Highland Chiapas, presented in Hilario's story as a contest between the Devil (Ladinos) and Jesus Christ (Pedranos), began with the founding of Ciudad Real, now San Cristóbal de Las Casas, in 1528. When the Spaniards invaded Highland Chiapas they encountered small, ethnic principalities, governed by nobles who controlled widely divergent territories (Calnek 1988: 9–13).

Archaeological and ethnohistorical studies suggest that before the Spaniards arrived in Highland Chiapas, women lived in kin-based societies where they fulfilled important productive and symbolic roles. Men and women in ranked patrilineal societies, such as existed in Chenalhó, complemented and depended upon each other; women's work was valuable to their households and protecting the community often superceded men's and women's relative positions.

The structural changes Mesoamerican state societies created seem not to have undermined women's importance in the domestic economy. Bernardino de Sahagún's writings about Aztec society suggest that while living under state domination, peasant women continued to have important productive roles. Women owned property, planted crops, hunted small animals, waged warfare, and were priestesses and curers (Sahagún in Nash 1978). Aztec and Maya states did, however, keep women out of the new predatory economy of war and tribute. Yet even while men controlled the spoils of war, women's productive and reproductive activities complemented men's and could influence success in battle. From sweeping, to weaving, to giving birth, women's household-based labor carried symbolic weight, paralleling and supporting men's activities on the battlefield (Burkhart 1992).[2]

We know something about gender ideology among K'iche', a stratified Maya society of Highland Guatemala, through the *Popol Vuj*, a document written by K'iche' elite men soon after Spaniards invaded Guatemala. In the origin story which forms an important part of the book, women are central symbols of the earth's and the group's fertility. Complementary dualism is embodied in the form of *Xmucané* and *Xpiyacoc*, Grandmother and Grandfather, the creators of humans. A contemporary expression of this couple is *totil me'il*, the mother/father ancestor/protector, a principal spiritual guide in Highland Chiapas.

Scholars have also used pre-Columbian murals, stone carvings, and clay figurines to probe gender ideology and roles. Recent studies confirm earlier findings (Proskouriakoff 1961) that as hereditary aristocracies began to stress lineage bonds in the late classic period, women became more involved in ceremonial affairs. Ongoing studies of classic Maya stone carvings suggest that women rulers let their blood (Lintel 25, Yaxchilan), and participated in vision quests and sacrifice. Struggles between elite women appear as important to the fate of their kingdoms as those between their kinsmen. Late classic period women rulers included Lady Ahpo-Katun of Piedras Negras, Lady Ahpo-Hel of Palenque, Lady Tok-Chan-K'awil of Naranjo, and co-wives Lady Xoc and Lady Eveningstar of Yaxchilan (Schele and Miller 1986: 143–144; Freidel and Schele 1993). Continued decipherment promises to reveal much more about the role of royal Maya women.

While male dominance existed in Mesoamerican state societies, considerable evidence suggests that the ideology of male dominance that Spaniards brought with them contrasted strongly with the gender ideology of Mesoamerican societies. *Marianismo*, the Spanish concept which ascribes moral superiority to women for being faithful and pure, had no known counterpart in Indigenous gender ideology. The Western dichotomy created between marianismo and *machismo*, a masculine ideal stressing physical courage and virility, and domination of women, negatively affected Indigenous women's status. Under the Spanish "development" strategy, gender roles also changed. Indigenous men often had to leave their families to fulfill tribute labor, while women took over much of their husbands' work, the Spaniard's work and continued on with their own. Nevertheless, the culture these women helped create owes much to their continuance of such traditional activities as weaving, pottery making, fruit collecting, maize cultivation, gardening, and treating physical and emotional ailments.

Archaeologists have also used pre-Hispanic art to learn about intoxicating substances. Their studies indicate that classic Maya courtly life could involve considerable drinking, smoking, ingesting intoxicating plants, and using intoxicating drinks as enemas (Schele and Miller 1986: 145, 155, 173–174). Throughout Mesoamerica and across classes Mesoamericans used intoxicating substances to cure illnesses and to arrive at a state of communion with the Gods.

From both Aztec and Maya codices we know that Mesoamerican societies had extensive knowledge of plants and used their flowers, fruits, or bark to make various fermented drinks. They understood both the medicinal and intoxicating qualities of alcoholic beverages. Central Mexican communities made *pulque* from the fermented juice of maguey, the century plant; Maya communities made various fermented drinks from maize, honey, flowers, wild fruits, and tree bark. Priests' accounts refer to these latter drinks respectively as *chicha, chilha, coyol, balché,* or Maya wine. They report that Mayas told them these drinks were medicine (Vallodolid, quoted in Roys 1931: 216). In Highland Chiapas Mayas made an intoxicating drink from honey (Calnek 1988: 15). Lacandon Mayas of lowland Chiapas used balché, a fermented drink made with water, honey, and the bark of the balché, a leguminous tree. In the early 1900s Alfred Tozzer (1907: 23–25) observed how Lacandones used balché in rituals. They offered prayers during fermentation (which took three days) and purified it by offering it to the Gods, calling it *ha* (water), water of the Gods.[3]

Aztec books and Spanish accounts report that *octli* (pulque), along with maize, was the staff of life in Central Mexico. One story attributes the discovery of pulque to a woman, Mayahuel, who discovered how to penetrate maguey to obtain the sap (Paredes 1975: 1146). Stories about Mayahuel describe her as a protector of crops and as a mother goddess with four hundred breasts to feed her four hundred children. Some drawings show her nursing a fish, a fertility symbol. Aztecs called the four hundred gods she protected *centzon totochin,* "four hundred rabbits." They associated these gods with the moon and drank octli during harvest celebrations held for them, thus linking the gods to drunkenness.[4]

While stories like those of Mayahuel extol the virtues of drinking, other Mesoamerican stories warn of the dangers of abuse. One such story tells of the beloved Quetzalcoatl (God of water to Toltecs, God of wind to Aztecs, empire builder to Mayas) who burned himself alive after he had fallen from grace by succumbing to several temptations, the most damaging of which was drinking with his sister. After looking at himself for the first time and seeing his drunken face, Quetzalcoatl felt unworthy to guide his people.

Some aspects of women's involvement in drinking in Chenalhó today seem to have pre-Hispanic roots. Fray Diego de Landa's description (1941: 92) of a typical Yucatecan Maya feast with balché could be a description of a contemporary Pedrano ritual feast, except that couples sat together, instead of dividing into same-sex groups :

> And they ate with dances and rejoicings, seated in couples or by
> fours. And after the repast the cup-bearers, who were not accustomed
> to get drunk, poured out drink from great tubs, until they (those cele-
> brating) had become as drunk as scimiters, and the women took it
> upon themselves to get their drunken husbands home.

From accounts of Aztecs' drinking by Alonzo de Zorita, a judge from 1556–1566, we learn that before the Spanish invasion nobles and priests were free to drink great quantities; sick people, postpartum women, and older men and women of whatever class had the right to drink a lot (Zorita 1971). Chroniclers' accounts suggest that rules, highly prescriptive and rigidly enforced, not availability and desire, set the parameters for drinking in Indigenous societies before the Spanish invasion. Commoners living outside the purview of authorities may have drunk with fewer restrictions than nobles; however, as gifts from the Gods, alcoholic beverages and rules about their use were not to be taken lightly. Pedranos still hold this idea. Before Spaniards started imposing their values and practices, Indigenous Mesoamericans maintained a strong sense of responsibility when drunk. Paredes (1975: 1150) suggests that these factors, combined with the need to maintain a strong defense and group solidarity against outsiders, made it unlikely that many Aztecs experienced debilitating dependence on alcohol.

The Colonial Era

From 1545–1824, during what Larson and Wasserstrom (1982) call the "forced consumption" period in Chiapas, clergy, settlers, and provincial governors used rum, appropriately named *"aguardiente"* ("burning water"), to exploit and control Indigenous people. Since bringing sugar cane from the Canary Islands Spanish colonists encountered problems in commercializing sugar, obliging them to convert to producing rum. The production of rum created its own market, at the center of which were

African slaves and Indigenous people, chained day and night to the sugar mills.[5]

Repartimiento, grants of labor to colonists, provided the structure for exploiting Native people throughout the colonial era. As representative of the king of Spain, the provincial governor of San Cristóbal stripped Indigenous leaders of their power and relocated their subjects into fifty-six villages, consisting of *cabeceras*, headtowns or administrative centers, and outlying hamlets. He divided the land among Spanish colonists in the form of *encomiendas*, land grants from which settlers could collect tribute from designated Native towns.

Four groups of Ladino elites—the *encomenderos* (holders of encomiendas) and their descendents, the Ladinos of Ciudad Real; the Dominican missionaries; the Bishop of Chiapas and his following of secular clerics; and the governor of Chiapas and his relatives and hangers-on—struggled to control Native peoples' labor during the colonial era (MacLeod 1989: 41). Initially colonists followed the strategy of surviving off Native labor, principally through extorting and taxing their production of cocoa, cotton, and cochineal (Wasserstrom 1983: 35–36). At times Indigenous households had to trade their own corn crops to acquire the cacao or cotton the colonial administrators demanded. Later in the 1680s the provincial governors instituted "forced sales at set prices," which forced women to elaborate raw materials (usually weaving cotton) into cloth and then sell their cloth to the governors' agents at below cost (MacLeod 1989: 43). By forcing Indigenous people to accept rum and other commodities in exchange for cacao, cochineal, and indigo, cash crops destined for the international market, these men created an artificial market. Eventually their parasitic dependence on Indigenous people transformed the inhabitants of Highland communities from multicultural, tribal people supporting themselves off their land to peasants burdened by excessive tributes and taxes, and dependent on rum and a money economy.[6]

We can only imagine how powerless people felt in the midst of such a radical transformation of their lives. As MacLeod (1973: 126–127) suggests, in addition to their fear of powerful encomenderos, Indigenous people must have been terrified by the large, often horned animals that these landowners introduced. Cows, sheep, pigs, goats, and horses plundered their *milpas* (corn and bean fields) and proliferated rapidly. As yet unaccustomed to eating these animals, Indigenous people often abandoned their milpas in despair or moved onto less productive mountain slopes. Food supplies consequently dwindled, leaving the animals to prosper while Indigenous people weakened in the face of yet another epidemic. The Indigenous population may have numbered about 250,000 at the time of the

Spanish invasion. Due largely to disease, the population in Chiapas declined from 114,400 in 1570 to 74,990 in 1670 (Wasserstrom 1983: 16).[7]

While colonists exploited Indigenous people's labor, Dominican friars were interested in both their labor and their souls. During the 1500s and early 1600s Dominicans controlled twenty parishes, demonstrating inspired missionary and entrepreneurial zeal. At first these men were appalled by Ladinos' blatant disregard for Indigenous rights. Fray Bartolomé de Las Casas, Bishop of Chiapas in 1542, went so far as to deny the sacraments to Ladinos who refused to make restitution of land, labor, and goods to Native communities (Wasserstrom 1983: 16). Although Las Casas was stationed in Chiapas for only a short time, during his tenure he devoted himself to reducing exploitation of Indigenous people by prohibiting usurpation of Native lands and the use of forced Native labor in sugar mills. After Las Casas returned to Spain to pursue reform through the courts, colonists managed to lure Dominicans away from their mendicant lifestyle in Native communities to the comforts of San Cristóbal, thus clearing the way for the unimpeded destruction of Native society.

Beginning in the 1570s Dominicans and Mercedarians began to get involved in the expanding agricultural economy. By 1590 they owned a good number of cattle ranches, sugar mills, and other valuable land holdings. Mercedarians and Jesuits, who arrived in 1667, made large profits from lending money to encomenderos and merchants. Not satisfied with merely maintaining their convents, of which there were six by 1617 (Trens 1957: 117), clergy instituted *cofradías*, brotherhoods, organized around service to a particular saint. The alms they collected and the zeal they inspired for the traditional Catholic mysteries in these cofradías served both their economic interests and their worry about the growth of heterodoxy.

After Las Casas left Chiapas, few defended Native interests. The Crown protested abuses to Indigenous people, but in the end it turned the other way in consideration of the taxes for financing public works that alcohol sales brought. Despite measures to control alcohol consumption and laws which put control of pulque in native hands in Central Mexico, the numbers of *pulquerías* and *chicherías* (houses where pulque and chicha were sold) and the demand for alcohol grew throughout the 1600s. The potential earnings from alcohol sales had become too attractive to let Indigenous people control the rum trade (Hernandez Palomo 1974: 31–191). Authorities, the military, and big landowners wanted a part of the profits.

Friars could have defended Indigenous people; instead they complained about how they abused alcohol. On May 9, 1796, a priest from San Cristóbal, Carlos Cardenas, sent a letter to Bishop Ambrosio Llano, discussing Indigenous people's alcohol use and abuse. His conclusion, that chicha is bad and rum beneficial, defended clergy's and colonists' interest in taxes from rum sales (San Cristóbal, Asuntos Civiles, 1796–1811).

> Everyone knows the innate predisposition of Indians to drunkenness. In their minds chicha is nothing other than rum of the earth . . . and as this drink is much more abundant than aguardiente, it is what the poverty of the Indian is inclined toward, in order to satisfy the insatiable thirst that he nearly always has to get drunk. . . . A chichería cannot be painted except with colors from hell. In it reign all types of abomination, blasphemy, *juramentos* (evil pacts or vows), and iniquities, robberies, lewdness, fights, murders, all this originates from selling chicha, and with it one drinks like it is water.

Two striking features of the sale and distribution of pulque in Central Mexico during the colonial period were informal trade within villages and women's important role in production and sales. In 1524 Motolinía observed that women represented an important sector in both sales and use of pulque (Gibson 1967, cited in Hernandez Palomo 1974). On November 2, 1667, the mayor of Mexico sent Viceroy Mancera a list of licensed vendors of pulque in Mexico City, all Indigenous women (Hernandez Palomo 1974: 19).

From before the Spanish invasion to the present, Central Mexican women have been in charge of dispensing pulque from their doorways. Their distribution networks took on an informal character. In Oaxaca, the vendor would greet local people, stopping by their house and offering them a drink and sometimes food. Recipients would pay in cash or kind, or promise to pay later.

Diocesan documents in San Cristóbal suggest that Indigenous women in Highland Chiapas also played important roles in producing and distributing fermented drinks. One diocesan document written between 1796 and 1811 responds to a proposal to limit the number of chicherías in the Highlands. It advocates registering chicha "factories," but describes the dependence of many women on chicha to support their families. The writer states that, while women made cigars previously, the rising price of tobacco forced them to abandon this business and rely on chicha as their sole means of support (San Cristóbal 1796–1811).

Work and ritual were deeply intertwined in Indigenous communities before the Spanish invasion. In colonial times clergy adjusted ritual drinking to Sundays and to the feast days of the Catholic calendar. Taylor's (1979) study of drinking in Oaxaca and Central Mexico concludes that Indigenous celebrations usually involved Native-produced drinks, and problem drinking did not extend to whole communities.

Influenced by contact with Ladino ways of drinking, Indigenous people participated more and more in a "time-out" style of drinking. They drank this way when in contact with Ladino society—in market places, on plantations, and on returning home after prolonged periods of wage labor. The "time-out" character that drinking took on increasingly after the Spanish invasion did not typify the way Indigenous people drank before contact with Spaniards. The fermented drinks Mesoamericans used required large quantities to become drunk, and once people reached a drunken stage strict rules guided their behavior. In contrast, distilled drinks require only a small amount to reach intoxication. Colonial records indicate that there were no similar rules to guide consumption of distilled beverages in "time-out" situations. Records from Central Mexico demonstrate that when drinking in a "time-out" manner Indigenous people adopted the Spanish view that alcohol could dissolve one's natural judgment and cause crime (Taylor 1979: 96–97). Spanish law allowed an offender to claim less responsibility for an offense committed while drunk than while sober. Violence in Oaxaca and Central Mexico during the colonial era was much more common in unstructured situations than in situations where alcohol signified social responsibilities (ibid.: 66).

The tendency to give men more leeway to drink, that both Mayas and Spaniards shared, continued in Indigenous colonial communities. While women and children drank during public ceremonies, women were not supposed to drink while their husbands were drunk. There is no evidence of a reciprocal injunction, nor of men being punished for periodic drunkenness, although women were apparently punished severely in Oaxaca and Central Mexico for drinking without their husbands' or lovers' consent (ibid.: 62, 87).[8]

Spanish ideas and substances transformed native societies, but Maya peoples were not pawns in the process. They have expressed a remarkably resilient and resistant spirit from the colonial era to the present day. During the imposition of Christianity, Mayas brought elements of both their own world view and Christianity into various relationships of tension or complementarity. Facilitating this process were a large number of elements common to both Maya and Christian rituals, including holy water, pageantry, incense, veneration of a cross, a hierarchy of religious officials, and alcohol use in ritual. Several of the new meanings Mayas created which persist to this day include: wedding the Virgin Mary with water and the moon, merging the Christian cross with the Maya World Tree and four-directional cross, and substituting rum for blood and water.

Since ancient times, Mayas have associated water with the Moon and a female principle. Both Aztecs and Mayas linked Ixchel, the Moon, with rain.[9] In the Dresden Codex (Thompson 1972) Moon appears in her watering aspect, holding an upside-down jar from which water falls to the earth. Kintz (1990) compares this to the *chaacs,* the ancient Maya rain Gods who watered the earth with their jars of water. Pedranos still consider water to be a powerful spiritual substance. They say that lakes forming after strong storms are emanations of the Virgin Mary (See Chapter 10).

A factor in forging an association with the Christian Holy Cross and rain was the occurrence of its feast day on May 3d, the end of the dry season (Thompson 1972). Prior to the Spanish invasion, Mayas associated the cross with rain, agriculture, and the great ceiba tree, the World Tree and the fifth world direction that stood at the center of the world. In ancient Maya cosmology dead souls and supernatural beings traveled from level to level by way of the World Tree (Schele and Miller 1986: 42). Inscriptions and carvings of this tree on ancient tombs indicate that Mayas positioned their kings at the center of the world. The most remarkable funerary monument known from the classic era, the stone lid of the sarcophagus of Pacal, a leader of Palenque, depicts Pacal, accompanied by Sun, falling from the World Tree into the underworld. The Tree's branches terminate in bloodletting bowls and streams of blood, likening sacrificial blood to the sap of the tree (Schele and Miller 1986: 268, 283–285). In many Mayan languages the word for sap means "the blood of the tree." Ancient Maya rulers and Gods made their way along the World Tree via the Tree's blood or sap. Symbols on ancient Maya inscriptions "declare that the blood of sacrifice is to the world of kings and gods as the sap is to the tree" (ibid.: 284).

Ancient Mayas associated blood in their rituals with life force, food, and healing. They cleansed participants and utensils in rituals often involving human or animal sacrifice. They especially desired children's blood, as children were freer of impurities. Ancient Mayas sacrificed children particularly in rites to the rain Gods (Landa 1941: 323). In former times in Highland Chiapas the ritual assassination of a child was a way to become a shaman (Cortes 1988).

Contemporary Traditionalists in Highland Chiapas seem to have substituted rum for blood. When cargo holders drink rum during fiestas, when shamans drink it or sprinkle it on branches in curings, and when sick people drink a sanctified potion of rum and other ingredients, they avoid the sacrifice of human blood to which their ancestors were committed. Phrases Pedranos use to speak of rum in drinking rituals demonstrate how they skillfully transferred their ancestors' ideas about the Gods of nature and blood sacrifice, depicted on the lid of Pacal's tomb, to rum and the Christian symbol of Christ dying on the cross. When offering rum to fellow Pedranos in rituals Pedranos say, *"Uch'an jtxujubal yok sk'ob totik nichim yanal te'e!"* ("Drink the drops from the hands and feet of the Father, the flowery tree!"). Traditional Pedranos say rum is:

sba nichim (the first flower)
sba yanal te' (the first leaf)
nichim yanal te'e (flower from the leaf of a tree, elixir from a flower, elixir from a tree) [sweetened, medicinal alcoholic solution, or possibly tree sap]
snichimal yok sk'ob riox (flowery hands and feet of God)
jtzujubal yanal te' (drops from the leaf of a tree)
jtzujubal ak'ob (drops from your hands) [hands of Jesus Christ, God]
jtzujubal avok (drops from your feet) [feet of Jesus Christ, God]

Some Pedranos I questioned about these phrases said that as well as representing drops of blood from the hands and feet of Jesus Christ, drops may also represent the good works of God, that he sent through his son, and other powerful beings, such as Earth. Taken this way the drops, like the World Tree, represent constant renewal and rebirth. They recall the drops of water falling from Ixchel's jar.

Contemporary woven versions of the ancient Maya symbol of the four-quartered universe moving through time also attest to the coexistence of Maya and Christian beliefs into the twentieth century. These designs incorporate a diamond figure, representing the four-cornered universe, with "spiny" appendages, like branches of flowering trees. In the crooks of the branches weavers put dots of brightly colored threads, which they call the "eyes" of the universe.

In spite of clergy's fears of their immorality, Indigenous people became devoted to their new form of Christianity based on collective salvation. The event that assured Indigenous acceptance of the new religion more than any other was the miraculous appearance of the Virgin Mary to Juan Diego, an Indigenous man in Central Mexico, on December 9, 1531. Gradually, Guadalupe's all-giving grace and forgiveness replaced the dual persona of Tonantzin, Aztecs' mother of all gods. In 1760 the Virgin of the Immaculate Conception became the principal patron of New World Spanish colonies. Today, over two hundred years later, a popular Mexican saying reveals the enduring appeal of the Maya duality principle and the power of the Moon/Virgin: "There are really two *jefes* (bosses) of Mexico—the President of the Republic and the Virgin of Guadalupe." Indigenous people have rarely questioned to whom they owe their allegiance.

Several revitalization movements in the eighteenth and nineteenth centuries, involving appearances of the Virgin Mary and women leaders, suggest that Indigenous people kept searching for a saint of their own who would defend their rights, and whom the Spanish religious authorities would accept (Bricker 1981: 68). Indigenous people interrogated about these appearances said that the Virgin came to do away with unjust tributes and to bring them prosperity. Her first reported appearance in 1711 was to an Indigenous woman of Santa Marta, Dominica López. Rumors circulated that the Virgin told Dominica that everyone who came to pay her homage would go to heaven, even if they had many sins, and that she would give them much maize, beans, and children. In Cancuc, a Tzeltal community, she came in 1712 to a thirteen-year-old-woman known as María de la Candelaria. This latter appearance led to an armed confrontation between Ladinos and Indigenous people when Catholic clergy refused to recognize the Virgin, although their predecessors had recognized the appearance of the Virgin of Guadalupe to Juan Diego in 1531. Pedranos took an active part in the revolt, providing its principal organizer, Sebastian Gómez. Gómez appeared in Cancuc carrying an image of St. Peter and announcing that he had been to Heaven where St. Peter, the Virgin Mary, and Jesus had given him authority to appoint literate Indigenous parish priests. They told him that they had come to liberate Indigenous people from kings, tributes, governors, and officials from Ciudad Real (San Cristóbal). The Virgin Mary replaced God as the head of the new church, and a native of Ocosingo became the Bishop. María de la Candelaria became the most important *mayordomo* (steward of a patron saint). About forty elders were under her. They renamed Cancuc "Ciudad Real" and decided that Ciudad Real should be known as "Jerusalem" and Ladinos as "Jews," because they had persecuted the mother of Jesus. Battles ensued in several townships. In Chilon Indigenous people took up arms against rum sellers, and eventually killed all the Ladino men. They took women and children to Cancuc where they forced them to serve Indigenous authorities as domestics. Eventually, despite a strong show of resistance, without guns and outnumbered by the Spanish troops, Indigenous rebels surrendered.

Independence through the Mexican Revolution

The replacement of the post of provincial governor in 1790 with a new form of administration, the *intendente*, put an end to governmental control of commerce and the encomienda system. The removal of taxation on trade between Mexico and Guatemala in 1797, independence from Spain in 1821, and the annexation of Chiapas to Mexico in 1824, brought a flood of settlers into the undeveloped lands in the Grijalva river valley. These liberals waged a struggle with Highland conservatives and clergy to control Indigenous people's labor, a struggle that characterized the rest of the century and precipitated a series of rebellions in the late 1860s. The struggle intensified during the mid-1800s when Ladino conservatives and liberals were on opposite sides in the war against French imperialism. Conservatives took the side of Maximilian and the French, Ladinos the side of Benito Juárez and reform. Conservatives forced Indigenous people to bear the brunt of much of the work of the war, including fighting, feeding and housing soldiers, and paying increased taxes. When liberals finally gained control of Chiapas in 1867 they assured Indigenous people that they were now free of onerous obligations to clergy, including religious taxes, and registering vital statistics (Rus 1989). Beginning in 1860, *jefes políticos*, assistants of the governor-intendent, governed Chenalhó. Indigenous people feared these men who, along with the *rurales*, ruthless federal police, kept down opposition. Finally in 1868 and 1869 Indigenous people in Chamula and several towns took up arms directing their wrath at landowners and priests. As in the revitalization movement of 1712, this movement began with a young woman's reports of visions of the Virgin Mary. In both movements women's symbolic dominance reflects their importance during stressful and transitional times.[10] In all their revitalization movements during the colonial era Native communities did not rebel against Christianity nor orderly government, but against unjust Ladinos (Wasserstrom 1983: 126–133).[11]

While Indigenous peoples succumbed to disease and liberals encouraged them to withhold ecclesiastical fees, cofradías began to weaken and clergy found themselves without revenues (Wasserstrom 1983: 46–147). To provide additional revenue bishops created new celebrations headed by new sponsors, mayordomos and *alféreces* (standard bearers) appointed by municipal judges. However, as with the cofradías, Indigenous people shaped this office into their own, creating a form of Christianity in stark contrast to the form that had evolved under clerical authority. Eventually priests reviled these offices, linking them to alcohol abuse (ibid.: 106).

In 1890 the despotic president Porfirio Díaz passed a law expropriating communal lands, paving the way for non-Native people to take over Indigenous lands. By 1911, the end of Díaz' reign, Ladinos throughout Chiapas had succeeded in depriving most Indigenous communities of their lands, transformed many Highlanders into lowland fieldhands, and exacted rents from Indigenous people who remained on their lands. Church officials recovered a fifth of the tillable land in Chenalhó, and big landowners snapped up at least a half. Before the late 1800s no Ladinos lived in Chenalhó or used the relatively unproductive lands around it (Arias 1985: 77). Ladinos who came to Chenalhó came as merchants on weekends or during fiestas.

During the late 1800s Chenalhó acquired a distinct ethnic identity. The effects of the Spanish invasion, including depopulation and political collapse, had all but erased the differences which characterized Indigenous communities before Spaniards came. Now villages such as Chenalhó contained Ladino homes, a church, shops run by Ladinos, and houses which religious officials occupied during their offices. The Ladino community in Chenalhó consisted of Ladinos who were fleeing poverty in San Cristóbal, which by the 1800s had become widespread. These poorer Ladinos followed wealthier Ladinos who had secured plantations in the late 1800s. After a brief period during the rebellion of 1869 during which they abandoned Chenalhó, the latter became shopkeepers, small farmers, or provided artisan and administrative skills.

Ladinos who found farming disagreeable turned to liquor sales to Indians— *"el comercio"* (Wasserstrom 1983: 129–130). Some Ladinos set up rum shops in Chenalhó. As the alcohol traffic spread, Indigenous people trying to support their familes on inadequate communal lands and small plots of private property fell increasingly into debt. Often they had to forfeit their lands or mortgage future harvests at a discount of about 67 percent (ibid.: 133). Indigenous people complained bitterly, but while priests commented on these complaints, they did nothing. It was much easier to attribute "native problems" to Indigenous immorality.

Much of the rum Ladinos sold to Pedranos came from distillaries in San Cristóbal run by a few prominent families. Moctezuma Pedrero, a scion of one of these families, had the best of both worlds by combining rum production with *enganche* during the early 1900s. "Enganche," "hooking" Indigenous people into debt through labor contracts, had been in effect since the 1500s, but in the last half of the nineteenth century it took official form. Through taxes and vagrancy laws enacted in the late 1800s and early 1900s, Indigenous people got into debt and the only way they could pay off their debts was to work for Ladinos. Ladino merchants bought off Indigenous people's debts and sent these people to work on plantations.

Enganche did not have as disastrous an effect on Pedranos as it did upon Chamulas. Ladinos usually sent Pedranos to plantations in the deep valleys to the north of Chenalhó, where they were not as far from home and did not stay away as long. Nevertheless, Pedranos like Tomás Arias, Manuel Arias' nephew, say:

"Well, in order to have workers available at the time they wanted them, they [hookers] sold *trago* [liquor] to them. One way that they sold it was to collect at that moment. If not [at that moment] they gave it to them on credit. This credit, let's say, they discounted in work . . . The laborers, well, they liked aguardiente, and their debts mounted. They [the landowners] deceived them. They said to them, 'You owe this much. You're going to pay it to me. You don't have to pay me right now. You're going to pay me in work.' But it wasn't true, it's only that they increased it at their whim, in order to exploit the campesino people. Although a person could say he doesn't owe it, it was already an order from the Mestizo hacienda owner. The campesinos NEVER GOT OUT of the hacienda, for not being able to pay their debt . . . They lived there like *baldios* [serfs]. Apparently, they [the hacienda owners] gave them a little bit of their maize and beans, so that they and their family could eat."[12]

Although the revolution, which began in 1910, arrived late in Chiapas and both revolutionaries and reactionaries used and abused Indigenous people, followers of Venustiano Carranza instituted sweeping reforms on their behalf. They outlawed enganche and abolished their debts. Manuel Arias, a young scribe at the time, joined the revolutionaries and began petitioning the state government for his people's rights. One of Arias' first challenges as a young scribe was to try to return the town government to Indigenous people's hands. In 1915 there was both a Pedrano and a Ladino president. Arias and other Native leaders feared that Ladinos wanted to take control of the township in the upcoming election. Arias and his associates petitioned General Castro, and came back with a paper declaring that Ladinos were to turn the town government over to Pedranos. Ladinos threw Arias and his cohorts in jail and a battle ensued, which Pedranos eventually won.

Despite these gains, after the revolution the revolutionaries withdrew, leaving the reactionary plantation owners to interpret the constitution of 1917. Chenalhó went back to belonging to the Ladinos as during the *Porfiriata* (reign of Porfirio Días). Arias' recollections of his people's struggles after the revolution speak to the experiences of Pedranos still striving for the respect and justice that the Mexican constitution guarantees them (Arias 1985: 97–98):

> . . . the Ladinos bought the things at the price they wanted; if the poor man or woman didn't leave their merchandise, they slapped them in the face, or complained in the presidency. Saturdays, Sundays, and fiesta days the Ladinos dragged the women of drunk men to the edge of the river to rape them. If a Ladino scolded you, you didn't complain, you bowed down, because if you answered back, they complained to the secretary to jail you. Indians were like dogs, like animals in front of their masters.

The Late 1930s to Present Times

During the 1920s and 1930s throughout Highland Chiapas Ladinos privatized administrative functions that before the Porfiriata were state-controlled. Although Pedranos controlled the town hall, Ladinos restricted the power of Indigenous officials to the Native population and gave a Ladino secretary power over the Native officials. During the 1920s in Chenalhó tensions reached such a level that Ladinos jailed many Indigenous leaders and lynched one.

While the constitution of 1917 outlawed enganche, *enganchadores*, men who "hooked" people to work on plantations, and alcohol producers restored debt contracting and controlled the officials directly charged with administering Native communities. Thus Ladino secretaries facilitated both alcohol sales and labor contracting. Bunzel, who undertook a study of drinking in Chamula in 1931 and 1932, a few years before enganche was effectively outlawed, quotes a coffee planter on the link between rum and plantations (1940: 363):

> Take aguardiente away from the Indian and what will become of coffee? Coffee plantations run on aguardiente as an automobile runs on gasoline.

Before 1930 there were no effective restrictions on the distribution of cheap rum to Highland communities. Between 1930 and 1940, Chiapas state governor Efraín Gutiérrez enacted several laws to prohibit alcohol sales and consumption in agricultural colonies, communal lands, Native towns and centers of work (*Legislacíon Indigenista Mexicana* 1958, cited in Maurer 1983: 350). Although these laws threatened Ladino interests, the governor and local delegate from San Cristóbal to the state legislature, Erasto Urbina, were determined to go with the general flow of reform that Mexican president Lázaro Cárdenas had initiated. They carried out a development project in Chamula which was to have a lasting impact on alcohol trade and consumption in that township and throughout the Highlands. In 1942 Chamula authorities made an alliance with the state government to enforce a law, enacted in 1937, which permitted only religious officials to sell liquor as a way of paying the costs of their service (Wasserstrom 1983: 177). These actions occurred at the same time as government officials were trying to instate local scribes, young men whom they had appointed to posts in the town government, in the township presidency. The regulation of rum sales compensated traditional authorities for their loss of power, conditioned upon their cooperation with the young scribes. Urbina and his young scribes became important figures as they traveled throughout the Highlands driving out Ladino alcohol merchants and threatening abusive labor contractors (Rus 1994). During this period the growing numbers of volunteers for religious office necessitated waiting lists. At the top of these lists were the young men who had come to power through their ties to Urbina (ibid.).

While making local gains from the reformist policies of the 1930s and 1940s, Indigenous communities let down their defenses and became bound to the state government and the economic and political elites whose interests it served (ibid.). From 1944 to the early 1970s their cooptation by state agencies and powerful Ladino elites became apparent as conservative politicians halted land reform and passed more and more laws against Indigenous peoples' interests.

Two laws enacted in the late 1940s provoked strong Native resistance. In 1946 San Cristóbal's municipal government tried to enforce transit duties and market taxes on Indigenous vendors transporting their goods to the city's market or just passing through San Cristóbal (ibid.). In 1949 the Chiapas state government enacted a new law taking away the right of religious officials to sell rum and establishing an official monopoly on rum sales. Indigenous communities responded to both laws through organized resistance. Following the enforcement of transit duties, young scribes from Chenalhó, Mitontik, Chamula, and San Andrés Larrainzar organized a blockade of roads to San Cristóbal and enforced a boycott of the city's market. In response to the monopoly on rum they managed to regulate the clandestine production and distribution of rum while at the same time convincing their people to resist bribes from government officials to inform on their neighbors. The scribes accomplished their goals by framing the defense of rum in religious terms. Although some of their own people were murdered as witches/informers during this time, the young scribes set a precedent for their future efforts to control their communities by appealing to religious traditions and beliefs. By 1954, the end of "La Guerra del Pox," "The Rum War," these young men had gained the respect of older leaders as well as a firmer hold on their communities (ibid.).

For the next thirty years scribes consolidated their power by serving alternately as president and as religious officials. As Ladinos gave up their shops, Chamulas took them over, eliminating the monopoly that the Pedrero family used to maintain debt peonage, but creating an internal monopoly. With the exodus of the Ladino shopkeepers, and the unacceptability of working with enganchadores, Chamula rum-sellers had to find a way to supply credit. They also faced the obstacle of excise duties, which took effect with the construction of the Pan-American Highway and which raised rum prices. Intensifying their connections to Ladino elites provided Chamulas one avenue of loans and credit (Rus 1994). One leading Chamula scribe, Salvador López Tuxum, received support to buy his first truck from Ladino elites. López Tuxum strengthened his economic and political base by transporting brown sugar from lowland plantations to the numerous illegal distillers in Chamula and by generating the cash flow required to loan money. During the 1950s and 1960s wealthy Ladinos helped many Native leaders diversify into money-lending and soda and beer distribution. Over the past twenty years the Chiapas state government has lent its support to these wealthy Native men through encouraging the consumption of beer and soft drinks in the Highlands. Many Highlanders have replaced rum with soft drinks in some or all of their rituals.[13]

Before the Spanish invasion in Mesoamerica, survival was a collective enterprise. Strict rules about drinking seem to have functioned to preserve group unity. When they invaded Mesoamerica Spaniards imposed a new ideology of land, labor, and natural resources that defined these as commodities, individually owned. Ladinos wielded rum as a tool of domination throughout the colonial era. Under these conditions preserving group unity has been difficult, as attested by the powerful Native leaders who today use rum to exploit their own people.

Ladino values and development policies also seem to have led to a devaluation of women's contributions to Indigenous and Ladino societies. Problems with alcohol and violence intensified with these changes, which are treated in the remaining chapters of this book.

As social relations changed, Pedranos have tried to cope with whatever new form exploitation took, but they have never completely converted to

Equipment to distill rum from chicha at a home in Amatenango.

Ladino views. During the critical period of state penetration in this century, Manuel Arias' astute leadership of Chenalhó prevented local Ladino elites from attaining the level of influence they have attained in other communities (Rus 1994). Pedranos' democratic values continue to clash with the unequal and competitive basis of capitalist relations in Ladino society. Traditional Pedranos still stress service to one's community, in place of personal advancement; and complementarity between the sexes, in place of sexual hierarchy. While most Ladinos see the unbalanced relations in their society as the inevitable result of progress and modernization, Pedranos view them as dangerous, precursors of envy that can bring illness and death.

Although they incorporated rum into their lives, Pedranos have never produced it; they buy it from Ladino shopkeepers in Chenalhó, Chamula distillers and Pedrano distributors in hamlets. Pedranos seem proud of their identity as a chicha-producing township. Women continue to sell chicha out of their homes in much the same way as described for Oaxaca in the 1700s. Highland women's continuing role in producing and selling chicha perpetuates informal trade networks, and offers their people an alternative to a seductive symbol of Ladino domination—rum. Although now made of sugar cane instead of maize, chicha still represents Native things to Indigenous people, as well as to outsiders. While probably neither sex has ever been exempt from the damaging consequences of their own or others' dependence on either chicha or rum, as with their ancestors' fermented drinks it takes a lot of chicha to get as drunk as one can on a little rum. Buying a few gourds of chicha in the market at one hundred pesos, Pedranos are less likely to use up their grocery money than if they buy rum at five hundred pesos for a small beer bottle. Some Pedranos say chicha is as easy to abuse as rum, but most agree that rum is sure to empty one's pocket and put one in debt. In addition, buying chicha helps support an Indigenous household, while buying rum lines the pockets of a Ladino or a well-off Native person from another township. Pedranos' ingenuity in substituting soda for rum over the past twenty years demonstrates their ability to take on new elements, while preserving their traditions. As in earlier transitions from sacrificing blood to chicha or rum, women's symbolic and productive roles have been pivotal (See Chapter 11). Nevertheless, while rum and soda distribution remain in the hands of powerful Ladino and Native men, both beverages remain integrated into structures of domination.

Indigenous people have responded to the Spanish invasion, expanding capitalism, and Protestant missionizing, with understandable wariness and distrust. At times they expressed their defiance against domination in organized resistance, but more often their responses have been embedded in a hidden symbolic discourse (Scott 1990). Pedranos' ideas about drinking form a core of this discourse.

To manage their fear of rum, Ladinos, each other, and powerful spiritual entities, Traditional Pedranos offer gifts of rum in rituals. Their gifts both perpetuate and reflect the cautious mindsets and precautionary behaviors their experiences have encouraged them to adopt.

Pedranos say that they offer rum so that all will be like one, and no one will have an edge over others. Tzeltal speakers in Guaquitepec attribute the same equalizing tendencies to rum when they offer a little rum to all present in court cases, saying, *"jun pajal yo'tan,"* "so that everyone's hearts become one" (Maurer 1983: 354). In their rituals and legends the people of Amatenango identify rum with the washings of the bodies of Jesus and the saints. In this form rum is a gift from the gods which releases people from their fears (Nash 1985: 210). Tenejapanecos tell a story which illustrates the Gods' punishment for abstinence: If people refuse to drink during their time on Earth, in the hereafter God will make them drink horse piss (Stross 1977: 3–5).

While rum maintains and restore well-being, Pedranos are aware that they use it to alleviate fear and embarrassment in social relations. Pedranos say they fear rum for its connection to envy and resentment, harbingers of illness. Even followers of Catholic Action and some Protestants, say that envy, fueled by resentment, is the primary cause of most problems, from physical and emotional disease to community conflicts. Pedranos link rum to envy and resentment on many levels. Resentment and rum are both hot. Rolling down the throat of a resentful witch, rum heats his petition further so that evil powers will hear his request to harm his victim. Later, envy comes in the victim's dreams, in the form of demons or devils disguised as an animal or the victim's own family. If the demons come with food or drink they force the victim to drink it. Then through the thin veil between sleep and waking hours the thirst for rum passes. In the Devil's hands rum becomes a tool to inflict pain and suffering, recalling how Ladinos have used it against Pedranos since the Spanish invasion.

In prayers to counteract envy, Pedano shamans return exactly the same amount of rum, in the same way it came, to the powerful beings. Before Zinacanteco farmers clear lowland fields they call on a shaman to pray. He holds a glass of rum and says (Laughlin 1993a: 59):

> There is still a pittance,
> There is still a trifle,
> Of the cause for Your fear,

Of the cause for Your shame,
The first of Your shot glasses,
The first of Your pitchers,
My Lord.

Prayers and formulas such as "the cause for fear, the cause for shame," demonstrate how skillfully Indigenous people deal with rum's dialectical role. When both personal and public misfortunes occur, Pedranos often say rum is involved, both in the cause and cure. In interpersonal disputes offending parties bring bottles of rum to people they have offended. Rum in this instance is called *melvo'*, "the water of sorrow," or "the water we drink together" (Guiteras-Holmes 1961: 90). An offended party who refuses to accept the rum several times may be set on using witchcraft. When public disasters such as famine occur, Pedranos say that God has sent it to punish them for feuding among themselves, for spending their precious money on rum and drinking too much of it. Pedranos examine themselves to see what they could have done to contribute to the problem and then gather together their experienced shamans to pray, with rum, to correct it (Arias in Guiteras-Holmes 1961: 251).

From Pedranos' accounts it would seem that rum is the most powerful of all substances in Indigenous communities. However, when pressed some Pedranos say that *moy*, wild tobacco, is the only essential ingredient in curative drinks that call for both ingredients, and is more powerful than rum as a talisman and weapon against evil. José, a Pedrano friend and translator, told me several stories about moy which illustrate its talismanic power. Two were about his uncle who was never without his moy. One story told about the time his uncle passed out on the trail home. Upon awakening in the dark the uncle didn't know which way to go. Then he saw a light rise up from his net bag lying on the ground. It was his moy lighting the way.[14]

I never heard comparable stories about rum, although they may exist. Through his stories José seemed to be cautioning me that however powerful rum may be, when people drink they lose their wariness of unseen dangers and are powerless to protect themselves if they encounter evil forces. In contrast to rum, which after a point debilitates, moy always empowers. It enables Pedranos to be ever vigilant and protects them when they are in trouble. "It accompanies us," José said.

Beside the talismanic power of moy and the signifying power of chicha, rum is forever a Pedrano stepchild. Pedranos adopted it with reservations, as Jesus first blessed it.

Pedrana carrying her chicha and chair to market.

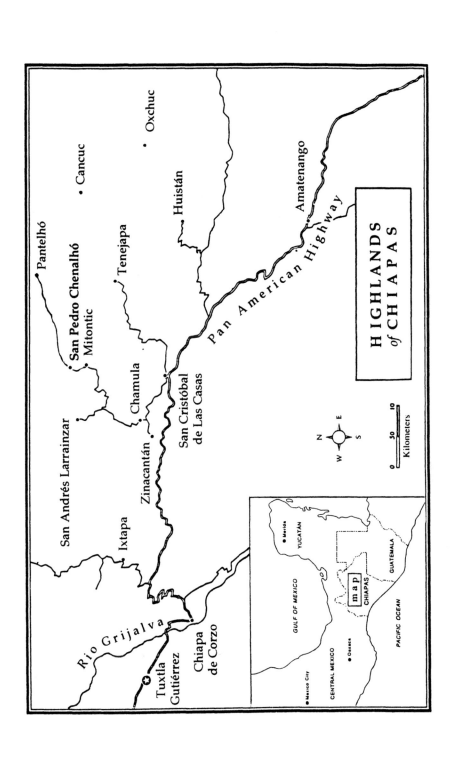

HIGHLANDS of CHIAPAS

Pan American Highway

Pantelhó
San Pedro Chenalhó
Mitontic
Cancuc
Oxchuc
Tenejapa
Huistán
Amatenango
San Andrés Larrainzar
Chamula
San Cristóbal de Las Casas
Zinacantán
Ixtapa
Rio Grijalva
Tuxtla Gutiérrez
Chiapa de Corzo

N E S W

0   50   100
Kilometers

GULF OF MEXICO
Mérida
YUCATAN
GUATEMALA
map
CHIAPAS
CENTRAL MEXICO
Mexico City
Oaxaca
PACIFIC OCEAN

Man from Tenejapa in carnival mask.

3 I Have Come
Crazy February

I started fieldwork in Highland Chiapas during "Crazy February," 1987. In-digenous people in the township of Chamula give this name to February because of the carnival season preceding Lent which occurs during this month. If I had known just how crazy February can be, I might not have plunged into life in the Highlands in this month. But looking back, my first impressions of drinking and gender relations during this time, however confusing, gave me an invaluable introduction to the complexity and rich-ness of Highland Chiapas.

"Crazy February" is a raucous time when Highlanders turn the nat-ural order of things upside down and make fun of each other and all the visible and invisible beings with whom they have had to contend since the beginning of time. During Carnival men can drink excessively, be obscene, and impersonate both historical and mythical creatures. They also dress up like women and Ladinos. Carnival rituals in Chamula comment on all as-pects of native life, from gender relations to the agricultural cycle, to the wider world, including Ladinos, foreign tourists, the state government, and the Mexican nation (Gossen 1986a). Like Chamulas, Pedranos com-ment on ethnic conflict, but their rituals also explore relations between men and women, and Indigenous people and Ladinos. In both townships, *paxyonetik* and their wives, *me' paxyonetik,* the couples who lead this fiesta, demonstrate what it means to be quintessential men and women, i.e., ca-pable of producing enough corn to feed one's family and surplus to offer to one's people and the Gods. At stake in all fiestas in Highland Chiapas, and especially during Carnival, is the continuity of time, traditions, and the natural order as Indigenous people see it (ibid.).[1]

A few weeks before I arrived in Chenalhó celebrants of the fiesta pre-ceding Carnival, the Feast of St. Sebastian, gathered in the town hall and warned fellow Pedranos of events to come (Bricker 1981: 136):

> They will appear here in a month's time!
> Lacandon will appear!
> Blackmen will appear!
> Crossbacks will appear!
> Abductors will appear!
> Evil creatures will appear!
> You see.
> Danger is on its way here . . .

During Carnival the ominous prophecy comes true. Six Blackmen, known also as "Turks," "Frenchmen," and "Monkeys," appear wearing blackface and monkey-fur headdresses with ribbons. Two of these men are called "Ladinos," and four pose as dogs of the Ladinos. The enemies of the Blackmen are the *jtzakeletik,* two abductors and their female companion, whom Pedranos gloss as *"novios,"* "lovers." The female impersonator dresses up like a Pedrana in a white cotton blouse brocaded with wool designs, a white shawl, also embroidered, a dark blue skirt and a string of gold beads. "She" announces,

> I am half a woman,
> I am half a girl.

The abductors wear knee-length red breeches, red jackets, and white shawls. Another two men, *kuruspatetike,* crossbacks, and *me' kabinal,* their female companion, assume enemy status during this ritual. Standing nude, except for a loincloth, crossbacks paint themselves by dipping the mouth of a soda bottle in anatto pigment and whitewash and making rings all over their bodies. They also paint crosses on each other's backs. The crosses and loincloth recall Christ's suffering on the cross and the circles, the wounds he received. The men joke with onlookers and warm themselves with cups of rum as they paint in the chilly February air. Me' kabinal dresses herself like a Pedrana and also paints circles on her body inside the house of a paxyon and a me' paxyon.

On the second day of the fiesta the Blackmen brutally torture and kill two turkeys. On the third day they get down to the business of tracking down their enemies whom they claim have abducted their sisters or wives (Bricker 1973: 141):

> Well, Passion (paxyon), did you see a woman
> and two men running away?
> My wife (sister) ran away.
> I am looking for my wife (sister).

They have sinned.
They are evil people.
They abducted the woman.

The paxyon refuses to open the door of his house and says, "You can't enter here, Ladino." But the Blackmen and the dogs force their way in. The dogs sniff at various girls and finally one of the dogs scratches the mat. Taking a stick the Ladino lifts off the mat, exposing the fugitives. The Blackmen fall upon the abductors, beating them with whips and feigning sexual intercourse with the one disguised as a woman. Meanwhile the Ladino announces (ibid.: 142):

"Watch carefully how this is done!

Look, children, so you will know how to do this when you grow up!"

The fugitives manage to flee to the house of another paxyon. Before leaving to look for the fugitives, the Blackmen pretend to attack me' paxyon for refusing to let them in and for condoning what the abductors did. At one point they throw a mat on her, suggesting that she was the woman on the mat between the two abductors (ibid.).

In the abduction and chase dramas, Pedranos reiterate two common themes in Highland stories and rituals—Ladinos dominating Indigenous people, and strong men controlling weak and promiscuous women. The image of womanhood men project is not that of a *batz'i antz* (true woman), faithful to her husband and dutiful to her parents. Instead, they depict women running around with other men and dressed at times like Ladinas. Pedranos base their ritual humor on behavior which deviates from norms. No adult is exempt from ridicule if he or she does not dress, speak, or behave correctly, but in public ritual men focus on women's and Ladinos' transgressions. Men evoke the most laughter during Carnival when they impersonate Ladinos hunting down Indigenous people with dogs, and men pursuing promiscuous women. Hilarity reaches its peak when they attack me' paxyon (the wife of the paxyon) and simulate intercourse in the streets.

Women spectators laugh as heartily as men when humorous acts focus on sex and deviant or powerful people, like the me' paxyon; in the privacy of their homes they joke about and pantomime sex and nonconforming people. Nevertheless, women fear deviations from norms. They find security in both sexes fulfilling their roles as the ancestors dictated. Women are keenly aware that heavy drinking, a focal point of rituals, often interferes with respectful relations between spouses and men's ability to do their part in maintaining their families and communities. As humorous as drunk men in drag, and men fighting over women, may appear, these scenes dramatize men's power to control women.[2]

I attended Carnival in Chenalhó after having spent one week in Highland Chiapas, five days of that living with Antonia and Domingo in a hamlet about a mile from Chenalhó (the *cabecera,* head village). Antonia and
Domingo brought me to town with them on the second day of the five-day
celebration. Antonia explained that if I liked I could go to a feast Catholic
Action followers were putting on at the same time as Carnival. Otherwise I
was free to wander around town on my own or hang out with them. Antonia apologized for being unable to provide a place for me to sleep. She
explained that Doña Consuelo, a Ladina, had rooms to rent and if they
weren't already filled with visitors, I could sleep there. And, too, there was
Padre Miguel, the local priest. He had some beds for visitors.

I found a room in Doña Consuelo's house only a couple of blocks from
the town square. Trusting that I would have more chances to get an in-
sider's view of fiestas, I contented myself with glimpses of women preparing
and serving food and drink from the doorways of the houses of the paxyonetik. Making my way back and forth between my room, the doorways,
and the town square where the public events took place, I had to pass a
corner of the market where groups of drunk Ladinos and Pedranos scuffled,
talked loudly, and bothered passers-by. While these men grounded me in
the moment and in why I was there, I needed a safe place to observe public events. I found my place among groups of women huddled against the
church door. Unable to converse in Tzotzil, I resorted to smiling and won-
dering about the women's lives. Antonia told me that many women, especially those living in distant hamlets, only come to Chenalhó for major
fiestas, relying on their fathers or husbands to travel back and forth for
supplies. Now these women's kinsmen were probably somewhere in the
market drinking chicha, leaving them alone to take in the sounds, smells,
and sights of Carnival.

I peered through the crowd to see a man, pretending to be a bull,
dance in the space in front of the church. The *castillo,* castle-like framework he carried, was studded with fireworks that ricocheted around us.
We crouched in the doorway of the church, while children ran in delight
and terror to the safety of the church walls. After we were sure that no
more bursts of sound and light were coming from the bull, we moved into
the street, where a dozen or so clowns surrounded us with their dancing
and banter. They were all men and boys, dressed in garish Ladino clothes.

Fortunately, most Carnival rituals don't overlap, so I was able to see
parts of Carnival in two other townships, Chamula and Tenejapa. After
Chenalhó, where there were a lot of drunks in the streets, I wondered
what I would see in other townships. At Zinacantán's fiesta of San Sebastián in 1985 Vogt (1985: 48) observed only a handful of drunks among

the estimated five thousand celebrants. In Chamula I, too, saw fewer drunks than I expected. Most drunks seemed to be in ritual roles, although I saw several drunk men and women onlookers. Perhaps more disturbing were several drunk tourists, whom Chamulas abide, but don't want disrupting their fiestas. At the fire walk that concludes Chamula's Carnival, I caught sight of a drunk woman tourist flirting with two Chamula men, who started to play with her. The three drew quite a bit of attention until the fire walk began and everyone turned to watch Carnival officials run back and forth along a path of burning thatch, the sacred path of God. The fire walk dramatizes the first ascent of the Sun/Christ into the heavens and culminates Chamula's reenactment of the creation, destruction, and recreation of the world. On this walk, and through tremendous sacrifices to serve their Gods, leaders of Carnival defeat the evil forces of the universe and bring Chamula to redemption and salvation in the embrace of the Sun/Christ (Gossen 1986a: 246–247).

My last Carnival experience was in Tenejapa, a Tzeltal township bordering Chenalhó. Although I went to Tenejapa to observe the fiesta, the ceremony in which I participated was not a part of Carnival. It was a change of office of mayordomos, older couples who hold the church keys and care for garments on statues of their important saints.

After walking around Tenejapa for a couple of hours, even more lost than I had felt in Chenalhó, I found Guillermo Monteforte, a film editor whom I had met when he was filming Carnival in Chenalhó with a crew from the Instituto Nacional Indigenista (the National Indigenous Institute). Fluent in Spanish, he got along with a wide variety of people. He had met a mayordomo, and the man invited us to join him in visiting the homes of the incoming mayordomos. We followed him through the decorated doorway of one couple's home. The large room smelled of *copal* incense,[3] pork, and rum. Men, seated on benches along the walls, were strumming violins and guitars. One man, who seemed accustomed to handling strangers, directed me to sit next to him on a bench near the musicians. I welcomed someone to talk with, but I became increasingly aware that there was a dividing line between men and women which started at the door and led to an altar. On their own side the women were talking, dishing up food, eating, and drinking. I was on the men's side.

After gazing longingly at the women's side and remembering how often women anthropologists report being managed by men, I decided to cross the line. I had drunk a couple of shot glasses of *pox* (rum), and was feeling more courageous than usual.

I got up from my seat, walked over to a group of four kneeling women, and knelt next to the drink pourer. The men had just taught me the Tzeltal toast in Tenejapa—*uchan iatik* (drink father) when toasting men, and *uchan me'tik* (drink mother) when toasting women. This was all the Tzeltal I knew, and most of the older women didn't speak Spanish. The drink pourer offered me a drink, then a bowl of tripe in broth and a chunk of *past*, steamed corn dough. The woman seated across from me pointed repeatedly to herself, then to me, and said "*jvix*" ("my sister"). Antonia had taught me *vixin*, the Tzotzil word for sister, and I took this as a sign that the woman was welcoming me to the women's side. When it came time to dance she took my hand and led me through the dances with the other three wives of the mayordomos.

I made it through the rituals in two more houses with my newfound friend, a woman who seemed in her fifties. I noticed that when the drink pourer handed the woman a shot glass of pox she took a sip or two, and then spirited it away into a plastic flask she carried with her from house to house. Eventually her teenage daughter took over pouring when her mother was too drunk to pour.

I got drunker and drunker. I didn't have a flask to pour my pox into so I just drank it down, afraid that I would offend someone if I didn't. I didn't like the burning feel of rum going down my throat. When it reached my stomach it made a nauseating mix with the churning pig entrails.

At the last house I realized that my partner and I were the only two women draining our shot glasses. My friend's daughter now had a distressed look when her mother refused to pour most of each glass into the flask. I linked arms, danced, and sang with my partner. In my drunkenness I felt euphoric, and confident that I was following her words and movements quite well. I know that I couldn't have been, because I could barely walk back to my room that night. I spent the night throwing up most of what I consumed. However, the next morning I didn't have a hangover, and I piled into a truck with the rest of Tenejapa to go to Pokolum, the original site of Tenejapa, for the largest gathering of Carnival.

Approaching Pokolum in an open truck took my breath away. Thousands of Tenejapanecos blanketed the green hills. As they milled around in the drizzling rain in their magenta and gold clothing, they adorned the mountain like blossoms on a tree.

I wound my way through the crowds for hours, never expecting to see my drinking partner again. But then I saw her, sitting on the soggy ground, drinking a beer. She waved her arms at me to come over. We greeted each other with "jvix," and she made motions for me to sit down. When I hesitated, she asked me to buy some beer. By the time I figured out where to buy beer, I heard that one of the last buses leaving the remote area was about to pull out. Afraid to be stranded, I apologized to my drinking buddy and left, reluctantly. She was a friend, of sorts, and I didn't want to say goodbye.

Drunken episodes and drunken bonds are confusing enough in one's own society. I don't profess to understand much about what happened between my drinking partner and me. My gut reaction is that she drinks often and a lot. Except for her daughter, whose distress was keen enough to penetrate my drunken perception, no one else seemed concerned about the woman's drinking.

Although excessive by American standards, the drinking I observed and participated in in Tenejapa had been patterned, peaceful, and obedient to ritual. But just before I left Tenejapa a darker side emerged. Walking around town with Guillermo, we passed the open door of the house of the *síndico,* where he and the judge were drinking beer. (The síndico heads the legislative part of the township government.) Neither man wore traditional clothes, nor did they seem friendly, although they motioned Guillermo to come in. Rather than ask Guillermo to join the drinking, as they had done many times before, the síndico ordered him to give them 10,000 pesos to buy enough rum to last out the fiesta, or they would put him in jail. Guillermo had already bought rum, beer, and sodas, and had shot photos of the fiesta for the town officials. The men seemed to have forgotten; Guillermo said that he could only afford to buy one bottle of rum. That eventually satisfied the síndico. A *regidor* (alderman) accompanied Guillermo to buy the bottle. Then Guillermo and the men, including two more regidores, went off to a nearby hillside to drink.

Several hours later Guillermo returned to town very drunk, and told me what had happened. On the hillside he drank with the judge and síndico while the aldermen served the drinks, without drinking themselves. Eventually Guillermo restored his good relations with the judge, and the síndico passed out. The regidores, who were dressed traditionally, seemed to function in this situation like "designated drivers" in American bars. They saw to it that Guillermo and the judge made it back safely to the judge's house, and they carried the síndico back to his house. While the judge and síndico had stepped out of ritual drinking roles in the síndico's house, as indicated by their non-traditional clothing and aggressive manner with Guillermo, on the hill with the aldermen's help, they seemed to restore order and balance to their drinking.[4]

That night in Tenejapa when I walked to the other side of the room and got drunk, I was just passing through and had nothing at stake. In contrast, at Antonia's house I brought my anthropologist's agenda. To her credit Antonia nudged me away from the acquisitive mindset, and the timetable which I tried to impose once I had settled down to serious study. In so doing she taught me a way of learning in which I often waited, sometimes patiently, sometimes not, for what she and other Pedranos decided to tell me, what Pedranos say comes from the heart.

Through stories and her thoughts, Antonia introduced me to Pedrano ideas about souls, the heart, and drinking. As the mother of three boys, Antonia is responsible for the care of her sons' souls. Pedranos say that mothers are guardians of sons' souls, and fathers of daughters'. But, they add, both parents share responsibility for guiding their children. Pedranos tend to make a causal connection between a father's or mother's error and the way children turn out, saying *"yich'ojbe stalel stot sme',"* "She carries on her father's and her mother's ways." But they also say that the way a child turns out is a matter of luck. Still, Pedranos consider chronically drunk and abusive parents as negligent in "being in the power" of their children's souls. And although a father is responsible for a daughter's maturity, they are likely to blame a mother more if a daughter is not obedient and respectful.

Antonia and Domingo are teaching their three boys what it means to be adults, to acquire the fullness of one's *ch'ulel* (soul), which is synonymous with the fullness of consciousness and knowing one's place in society. When a child is still maturing Pedranos say, "He already has a little bit of his soul" (Arias 1973: 29). One's soul never fully unites with a person, Pedranos say. One can call up one's soul and control it to some extent, yet it is a free agent in many ways.

Pedranos say there is a close relationship between the heart, mind, and soul. The heart is the seat of impulses, attitudes, and emotions, and is often equated with the soul. For example, when you and I are in agreement, *jmoj ko'ontontik,* our hearts agree. When I am thirsty, *takin ko'onton,* my heart is dry. When someone is drunk, *ch'ay yo'on,* he has lost his heart. One thinks in the heart, and hearts can be either small or big. A small heart is quick to anger. Although one can't know a person's heart size until he or she is mature, most Pedranos try to make their hearts grow big, and therefore slow to anger. Eventually thoughts reach the mind, which Pedranos say is the head of the heart. Knowledge of right and wrong resides here. Many times mind and heart disagree. At such times liquor is often an aid in quenching the heart's anger, thus ensuring collaboration with the mind.

Traditional Pedranos say that the soul leaves the body when one drinks to excess. While the body is passed out, a person's soul walks about courting danger. In this state he is out of balance with the world, and not responsible for his actions. As soon as the drunk person regains consciousness his soul comes back, and within an acceptable time most people go back to doing what others expect of them. Still, as I walked around sprawled-out bodies in Tenejapa and Chenalhó during Carnival, they looked pitiful to me. I knew that many of these drunks didn't go back to their milpas on Monday. It might have been Tuesday or Wednesday before they made it back to work.

Pedranos value predictable behavior between the sexes and the generations. In their dealings with each other, Pedranos practice self-restraint and mutual deference, and they do not impose their categories on the world. They are reserved with non-kin and strangers. Even with close kin they say it's dangerous to show strong emotions, especially anger. Individual coping and service to the Gods are the best ways to ensure prosperity and good health. Norms and values about control and expressing emotion are part of a strong body of traditions to which Pedranos constantly refer their actions. They tell their children, "This is how the ancestors did it. Now you do it like they did, and everything will work out well."

To help her boys find their place in Pedrano society, Antonia is teaching them how to behave with girls and elders. Believing that heavy drinking often leads to disrespectful and unpredictable behavior, Antonia tells her boys not to drink when they grow up and to stay away from those who drink too much. She tells Felipe, her seven year old, "God doesn't like it if you drink too much. Also, people will criticize you if you drink and are a believer in the word of God." Antonia hushes her boys so they can hear voices on nearby paths; the boys can tell if the passer-by is drunk or sober. When Antonia isn't watching, they pretend to be drunk men dancing and singing on the road below their house. They recognize the song-prayer of a drunk neighbor lamenting her existence by the evening fire. As they sit around their fire they imitate how she sways in front of hers; they muss each other's hair, and weep and wail about something Antonia won't let them do or give to them. Four-year-old Sebastián puts his whole body and soul into his woeful lamentations:

> Ooooooh, I am nothing more than a poor dog!
> My mother won't feed me.
> Ooooooh, I am nothing more than a poor snake!
> My mother won't put clothes on me.
> Ooooooh, I am a poor thing!
> My mother won't give me coffee.
> Ooooooooooooooooooooooooh. . . .

Attending to the sounds and sights around them and listening to the stories their parents and other relatives tell, the boys have learned that no one can predict what a drunk will do. Of all visible and invisible entities, the boys most feared bulls, the Devil, and drunk men.

During the time I lived with her, drinking didn't affect Antonia on a daily basis. However, during her childhood her father had been a heavy drinker, and her mother had drunk at times, too. Her oldest brother, Lorenzo, has been a compulsive drinker since his youth, and Domingo was a drinker before she met him.

Hilario, Antonia's father, started drinking when he was fifteen. The first time he got drunk was on a market day in Chenalhó with another boy. They bought some chicha, got drunk, and shouted with pleasure. Hilario said he never forgot how he felt that day, the pleasure of being numb to pain. He continued drinking until about eight years ago when he stopped, mostly for health reasons. Throughout his life Hilario fulfilled his major responsibilities, and one year he served a religious cargo, but according to Antonia, he got very angry when he drank around the house. Although Antonia's mother also drank and at times got drunk, María didn't lash out in anger. Instead she sang songs. One particular song her mother sang stood out in Antonia's memory.

"I remember that my mother and father had gone with Francisco to ask for a wife. My brother was a drinker and poor. My mother and father and my brother's godfather went with him, as is our tradition. But the girl's parents refused Francisco's request and everyone came home very discouraged. When they got home I was there. I was very little then. They all began to drink, got drunk, and sang. At one point my father was going to hit my mother, but she hid behind him. She grabbed him around the waist and laid her head on his back and sang. She just kept singing over and over,

> I am a drunk woman,
> I am a drunk girl,
> My father doesn't want me.
> My mother doesn't want me.
> I am an unappreciated woman,
> I am an unappreciated girl."

When Antonia finished reciting the words of the song (as she was too embarrassed to sing it), she clapped her hands together, bringing one hand down to her side while the other remained in the air. I asked about the meaning of the hand motion, and Antonia said that women make this gesture to vent their anger. Antonia didn't say much more about the song, except that most older women sing it when they are drunk, and perhaps for this reason people say that women are like little children when they drink. Antonia said that women improvise on the basic words, personalizing them, but they usually make the hand motion at the end.

Although Antonia doesn't blame any of her relatives for their past behavior (she says people have to make their own mistakes), she adds that drunks are crazy and you never know what they will do. Some just sit, sing, or shout. But, she cautioned, others hurt themselves or family members: for example, by spilling a pot of boiling water, thus burning a small child playing by the fire.

Explaining why her people drink, Antonia said that one reason is because they must constantly ask for things. For example, if one is a paxyon one must ask relatives to help prepare for and assist at Carnival. If one is a boy desiring to marry, one must ask the parents of the girl for permission to marry her. Although Pedranos are constantly petitioning for favors, loans, or advice throughout their lives, they are usually embarrassed to ask. Petitions often involve reciting formal chants in a respectful falsetto voice (McGreevy 1983). Some Pedranos have trouble speaking well in the high voice and almost all Pedranos forget some of the words to petitions. Drinking rum is one way to get up the nerve to petition, and to overcome embarrassment if one doesn't do it well. Antonia explained that her people say after three

cups of rum a petitioner's words become heated and strong enough to overcome timidity and embarrassment. And as the one petitioned drinks, too (or at least accepts the rum for later use), he or she is likely to lose any resistance to fulfilling the petitioner's request.[5]

Sometimes Antonia taught me by sharing her impressions or reports of things she had seen. Her reports were often about disturbing incidents or something that didn't fit with her people's traditions. While I would be studying by her side, Antonia might look up from her weaving and break the silence. One afternoon Antonia told me about two drunks she had seen on market day in Chenalhó.

"I saw something very sad last Sunday in Chenalhó. I was walking in the street behind the market and I saw two boys, only fourteen or fifteen. They were lying in the street, passed out. The flies were licking the chicha off their lips."

Sebastián, Antonia's four year old, made this drawing of a drunk man collapsed on the ground with a bottle of rum by his side.

We talked about what a sad sight the boys were, how even young boys were getting drunk these days. When I finally went back to my reading, all I could see on the page before me were the two boys, flies swarming in their mouths.

I had never seen many men or women face up or face down on city streets before coming to Highland

Chiapas. When I'd seen a drunk man in this position on a street in Buffalo, I concluded he was an alcoholic who had "hit bottom." In Highland Chiapas I tried not to label drunks in the same way I did at home. I understood that passing out was not always a disgraceful end to a session of ritual drinking, and that family members usually stayed with drunks until they sobered up enough to walk home or board a bus. But I had rarely seen a man staying by a drunk woman, and the image of the two young boys, abandoned in a street, together with the words of María's song, haunted me.

"Go help your father."

Seven-year-old Felipe dropped from the *níspero* (a medlar tree, with fruit like crab apples), where he had been eating the not-yet-ripe fruit, and went to help Domingo with a load of *ajan. Ajan* (*elote* in Spanish) is corn before it hardens, what Americans eat in the summer and call sweet corn. In Chenalhó this special treat is ripe in October and November. Pedranos roast a few ears carefully in the fire, or steam many in a pot. When the ears are ready they pick off the kernels one by one, savoring them.

Domingo entered the kitchen house, where Antonia was weaving and I was studying Tzotzil. Antonia laid down her loom and went over to the grinding table while Domingo rested by the fire, waiting.

" Do you want to drink matz', or do you want to eat first?"

"Give me your matz' first."

"I'm going to mix it."

Antonia grabbed a handful of corn dough and mixed it with hot water in a gourd. She worked out all the lumps with the fingers of one hand and gave it to Domingo saying, "Here."

Domingo drank his corn gruel in a few swallows and returned the gourd to Antonia.

I heard and saw this exchange countless times in every Pedrano home where I stayed. For me it symbolized the cycle of obligations that men and women fulfill. When a man tells a woman he wants *matz'*, a mixture of coarsely ground corn mixed with hot water, he refers to it as *her* matz', as she is the manager of corn at this stage. The server of food and drink, usually a woman, retains ownership of the substance until she gives it to the one who will drink it. At that point she calls it *your* matz'. In the act of handing her husband or a male relative the corn which he raised for them, transformed now into food, a woman completes the cycle of mutual interdependence that binds them and reaffirms their relations to each other.

More than any other eating or drinking act, drinking matz' signifies that one is a *batz'i antz* (true woman) or *batz'i vinik* (true man). Like wearing Pedrana clothes correctly and completely, or raising enough corn to feed one's family, it makes one a true woman or man. The first drink Antonia offered me in her home was matz'. I drank it, but worried because the water wasn't boiled. I gave up drinking matz', painfully aware of its importance to Pedranos. I often felt bad for not giving Antonia and Domingo the pleasure of seeing me drink matz', but I rationalized that I was trying to eat and drink many other new substances and couldn't afford to drink unboiled water. No one pushed me to drink matz' and I turned to my old stand-by, coffee. Since neither Domingo nor Antonia liked coffee, I made it for myself in a small pot, sharing it with the boys when they wanted some. Sometimes we made lemon tea from a lemon grass plant near the house. I bought sodas for special occasions. The only time we had rum was when Antonia bought a liter to keep on hand for pain when she was pregnant. Domingo used it a few times to wash cuts on his leg from working in the milpa, and once or twice we all drank a cup. Like drinking matz', drinking rum also balances relations in Pedrano households and communities, but unlike drinking matz', it sometimes leads to disrespect or violence. Antonia and Domingo have seen enough of the disrespectful consequences of heavy drinking. They have decided that rum is something they can live without.

Domingo's return from the milpa in late afternoon or visits from neighbors broke up long days around the house with Antonia and the boys. If no one had heard any new gossip on the way to the milpa or at the waterhole, rehashing my adventures in other townships was always worth a few laughs. When I returned from my Carnival adventures Antonia and Domingo wanted to hear every detail of my experience, and took the story of my drunken night to Antonia's parents in another hamlet. In more serious moments we would talk about our lives. Antonia and Domingo didn't talk readily about the past, but when I asked they would tell me.

Piece by piece Domingo told me the story of his past drinking. One day I happened to be around when he told the whole story at once. Domingo had just finished eating and was talking with the boys when Antonia hushed them. A few yards from the door an old woman's voice called,

"Young woman?"

Before rising to meet her visitor, Antonia replied, "I'm here. Come in." The woman hung back until Antonia came out of the house to greet her again and urge her to enter the house. Pedranos speak words of greetings from a distance, with walls and sometimes even shawls drawn over mouths, to separate them. Irrespective of sex, age, or personality, greetings are shy and soothing. The neighbor came inside and sat on a little chair that Antonia set by the door on her way out to talk to the woman's daughter, who had remained outside. The daughter was learning to weave, and had brought a blouse she was working on to show Antonia. Domingo and

I remained seated close to the fire, the area reserved for members of the household. Domingo greeted the woman in a high voice and she reciprocated. As they chatted their voices settled into lower tones.

I understood enough to know that the woman was worried about her son's drinking. I knew her son. He helped me carry my things up the hill the day I first came to Antonia's. One Sunday in Chenalhó I lent him money. Once he came here drunk when Domingo was gone. Although he never entered the house, he lounged in the doorway while Antonia wove and I wrote. He addressed Antonia with her Spanish name, instead of "sister". He asked me if I had come to help the *"pinche indios,"* "low-life Indians."[6] The way he put his own people down and slouched in the doorway, instead of staying respectfully outside, intruded into Antonia's home as Ladinos did when selling skirt lengths or buying pigs. While Antonia did not order him to leave, she also did not get up from her loom and offer him the beans wrapped in two tortillas that is every visitor's due.

After he left, Antonia told me he had asked her for the money she and Domingo owed his father. She told him she didn't have it.

The man's mother stared at the fire while she spoke.

"My son drinks too much. He drinks in the market, at the plantation, visiting, in the house. He drinks up about five to six thousand pesos of rum three times a week. He doesn't buy my clothes or my medicine. I tell him I don't want him spending his money on rum. But all he wants to do is drink. He doesn't eat. He just drinks rum. He gets crazy when he's drunk. He scolds me and tells me, 'Get out of here. I don't want you here.' Sometimes he says he's going to hit me. My daughter and I run to my married daughter's house. After he's asleep we come back quietly."

The woman stretched her legs toward the fire and arranged her shawl over her chest. Domingo moved some logs while gathering his thoughts. He began to tell the story of how he stopped drinking. It was a rare opportunity to get the whole story, and I asked Domingo if I could record him. He agreed.

> I'm going to tell you how it was when I was a drunk. I was quite a drinker. It's terrible what I did before. I was in debt at three bars in Chenalhó. I was in debt in the hamlet with rum sellers, too. I got drunk, but I wouldn't stop at that. I wanted to fight and I knew how to fight well.
>
> My mother told me that I drank too much. I would get drunk for two or three days at a time. Sometimes I would get home at two or three in the morning. My mother got angry and said:
>
> "Don't you have ears?" and she pulled my ear.

I was a grown man when my mother hit me another time. This time blood came out of my nose.

"O.K.," I said. But I wanted to hit my mother.

Sometimes I got into fights in the village. I went to jail four times. The fourth time they did something terrible to me. They beat me with a leather strap, and pus came out of my foot. I was a pitiful sight. I couldn't sleep for three weeks. I lay on my back on my bed, and I couldn't turn over on my other side.

Well, when the sun came up over there, I said to God, "My Lord, I'm pitiful. Look at my body. I'm ashamed of myself. I've committed a lot of crimes. Forgive me," I said and I covered my face with my hands.

I cried a lot because I was so poor. I didn't have any clothes. The ones I had were torn. I didn't have any money to buy clothes.

One day I saw a man who's a Catechist. He had told me once before about the word of God. "Let's go to Church," he told me. At the time he said this to me, I didn't pay any attention to the word of God.

Then, four weeks after I saw him, I dreamt I saw the apostle St. Peter looking at me. I was standing on the first step of the church. In front of the church in the town square I saw the ancestors sitting. I saw them clearly. I was looking at St. Peter far away and I saw him coming close to me. I heard the sound of his shoes. I saw that it was the Lord St. Peter, but he was very tall, like a big Mestizo [Ladino]. "I wonder where he's going," I said.

Then I saw that he had stopped on the first step of the church. He beckoned me with his hand saying, "Domingo." I was afraid.

"Domingo, take it," the apostle said.

"Teacher," I said, because he was a big Mestizo.

"O.K., come in. Let's go over there," he said.

I walked over to where he was. He embraced me and carried me in his arms into the church where the ancestors were. They were all big men. Their arms were this big. [Domingo made a large circle with both hands.] Their hair was white and they were very old.

The apostle began to talk with the ancestors.

"What's on your mind?" said the ancestors.

"Well, I have a little something to talk to you about. I don't know what you're going to think," said the apostle. "It's that I want you to be sure in your hearts. I want your hearts to be in agreement. This young man is going to be in charge of making the balls of incense," St. Peter said.

"That's fine. That's what we're thinking in our hearts, too. We're in agreement, if you're in agreement, too," the ancestors said.

"Good," St. Peter said. Then he blessed me three times on my head. He touched me on my head and my heart. That's how I accepted my cargo in my heart.

Then he pulled me over to a special place, a chair where he sat me down. I made a lot of balls of incense. It was quite hot and I sweated a lot in my dream. The smoke of the incense rose up. That's how the saints received the incense.

That's what I saw in my dream. Then I woke up and opened my eyes. Later in another dream they told me that I was going to enter church to hear masses. About three or four weeks later I went into the church to listen to the word of God.

But it's difficult to give up bad things. I listened to the word of God, but I wanted to go to sleep. I was thinking that the chicha in the market would be gone by the time I got out there. "I'm not going to get any of my uncle's chicha," I would say to myself.

I started listening to the word of God little by little. After I had been going to church for one year, I still drank a little. But after two years went by it was as if I had forgotten rum. Three years, then four years, until today. It's been twelve years since I got drunk. It's been a long time since I gave up rum. I just listened to God and read the Bible. I only know how to read a little, but God helps me. My heart is with God. My heart became big and strong when I began to preach the gospel. Although I drink a little and sometimes lose myself, I'm only human, too.

But, truthfully, I don't drink anymore. With the power of God, I don't feel like drinking anymore. One time when I was in the village I saw a barrel of chicha standing nearby. But I didn't feel like drinking any. To be respectful I said to the people, "Let's drink sodas." Some people saw that the chicha was sitting there, and they began to drink it. But others said, "It's true, what Domingo says. He's been in the township for a long time. He should know."

Well, that's how I'm still going around every Sunday. Although I walk around with friends, it doesn't matter to me if I don't drink. I can take it or leave it. Some ask me, "Doesn't it make you sick and that's why you don't drink, Domingo?" "No, it doesn't make me sick and I don't feel like drinking. That's how I'm carrying on in my life," I tell them. When I go to the village it doesn't matter to me if people are sitting there drinking. I make *la acción*,[7] if I can. The others have to drink because they don't understand. People are different. That's how it is.

Domingo and his neighbor moved on to miscellaneous gossip while Antonia ladled some beans into two folded tortillas. She held the tortillas out to her guest for several seconds, urging the woman to take them. Pedranos politely refuse food they receive in other households, at least two times. Antonia also gave the daughter her food while her mother got up to leave. Each woman, carrying her tortillas, bid us farewell in a high voice, first the neighbor, then the daughter, to each of us in the same order— Domingo, Antonia, and then me.

Domingo lowered his head over his arms. He was tired and hungry. He had just given his advice and support to a neighbor, his burden as a Catechist. I could tell by his smooth forehead that although he was tired, he was at peace in that moment.

Domingo hasn't always had a big heart, but since giving up rum and becoming a Catechist, his heart has grown. Domingo remembers his childhood as a time of hunger. His father died when Domingo was only six, causing Domingo to cut short his brief school career to work on his family's land with his older brother. Neighbors took pity on Domingo and gave him work in their milpas. When he was about twelve, Domingo tended cattle on a plantation. Eventually he returned to Chenalhó and hired himself out to work in milpas again. By the time Domingo was fourteen he was drinking regularly. Domingo characterizes the period from eighteen to twenty-two as his drunken years. Over these years he developed a pattern of drinking which began every Sunday and continued on until Tuesday. This had been his father's pattern, as well. While in Chenalhó Domingo would get in fights and spend all his money on rum. Once back home he would wake up with severe hangovers which kept him in bed for days. He said his heart felt dry and sad.

When he was about twenty-two, Domingo says he began to realize that his drinking was contributing to his family's poverty. His only sister had died, and there was rarely enough food. Standard fare for dinner was greens and tortillas, no beans. About this time Domingo had the dream he described to his neighbor. Not long after the dream and becoming a Catechist, he asked Antonia's parents if he could marry her. Although relatively poor, Domingo was no longer a drinker and otherwise upstanding. This made it difficult for Antonia's parents to reject his petition. They accepted Domingo's petition, and a few months later he moved into their house to begin his bride service. Antonia gave birth to her first son while they were still living with her parents. After four years living with Antonia's parents, the young couple moved to their present home. For weeks after Antonia left her parents' home to live alone with Domingo, she cried every day. She has never made her own *komen*, the instrument with which weavers begin weavings, in part because this gives her a reason to visit her mother and sisters who share the same komen. While Antonia starts a weaving and the other women continue theirs, they chat about the rising price of thread, a sick neighbor child, a bride petition that a young boy has begun in the hamlet. Antonia tells me that elders say a woman should be sadder at the death of her husband than of her mother, but it seems that Pedranas are sadder when their mothers die.

Through Antonia's weaving, Domingo's Catechist work, and their joint work in subsistence farming the young couple have created a stable, productive household. They live well together, except for the times when Domingo's pride[8] and envy from his drinking years dominate him. Pedranos value humility and keeping one's strong emotions in check. Domingo struggles to conform to these traditional values as well as the ones he reads about in the Bible. "Rum is the Devil's, the spirit of Satan," Domingo tells me. He points to the Bible which he says warns against excessive drinking, violence, and coveting another man's wife.

However, when we talked about rum in traditional fiestas, like Carnival, Domingo and Antonia told me that in this context rum is not the Devil's, but God's. "It's always been our tradition," they said. "When leaders of fiestas drink, they do so because God wants them to. God wants the fiesta to be joyful. Merriment and rum come from God," they said.

In spite of the heavy symbolic weight and promise of release from physical and emotional stress rum holds in traditional society, many Pedranos, like Domingo, have decided to limit their drinking or stop completely. Domingo's decision to limit his drinking to a gourd of chicha, a cup of rum, or one to two beers, three or four times a year, reflects self- and community-reflection as well as outside religious influences in Chenalhó. Before the critique of drinking and Indigenous traditions began developing in Highland townships with the expansion of Protestant churches and Catholic Action, religious traditions for the majority unified Maya beliefs and Catholic doctrine in a common arena where complementarity rather than conflict was the rule. Today followers of Acción Católica (Catholic Action), like Domingo and Antonia, respect many of the old traditions, such as saints' fiestas in the town center and traditional ceremonies in the hills, but also follow the teachings of Jesus and his apostles.

After his neighbor's visit Domingo was primed for talk. I took the opportunity to ask him more about his drinking. I had been wanting to ask Domingo about something that happened during Carnival in Chenalhó. As I expected, the Catechist feast was dry. This gathering contrasted with celebrations in official houses where drinking was ritually prescribed and where most men in attendance, and some women, were in various stages of intoxication, depending on the time of day. However, the second day we were in Chenalhó Domingo drank a couple of beers at a fellow Catechist's home.

"Domingo, do you think it's O.K. to drink a little, even though you once had a problem?"

"At times I do 'the action,' or I drink a little. But, truthfully, it's only an action. My heart doesn't want to. I don't drink hardly anything. I see what it says in the Bible and I respect it. And also I pray to God that I don't go back to drinking again. That's the way I'm living each day. But I can't say I'm a perfect person. Like I told you, I can't tell if I'll lose myself again. Because I know that I'm only human. I'm nothing more than this.

"But my dream came true. My dream showed me that it's going to help me. It touched my head and my heart, and my heart changed. I don't think about drinking rum anymore. I used to think about rum. 'I'm going to drink rum. I'm going to fight. I'm going to get drunk,' I used to say.

"So now if someone scolds me I only say a few words and I think how bad off he would be if I hit him. That's what I say now. Before it wasn't like that; I could kill, because I really knew how to fight."

Domingo's dream changed his heart, or mindset. Traditional Pedranos say that higher spiritual powers come in dreams to commission people to serve their communities or to admonish them for doing something bad, like drinking too much. When St. Peter came to Domingo in his dream he gave him both a cargo and a way to control his drinking. Domingo interpreted the responsibility St. Peter gave him, to care for the incense, as his calling to be a Catechist. Although Domingo didn't tell me so, it is likely that the incense St. Peter gave him symbolized not only his cargo, the new center of Domingo's life, but the blood of Christ. Realizing that he had not been able to deal respectfully with rum, which his people associate with ritual sacrifice, Domingo may have let St. Peter give him an appropriate sacrificial substitute, incense. Through accepting the incense Domingo received absolution and "let go" of his efforts to control rum. In doing so he restored his relation to ideal Pedrano values—humility, surrender, and service—and let St. Peter lead him.[9]

Surrender and humility do not come easily to Pedranos who have been compulsive drinkers. As the months passed, I heard more stories like Domingo's about men's struggle with pride, envy, and rum. Domingo opened these subjects, and also the importance of dreams, to me. Stories older women drinkers told me focused on the power of dreams, and their physical and emotional suffering. In contrast, younger women struggling to raise their families under difficult economic conditions told me stories of the disruption that heavy drinking caused in their households.

While Pedranos differ in their relationships to rum, they share a commitment to following strict rules in all social relations and relations with their Gods. Like American alcoholics and their families who follow twelve-step programs, Traditional Pedranos follow well-defined guidelines to stay on the "right path." For example, even if their hearts don't feel like giving, Pedrano hosts offer a gourd of matz' and beans wrapped in two tortillas to all visitors, except particularly obnoxious drunks. At Alcoholics Anonymous meetings, recovering alcoholics go out of their way to shake hands with other recovering alcoholics whom they may not particularly like. Food and welcome create good will in both cultures, and underscore the commonalities between members, making it easier to stay on the proven path. Pedranos take their responsibilities in this regard seriously. They say this work helps their hearts grow and their communities stay balanced.

4

Making One's Soul Arrive

Child Rearing and Household Relations

"Uh! Cristina, look!" Felipe stops abruptly on the trail and points to the top of a sweet gum tree. His eyes are wide, ears strained. He touches my arm to stop me, make me listen, too. I can't see the bird but I hear its song: cooo-eeen, cooo-eeen. We listen and rest, but not for long. I want to get where we are going, Felipe's grandparents' house. Felipe, in contrast, wants to collect branches and vines, veer off into adjacent milpas to search for signs of dreaded bulls, listen to birds.

I climb with my eyes on the trail, fearful I'll trip over a rock or step on a snake. We are following one trail in a web of paths that rests lightly on these mountainsides. Our trail just grazes the earth's surface, but takes us where we are going, on this day to another hamlet, other days to the waterhole or on special occasions to a sacred cave.

While we rest, my eyes take in the whole valley and the mountain ridges beyond. Chenalhó extends as far as my eye can see, to where the distant ridges meet the sky. It wraps around another township, San Pablo Chalchihuitan, which I know by its bright pink church. Antonia tells me that some Pedranos say Pableros eat snakes. I chalk this up to Pedrano provincialism, but the pink church strikes me as eerie.

Before the Dominican friars built this church and re-settled Indigenous people around it, the people who once stood where I am looked out over the same mountains. But one outcropping of rock over there signaled the mouth of a spring, another the entrance to a sacred cave. Chenalhó derives from *ch'enal* (cliff) and *vo'* (water), which roughly gloss as "water of a rocky spring." Before the Spanish invasion landmarks in hinterlands like Chenalhó were not buildings but features of the land: springs, mountains, caves, and lakes. In these sacred places dwelt beings other than humans—the family of Earth Lord, and totil me'il, the father/mother ancestor/protector. Ancient Mayas conceived of the universe as a square room with a legless tabletop,

the earth, suspended halfway between the ceiling and the floor. Above the earth were thirteen layers of heaven and below, nine layers of the underworld (Thompson 1970). Manuel Arias stated that the world is a square, like a house and field (Guiteras-Holmes 1961). The sky rests on four pillars, like a house. Each day as the sun descends in the west totil me'il, on their knees, deliver the setting sun to those waiting for it in the underworld. Then at dawn, on their knees again, they receive the rising sun and deliver it to the sky. Totil me'il also watch that Pedranos' animal spirit companions don't stray from their protective corrals on Earth Lord's mountain. Traditional Pedranos invoke totil me'il, Earth Lord, Sun, Moon, and a pantheon of Maya deities and Catholic saints in prayer, but only after invoking *ch'ul banamil,* the sacred Earth, source of all good and evil. Then, as now, Traditional Pedranos say that ch'ul banamil—although composed of many parts, each with its special powers—is the supreme power, ageless and everlasting:

> The earth is the caretaker of tradition, the goddess of righteousness, and the guardian of the moral order. The cleansing of sins is one of her favors, and it is only after man has been chastened that he can expect to be allowed to continue his human existence. She is the cause of all harm that may befall the entire group. Only by obtaining her permission may man occupy her with his home and fields. Any change of residence, any enlargement of the milpa must be her gift. She punishes and destroys. There she commands continual respect and sacrifice. Her protection can be acquired only with constant care and vigilance and is forfeited by the slightest breach or misdemeanor. She is man's conscience and appears to him in the guise of a woman, and her commands are strictly obeyed (Guiteras-Holmes 1961: 290).

Three times a year Traditional Pedranos make pilgrimages, *mixaetik,* to *ojob-anjel,* sacred places where the powerful beings other than people reside, to offer to them incense, music, liquor, and food. In return these beings send rain and good crops. Pedranos say that if they do not placate Earth with periodic gifts, she will not reciprocate with her gifts to them. Their relationship with her is a model of reciprocity and complementarity that they apply to relations among humans conducting their affairs on her surface. Antonia gave her thoughts about this relationship during one of our Tzotzil lessons. As if it was just another word I wanted her to teach me, I asked:

"Antonia, how do you say 'life'?"

Antonia looked up from her weaving with one of her "You're not going to like this" looks, laughed a little nervously and said:

"How about *banamil?*"

O.K., Antonia, I thought. I already know what banamil means. It doesn't mean "life."

Antonia went back to her weaving and I went back to biting my fingernails. How could "earth" take the place of "life"? I asked myself.

Later that day Antonia offered me some of her thoughts about "life," perhaps realizing that *la vida* is a significant word for Ladinos and Gringos.

"Look, Cristina, when I think of my life I think of how I am passing over the earth from year to year, and with whom. Well, I think of a few years, like three or five. These are like chapters in the books you read. I'm changing in each chapter, different things interest me. But it's not important what happens just to me. What matters is that I follow the traditions and serve my people, that I show respect to people and God, that I pass well over the earth."

Felipe and I have come upon a sacred cave marked by three crosses. Felipe stands still, holding this place for a while in his wide eyes. Antonia's eyes widen in much the same way when observing something that interests her, or when speaking of important or frightening things. Pedrano elders say that while ordinary people's eyes are open, powerful people's eyes are wide open so that they can see everything. Elders who guard traditions and know *sjam-smelol*, the ultimate reality/raison d'etre of things, say that contemporary Pedranos see and know only a fraction of what the ancestors saw and understood. Today the ancestors need human cooperation to understand the rapid pace of events on the earth's surface. But long ago they saw and understood everything in the earth and sky.

Ladinos and Gringos often assume that wide-eyed countenances indicate childish, naive, or stupid minds. I don't know if the old wisdom about seeing is connected to the way Pedranos look at things today. I know that I wish I could hold things in, as they seem to do.

It has started to rain and we run the rest of the way. The sight of smoke trailing from María's and Hilario's housetop assures me that I'll be dry again soon. Dusk is blotting out my landmarks. Only Felipe's white tunic bobbing ahead on the trail signals the way. Felipe keeps me in sight as he skims over the slick trail.

Antonia sent me ahead with Felipe because she has to wait for Domingo to return from the milpa with a load of new corn to give to her parents.

Their supply has run out. Domingo will light their way with his flashlight. The burro will follow with Sebastián and the corn and, at the rear, Antonia and the baby.

Felipe throws his net bag on a pile of corn by the door and joins his two cousins near the fire. I greet Antonia's parents, two sisters, and brothers-in-law, and unload my net bag and backpack. I've brought my sketchbook, camera, notebook, and tape recorder, ever hopeful that something will happen I can record. They stay inside my pack as I take the chair that María has placed for me next to Hilario. I extend my hands toward the fire beside Hilario's bony, outstretched fingers.

"It's been a while since I've seen you, Hilario. Are you still sick?"

"I'm still sick. All I do is cough, all night long."

"Ahhh. You poor thing. I'm so sorry you're still sick."

"Well, I'll get better if God wants it."

"Yes, if God wants it."

"Tzk'an riox," "If God wants it to be," is a common Pedrano response to the unknown. Pedranos have long lived with forces and beings they can't control. While they competently control their tools and work, the boundaries of illness, the weather, and other people are not so clear. These fade into the realm of the invisible where powerful beings are in charge.

Hilario has met these powerful beings in dreams. Fifteen years ago he had a dream that the Devil, disguised as a snake, wrapped himself around his waist. Hard as he tried, Hilario could not get the snake off his waist. Not long after, he developed *aire* (a kind of air or wind which may enter a person's body and make them sick), which still bothers him today. But in the dream that Hilario says brought on his current illness, the Devil took the form of two men. The men seized Hilario and tied up his feet and hands. They told him that he would stay tied for eight years. Hilario says that the ropes in this dream are the illness that now, ten years later, still binds him.

We warm ourselves in silence. I can barely make out the interior of the kitchen in the firelight, but I could be in any Pedrano home, so similar are people's possessions and ways of organizing them. Here I expect to find at least one backstrap loom hanging from a peg on the wall, with a weaving in progress. Even in the dark I can recognize María's tight, fine work hanging from the house post behind me. A large table which supports the *cho'* (stone mortar and pestle) takes up most of the space along one wall. Stacked at the back of the table are bowls and gourds of assorted shapes and sizes, a napkin-lined gourd with day-old tortillas, a ball of matz' in a plastic bag, salt, chiles, and some dried lemon grass. Pots for cooking, and jugs and buckets for hauling water, fill the space below the table. Against a neighboring wall a small table holding the *molino,* the metal grinder used to grind corn, seems to have grown up from the spot on its tree-branch legs. Sooty rafters support large clay containers, weaving tools, and farm equipment. Net bags and gourds containing eggs, thread, matches, money, an old transistor radio, and a homemade kerosene lamp hang from the rafters.

María offers me a shallow basin of water in which to wash my hands, and asks me if I want to eat. I tell her yes, forgetting in my hunger that I should decline at least once. María and her daughters are making tortillas, the second time this day. Antonia's family is small, so she only makes tortillas once a day in the morning. But here there are two daughters, two sons-in-law, and two grandchildren. The women have to make about two hundred tortillas a day to fill everyone's stomachs.

In spite of the hard work involved in making hundreds of tortillas, Pedranas are usually relaxed and jovial around the fire in early morning and evening. At Antonia's house I wake up to the familiar sound of Antonia grinding. Like her boys, if something has scared me in the night or is bothering me, I know that around the fire I will tell my dream or problem, laugh at something Sebastián says, fill my stomach, and reaffirm that I am not alone. I make my way in the dark across the yard between the sleeping and kitchen houses. After putting water on to boil I relieve Antonia at the grinder, and she prepares the fire to cook tortillas. When the logs are blazing Antonia lays a large pottery griddle on three old pieces of crockery lodged between logs. Then she adds water to the corn that has spilled out of the grinder and forms a heap of dough. This she puts on a small table next to the three-legged stool on which she makes tortillas. From the corn mound she plucks hunk after hunk of dough, slapping them into flattened circles on a small piece of plastic. She lays these gently on the griddle. If I have ground the dough fine and she has patted it paper thin, the tortillas puff up in the middle. After a few minutes on each side she places them in a wide-mouthed gourd. When she gets hungry she stops to ladle some beans into two hot tortillas. I rest, too, and have a tortilla and my first cup of coffee. We listen for the sound of a neighbor woman's hands echoing ours. If all we hear are roosters crowing, we know that something is wrong. Is she sick? Did she give birth? Did she have to flee in the night? Is she hung over, or worse, lazy?

Between five and six A.M. the boys enter the firelit kitchen, rubbing their eyes as they search for blocks of wood. Domingo is usually the last to join us by the fire, unless he has to work in the milpa or travel to a meeting of fellow Catechists. He takes the baby off Antonia's back and draws a chair near the fire. The boys move their wood blocks closer to their father's chair. Talk is the major form of entertainment in Pedrano homes, and tortilla making leaves women free to engage in it.

Felipe and I have come while the women are in the last stages of tortilla making. María is seated on a block of wood by the clay griddle as her two daughters, Marcela at the molino and Anita at the cho', supply her with ground corn. Marcela, small son curled on her back, makes her body and her child's one with the handle of the molino. In the daily repetition of familiar movements, she is free to joke with her sister or to think about a weaving that she is planning. When her son begins to cry, Marcela leaves Anita to take over at the molino. Then she draws a block of wood near the fire and sits down to nurse him. With Marcela to turn the tortillas, María is free to serve Hilario, Felipe, and me.

Hilario and I sit on wooden chairs like the kind I sat on in kindergarten. The women and children sit on wooden blocks worn smooth by the weight of at least two generations. Our blocks and chairs bring us almost as close to the fire as the old cat who makes a bed in the ashes. On the ground by our feet are corn husks and cobs, bean shells, and a few gum wrappers.

As we eat María keeps us supplied with hot tortillas, while Hilario roasts chiles in the hot coals. María takes three pottery bowls from the table and ladles beans into them from the pot in the fire. Watching María ladle, I remember the morning at Antonia's house when I spilled a whole pot of beans in the ashes. It took me months to learn to handle pots without hotpads, but only this one time to learn the value of beans. While Antonia was busy in another part of the kitchen I started to scoop up the beans that lay on top of the pile and put them back in the pot. Just as I was about to toss the bottom layer of beans caked with ashes out the door, Antonia rushed over and began to wash each bean and put it back in the pot. When we had finished, twenty minutes later, every bean was back in the pot.

María and Hilario dip their tortillas into the same bowl of beans, while Felipe shares his beans with his cousins. I dip my tortillas into my own bowl, wishing I had someone with whom to share. Now, no one takes much notice of my eating, but the first time I ate here all eyes were on my hands, until finally Hilario broached the question on everyone's mind:

"We have heard . . . is it true what we have heard, that your people don't eat tortillas?"

This day was the first time I heard this question, and it struck me as strange. I wondered if this was Pedrana small talk with Gringos, or if people could not fathom life without tortillas. Eventually, after eating in other households and hearing the same question, I understood the importance of corn for Pedranos. Corn constitutes roughly 80 percent of Pedranos' diets. On ordinary days Pedranos consume it as *vaj* (tortillas), matz', and *ul* (boiled corn dough and water). To eat tortillas or other corn products is *ve'el*. Ve'el differs from other verbs that denote eating foods not necessary for human survival. For example, *ta jk'ux chenek'*, "I eat beans," or *ta jti' ti'bol*, "I eat meat," refer to acts which animals as well as humans can perform, and which are not necessary for human survival. The only food that is a given in Pedrano households is corn. Sadly, in many households even corn is in short supply before the next harvest.

When Hilario asked me how I would fill myself once I returned to my home, he was speaking about a sense of fullness I had not experienced before with food. Growing up female in a middle-class home in the United States, I was never hungry. In fact, I learned to watch how much I ate, not to leave the table full. Growing up female, or male, in Chenalhó is to have one's heart hurt from hunger and yearn for fullness. Every food but corn, beans, and chiles is a treat, and even these three foods are not always available.

When Pedranos eat they savor each kernel of corn, each gourd of matz'. Filling oneself with corn in Highland Chiapas is synonymous with filling oneself with life. Jacinto Arias explains (Arias 1985: 27):

> . . . our flesh, our bones, the blood that runs in our veins would not have force or vigor if it weren't for the corn we eat: the matz' and tortillas that is our destiny brought from the Gods to feed us of that divine brightness of shade, that grew and multiplied from a grain dropped from the sky.

Pedranos say they do not know exactly how humans came to be; however, stories they tell are similar to those K'iche' Mayas recorded in their sacred counsel book, the Popol Vuj. Arias refers us to the Popul Vuj for a description of how the gods made humans from corn (Arias 1985: 25–28):[1]

> . . . and from grinding yellow and white corn cobs *Ixmucané* [Grandmother] made new drinks, and from this food came the strength and the fat that created the muscles and vigor of man. The progenitors *Tepeu* and *Gukumatz* made this. From yellow and white corn they made man's flesh, of corn dough they made his arms and legs. Only corn dough entered into the flesh of our fathers, the four men that were created.
> . . . It is said that only these men were made; there wasn't a mother or a father. Only these ones called sons . . .
> Later women were made from the four men. God himself carefully made them during the men's dreams and the women appeared at their side truly beautiful.

Pedrano weaving designs depicting a woman and a man.

Although K'iche' tales say that women came later than men, contemporary stories from Highland Chiapas focus on the complementarity of male and female principles. A Chamula origin story says that when God made people of clay, one part of the new creation was a woman, another part a man (Gossen 1974: 147–153). Chamula tales also say that Sun was born from Moon's womb. In a version of this tale told by a Chamula man (ibid.: 37), Sun threw boiling water in his mother's face, diminishing her power and brightness. In a story told by a Chamula woman (Rosenbaum 1993: 191–193), Moon/Mary fled with Sun/Jesus, still in her womb, to protect him from demons who didn't want him to be born. The demons eventually killed Sun, but he rose to heaven where he and Moon lived on. Pedrano tales say that Our Mother gave birth to three sons, one of whom was called *kox*, Sun. Kox rose to the sky after turning his brothers into pigs for having always mistreated him (Arias 1985: 43–50). Sun's rising to his apex in the heavens made it possible for humans to live on the earth.

Gender complementarity also seems to characterize numerical associations with the sexes. Three was the sacred number for women among ancient Mayas, while four was the number for men, corresponding to the four sides of the milpa. The three hearth stones that support a woman's *semet*, the clay griddle on which she cooks tortillas, symbolize her being. The symbol of a woman that Pedranas weave into their cloths is a figure with three fingers on each hand and three toes on each foot. The symbol for a man has four fingers on each hand and four toes on each foot.

Ancient Maya associated four with the four world directions and their associated colors: east, red; north, white; west, black; and south, yellow. Some of the Gods, such as the *chaacs* (rain Gods), the *pauahtuns* (wind Gods), and the *bacabs* (sky bearers) had a "four in one" aspect, each occupying one of the four directions. And at each of the directions stood a sacred tree represented by a cross (J. E. S. Thompson 1954: 225).

While four was important in ancient times, in contemporary Chenalhó the number three is as important as four, possibly more important. Although there are four principal saints in Chenalhó—St. Peter, Holy

Cross, Our Lady of Rosary, and Immaculate Conception—there are three major annual fiestas (Carnival, St. Peter's Feast, and the Feast of the Souls or Day of the Dead), three annual masses to the hills, three crosses at sacred places, and three pine branches offered at three corners of the village during masses. Pedranos eat three daily meals, decline gifts of food three times before accepting, process around the town square three times during fiestas, drink three cups of rum to seal agreements or to make one's words sufficiently powerful in prayer, offer three candles for prayers to stop drinking, and limit their drinking to three times a year as a way to deal with compulsive drinking. I found that it usually took me three times to be able to talk to someone, to secure their confidence. It was not until my third trip to Chenalhó that I believe Antonia saw me as someone whom she could trust.

Pedranos say that men and women are indispensable to one another. Without *jnup/jchi'il* (my complementation, companion, or spouse), one cannot be a true woman or man (Arias 1973). True men plant and harvest corn. True women transform corn into food for humans. Learning to cultivate corn and to transform it into the foods that sustain human life identifies men and women as true people. In San Pedro Chenalhó men typically work in the corn and bean fields and women work in and around the home, gathering greens and fruits, preparing and serving food, tending children and animals, and weaving and embroidering. Many women work in the field during some part of the year, and men assist in child care and household chores. Good husbands help with household chores. Men stack and reorganize corn in its bins in the house and cut, carry, and stock firewood on a regular basis; when needed they shuck and grind corn, carry babies and care for children, feed chickens and other animals, collect fruit from nearby trees, buy the kerosene for lamps and starting fires or an item of food the family needs, comfort children who wake up from bad dreams and lead them outside in the dark to urinate. Some men don't help when they could, arguing that these latter tasks are women's work. But they know that they can count on their wives to work in the corn and bean fields, and therefore mutual help is in everyone's best interest.

Pedranos say men should treat women respectfully, as women's household-based work is important to all. But elders also say that younger women should not question their father's and husband's authority, that they should stay close to home and not deal with strangers. Young women generally comply with this expectation. Their compliance has kept marital friction down.

Before a boy and girl marry, their parents, godparents, and other relatives advise them on how to be good spouses. They continue to advise the couple throughout the marriage petition process, but at the final visit to the girl's home the boy's father, mother, father-in-law, mother-in-law, and other elders tell him explicitly how to treat his wife.

"Don't make problems for your wife, respect her. Don't scold your wife. Talk in a good way. Talk with a soft voice. Work hard so you both can eat, so you can buy the things your wife needs in the house. Don't drink. If you get drunk, you will spend all your money and not go to your fields in the morning. Don't take advantage of your wife, you didn't marry her just for sex. Your wife is to care for, to buy clothes for, to buy medicines for so she doesn't get sick."

After a girl marries, she and her husband usually stay with her parents for a year or more while her husband completes his service to her parents. Before she leaves her home to go live with her husband's family, or to a home of their own, her father and mother instruct her:

"Look, daughter, be obedient. You always have your duties. Take care of your husband. Grind for him so that your husband doesn't suffer from hunger. Also, obey your father-in-law. Give food to your father-in-law with all your heart. Always ask him if he wants tortillas or matz' or whatever. If you and your husband both respect each other, you will be happy when you do your work. You will be very happy when you work your fields. In this way you will be true men and women."

The many times I watched Antonia and her mother and sisters carry out the laborious work of feeding their families I wondered if this work anchored them, as it seems to anchor their children, husbands, and me, and if they feel that their families appreciate them. Pedranas seem to be thoroughly grounded in the tasks they carry out so capably and respectfully. Although they learned the movements when they were girls and could do them in their sleep, they don't carry them out mindlessly. Making tortillas, Pedranas seem to focus on each one, not on the hundreds that they have to make. Tortillas rarely burn on the fire, babies seldom wait long for a breast to soothe them.

Still, women go on with their work even if men do not, and their work never seems to end. Pedranos do not bear out their ideal gender complementarity in daily life. If a male member of the household is sick or sleeping off a drunk, the women let him sleep. But if the women are sick or drunk or just feel like sleeping in, they usually still get up to make tortillas, unless they live in an extended-family household where another woman can take over for them. When Pedranas entertain women visitors they don't stop whatever they are doing, whether it is weaving, embroidering, cooking, or child tending. In part they continue working because they find security in their work, but also they fear that their visitor may think they are lazy and, worse, start a rumor to that effect. They can be sure that their visitor has come for a reason, however much both women may enjoy a chance to talk.

Women's work in subsistence labor is taxing enough, but today more and more Indigenous women are taking on additional work to help their families survive. Pedranas are playing a more significant role as steady providers through selling agricultural products, and making and selling weavings, pottery, and chicha. Maya communities excelled in these activities before the Spanish invasion and like other valued traditions, turn to them in crises. Their efforts defy predictions that the development of industrial production would eventually eclipse these activities (Nash 1993).

Since the debt crisis began in the early 1980s men's role as principal breadwinner has been weakening. Reduced credit and soaring prices, combined with the rising population, threaten the intensive agricultural methods that Indigenous farmers adopted in the seventies in an effort to maximize productivity of their land. To feed their families many men have been either selling their labor to neighbors or increasing the time spent as wage laborers on coffee, sugar cane, or cattle plantations, often far from home. Although many Pedrano households must depend on some plantation work, they still do not consider it as honorable as relying on their own land to provide most of their food.[2] Also, work on plantations and wage labor in nearby cities such as San Cristóbal is no longer readily available. Many Highlanders have become part of the salaried work force, traveling long distances for long periods of time looking for work, in cities like Villahermosa or Cancún.

Although there has been less out-migration in Chenalhó than in neighboring Chamula and Zinacantán, an increasing number of Pedrano households are growing non-traditional crops, such as coffee. Some are turning to coffee as the panacea for their problems. But they are discovering that coffee prices fluctuate. At the beginning of 1988 one kilo of coffee sold for 2,500 pesos, about one dollar. By September the price had fallen to as low as 1,500 pesos.

Like their husbands, women, too, are more or less dependent upon the demand of cities. This dependence is especially poignant for weavers trying to cater to tourists. Making one's own products to sell is risky. For example, women must consider the cost of materials. Inflation is increasing the price of thread. Transportation to town to sell their work is another cost. Arrangements for child care, and the possibility of increased marital tension from women's greater involvement outside their homes and communities, are additional difficulties for most women (See Chapter 11). Some women in townships close to San Cristóbal, like Chamula, have chosen to stay at home and sell to a middle person. But in 1988 a woman could only expect to make about 1,000 pesos a day (less than U.S. $0.40) for embroidery (Rus 1990). Other women, like Antonia, have joined the cooperative movement, which has been growing steadily since the early 1970s. Still, only a small percentage of the 400,000 Indigenous people in Highland Chiapas belong to cooperatives of one kind or another (Eber and Rosenbaum 1993).

Despite diverse survival strategies, the majority of households I visited from 1987–1989, including María's and Antonia's, did not raise enough corn and beans to feed household members and at times had no money to buy these foods. If a household raised eggs, they sold them for cash. Chicken was a luxury eaten only during healing ceremonies or other rituals. Beef and pork were rarely affordable. Everyone knew of at least one family that for periods of time lived on tortillas dipped in hot water with salt. When a family had money, they spent 85 percent of it on food.

Power relations are changing as men are losing their capacity to fulfill their roles as batz'i vinik. Women's relative economic independence increases their leverage; men know that they need their wives' contributions to support their households and that their wives do not have to put up indefinitely with unjust treatment. However, at times men also tighten their control and oppress women.

When men are jealous or demanding and do not fulfill their responsibilities to them or their children, women know that the obedience required of them as wives, daughters, and sisters is unfair. Some mornings I woke to hear Antonia slapping the dough extra hard. Her usually fluid movements were staccato. Her bare feet struck the ground. Instead of deftly placing pots in the fire with lids on straight, she let them fall where they would. When she poured water over the beans she sloshed some onto the ground. On these days Antonia didn't tell me what was bothering her right away. Later in the afternoon or the next day she might tell me that Domingo was angry because she was talking to a strange man in a truck going to the market, or because she wouldn't give him some of her weaving money to trade the burro in for a horse.

When María is sure that Hilario and I cannot eat any more beans she takes our bowls and places my table in front of her sons-in-law. Andrés and Moisés have spent the day in their milpas. Andrés pulls his T-shirt up to his face and wipes the amber beads of sweat. Anita and Marcela prepare their husbands' food and tell them about their days. Anita begins.

"I have money. Arturo's wife paid me for the embroidery I put on her shawl."

"That's good. How much did she pay you?"

"Five thousand pesos. Even though it took me longer than I thought, that's what we agreed on. I'm buying some thread at the market tomorrow. I'm buying one thousand pesos worth."

"O.K., but give me eight hundred pesos. I'm going to pay the elders when they come to collect for the mass for the hills today."

Anita goes to the sleeping house for some loose change Arturo's wife gave her. She sorts through the coins, but can't find one two-hundred-peso piece (worth about five cents U.S. in 1987). Pedranos rarely lose track of money, and Anita is sure that someone has taken it. It could only be a child. But which one? Could it be Felipe? He and Sebastián are the only ones who can go off to a store by themselves. Anita returns to the kitchen and announces, "Two hundred pesos are gone from my bed."

The children, tussling on a reed mat where they will eventually sleep, fall silent. Felipe draws the blanket up over his head and pretends to sleep. His cousins follow suit. Everyone is quiet, waiting.

"Who has my money?"

The children lie still. Finally Felipe crawls out from between his cousins, sits up and fishes under his belt. Head lowered, two hundred pesos clutched in his hand, Felipe walks over to Anita and hands her the coin. She grasps the hand that holds the money, half to keep Felipe's attention, half to let him know that his crime is not so great as to banish him from the fellowship of this household. But now he has to listen as every adult present tells him what they think about his actions. María begins.

"Grandson, you took your aunt's money. It isn't yours. You don't need money. Your mother buys you bread or fruit in the market. Obey your aunts and uncles. Help them, don't take their money. Think before you do things. Behave yourself. In that way you'll bring your soul to yourself. In that way you'll make yourself into a man."

When everyone but Hilario has spoken, Felipe falls against the old man's frail chest. Felipe's eyes stay riveted on the heaving motion of his grandfather's chest as he speaks. Hilario speaks in the same gentle but firm tone the others have used.

"Now you've heard what we've said. Now you know that you weren't thinking before. Now I have nothing more to say. Go to sleep there with the others. Don't be afraid. Bulls and horses won't come to kick you in your sleep."

Felipe shuffles back to the mat to join his cousins, who have been propped on their elbows listening. They open the blanket for him. He is mercifully asleep by the time we hear the mule's heavy hoofs approaching the door.

Antonia shoos the dogs away from their command post at the door and enters, pulling Sebastián behind her. He has been fighting off sleep on the trail, and wastes no time burrowing under the blanket with his brother and cousins. Never completely awakening, the children realign their bodies to make room for one more.

Antonia greets us one by one as she unloads several net bags. One bag holds a ceremonial blouse that Antonia has been working on for months. Antonia wants her mother's opinion on her work. Domingo follows Antonia with the corn. He greets his father- and mother-in-law with the high voice and lowers his tone to greet his brothers- and sisters-in-law. Domingo produces several ears of corn from a large net bag and hands them to his father-in-law. Hilario wastes no time placing a choice ear in the intersection of two logs. María roasts two more ears on the other side of the fire.

I wonder when the story about the money will come out. It is some time after Antonia and Domingo finish eating that Anita tells her sister what happened. Antonia glances over at the blanket and sighs. Hard as Antonia tries to make Felipe be responsible for his actions, he invariably copies other children. If a child at school has gum, he wants it too, even if he doesn't have money to buy it. Like most Pedranos, Antonia rejects thievery. Once when the corn supply had nearly run out, Antonia dreamed that she and Anita were creeping around in a neighbor's milpa in the moonlight stuffing corn into their net bags. When they couldn't stuff any more corn in their bags or shawls they fled to the road, where a policeman from the hamlet stopped them and led them to jail. Antonia was still upset when she told me about the dream the next morning. In the visible world Antonia would never steal from anyone, least of all one of her own people. The Devil must have encountered her soul while she slept and tempted it into the neighbor's milpa, she said.

When children reach Felipe's age their mothers ask them to care for younger siblings and help with household chores. Parents are realistic about what their children can accomplish and tell them clearly what they expect of them. While Felipe often forgets what Antonia asks him to do, when his heart is in the task he is a great help to her. Felipe often accompanies Antonia to the waterhole and cares for the baby while she washes. Descending the trail, carrying his brother on his back and a load of wash on one arm, Felipe beams proudly. When Antonia is in a rush to finish a weaving, she keeps Felipe home from school to play with the baby while she works. On one such day when his grandmother was visiting and Felipe was balking, María took him aside and explained.

"Grandson, you're helping your mother because she's earning the money to buy your clothes and shoes. Your little brother cries and she has to stop her work and take care of him. Take care of your little brother. This is what your mother wants you to do. This way your mother can work fast. Then she can buy things for you and your brothers."

Girls and boys of Felipe's age bear the weight of clay jugs on their backs without complaining as they accompany their mothers on daily trips back and forth to the tank of water, often a half mile or more each way. They know that the water they carry back to their houses will cook their beans and quench their thirst. Beginning at five or six years of age girls and boys begin helping their mothers make tortillas. At this age mothers will also begin to teach daughters and interested sons how to embroider. Felipe's and Sebastián's teachers and schoolmates are beginning to take on some importance in their lives, and will remain important as long as they attend school. Nevertheless, socialization occurs primarily at home (Modiano 1973). When school is not in session or their parents need them, Felipe or Sebastián go with their parents on their daily rounds.

The first chilly dawn Domingo asked Felipe to accompany him to the milpa, Felipe was torn. After changing his mind several times and breaking down in tears once, he managed to separate from the fire and his mother. In the milpa he played and helped his father with simple chores. When they returned that afternoon Felipe came home like a man. He sat down by the fire, asked Antonia for his matz', and filled our ears with stories about animals and people he encountered on the road.

Arias (1973: 29) describes child rearing among his people as helping children remember what "they have temporarily forgotten." After they are about five years old, parents expect children to think things through before they do them. When Pedranos of all ages talk, it is customary to tell the other what one is about to do, the assumption being that one has thought out what one intends to do sufficiently to be sure that it will not be offensive to others, or in the case of a child, prohibited. Then the others around the person say something to the effect of, "O.K., so do it."

While parents tell children to be responsible for their own actions, they do not tell them to be responsible for others' actions or to make up for what others don't do. Pedranos of all ages seem to be able to detach themselves emotionally from family members who are not conforming to what others expect of them, without blaming themselves. Living in a subsistence economy with a fairly strict sexual division of labor, beginning in childhood, clarifies each household member's role and importance for survival of the group, and makes dependence on others necessary. Just as they do not accept the sole responsibility for keeping a household running, women do not usually accept the sole responsibility for monitoring the emotional tone of households. Pedranos say that both parents should nurture children's and each other's spiritual growth. Most spouses show pleasure in each other's company. Although men have considerable power over women, they explain this power as an extension of the economic and moral support they provide for their households, rather than power to make their wives do what they want.

Pedranos value large and close families, but they have a tenuous hold on their children. The infant mortality rate is high in Highland Chiapas. In their 1988 census of a Chamula hamlet Diane Rus and Jan Rus (Rus 1990) found that one-fourth of the children die before age five. In my 1988 census of a hamlet in Chenalhó I found that of the forty-five women I interviewed, twenty-five women had lost seventy-five children between them.[3]

Neither Antonia nor Anita have lost any children, but they fear that their children may get sick and die. Parents, especially mothers, constantly watch a baby's and toddler's movements because they say its soul is still not firmly attached to its body, and evil forces can easily injure it or lure it away. Mothers watch to see that young ones do not fall and perhaps jar their souls out of their bodies. If this happens, they can experience *xi'el* (fright), resulting in diarrhea.[4] When Antonia first carried her baby to her mother's house, she paused where the path divides near the pitch pine stand and laid sticks across the path that they would not be taking, to make sure the baby's soul would not go the wrong way. Although Antonia is a follower of Catholic Action and familiar with the Christian concept of soul, she says it can't hurt to follow the old ways, because her people need as many safeguards as they have at their disposal.

Infants remain like an extension of their mothers' bodies during their first years. Fathers are only close to their children at intervals during the day and while sleeping. Children sleep between their parents until another infant replaces them or they are old enough to sleep with older siblings. Weaning can occur as late as four years, if no new baby has arrived to take a nursing child's place. When Antonia weaned Sebastián at three and a half years of age, she rubbed a foul-smelling ointment on her nipples to discourage him from nursing. Sebastián cried pitifully and when I arrived, a half a year later, he was still trying to climb on Antonia's lap when the baby was at her breast. Sometimes in his private laments he sings about killing his little brother. At such times Antonia might nuzzle him a little and tease him with her breast, but she makes it clear that he is not welcome on her lap. Now Sebastián's place is on a wood block next to his father. If he wants affection he can sit between his father's legs, hug and kiss Felipe or the baby, or climb on his grandmother or grandfather's knee. María often holds Sebastián when he comes to visit her. At Sebastián's house, he let me hold him. Sebastián had figured out that I was a kind of woman, but not one like his mother and grandmother. When he was still trying to peg me—tall, pale, woman-like person who sleeps alone—he asked me, "Cristina, would you like to marry a rabbit some day?"

Sebastián rarely worried if he couldn't understand me when I talked, nor I him. We rocked back and forth and made the sounds of buses lumbering down the road or helicopters whirring in the sky. Perhaps Sebastián sensed that I, too, had to learn new ways of being in the world. While the others seemed more or less comfortable with themselves, we were like the naked snakes about which Sebastián sang, waiting for someone to clothe us in new skins. One day when I was particularly impatient about my progress in Tzotzil, Antonia compared me to Sebastián:

"Look, you have to remember you've only been here a few months. Think of Sebastián. He has been with us four years, and three of those he was at my breast, drinking not only my milk but my thoughts. But you, you only drink coffee. Sebastián knows how to talk now, but he still has much to learn about how to be one of us. He only knows a little. You, too, have to be with us for a long time to understand us, to be one of us."

While the other adults talk and the children sleep, Marcela nurses her son. I smile at her across the fire. Marcela blushes and presses her face against her child's head. Although a married woman, Marcela is a teenager, and around outsiders she still seems embarrassed about her relatively new roles as wife and mother. When Marcela finished sixth grade in the hamlet school she was not interested in going on in school. Even if she had been, it is doubtful that her parents would have let her, as it would have meant traveling a long way back and forth to the secondary school in Chenalhó each day or staying all week in Chenalhó in a relative's home or in a Ladino's home as a servant. Parents fear that at school girls will talk with boys, "fall in love," and elope. When this happens Pedranos say, "*sk'opon sbaik*," "they have spoken." Sk'opon sbaik is a loaded term which can mean any of the following: "their eyes met," "they merely spoke," "they are in love," "they went off together," "they made plans to marry," and "they had sex on the spot." Elders see a boy's question, "Where are you going?" as tantamount to an invitation to elope. Proper greetings on paths and roads should go:

Girl: "Pass, uncle." (She steps off the trail.)

Older man: "O.K., I'm going, young woman." (He proceeds up the trail.)

Girl: "Go then, uncle."

Romantic love is not a part of Pedrano marriages, but children know about it from watching Ladino couples on buses and in Chenalhó, or catching a pair of Pedrano lovers. They see them put their arms around each other and kiss on the lips. Today some teenagers, even in remote hamlets, speak to each other on the trails, and if they desire each other they may go off together, only to return a few hours or days later to begin the formal bride petition. Until quite recently, this elopement was about as bold a statement of independence as Pedrano teenagers make (see Chapters 9 and 11).

If a man, even a household member, approaches a young woman in a way she doesn't want or she knows is not correct, she usually tells her mother or father immediately and without shame. No one blames her and she doesn't blame herself, because she knows she was not doing anything wrong.

By the time Marcela had graduated from sixth grade she could speak Spanish and was a good weaver, making her own and other women's clothes. It made sense to Marcela and her parents that since she had accomplished the primary objective of education, to learn Spanish, she was now ready to get on with the business of making herself into a woman.

Like most young women at fifteen or sixteen Marcela didn't yearn to get married, I learned from Antonia, who told me about her marriage. Marcela was at the grinder as usual the morning a terribly beautiful man's voice drifted over the icy dawn air from far down the path, gaining in urgency and sweetness as it came closer. Anita was helping María make tortillas. Marcela rested her weight on the handle of the grinder and listened. She looked at her mother, who looked at her father, who lowered his eyes. Hilario knew there was no way out. A few weeks before, a boy named Moisés and his father stopped Hilario in the market in Chenalhó and offered him a bottle of rum. He had to drink it. Normally he would have accepted the rum gladly, but this time he didn't want it. He knew what it was about.

Now Moisés came down the path singing his petition. He knew it well. His voice was high and sweet and he didn't miss a word. He came with his father and two uncles, early so as to be sure to find everyone at home. They were carrying net bags of corn, bananas, pineapples, limes, oranges, and roasted meat. Moisés came in shame expecting to be rejected, to have his gifts returned. He knelt by the door with his arms outstretched and asked for Hilario's and María's pardon. Marcela had moved away from the molino and stood by the fire with Anita. Marcela covered her open mouth with her shawl and gaped at Moisés and his helpers. She stayed that way during the discussion that followed, as if she was watching an event that had nothing to do with her.

When Moisés was about to leave his petitioners said,

"Well, then, that's fine. That's all we have to say. Pardon us, but we're going to leave here all the things that we've brought. You see where we're leaving the things. It is up to you if you throw them away or use them. But we didn't bring these things for you to throw away. We want you to eat all the things that we've brought."[5]

María and Hilario were hard pressed to turn Marcela's suitor down. Moisés was not a known drunk, an adulterer, or an old man. Marcela was of age, fifteen. Moisés had come with all good intentions and a retinue of recommenders in tow. Before Moisés made his next visit, her parents asked Marcela how she felt. She told them she was ready to marry.

Pedranos launch their children into adulthood gradually. During their first years of marriage Marcela and Moisés practiced being a couple under María's and Hilario's watchful eyes. Although Marcela and Moisés have had one child, María and Hilario still have not begun to treat them as adults.

"Has your sleep come?" María asks me.

I nod sheepishly. María, like Antonia, knows my limits. She tells Marcela to go with me to prepare the bed. While I hold a candle Marcela places my sleeping bag on a *petate*, a reed mat, arranges some shawls for my pillow, and tells me that she will be going back to the fire. For the next hour I lie awake, like a child put to bed too early. Every now and then a burst of laughter from the kitchen penetrates my thoughts. I am thinking about how it is for Antonia, Anita, and Marcela to have husbands they did not choose. I know that if Andrés, Moisés or Domingo don't do their work, scold their wives needlessly, drink a lot, or take up with other women, María and Hilario will tell the men to leave, or Antonia to come home. And the girls will not blame themselves if things go badly. After all, they didn't choose their husbands.

Nevertheless, I wonder about their desires. Pedranas' feelings seem muted and private, and contrast sharply with the assertive style of expressing feelings to which most Americans are accustomed. Pedranas seem most expressive with their babies, especially when they think no one is watching. Babies seem to provide a constant source of amusement and sensual pleasure to women. But knowing how quickly children fall sick and die, women also fear the difficult and often sorrowful work of raising children who may only die. Yet children are important to couples. Not only do babies provide a source of enjoyment and an outlet for affection, but as they grow up they perform important household work. Women also find children a source of security when they must go out of the house. A woman alone is often afraid, but with a child by the hand or appended to her body she seems to feel safer. On a community level, children are fortifying, for they assure the continuation of the group.

As a woman ages, her husband and children respect her wisdom, accomplishments, and her increased heat.[6] Her community recognizes these when she serves a religious cargo. María poured her heart into the cargo she and Hilario served before he became sick. Now that her husband can no longer serve his people or her, she spends her days weaving to earn money to support them and to buy the candles, incense, and rum for traditional cures, and medicines doctors prescribe. She is an accomplished weaver, often advising younger women on their work and how to resolve conflict in their cooperatives. María carefully weighs her personal interests with her family's and community's needs as she decides which traditions serve her well, and which are unjust or no longer working. She is a model to her daughters of how to balance household and community.

However, not until recently has María had a voice beyond her household. The weaving cooperative is one bridge she and her kinswomen are creating to make the transition from subsistence to a market economy, and from a position of power in her household to a greater public role in her community.

I am the last woman to get up in the morning, as usual. The women work around Domingo, who is still sleeping on the reed mat where he and Antonia slept the night before. They are making *k'oxox vaj*, toasted tortillas. This usually means someone will be traveling.

Andrés is the first man to enter the kitchen house. He is wearing pants and a shirt, clothes that let him fade into the Ladino world. Anita looks up at him from time to time as she places cooked tortillas below the semet to toast in the embers. Marcela is grinding beans for her brother-in-law to eat with his toasted tortillas. The creaking of the molino fills the silence between us.

When Andrés has finished his breakfast and the other men are eating, he sits as high as he can in his little chair and clears his throat. I sense that this is not just any farewell, but I don't know where Andrés is going. He speaks first to María, in a voice like the one I imagine he used when he came here as a young suitor.

"Well, mother, I have to be going now. Pardon me that I have to go away for awhile. It's just that it's time for me to go to the plantation. I won't be back for Christmas. If God wants I'll be back when the new year comes, when the cold days come. I'm not going to get rich. But I'll be coming back with a little money."

After María has given him her blessing, Andrés makes a similar personal farewell to Hilario, Domingo, and Antonia. Antonia is the last to bid him farewell.

"I understand that you're going to the plantation. I know that you're going to suffer. You have to sleep on the floor there, and the food is not like here. The men get drunk on Sunday and sometimes there are fights. But, don't be afraid. You're going because you have to. Pray to God that he looks out for you, that you don't have to suffer too much. May God go with you."

Andrés is crying as Anita hands him a napkin filled with tortillas and beans, and a plastic bag of matz'. He tucks the food carefully into his net bag. This and a small gourd of moy are all he will carry. He places a wad of moy in his mouth and cradles it in his cheek as he walks. If he senses danger, he will spit a little on the trail ahead. Households protect, shelter, and comfort; the outside is replete with visible and invisible beings that can bring sickness and death. Machetes may protect people from visible beings, but only the powers of moy protect them from invisible beings.

Anita stays crouched by the fire toasting tortillas as Andrés walks out the door. She lifts her shawl to her eyes and cries quietly. I decide to ask Anita if she will miss Andrés, assuming she will say yes. She laughs and replies, "Why should I? Now I can work without interruption." Sometimes I ask foolish questions, and sometimes Anita plays with me. This time I think there is truth both in what she says and in her tears.

Watching Pedranas interact with their husbands, I know that their men are not just interruptions to them. Yet more than once I've been with Antonia when she has just sat down to weave and Domingo comes home wanting to eat and talk. Antonia tosses me an ironic look as she lays her weaving aside and says, "It seems that *'El Señor'* has come home." But once she has served Domingo his food, she seems to enjoy their talk. And when

she settles back to weaving, she laughs and chats with the boys and Domingo. Pedrano couples often behave like best friends in the privacy of their homes.

With Andrés gone for several weeks, Anita will surely take advantage of the extra time to weave, and perhaps win a prize in her co-op's competition. She and Marcela may help Moisés carry firewood, but when a man leaves home to do wage labor it becomes clear that women and men can survive without each other. However, in a hamlet a woman can survive without marrying by selling her weavings or agricultural products to buy corn. In contrast, a man cannot buy tortillas.[7]

Despite liking free time for weaving, Anita depends upon Andrés. They make all their decisions together. They discuss how to conduct themselves in the world ou ide. Everyone has said that Andrés is going to suffer, and she fears that something bad may happen to him while he is working for them on the plantation. He could get sick and die there. On his way home robbers could leap from the side of the road, kill him with a machete, and take his money. Even if nothing bad happens, Andrés will be with strangers. And every day his heart will hurt.

Tzotzil has no word for "family." The closest words Pedranos and Tzotzil speakers from other townships were able to give me for "family" were *utz alal* (one's consanguineal kin), *jchi'iltak/compañeros* (Sp.) (friends), or *yol xnich'on sbaik* (a gathering of relatives excluding co-parents and neighbors). Nevertheless, *sna* (the household) is the focal point of life for Pedranos. Although Anita's family is not his, Andrés is now a part of her household. Alone, far from Chenalhó, he will yearn for the fellowship, food, and drink of the household to which he belongs.

Laughter, and pleasure in food and drink and the company of others, may be coping mechanisms Pedranos employ to deal with the vagaries of nature and the stresses of living on the bottom of the social order in Mexican society. But in these ways Pedranos demonstrate their commitment to their families and a vision of wholeness, of belonging to others. Even when disrespectful or drunk Pedranos shatter households, Pedranos reaffirm who they are, and who and what matters to them, through their ordered and familiar reunions around the fire. Household rituals integrate Pedranos into a social and economic whole based on communal traditions rather than individual rights. Like the telling of dreams, household rituals are litanies invoking the daily cooperation of men and women and invisible beings.[8]

5

"Before God's flowery face"
The Feast of St. Peter

There is no town in the Indies great or small, even though it be but of twenty families, which is not dedicated thus unto Our Lady or unto some saint, and the remembrance of that saint is continued in the minds not only of those that live in the town, but of all that live far and near, by commercing, trading, sporting, and dancing, offering unto the saint, and bowing, kneeling, and praying before him.

The Indians of the town have their meetings at night for two or three months beforehand, and prepare for such dances as are most commonly used amongst them, and in these meetings they drink of both chocolate and chicha. For every kind of dance they have several houses appointed, and masters of that dance, who teach the rest that they may be perfected in it against the saint's day. For the better part of these two or three months the silence of the night is unquieted with their singing, their holloaing, their beating upon (drums and using as trumpets) the shells of fishes, their waits, and with their piping. And when the feast cometh, they act publicly for the space of eight days what privately they had practiced before. They are that day well apparelled with silks, fine linen, ribbons, and feathers according to the dance. They begin this in the church before the saint, or in the churchyard, and thence all the octave, or eight days, they go dancing from house to house, where they have chocolate or some heady drink or chicha given them. All those eight days the town is sure to be full of drunkards. If they be reprehended for it, they will answer that their hearts rejoice with their saint in Heaven, and that they must drink unto him that he may remember them.

> Thomas Gage (1981: 243) a Dominican friar assigned to a
> Pokomam Maya town in the 1630s, describing a saint's feast

San Pedro Chenalhó, as seen from the road to Pantelhó and San Cristóbal de Las Casas.

We are here. Chenalhó. Today marks my formal debut in Chenalhó. The past four months I have limited my experiences to life in one hamlet, with visits to Antonia's parents, the market in Chenalhó, and San Cristóbal. At my request, Domingo has come with me to Chenalhó to petition on my behalf for me to stay with the couple who are leading the most important fiesta of the year, the Feast of St. Peter, the patron saint of Chenalhó. I feel forever indebted to him. Now, at close hand, I will see how Pedranos use rum in rituals, and how Ladinos and Pedranos carve up social space in the township center.

Domingo and I arrive at the door of the standard bearers' house. The *alperes* (standard bearer) and *me' alperes* (madam standard bearer) emerge from the cavelike interior, lit only by two cooking fires. Domingo greets his relatives respectfully and begins to petition on my behalf. He tells them that I've come to see how women make the fiesta, that I have learned to grind corn, and that I even got drunk once in Tenejapa during Carnival. Angélika, madam standard bearer, has been smiling at me throughout Domingo's petition, and now she laughs. Several women leave their crouched positions by the fire, while men in various states of inebriation move their intimate huddles closer to the action. Domingo and I soon find ourselves inside the house, a little island in the sea of helpers who have come to assist Angélika and her husband, Victorio. I scan the crowd for friendly faces. Two young women at the front of the crowd crane their necks to get a better look at me, then hide behind their shawls to giggle.

Victorio and Angélika give me permission to live with them during the fiesta, although Angélika tells Domingo, apologetically, that there is just not sufficient space on the floor for me to sleep. I will need to sleep elsewhere, but I can stay here from early morning till late night. At first I am disappointed, but then knowing myself and remembering Carnival in Tenejapa, I realize I may welcome some time alone. On the bus ride returning to Domingo's house, I think about Doña Consuelo's house where I stayed during Carnival, and hope that she will have a room for me.

Antonia and Domingo knew that nothing they said could prepare me for the feast of St. Peter. Still, on the eve of my departure they gave me some instructions on how to behave. They aimed their comments at keeping me from offending anyone or embarrassing myself, but from Antonia's tone I could tell they feared their advice was fruitless.

"Cristina, you may not be able to find a place on the fire for your coffee pot. There are many pots of beans, and people toast their tortillas on the side of the fire."

Domingo interrupted Antonia with a comment I couldn't understand. I asked him what he said, but he motioned for Antonia to tell me.

"He said that you have to be careful when you walk around, that you don't step over bowls of food."

Antonia explained to me that elders say when women's genitals pass over a plate of food, if a man eats the food it can weaken him. She also tells me that when they butcher three pigs for the fiesta all women must spit salt and water into the pork fat, although she thinks that doesn't include me. The spitting counteracts any weakening effects on men who eat meat from the power of women who are pregnant or menstruating. It also ensures that the lard will not be too liquid.[1]

Armed with advice and the new blouse that María made me, I make my way to Chenalhó alone. Domingo and Antonia will come later for the most important days of the fiesta.

My arrival at Angélika's and Victorio's is just one more coming in a flow of bodies in and out of the house that they are borrowing for the fiesta. One of the two girls I remember from my last visit is the first to notice me. She takes my things, draping them over her sturdy body, bombarding me with questions:

"Is this your camera? How much did it cost? You can put your coffee here. Where did you buy the little pot and spoon? How much did it cost? Lend me your glasses. I want to see how I look in them. How do you write with this pen? Write 'I love you darling' in English."

I soon discover that Josefina is Angélika's daughter. I am relieved, although surprised, to learn that Josefina goes to secondary school and speaks Spanish well. I barely speak Tzotzil, and have to rely on translators to talk in depth with Angélika and most other women. Josefina jumps at the chance to be my chief translator.

While I expect to find Angélika's cargo important, I am surprised to see that her children's help is indispensable as well. When cargo-holding couples live far from Chenalhó, they often call upon extended kin to tend their animals and milpa while they leave in order to serve their cargos. Because Angélika and Victorio live on the outskirts of town, they do not need to call upon kin to help them. The responsibility of keeping an eye on the house and feeding the animals falls to their children. In addition to this work, all of Victorio's and Angélika's children but Alejandro, their second eldest who works in San Cristóbal, carry out ritual work as well. Enrique, the couple's eleven-year-old son, usually accompanies his father to various houses or to the town hall carrying bottles of rum in a net bag. At the appointed time he produces a bottle for his father to serve to others. The rum his father receives, but cannot finish, Enrique pours through a funnel into an empty bottle. Pancha, Angélika's and Victorio's second eldest daughter, assists her parents dispensing chicha and rum and providing it to the drink pourer, as well as selling it to those who come to buy. She orients me to women's work and other events inside the house. Reina, the eldest daughter at twenty-five, is just as busy as Pancha in her role as *me' cho' vaj*, the assistant who unwraps tamales. She smiles at me often from her station near the head cook who directs her in her work. Pancha tells me that Reina is pregnant, a fact that hasn't escaped me.

The house that I call home for the time I am with Angélika and her family is on the main street of Chenalhó. It is one of several whitewashed, tile-roof, dirt-floor houses that religious and political officials borrow for fiestas. Each house consists of one big room, which is home for about forty helpers. For about two weeks during the Feast of St. Peter and Octavo, another feast which tags on its heels, helpers are together day and night. They prepare and eat food, wash and clean themselves and cooking utensils, carry out numerous rituals, and sleep, all in this one room. Pedranos do not find each other's company annoying; instead they say that fiestas are the happiest of times because the largest number of people to whom one belongs gather together in one place.

The left half of the house where the standard bearers of the Feast of St. Peter and their helpers stay during the fiesta.

Seated on a sack of corn, surrounded by helpers' children, one of the first things I do is draw the layout of the house. A platform in the center divides the room into two equal parts. When women prepare and allot food, they occupy most of this space. Women divide into two work groups, stationed by two fires. Although they tend to stay on the side of the house where they work and sleep, they frequently cross over to opposite sides or meet halfway near the front door to sort beans or make tamales. Men congregate near the front door to eat, drink, play, and listen to music and dress Victorio in his ceremonial clothes. Families share the same sleeping space on the floor, but men and women eat separately. While men and women serve cargos and assist cargo holders as couples, women spend most of their time with women and men with men.

Not long after Josefina helps me settle into the liquor corner where her family store their personal belongings, Angélika offers me a gourd of corn gruel. I thank her, but say I would like to make coffee instead. In spite of Antonia's warning, I brought my coffee pot to the fiesta. I anticipated drinking less and sharing my coffee with others, but I never thought that my whole coffee supply would be gone within an hour of my arrival.

Angélika dismisses my coffee pot with a glance and sends Josefina to bring a metal can used to boil water. As I watch the water boil I look around at women helpers and their children drinking corn gruel, resting, embroidering, combing each other's hair, or chatting. It strikes me that this is the Pedrana equivalent of a "coffee break." But only I, it seems at first, am having coffee.

After the water has drained into the first cup I look at Josefina as if to say, "Should I offer this to someone?" She takes it from my hands and gives it to her mother. Indulging me in my ridiculous drip method using a strainer, Josefina helps me prepare enough cups for every woman and child in the house. It takes about an hour. When we have finished serving everyone, I sit back to savor my quarter cup and realize that for the past hour Josefina has introduced me to every woman and child, and I am no longer a stranger. I have met *me' pan vaj*, the head cook; *me' xchi'il me' alperes*, Angélika's personal helper; *kabilto antz I and II*, the two women who serve food and drink to other women; *me' ulubil* the preparer of *ch'ilim*, a special toasted corn drink; and *me' jriox*, the old woman who prays when Angélika and Victorio pass their cargo to the new cargo holders.

Preparing food and drink is the most important activity in the standard bearer's house during the days preceding the fiesta. Each morning around five A.M. a procession of men and women helpers carries baskets of cooked corn to an electric grinder owned by a local Ladino. There they pay Don Roberto for the use of his grinder and the assistance of one of his workers.

Back at the house two work groups of women ready themselves to make tortillas or tamales. I move out from my place in the corner to help them. Tamales for fiestas take the form of leaf packages containing several hunks of corn dough, with or without beans and salt. When the dough is plain it is "*taki vaj.*" When it is filled with salted, cooked and ground beans and rolled up jelly-roll style, it is "*chenk'ul vaj.*" I am struck by the plainness of fiesta food. Even Pedranos say that taki vaj is relatively tasteless. Still, when Reina describes the "*comida particular,*" "personal meals," that we will soon be having her eyes light up and her voice is animated. Unfolding a tamale that she has just wrapped, she explains,

"Well, after we cook the taki vaj I take the leaves off, like this, and then me' pan vaj puts about eight or ten taki vaj in a basket for each person. Then we sit down and eat by ourselves. You'll see."

I already know that "by ourselves" means out of separate bowls. But until the first "personal meal" I don't realize the importance of these meals. I sit waiting with other women while the two male servers collect baskets of taki vaj and bowls of beans from me' pan vaj, and deliver them to all the men and boys.

Some men share tables while others balance their bowls and baskets on wooden blocks. When they have eaten their fill, they pour the remainder into a plastic bag or container and return their bowls and baskets to the area where the head cook rests between servings. They hold out their bowls to an available woman on the fringes of the area who sets it down near me' pan vaj. After a few women helpers wash dishes, the two women servers begin to serve women and girls, in the same way their male counterparts served men and boys.

While it is customary for men to eat first, when women sit down to eat they do not seem hurried or resentful. They take their time and enjoy the fruits of their labor.

I discovered that no one can eat or drink everything that one receives during the days of fiesta preparation. Every helper brings net or plastic bags, or old containers, in which they store tamales and beans after each meal. Reina asks me if I'll be giving Antonia some of my food when she comes for the fiesta. I had thought of saving pork for Antonia, but not other food. Relating her memories of the fiesta at which her parents officiated when she was fifteen, Antonia focused on the pork banquet her parents served. I never saw her so excited about a memory as at that moment. During the fiesta men butcher a pig, and prepare blood sausage and pork that Angélika and Victorio will feed their helpers and political officials, and sell to passers-by. Later Angélika explains to me that men must do this work because women and important cargo holders should not cut meat nor tend its preparation.

"We aren't permitted to do this. If we touch or cut the meat, then we cut people, too."[2]

Our meal of pork at the Feast of St. Peter consists of two pieces of roasted pork, eight tortillas, and twelve taki vaj, plenty for both Antonia and me.

My plastic bag begins to bulge with tamales and beans, and I soon realize what the overabundance of food might be about. After eating basket after basket of taki vaj there is no doubt in my mind that taki vaj represents the least manipulation of cooked corn necessary to distribute it for consumption and storage. Uncooked corn would not be fit for human consumption. Tortillas just don't suffice. Although eaten at other rituals, they spoil quickly if not toasted, and also, unlike tamales, they do not make neat packages. Taki vaj and chenk'ul vaj, which unite corn and beans in its own package, are preferred foods that assistants can make in great quantities, and that helpers can redistribute to kinsfolk who stop to see them during the fiesta.

Amassing enormous quantities of corn and beans and carefully selecting a knowledgeable specialist to cook and allot them, Angélika and Victorio demonstrate their gratitude to their helpers for supporting them during the fiesta, and to the saints and other spiritual entities for providing abundant crops. In consuming what they can eat and distributing to others what they can't, helpers stand for the whole community of Pedranos, thus spreading the wealth that the Gods have given and proclaiming the importance of the standard bearer and his wife.[3]

Angélika and Victorio chose their helpers carefully, especially me' pan vaj, the most important assistant. Angélika asked one of her sisters to be her cook soon after she received her cargo. A good cook needs to know how to make the food increase in her hands, but she also needs to judge how much corn, beans, and other foods the cargo holding couple need to have on hand. Me' pan vaj's work began before the fiesta, when she advised Angélika about the quantity of food needed and prayed to God to help her in her work. Me' ulubil's work also begins before the fiesta when she toasts corn. She brings the corn with her to the fiesta, and combines it with sugar and water when the morning arrives to make the drink. Similarly, a good drink pourer must know how to increase the rum and chicha in his hands, and like me' pan vaj, prays to God to help him do this.

Angélika was confident in all her helpers and in God. In her dream God told her:

"When you see that you don't have money or what you need and you are gathering your helpers together and you have to give them something to eat, give *all* the corn and beans. Don't deny anyone anything. Let them drink! Let them eat! Give all your corn. I will replenish your pot. I will give you everything so that your pots are full. Don't deny anything to them although you see that they are taking the beans. Don't pay any attention, because I know it. Señora, don't do anything bad, because you are in the center."

Assistants in Angélika's and Victorio's house act like one big family. The efficiency and good humor with which they carry out their duties creates a feeling of well-being and control. Once the fiesta is underway other events take precedence, and we rarely eat all together those "personal meals," ironically so communal. But celebrants sustain a feeling of well-being that keeps everything from falling down when an occasional drunk

Angélika's helpers making tortillas during the Feast of St. Peter.

gets out of hand, or ritual events tumble on top of each other in a relentless progression. We no longer consistently sit down together to eat our "personal meals," although women still share cooking for their families and dignitaries and maintain a stable home base for celebrants. In their public prayers and recitations, cargo holders verbalize what they practice at these ritual meals and daily when they gather together around the fire in their respective homes. They tell the Gods and each other that they have come together at this special time and that they will continue to come together the same time next year and every year after that. The standard bearer and his wife are to fellow Pedranos what good parents or older siblings are to children. They stabilize the "family" by carrying out an ordered, expectable sequence of events.

The delight with which most Pedranos both talk about and consume food and drink during fiestas encouraged me to see these substances as closely related and symbolically important. Rum and chicha, however, stand out from other drinks and food in the greater heat which they promise and their many-layered symbolic roles. Admirers of rum's virtues say that it brings warmth, courage, contentment, spirit, and intelligence. In a special ritual conducted to protect the village, participants drink three bottles of rum so that all will forget their disagreements (Arias 1985: 148):

> so that they forget their machetes and knives and that cold water
> falls over their pistols and guns and freezes them so they can't be
> fired, so that the hands and feet of those who guard rancor and
> anger in their hearts stay tied, embraced, and immobile.

While I turn to coffee to keep me going, many Pedranos say that for them rum is the gas that makes their motors run. Rum and chicha play a part in almost all public transactions and fiesta drinking events in Chenalhó. Long before I came on the scene, rum had fueled the preparations for this fiesta as it has all fiestas before it. Angélika and Victorio began preparing for this fiesta before they took their office from last year's standard bearer and his wife. Angélika says it has been a joyful year for her, although demanding. She suggested taking on the cargo of St. Peter to her husband after a dream she had in which St. Peter came to her and said,

"'We will take care of each other well. You are going to carry me,' he said.

"This St. Peter wants me to carry him! I saw him clearly. He was very little. He has his necktie, his hat with ribbons, his sandals, and his bag. I saw it all well. I had to accept when he told me that I had to carry him. But I told him that I didn't want to carry him. Well, I didn't know [if he was really St. Peter], because it was in my dream."

The "Lord of the sky" had come to Angélika once before, when she accepted me' paxyon, the most important female cargo in Carnival. He reassured her:

"'Don't be afraid, Señora. You are O.K. here, as my servant. Don't be afraid about my work, I will help you. This is the way my fiesta begins. All my children have done it for me,' the Nazarene said.

"I thought it wasn't God. But it was God whom I saw because he shows us everything very clearly. That's how I know it was the true God I saw."

When he came to her about her present cargo, God told Angélika:

"'Well, Señora. Don't be sad. Don't let your heart become sad. Now, if you feel something bad, or you don't have money, come and talk to me and I will give you my blessings, because I am God,' he said. 'I've given you all that you have. There's corn, beans, money. Use all of it,' he said. 'It's for all my children on the earth,' he said. 'If you go in another land, I'll go with you, you'll go in my hands. Because you're my servant, and also you will be very pure,' he said. 'Don't be afraid. I myself will make sure that you get by. Nothing bad will happen because we'll oversee it together, you can triumph. Although you don't have money, don't be afraid. You're poor, but look at Victorio. He comes to my house. He talks to me every day. It's very good that he worships me. If you, too, remember me in your heart, every day will go well for you. In that way you'll have money. But only if you worship me, if you always follow me. But if you forget me, you'll only have enough to survive. Always I have money beneath my feet. I have a purse and shoes. Here in my hands you'll never have any need. Because I love all my children. I love you,' he told me.

"When I dreamt, I saw many things there. I saw everything: for example, the large container [of chicha], tobacco, chile, corn, *cruzador* [a man with a cross on the front of his garment]. It was all there. But that was the harvest of the Lord. He gives everything to us when we work hard. Now, if we don't work, he doesn't give it to us, [he gives us] only a little.

"He gave me a small gourd. Then he went to bring something in a metal drum and I took it [chicha] in my shawl. I forgot about my fear. I never had any more fear about my cargo. I never worried about it. The chicha and rum just came."

With her past successes in other cargos and St. Peter's words in her heart, Angélika went to talk to Victorio:

"'Let's take a cargo,' I told him. 'I like St. Peter. I want to see him with my own eyes. I want to see many flags passing before my eyes,' I told him.[4]

"'I'm not going to take a cargo,' he said the first time. 'If you want to take a cargo, you can do it in your soul.'

" 'But, why do you say this to me?' I said, because I was a little hurt.

"So, little by little he thought about it. 'O.K.,' he told me. 'If you'd like to, we'll do it. Let's do it.' "

To fulfill their cargos Angélika and Victorio have had to arrange for many helpers. They have also had to borrow money, as no Pedrano has enough to buy all the rum, chicha, corn, beans, skyrockets, pigs, and other items fiestas require. Sometimes they borrowed 10,000 pesos, sometimes 50,000. They borrowed corn and beans and returned it in kind. After their harvest was in, they sold corn and beans to earn money to pay their debts.

Angélika and Victorio have had to visit all the homes of prospective helpers, and those from whom they hoped to borrow money. Pedranos say it is difficult to ask for favors. Many fortify themselves with three cups of rum before venturing off to ask for a favor. It is after the third cup that anxiety lessens. When a person must remember exact words of prayers or petitions, rum relieves her anxiety about forgetting, and in case she does, it makes her feel less distressed about forgetting.

Modesty and the *vokaroil* (a gift of rum) characterize Pedranos' requests for help. Pedranos value modesty for both sexes, not just for women. In contrast, Ladinos and Americans say modesty and cooperation are more appropriate attitudes for women than for men. While Pedrano petitions sometimes seem self-abnegating, minimizing oneself and one's resources seems less a reflection of self-worthlessness than a strategy to equalize relations between the one petitioning and the one petitioned. By accepting gifts of rum Pedranos acknowledge the effort involved in making the gift. They show their respect to the donor in phrases such as, "Thank you, now I have drunk of your and your husband's labor." Modesty, respect, and three cups of rum help make both parties' hearts equal.[5]

From my vantage point in the corner among sacks of corn and containers of liquor, I watch Angélika and Victorio managing their supplies and overseeing the general operations of the house. When I arrived, the liquor corner in the southeast part of the house held one twenty-liter glass jar of rum, two barrels of chicha, a case of Pepsi, and baskets of bottles, some full of rum, others waiting to be filled from the glass jar. At various times during the fiesta more barrels of chicha and jars of rum arrived. By the end of the fiesta, eighteen fifty-liter barrels of chicha and thirteen twenty-liter jars of rum had arrived. Although Victorio and Angélika make chicha to sell on market days and out of their house, they could not make enough for the fiesta. They had to buy chicha from a man in another hamlet, who transported it to Chenalhó on horseback, two barrels strapped on either side of each horse's back, "nine horses" of chicha. Rum they purchased from a Chamula man. He operates a still and sells to fellow Chamulas,

Pedranos, and Migueleros, residents of a small township which lies in a curve between Chenalhó and Chamula.

I also watch Victorio when he is drinking in the house during the fiesta, and how Angélika cares for him when he is drunk. At the end of a day's drinking Victorio usually passes out in a little chair. When Angélika decides it is time to go to bed, she tips Victorio's chair so that he slips off it onto the reed mat she places beside the chair. Then she lays a shawl under his head and a blanket over him. Sometimes Victorio awakens and insists on staying up and having a cigarette,[6] or drinking some more rum. Other times he sleeps until five A.M. or when Angélika awakens him.

Josefina tells me that her mother stopped drinking before Josefina was born, and only makes la acción when she has a cargo. Her father drinks in his work as a shaman, in his cargos, and also whenever he wants to. She tells me her parents make chicha and sell it in the marketplace on weekends. I had heard a rumor to that effect, but it seemed too fortuitous, that the leaders of the fiesta that I chose to observe would also be chicha makers. But I discover that it is true when Josefina takes me to her house to feed the turkeys and chickens. Before I had any idea who he was or that I would come to know his family so well, I had asked Victorio if I could sketch the horse-drawn chicha mill.

Drinking in the standard bearer's house, like eating, is usually convivial and festive. Besides providing pleasure to their assistants, rum is the way the cargo holding couple pay their helpers. While all adult men and women receive equal portions during ritual drinking events in which they participate together, men participate in many drinking rituals without women. Older women do most of the official and unofficial drinking in the

Angélika's and Victorio's horse-drawn press for mashing sugar cane to make chicha.

standard bearer's house. Most women under fifty do la acción, and pour the rum and some of the chicha they receive into containers to carry home. Some older women drink a lot, but, as Angélika tells me after the fiesta, they never cause any problems. They just sing and dance.

The stability and security I feel in the standard bearer's house contrasts sharply with my uneasiness in the streets. During the days leading up to the fiesta and during the three major days of the fiesta, Pancha and Josefina ask me to *"pasear,"* "walk around town," with them. This is the grand pastime during fiestas and whenever Pedranos visit Chenalhó or other villages. It involves strolling up and down the streets to see what is happening. The girls love it. I am less enthusiastic, especially when I am dressed like a Pedrana. I become a spectacle, although one that gives Pedranas and Ladinas some pleasure. To Pedranas I am trying to be a true woman. To Ladinas I am dressing up like "our Inditas."

I usually have my fill of each foray in less than an hour and head back to the standard bearer's house. In the streets and at the market the traditional fiesta coexists with the Ladino popular fiesta in a mishmash of hawking vendors, processing dignitaries, reeling drunks, cavorting clowns, and music blaring from a loudspeaker.

Some of the most notorious drinkers at fiestas are musicians, who sustain themselves through all-night jam sessions with rum. There are two traditional types of musicians in Chenalhó, a string group, *sonovil,* and a drum, flute, and cornet group, *jvabajom.* While jvabajom members specialize, each sonovil knows how to play guitar, violin, and harp. Sonovil groups, of which there are three, wait to be invited to play for a particular fiesta. There is only one group of jvabajom and they play at every fiesta. Both groups entertain throughout the entire fiesta, and their only pay is rum and food.

Traditional Pedranos say that song is God's favorite sound and that rum heats, and therefore empowers, musicians' words. One musician stood out among the fiesta personnel because he didn't drink. I wondered how Pablo could manage to avoid drinking with so much pressure around him, and a history of problem drinking in the past. Watching Pablo interact with the other musicians, it became clear to me that they respect his decision not to drink, as do Victorio and Angélika, who asked him to play for them. But some of his friends, who find Pablo strolling around the market, have a hard time accepting that he will not drink with them. He has to put up with their insistence and occasionally their ridicule. After the fiesta Pablo tells me how he handles this:

"It is difficult, because those people who know I don't drink say,
"'Why aren't you drinking?'

"'I can't, because it does me a lot of harm. . . . If it were food I would eat it. If it were soda I would drink it,' I say.

"'Yes, but you know we're friends,' my friends say.

"'Yes, we're friends, but if you're going to invite me to a soda, I'll drink with you right now. It's been a while since I quit rum,' I tell them. 'Rum, no more,' I say.

"'Well, then, if you don't want to drink rum, you'd better go right over there to the church. Stop there in the church so we can incense you, because you're going to be a saint,' they say.[7]

"'Thank you,' that's all I say. Because men who drink rum, they don't know any better. . . . Only God knows. God left rum on the earth, but God said,

"'One can't drink a lot. You are going to drink one, two, three cups only. If you are going to drink a lot, you are going to die,' God says.

"I think it's better to play my music in the fiesta sober, so it goes well. I watch how they do it. When I'm drunk, I don't see how the fiesta goes. Who's to blame [if the fiesta doesn't go well]? I'm to blame.

"The standard bearers know how I am . . . they give gifts of rum, three bottles to each musician. Because they already know that I'm not going to drink, I say,

"'Give me 1,000 pesos. Throw me 500 pesos for my expenses. I'll buy soda, because I'm not going to drink rum.'

"They only give me money now. I give it to my wife to buy what she wants to eat. Right now we're happy."

Ladinos from other townships also come to Chenalhó to celebrate the popular fiesta, and some come to the standard bearer's house to buy rum, knowing that it will be strong. Victorio and Angélika serve *nich pox* (flower of the pox), a strong rum, as well as *sikil pox*, a watered down version.

Pedranos have less tolerance for drunk Ladinos than for one of their own. The only time I saw Angélika take action with a drunk, Ladino or Pedrano, was when a Ladino came to buy rum and secondarily to get a look at me. Flanked by several women helpers and speaking from the security of her house, Angélika met the man at the door where he was trying to get me to drink with him. She raised her voice louder than I had ever heard her speak, telling him they had no more rum and he should not bother us. Knowing how Pedranos frown on scolding each other, I thought that Angélika may have seen this as her chance to get back at Ladino men for some of the abuse she and her daughters have suffered at their hands. And, too, maybe she felt it was her duty to protect me from potentially dangerous Ladinos.

In the days of preparation for the fiesta I drink along with others as we eat, orderly and controlled. Angélika, Pancha, or Reina allot rum and chicha to me' pan vaj's son and to the head male servers, who serve men and sometimes women, and to the two women servers, who serve women. When serving both men and women, men or women servers serve senior and junior men first and then senior and junior women.

Before the fiesta several people advised me to buy a plastic container into which I could put rum and chicha that the drink pourer and others offer me. I bought a one liter container for chicha and a smaller one with a strap for pox. At the beginning I try to drink what the drink pourer offers me, but it is impossible to drink it all without getting drunk. I decide that I already give people enough to talk about without that, too. Women my age and women with small children usually do not make more than la acción when the drink pourer serves them a cup. I follow their lead, taking the first cup of the event that the drink pourer offers me, then making la acción from that point on. Like my plastic bags, my plastic jugs get fuller and fuller, and I wonder what I am going to do when they are full.

I don't have to worry, as the ritual drinking that fills much of our time in pre-fiesta days moves into the streets, the town hall, and the marketplace once the fiesta has begun. Men and women still drink in the standard bearer's house, and in fact some men who drank moderately before the fiesta began, drink more as time wears on. But now in addition to offering liquor as a way to show gratitude to helpers and make their work lighter, the offer of a cup of rum often signals a ritual event that Victorio or Angélika must perform at a particular time.

The Feast of St. Peter features a special meal that the standard bearer and his wife serve the civil authorities on the principal day of the fiesta. The all-male feast consists of pork and tamales, and takes place in front of the standard bearer's house. Victorio's two servers scurry back and forth between me' pan vaj and the table, carrying heaping bowls of pork and baskets of plain and bean tamales. Two drink pourers are equally busy serving shots of rum to each authority. Most of the authorities give their shot glasses to their sons or another young male relative, who pours the rum into a bottle. The two servers present each guest with a leaf and red flower.

After the meal Angélika and Victorio participate in the first of four *juramentos* (oaths of office) that will take place during the fiesta. Each time, Angélika and Victorio kneel to receive the white and red banners of Santiago. Angélika's personal helper adjusts the hem of her skirt, while the regidores hold the tips of the banners, which form a Lorraine cross, toward first Victorio and then Angélika. Touching the cross to their faces and chests, the couple make the sign of the cross three times.

After passing their obligation to the new standard bearer and his wife, Angélika moves inside where me' jriox, the prayer assistant, awaits her. Meanwhile Victorio stays outside with the authorities and *jriox*, the man who will pray in response to me' jriox. I am outside with a crowd of on-lookers, and don't know what is about to happen. Later I learn what went on inside the house, when I attend the Fiesta of San Nicolás a year later. This time I make sure to see me' jriox pray. At the outgoing standard bearer's house, I meet Ernestina, the standard bearer's daughter, who like Josefina, takes us under her wing. We have only dropped in to visit and I am hesitant to ask if I can take photos or record. Margarita, Ernestina's mother, gives me permission in exchange for some copies of the photos. Me' jriox, however, isn't interested in my recording her prayer. Ernestina suggests that me' jriox is an old lady and is probably afraid of my equip-ment and me. I wonder if it is because me' jriox sees her prayer the way many Pedranos see their images on photos, as their souls incarnate. Recorded and taken to parts unknown, a soul can be lost, thus endanger-ing its owner. Me' jriox may be risking more than her own soul, as her prayer is for Margarita's and her husband's souls. Besides, some photogra-phers have put images of her people on postcards; me' jriox may suspect that I will make copies of her prayer and sell it. Although me' jriox doesn't know what is marketable in my country, she knows that my people com-moditize most things. Why not prayers?

The two knowledgeable prayer-givers face each other reverently, heads slightly bowed, hands together in front of their bodies. Jriox, the standard bearer's prayer assistant, stands a few feet in front of the doorway facing the inside of the house. The standard bearer and other town au-thorities stand behind him. Me' jriox stands about five feet from the door, facing outside. Margarita is directly behind her with her head bowed. Dur-ing the prayer, which lasts about half an hour, I am crouched near Ar-mando, a well-known healer who is *kabilto vinik* (one of the two male servers in the standard bearer's house) in the fiesta. Always helpful, Ar-mando tries to answer my questions.

"Armando, would you do me the favor of telling me why me' jriox stands inside and jriox stands outside?"

"Ah, you want to know this. Well, the woman is inside because the woman controls the house and the man is outside because, well you know, he has his 'office' outside of the house."

Jriox begins praying first, then a few minutes later me' jriox begins. As they pray helpers and onlookers listen, talk, and carry on with their work. I want to know what me' jriox is saying, and I ask Armando if he would translate her prayer as she speaks. As prayers in Tzotzil are spoken rapidly, Armando gives me a condensed Spanish version:

> Now her cargo has passed.
> Thanks to God now it has finished.
> Now she has left it for a new obligation.
> We are going to see if it passes or not.
> If God wants, it passes.
> Thanks to God,
> For the other is content.
> Now she is content because her cargo has passed.

When me' jriox finishes her part she makes the sign of the cross. Then one by one the authorities standing outside approach her to salute her and the standard bearer's wife. They extend their fingertips toward me' jriox' outstretched hands and lightly touch her fingertips. Then each man touches Margarita's bowed, shawl-covered head with the tips of his fingers. The men say "vixin!" (sister) to each woman, and the women re-ply "*jbankil*" (older brother). One drunken official dances on his toes to-ward the women, bows absurdly low, and salutes Margarita with "me' alperes" instead of "vixin." He seems pleased with the laughter his parody brings.

Tired from her work, me' jriox takes a seat that Armando places in front of the baskets of food. The head female server, Armando's wife, of-fers me' jriox several baskets of taki vaj and chenk'ul vaj. Her young grandson accepts the baskets for his grandmother and pours the hunks of corn dough into two plastic bags. Armando offers me' jriox two bottles of rum, which her grandson pours through a funnel into her own bottles. It seems that this time me' jriox can accept her rum without putting a cup to her lips.

While rum and chicha are the drinks of choice at most fiesta drinking events, women serve ch'ilim and coffee at two events, and over the past ten years soda pop has been growing in popularity as a substitute for rum in some rituals. While most Traditional Pedranos still consider rum the most symbolically powerful drink, some fiesta celebrants maintain that gifts of soda during fiestas are as fitting for helpers and saints as rum. In 1987 in Chenalhó a soda cost from 250 to 500 pesos and a similar size bottle of rum 500 pesos, making gifts of rum and soda almost equivalent in mone-tary value.

Each year, on St. Peter's own day, authorities and their wives from the neighboring township of San Miguel Mitontik and two Pedrano communi-ties carry their saints' statues to Chenalhó to accompany St. Peter. In a grassy area near the crosses that stand on the south side of town, I wait with a crowd of Pedranos for the contingent from Mitontik to arrive. It is hot. I look longingly at the red, yellow, and orange bottles of soda stacked in cases. Amid much fanfare Migueleros come, bearing their Archangel Michael, who rests on a platform supported by two wooden poles carried on the shoulders of two Migueleros.

The entourages from Mitontik and Chenalhó meet in the middle of a U-shaped area, formed by benches. Angélika and her helpers incense the statues, as celebrants greet each other and pray to each other's saints. When the formalities are over, everyone sits down on a bench and waits to receive a bottle of soda, Sin Rival for Pedranos and Pepsi for Migueleros. In past years the standard bearer and his wife used to give rum to the authorities from Mitontik, but since the last president took office Mitontik has been dry. The president led a vigorous prohibition campaign, arguing that Migueleros could move out of poverty if they would stop drinking rum. He won the people over and enacted a "dry" law when he took office.

The month before I participated in the Feast of St. Peter I attended the Fiesta of San Miguel, to compare it with fiestas where alcohol is served. Antonia suggested that I take Felipe with me, so that he could see Mitontik and how Migueleros celebrate fiestas without alcohol. When we arrived the town center was full of people drinking sodas and fruit-flavored drinks; however, not everyone was sober. On the outskirts of town where we waited for the bus to return to Chenalhó, several stands were crowded with men drinking chicha, rum, and beer.

Rumblings of discontent surface from time to time in Mitontik, but Mitontik has successful models to follow. Several other Highland communities have voted to go dry, most notably Oxchuc, a Tzeltal community. It has sustained a dry law since the early 1980s. Drinking goes on there as well, but not in fiestas or in the marketplace.

On the principal day of the fiesta, Angélika changes office with the incoming standard bearer's wife in the church, exchanging Sin Rival instead of rum. Although I watch Angélika dress for the event I do not take notes, but turn to my memories of when Margarita's helpers dressed her.

Ceremonial clothes are longer and bulkier than ordinary clothes, and are difficult to put on without help. Three women formed a circle around Margarita. Her personal helper and the two women servers secured Margarita's skirt with a rope, adjusting the pleats so that they fell neatly. One of Margarita's helpers produced a tiny gourd and served Margarita a cup of rum, which Margarita drank down. Then the other two women and the drink pourer drank a cup. Next the women helped Margarita put her ceremonial blouse over her ordinary one, placing her at the symbolic center of the universe. The designs that encircle Margarita's neck and adorn her back, breast, and arms show that she holds a religious office and that she is in a position in time and space to request assistance from powerful beings.[8]

Once dressed, Margarita placed a bottle of rum in front of an incense burner near the pot of corn gruel. *Tot ulubil* (the corn gruel maker was a man at this fiesta) took the bottle and offered Margarita a small gourd, which she drank. Then Margarita's helper offered the corn gruel maker a gourd, which he acknowledged and drank. While acknowledging drinks, Margarita and tot ulubil kept up a friendly banter.

At the Feast of St. Peter I ask Angélika to pose for me in her full ceremonial attire, after she is fully dressed. She chooses to hold a bottle of rum in front of her heart. I have just watched kabilto antz and another helper transform Angélika from one of them into a symbol of her people. In this moment, the bottle of rum by her heart, her shawl shielding her radiance, Angélika seems to have moved beyond us, to a secure, peaceful place. Perhaps she is remembering what St. Peter told her in her dream:

"Señora, don't do bad, because you are in the center. Don't be afraid, Señora. I, myself, will see how you pass."

Angélika's mood in this moment, and managerial skills at other times, seem to draw from her confidence in St. Peter to come through with his promises. After all, she is coming through with hers.

After Angélika's helpers dress her, the men dress Victorio. An older helper sets two bottles of rum on a reed mat in front of Victorio, who is already intoxicated. Victorio plants his feet as firmly as he can on the mat and waits for the men to begin. Between cups, several men help Victorio into his knee-high red breeches, high-back sandals, a white-and-red shawl and cloth turban, a purse, and a broadbrimmed black felt hat.

Finally everyone is ready to proceed to the church, one of the nine times Angélika will go to the church to incense the saints. *Me' tzebetik*, "mother of the maidens," joins Angélika and her entourage on the street, partway to the Church. Sprinkling laurel leaves as she walks, me' tsebetik leads the procession into the church. The first time I saw her leading a procession at Carnival, I was surprised that her skirt was faded and her shawl worn. Under her shawl she wore a tattered sweater. Me' tzebetik is a widow, and her cargo does not bring her any material rewards, except food during fiestas. She is responsible for gathering laurel leaves which she sprinkles in the path of all processions, as well as branches that crossbacks, male actors in Carnival, use in mock curative rituals. Her cargo could last for many years if she carries it well. The last me' tzebetik drank a lot, and eventually lost her cargo because no one could depend on her to turn up for every procession.

Behind me'tzebetik comes Angélika, who is surrounded by helpers carrying incense burners. I follow the women toward the front of the church, where they incense the image of St. Peter and other saints' images. While the women incense the statues, men hoist the images onto wooden platforms to carry them around the park. At the back of the church they wait for the authorities and standard bearers to finish praying in the front pews. There four young people carry the statues of St. Peter into the street: two girls carry "Big St. Peter," and two boys, "Little St. Peter." Celebrants parade three times around the park to the music of jvabajom and the tipsy dancing of the alperes and his captains.

Me' tzebetik leads the procession back into the church, where Angélika's change of office will take place. Just inside the door of the church before the banks of pews, Angélika and the incoming me' alperes lie face down on reed mats, their heads covered by their shawls and their legs by their long skirts. Angélika's helper places an incense burner by her head and then moves to Angélika's feet, where she tucks the hem of her skirt around her ankles. The regidores wave the banners over the women while dancing around them three times. Jvabajom and the incoming and outgoing standard bearers join them. After circling the women, the men go outside to the three crosses in the park which face the church. Circling the crosses three times, they begin the ceremony releasing Angélika's soul of its burden and passing the obligation to the soul of the incoming me' alperes.

Angélika's helper taps her legs to signal her that it is time to get up. I follow the crowd of onlookers, mostly women, to the right side of the church where the image of Santa Lucía stands. Here under Lucía's gaze Angélika will pass her service to her *k'exol,* her replacement.[9] Angélika is veiled as she faces the wall flanked by the two outgoing captain's wives. Her unveiled replacement faces Angélika, flanked by the two incoming captain's wives. Angélika and the new standard bearer's wife "cross their heads" three times by touching each other's cheeks.

At this point Josefina, hair recently curled in Ladina style, produces a bottle of apple-flavored Sin Rival from her net bag, removes the cap with her teeth and hands it to her mother. Angélika receives the bottle from Josefina and exchanges it with her replacement. Each woman pours the other three shots from her bottle, saying, "Try a little"; then Angélika says:

> Now we are changing.
> Here you are going to receive your cargo
> and your commitment to make the fiesta.

Thus you are going to receive the cargo of me' alperes.
Your commitment rests on you and in your power this day, this year.
Now you have your cargo during this day and this year.
We will see if you fulfill this year here on the earth.
Thus my cargo has passed.
Now I am going like a branch and its leaves.

With these words Angélika mourns the loss of her cargo, for during the time she serves it she is connected to something bigger than herself and her household. Like a branch severed from the trunk of a tree, Angélika goes on without a direct connection to the divine, the nourishing roots of life itself. After this day when Angélika greets a *pasara*, another woman who has held a cargo, she will salute her differently than a woman who has not held an office and therefore remains a *tze antz*, "a raw or crude woman." Bowing slightly, Angélika will extend her right hand to touch the finger tips of the woman. She will say, "*Ya'a sasain ya'a*" ("I am saluting you, grandmother") (McGreevy 1983: 5).

After Angélika and her replacement have finished drinking, they offer the remaining soda to women onlookers. I join the women in receiving my cup and toast them with, "*Ta xkuch'*," "I am drinking." When her bottle is empty Angélika gives it to Josefina, who puts it in her net bag.

The outgoing women bid farewell to the incoming women with "We'll talk again soon" and "I'm going." They pause at the door, face the altar and cross themselves. Turning around, they also cross themselves facing the three crosses in the park. Helpers who carry incense burners for both Angélika and her replacement dump the ashes from the burners at the feet of the crosses, and then the entire entourage of women proceed to their respective houses.

The last ritual event with liquor takes place just before helpers return to their homes. Although many men are drinking the last of the liquor supply, the tone is subdued as Angélika and her helpers prepare the last meal of the fiesta. The meal, consisting of tortillas, beans, and a raw green, recalls the first meals of the fiesta before we began to eat tamales instead of tortillas. Like these first meals, it smooths the transition from public fiesta meals of tamales to private family meals of tortillas.

After everyone has eaten and women helpers have washed and dried borrowed bowls and baskets in the back yard, Angélika sets a small table near the front door, in the public space. She places a beautifully brocaded cloth on it, an incense burner underneath it, and two bottles of pox at one end. Then she and Victorio assemble their most important helpers around the table.

The head cook, the atole maker, her husband, the two server couples,

Angélika (on left) exchanging office with her k'exol (replacement).

and Angélika's personal helper join Angélika and Victorio around the table. Amidst much discussion about the piles of money, Victorio and one of the male servers count the profit from selling pork, rum, and chicha. They lay the 240,000 pesos in several piles on the table. Victorio offers the first handful of bills, payment on a debt, to the other male server's wife. As her husband had to go to San Cristóbal, she receives this payment for her husband as well as herself. No helpers expect to be paid, but Victorio and Angélika give me' pan vaj 2000 pesos, in honor of her important work. Although worth only about one dollar in 1987, 2000 pesos was a help to me' pan vaj, who is a widow. The only other helpers to receive money are me' ulubil, who also receives 2000 pesos and a barrel of chicha, and kabilto antz and kabilto vinik I and II, who receive 1000 pesos each. Angélika and Victorio take 2000 pesos and divide it between themselves while Angélika and her daughters dispense rum to the female servers, and Victorio dispenses rum to the male servers.

When Victorio finishes distributing the money, the male server begins to serve shot glasses of rum. Me' ulubil and her husband drink their cups, as does Victorio. Other helpers put their rum in bottles to take home. Each answers Victorio and Angélika with "I am drinking" as they accept the cup and "I have finished" when they hand it back to the drink pourer. When both bottles are empty the assistants gather their things together and say goodbye to each person remaining in the house.

Accompanying Angélika in her ritual work, women's work took on new meaning to me; it seemed to be as much about the regeneration of life and the reaffirmation of proper relations between people, and between mortals and the Gods, as it was about material survival. In this sense Indigenous women in communities with strong religious cargo systems, such as exist in Highland Chiapas, have access to sources of power and prestige that Ladinas and Indigenous women who have lost their connection to their communities no longer have (Rosenbaum 1993: 154).

Angélika asserted and demonstrated that her cargo is as important as her husband's in a myriad of ways. Relating accounts of her dreams in which the saints charged her with her cargos and guided her in daily life, Angélika established her direct communication with the Gods. Angélika's dreams have empowered her so that others must work through her, as well as Victorio, to secure good crops and prosperity in all things. In carrying out ritual duties that also support Victorio's status and power, Angélika may validate herself in part through Victorio and other Pedranos. But her work, her respect for traditions, and the approval and caring she receives from the invisible beings seem to be her most important sources of personal strength.

By monitoring the fiesta from their houses, and in the examples they set in their public rituals, women cargo holders and their assistants make strong statements about taking responsibility for themselves, their communities, and powerful substances. Women don't just react to their husbands' or Ladinos' actions or imitate them. Although Padre Miguel, the priest in Chenalhó, does not let Pedranos exchange rum in church, women could move the site of their change of office if they wanted to use rum. Instead they stay where their beloved saints can witness them, turning what others might see as a restriction into a statement about soda as a valid replacement for rum in an important communal ritual.[10]

In Pedrano public rituals men try to put the focus on themselves and rum and meat, substances over which they exert considerable control. They demonstrate their power through memorizing long prayers or petitions and in drinking. On the surface they appear to have succeeded in putting themselves at center, but in dramas about gender relations during

Carnival and in defensive attitudes they have developed toward using rum in public rituals, they reveal their insecurity and ambivalence about women's power.

Studies by feminist scholars of women's symbolic roles in diverse communities support what Pedranas say and publically dramatize to their kinsmen and women.[11] Rosenbaum's (1993) study of gender relations in Chamula demonstrates the constant work it requires for men to perpetuate the ideology that they are in control. In her analysis of Trobriand women's exchange relations during mortuary rituals Weiner (1976) urges scholars to extend notions of power beyond social contexts to the articulation between social and cosmic orders. Trobriand and Maya peoples articulate these realms closely. In both cultures women obtain power through the duties they perform in support of their deities or ancestors during rituals. Weiner argues that any study that does not include women's roles as they see and experience them, is only a partial study (ibid.: 228–229):

> Whether women are publicly valued or privately secluded, whether they control politics, a range of economic commodities, or merely magic spells, they function within that society, not as objects but as individuals with some measure of control. We cannot begin to understand either in evolutionary terms or in current and historical situations why and how women in so many cases have been relegated to secondary status until we *first* reckon with the power women do have, even if this power *appears* limited and seems outside the political field.

Much as Trobriand men must work around Trobriand women's exchange of yams, grass skirts, and banana leaf bundles, key symbols in mortuary rituals, Pedranos must work through, around, and in opposition to the limitations Pedranas set up through their control of all food and beverages in fiestas. Before and during the fiesta Angélika and her assistants controlled the preparation and distribution of corn, the major symbol of fertility and regeneration and the primary object consumed and circulated during fiestas. Pedranos' deepest sentiments and values cluster around corn and to a lesser extent chicha, substances which women prepare, serve, and in the case of chicha, sell. When speaking of maize during rituals Pedranos refer to it as *"sbek'tal xojobal kajvaltik,"* "the Body and Emanation of Our Lord" (Arias 1973: 19). In their legends Pedranos say the spirit of corn is *xob*, Earth Lord's daughter; subservient to her is *anjel*, the male force in the earth who cares for milpas. During planting rituals women symbolize their power over crops by pouring the grains of corn for new plantings from one basket to another three times, or by stepping over the basket three times (Guiteras-Holmes 1961). By the fire, transforming the dough that they have ground from raw corn into tortillas for their families, they control the transition from raw to cooked and cold to hot, important symbolic categories for Pedranos. Putting a ceremonial blouse over their ordinary ones at feasts and heating their words in prayer, women place themselves at the symbolic center of the universe where the Gods can hear them. No longer raw women, they are essential humanness, the spirit of their people.

Events at the Feast of St. Peter left me unresolved on some issues about drinking and gender relations, but they convinced me that Pedranas are not passive puppets responding to their husbands' needs and demands, nor are they merely reacting to changes imposed upon them from outside their communities. While Pedranas may obey their husbands and fathers at home and in the courts, in the interface between the social and cosmic realms they take their orders from the Gods. There they are equal partners with their husbands.

6
"Now I am going like a branch and its leaves"
Drinkers and Their Families

Ah, I feel content, because now I've done the work of our flowery Lord of the sky. I passed in his feet and in his hands. I carried him and embraced him for a day and a year. Now I've fulfilled my work before him. It's good that I fulfilled my work, because they say it's best to do this. They told me, "Nothing went badly." My husband didn't do anything bad when he drank. He didn't get angry. Our hearts were equal, content. . . . Now we are returning everything we borrowed because of our work for St. Peter. Also, because I want to be in his hands. You see, I am the daughter of St. Peter.

Angélika

While my original reason for being in Chenalhó in June 1987 was to observe the Feast of St. Peter, something unexpected happened two days before the principal day of the fiesta that gave me another reason. Reina gave birth to her baby. After staying with her the night she gave birth, I spent the rest of the time I was in town going back and forth between Reina and the fiesta. I brought her tamales, gifts for Daniel, her new son, and news from outside. When I'd come back to the fiesta, Angélika would ask me about Reina and her baby. I kept asking myself how Angélika could be too busy to walk a few blocks to see a daughter in need or to see a new grandchild. But at the same time, I was moved by the devotion Angélika expressed in her ritual work and the dignity and good humor with which she carried it out. Later, when we talked about the fiesta, she explained how she saw her role. She told me that she had to go on with her work because St. Peter and her people depended on her to fulfill her duties at prescribed times, so that the world would continue and her people would prosper. Knowing I was with Reina made her heart less sad that she had to wait to see her daughter and new grandson.

Early one morning at the end of the fiesta, Reina fled to a nearby
hamlet with the father of Rafaela's father. She explained to me that he and
his wife felt sorry for her and invited her to live with them. They had sent
for their son who was working on a plantation near Tuxtla. I visited Reina
at their home and thought she seemed content there. But the days and
weeks passed and Rafaela's father never returned. Eventually Reina went
home, explaining that her mother had called her home because her father
was beating her. Later when I heard her in-law's story I understood why
they may have wanted Reina. Another son in his twenties had recently
died. His wife, who had been living with them, returned to her parents'
home with her baby soon after her husband's death. This left the couple
without the son's or daughter-in-law's labor and bereft of the joy their
grandchild brought.

In the weeks after Daniel's birth rumors flew about Reina. One of the
first rumors implicated me, saying that I had taken Reina to San Cristóbal
with me. But I had only gone back to Antonia's house. Once there, I told
Antonia what had happened, that Reina had asked me to help at Daniel's
birth. Her reply surprised me.

"How good that she wanted you! I wouldn't have."

When I described to Antonia how Reina had given birth, I understood
why Antonia said this. Reina had knelt, fully clothed, gripping the side of
a bed. The midwife was behind her and I was at her side, wiping her brow.
Antonia shook her head and said,

"How sad that she didn't have a husband to hold onto."

"But, Antonia, how do women give birth here?"

"Like this. The woman kneels, like Reina, but instead of holding onto
a bed she puts her arms around her husband's neck. He puts his hands
around her waist as she labors. The midwife or her mother kneels behind
her and receives the baby when it comes out."

I had trouble picturing Antonia's description. Finally, she sat me down
in a little chair, knelt and put her arms around my neck. Although we
were laughing, in that position I understood why Angélika had jokingly
referred to me as Daniel's father. In the absence of a husband, the bed and
I had been Reina's symbolic husband.

After the Feast of St. Peter I paid regular visits to Angélika and her
daughters. I felt as if the time we spent together at the fiesta and the night
I stayed with Reina had forged a bond of sorts between us. As events un-
folded during the fiesta I barely had time to ask myself if what I was doing
was right. I was only aware of basics: the fiesta must go on and Reina's
baby must be born. Nevertheless, events during this time had a strange

rightness about them. Later I realized that Angélika and her daughters had been teaching me about important Pedrano issues, especially how Pedranos view control and community.

It wasn't until a few weeks after the fiesta that I began to understand how ritual drinking during the fiesta related to non-ritual drinking then and afterwards. It was a July afternoon and I had just come into Chenalhó on the bus. I made my way up the hill to Angélika's house, hoping she would be at home. I found her seated by the fire with her children eating the midday meal. She asked me where I had been and when I had arrived and told me to sit down. Then she told Josefina to make me an egg, my gift of food when I visited. Josefina fried my egg on the semet, tucked it between two toasted tortillas, and handed it to me. As she worked I focused on the three deformed fingers on her left hand.

"Josefina, what happened to your hand? When did it happen?"

Josefina stuck her hand in the pocket of her dress.

"Oh, it's been almost a year. One day when my brother was drunk he ordered me to bring him more rum, and when I didn't, he hit me. I fell on my hand and that's how my fingers broke."

I couldn't stop looking at Josefina's pocket. How had I missed those fingers? As her other hand turned the grinder and her mother and sisters made tortillas, the stories that I had suspected, but didn't want to hear, spilled out like corn from the grinder. Angélika was first.

"Once, many years before Josefina was born, I separated from my husband. He really used to hit me. Once he just missed hitting my baby's foot. I went to my parent's house but my father didn't want me, because he was afraid my husband would kill him.

" 'Get out of here, go to your brother's house,' my father said.

"Then I went to stay with my brother. I stayed with him a week. He gave me food—meat, shrimp. He didn't ask me for anything. My brother was very good. Now he's dead; he died from drinking too much.

"Before I stopped drinking I didn't drink in the town center, but I drank a lot with my sister at her house. Once my sister wanted to pray with candles and rum for a horse she had just bought. We drank the rum and I got good and drunk. On my way home I had to walk through the river because there was no bridge; the river was wild before. I waded through the river carrying my baby and dragging my son by the hand. Eventually I got to my house where I saw my husband. He was running outside of the house looking for a gun. He wanted to kill his brother-in-law because the two of them had been drinking together. I took the gun away from him and told him,

" 'It's no good to kill him because you'll go to jail.'

"Then he hit me and I fell. I nearly died. But God was with me. He protected me. He gave me medicine in my dreams."

During and after my visits to Angélika and her daughters I thought about the contradictions between what I had seen at the Feast of St. Peter and what I heard and saw afterwards at Angélika's house. During the fiesta I never heard Victorio raise his voice to Angélika, much less hit her. He was drunk much of the time, but over the seventeen days or more during which he was in charge of the fiesta he seemed to have his mind on his ritual work. Later I realized that there had been an undercurrent of tension between Victorio and Angélika over Reina, but I never felt it at the time. The couple didn't let their family problems detract them from fulfilling their responsibilities to their people and the Gods.

After the fiesta Victorio drank non-stop for twenty days. He was neither curing nor working in the milpa. He was scolding and hitting Angélika again. He told her that she could take care of the bulls because he didn't want to be with her any more. He was going to the plantation. Then one of Angélika's neighbors told her he saw Victorio talking to another woman, who was looking for a man.

"Now that his cargo is over he's drinking nothing but rum every day. He told me, 'Who cares now that my cargo has passed? There's no reason to be ashamed now.' He left it like that.

"The day before yesterday he fought with his friend, Alonzo. They fought with sticks of wood and Alonzo hurt his ear. He bled a lot in his face and head.

"'Look at what you're doing; you're going to commit a crime,' I told my husband. 'If your friend accuses you, they're going to drag you away and you're going to jail,' I told him.

"At that point Victorio became afraid. Another man came to defend Alonzo and Alonzo went running down the road to hide. From there the police got Alonzo and threw him in jail. Then they let him out. Afterwards Victorio and Alonzo went to settle things, but the authorities didn't say anything and it was left like that.

"I told Victorio:

"'This happened to you because of drunkenness. Why don't you give up rum? Why don't you cut down a little? You've got to put yourself back together.'

"From there he ran me out of the house. He told me I'm good for nothing. He told me he wanted to find another woman."

The girls told me that about two years ago their parents had separated briefly but got back together. Now it had happened again. During our talks in the kitchen I was aware that Victorio was camped out alone in the sleeping house several yards away. Angélika and the children had staked their claim to the kitchen house. The girls told me that none of the women in the household was making Victorio's tortillas or washing his clothes. Victorio had bought a tortilla press and was going around in dirty clothes. A few times after his binge ended I was there when Victorio brought his family some choice morsels of chicken from a curing he had done. On those occasions Angélika told him to sit down as she and her daughters fed him tortillas and beans. After that the girls told me they sometimes washed their father's clothes, and several times I found Victorio eating by the fire when I came to visit.

Soon after their break-up Angélika took the matter to the town hall. I asked her what happened.

"The síndico said we can't divorce because we're pasados. The síndico said that since Victorio had held cargos people will be ashamed to go to him for advice if we divorce.

"*Pasados* [people who have held cargos] have to get everything ready for fiestas. They have to go to many hamlets to find men to take cargos. Seven years ago I did Passion of Jesus Rasereno [Jesus of Nazarene, Fiesta of Carnival]. Then I did regidor. Then I did *alcalde* (one of five who serve as judges under the supervision of the síndico). Then we decided to be standard bearer of the Apostle St. Peter. This cargo just passed. My husband and I have done all this together over many years.

"The authorities said to my husband:

"'You know everything about cargos and have already completed several. Why did you do that to your wife? Why do you make your wife stay in the other house? Your wife is not to blame. You are. Watch what you're doing this time. If you go looking for trouble again, if somebody hits you with a stick, if you bleed, whose fault is it going to be? Yours,' they told him.

"That's how the síndico settled it in the town hall. The síndico says my husband is crazy. I say he has the Devil in him."

Although Victorio's drinking was important to my understanding of his wife's relation to alcohol, I also wanted to know what had led Angélika to stop drinking. I wondered what her first experiences with alcohol had been like, what the medicine was that God gave her in her dreams.

On another visit I asked Angélika if I could record her telling me about her life. My first questions that day were about Angélika's childhood.

"Did your parents drink, Angélika?"

"My father and mother both drank. They would drink on Saturdays when they went to market. They got drunk when they ran into a lot of relatives and friends. When they returned home it would be Monday, Tuesday, or Wednesday.

"Ah, we cried when our parents went off. We were happy with our parents at home. We kept a look-out from high rocks to see if they were coming or not. If we didn't see them we cried. I remember sitting on top of a rock, crying and saying:

"'I'm just a little girl. I don't know how to take care of myself. Who knows if mother and father will come home drunk and hit me with a rock. Who knows if they'll hit me with something else. Maybe mother will kill me!'

"I sat there on the rock worrying because my parents went to the town square. Meanwhile my sister and I took care of each other. We were used to that, because we knew that if our mother drank, she'd get drunk and stay away a while.

"But we kept watching. If we saw our mother coming down the road drunk we'd go to meet her. We'd carry a pitch-pine torch to light the way.

"When my parents got home they wanted to warm up. We made the fire and heated water, hoping this would keep them from scolding us. They didn't say anything to us if we were obedient daughters. When they felt like being nice to us they bought us food in the market. Sometimes they brought us chittlings, shrimp, or fish.

"Sometimes they kept on drinking at home. They didn't get drunk every day, just once in a while. They would drink every week, or every two weeks, or every twenty days. Usually they would drink when they ran into friends who'd give them rum."

"Did your parents scold you, Angélika?"

"My parents would get mad at me. They would hit me with a strip of rawhide or with sticks of burned wood. If we didn't obey my father, he would be fierce, like a dog. My parents felt like hitting me for any little thing. If our jug broke when we went to the waterhole, they hit us. Just for that! My parents scolded us if we made thick tortillas. They wanted light, thin tortillas. They wanted the belly of the tortilla to rise. We made tortillas in our hands. We didn't make them on a piece of plastic. Beautiful tortillas came out the old way.

"'Grind the dough fine! Don't burn my beans! If you don't burn your corn, your beans, I won't scold you,' my mother said. 'If I just hit you because I feel like it, God will punish me.'

"So she only hit me now and then. But when my three older sisters were growing up they didn't obey. They annoyed my mother because they played so much. They played constantly.

" 'Your sisters just barely obey me.'

"My mother talked differently with them. Once she choked one of my sisters around the neck. Then she kicked her.

" 'Behave yourselves,' she said to them. 'Obey orders. Don't go wandering off. If you go off somewhere you won't be here when I need you. When you have husbands some day, obey them, too. I'll give you over to them with my own hands; I don't want you eloping. I don't want you to shame me like that. If you do what I tell you, you won't be ashamed.'

"It was rum that made our parents scold us. But I was pretty obedient and they didn't hit me much. My father only scolded me now and then.

"Once we were teenagers, we knew how to work hard. We worked so we wouldn't be hungry. Our father couldn't afford to lose his corn crop.

" 'If we lose the corn crop it's because you're lazy,' our father said. 'One day when you have husbands, if maybe they don't take care of you or honor you, if you come back to us, you'll have a way to support yourselves. You'll be used to working with a spade in the milpa and you can plant corn. If you have a good crop you'll be able to support yourselves by selling some corn. That way you won't go hungry,' my poor father said.

"We helped my father with his work. I worked hard for him. I'd get up at dawn. Then we'd eat, and afterwards we'd go off to work in the fields together. That's the way I grew up.

"We filled a lot of pots of beans from working my father's fields. His corn also grew well. The earth was very good before. In those days the sacred earth didn't need fertilizer. Now it's worn-out and dry. It doesn't want to give us much food."

As we talked Angélika vacillated between defending her parents and frankly describing the abuse she suffered at their hands. Even when they abused her it seems that Angélika longed to be with them. Nevertheless, the times her parents came home drunk and angry Angélika and her sisters resigned themselves to abuse. When I asked Angélika if she ever talked to someone about her problems she said,

"No. Nothing that bad happened. Nobody died. That's just the way it was. We were like that."

Angélika and I moved on to other topics and I neglected to go back to her childhood that day or any other day. Eventually when Antonia helped me translate Angélika's description of her marriage to Victorio, the picture of Angélika's childhood filled out. Like many women of her generation, Angélika married young.

"When did you get married, Angélika?"

"I was twelve when I got married. I got married according to tradition.

No man spoke to me before I married, not in the town square, on the path, nor in my home. My husband came to my house to ask for me five times. He knelt outside our door with his three net bags of gifts and said,

" 'Give me your daughter because I want her to be my companion and I want you to be like my father and mother.'

"My parents said to each other:

" 'We'll see if he appreciates our daughter. If he doesn't she'll have to come back to us.'

"At the time I was grinding corn inside the house and thinking:

" 'I'm too young to marry! I just barely know the things a woman has to know. I'm so little I have to stand on a wood block to reach the grinding stone. My skirt only takes two and a half yards of cloth. I don't look like a woman yet.'

"But finally my parents said, 'We accept your petition.' And they delivered me into my husband's hands.

"My husband and his helpers brought all the gifts tradition requires. They brought bananas, pineapples, oranges, meat, *pinole* (a drink made from parched corn, sugar, and water), bread, and one *garrafón* (glass jug of 17–20 liters) of rum. My sister and I divided up the rum into bottles for all the guests. If they were present they would finish their rum. If they weren't we would keep their rum for them. When everyone was drunk we ate. My husband and his brothers divided my gifts of food.

"I didn't sleep with my husband until one week after the feast. Each day at dawn in my parents' house my husband would go bring firewood. He would come grunting down the path with the wood. This lasted a week. Then we got together to sleep, like husband and wife.

" 'Now get together, because he's your husband,' my parents said.

"I accepted my parents' decision with difficulty because I didn't know the man. He came from another place. I was close to my brother and my little cousin Cristóbal. Cristóbal and I slept together. We went to gather firewood together. We fetched water together. We went everywhere together.

"After I married it was as if I no longer had a companion. I was used to my little cousin. I was used to the place I always ate and bathed and got water. Where I went to live with my husband I was very sad. My husband's house wasn't the same as mine. I didn't know his family's ways. My husband and his grandmother ordered me to eat, not to be sad.

"I worked all the time. I regret that I never learned to weave. I worked in the field with my husband instead. We planted corn. The sacred earth gave us corn and many pots of beans. We had a little house for the corn. We'd sell some of our corn and buy meat, my blouse and skirt, and later a bull."

Angélika had eleven children, of whom six died. She told me how they died, this one from diarrhea, that one from cough. Through tears and laughter Angélika told me that, like Reina's child whom she held in her arms, she, too, had been born during the Feast of St. Peter, some forty-five years ago. While her sister had had to pull out of her cargo as me' pan vaj during this year's fiesta because her daughter had taken ill, she couldn't be with her own daughter when she gave birth because of the importance of her cargo. But God helped her find another me' pan vaj and sent me to be with Reina.

I felt privileged to hear Angélika's story and didn't want to push her in directions she didn't want to go. But she seemed to welcome the chance to talk, especially about her pain. I broached the subject of her own drinking.

"Angélika, what did you do when you drank rum?"

"At times I would bring a gift of rum to Victorio's grandmother and she would tell me to drink it. She drank a lot of rum. She would tell me to drink her rum. I would accept it. Later I would also drink secretly, because my heart wanted rum and chicha."

"How did you stop drinking, Angélika?"

"It's been a while since I stopped drinking. Reina was little, hardly walking. My dream cured me. They gave me medicine in my dream. It seemed more real than a dream, but it was a dream. I saw her. She came out of the sky. She came close to me and I went toward her. I went on my knees to see the Moon, to ask her for a favor. I said:

"'Lord Jesus Christ, Lady Mother, Holy Mary, Virgin of Guadalupe,' that's how I addressed her. She talked to me:

"'Why did you get drunk? Who told you to?'

"'Nobody told me to. I made myself. My sister gave it to me.' That's what I told her.

"'Why did you get drunk? I'm talking to you,' the Moon said.

"'Not because you told me to. I did it to myself.'

"'But that's exactly why you're going to stop. Rum is not food. You can't fill up with rum. Give it up! If you die from a blow you won't know what hit you. If some man kills you, you won't know what hit you. You didn't feel it when your husband hit you because you were drunk. See? He hit you. You almost died! When you're drunk you don't feel it if you are hit. You don't feel it if you die by a blow from a stick. What good is rum? Give it up!'

"'Look at your companions. They fall on the ground. They lie there face up. Their skirts rise up to their breasts. I'm ashamed for them. Sometimes you lose your clothes or money. At times you leave a net bag behind in the road.[1] You're all going to embarrass me,' said the Mother of the Sky. 'I come to beseech you not to drink. Give it up! Rum is going to rot in your heart. Throw it far away on the earth. It's not good food,' that's what she told me.

"We arrived at the house of the doctor. She gave me the medicine, as if she were a doctor.

"'You've been here a long time. Don't drink! If you go back to drinking, hire someone to carry you,' she said. 'You can't drink here. It's your fault if you drink. It's not as if it's good food. Give it up! I give you this medicine, because your husband hit you. Drink it.'

"She gave me the medicine. I drank it and from then on I gave up drinking. That's how I gave up drinking. The Mother of the Sky counseled me well:

"'Talk to me. My image is there in the church,' she said. 'Remember to talk to me,' she said.

"From then on I obeyed her orders. I followed her advice because she's Our Mother, Holy Mary. That's why I don't want rum. . . . My heart doesn't crave rum. I threw it out of my heart. It's been many years. I no longer drink when I take part in a fiesta. My heart doesn't want it. I don't drink alcohol, beer, tequila, chicha, strong rum, or weak rum anymore. I never went back to drinking. I stopped for once and for all. When we get together for fiestas I don't drink even a shot of rum. I only give it to my friends, because I don't want it. My heart doesn't want it.

"'Drink it,' my friends tell me.

"'No, I don't want to.' They can see that I don't want rum.

"Now, if I see people drinking it doesn't bother me. When I'm around rum being served, the reek of it smells bad to me. It seems like poison. It spreads through my body. My stomach hurts. My heart doesn't want it. I want coffee.

"'It's not like it's meat,' I say. 'If it were food, if it were a good meal, that's something else again.'"

Angélika added that God also spoke to her in her dreams. He told her that there would be no medicine in the clinics to stop drinking during the time that her people lived. She could drink after she leaves this world for another, he said, but drinking was just not workable in this world.

"Like Moon and flowery God say, it's no good to get drunk. God doesn't want us to drink because we aren't free that way. Our Lord knows that it's not freedom to be drunk. It's good to be sober, to be happy. You know where you're going. You know what you're doing. You understand if someone says,

" 'Take care of your pig. Take care of your chickens. Sell them sometimes, you'll earn money that way.'

"If there is a sickness, a problem, a cargo, we're on top of everything.
If we have to give speeches we know how to give them well. We know
how things should go."

Each time I visited Angélika my affection for her grew. Simultaneously, my feelings about her situation became more complicated. Some of
this confusion was because my talks with Angélika that summer were my
first attempts to ask in-depth questions in Tzotzil. Perhaps because she was
a talker, as Antonia suggested, or because she felt indebted to me, my
many questions didn't seem to bother her. If I repeated a question she
would laugh and say, "But I already told you that!" Helping me transcribe
my interviews with Angélika, Antonia was moved by Angélika's words
about her service to her community. While we were listening to one of the
tapes, Antonia stopped weaving and said,

"I would like to serve a cargo in the Feast of St. Peter one year like
Angélika. I could show my people how we can do the fiesta with soda instead of rum."

I, too, was moved by Angélika's words and Antonia's response. While
interviewing Angélika, dressed in her torn sweater, shelling beans and
pouring out her problems, I still saw Angélika standing in her ceremonial
blouse at the center of the universe. Talking to the saints about the welfare
of her people, Angélika communicated clearly and eloquently; later, talking into a tape recorder about craziness and pain to someone who barely
knew her language, it was no wonder that she wasn't always clear.

Translating Angélika's dream with Antonia's help, I was impressed that
Angélika stopped drinking by surrendering to the Moon Virgin. Later Angélika admitted that she sneaked a few drinks on the sly after her dreams, but
she never went back to drinking as before and eventually stopped completely. That summer I didn't ask many questions about Angélika's own
drinking, perhaps because Victorio's drinking was a pressing issue. That she
had stopped drinking, once and for all, with help from the Mother of the Sky,
seemed to be what Angélika wanted me to know about her drinking history.

Angélika often turned to invisible beings, especially the Mother of
the Sky, for comfort and direction. In return for their support she served
them in cargos and thanked them in prayer. Even when she had to prepare food for the *mixa* (mass for the hills) in which Victorio was an important participant, while they were still separated, she undertook the work as
her service to the saints and her people. (Conveniently, this particular

mixa happened to fall at the end of Victorio's long binge and may have contributed to bringing his drinking under control again.)

After finishing Angélika's interviews, Antonia helped me prepare survey questions that I used to interview women in Chenalhó and in several hamlets. While working on questions Antonia and I talked about drinking in general and drunk women's songs, specifically. Women's drunk songs fascinated me and I wanted to record some. I thought about drinking with older women in order to record them singing, but that would not be ethical unless I got drunk, too. Although I enjoyed feeling high and losing some of my self-consciousness among Pedranos, as a woman field worker doing research alone, I felt most comfortable being sober. After my experience in Tenejapa during Carnival, I rarely drank much rum or chicha. Partly this was because I lived with Antonia and Domingo, who only drank on special occasions. But another reason was, as alcoholic beverages go, I do not like rum. Out of politeness I would usually accept one cup and then excuse myself from drinking more. If my host ignored my excuses, I would either make la acción and offer the drink to someone else, or if I had a flask with me, pour it in that to carry home. Another reason I didn't get drunk was that I feared stories might circulate about me and ruin my chances to speak with Protestants, who frown on drinking.

One of the first interviews I conducted during my household survey encouraged me to use my survey to open doors rather than to get comparative or statistical data. Carmela, a young Pedrana from Chenalhó, had agreed to help me the day I interviewed a group of women gathered on the front porch of a store in a hamlet near Antonia's. The last woman we interviewed in the group was Pascuala. As with the other women, we asked Pascuala to tell us what advice she would give her children about drinking. Although she gave us a typical response from a Traditional woman, "Don't learn to drink rum yet, you're still children," she also said she would tell her children why she had started drinking.

"'I learned to drink because your sisters died. If they hadn't died I wouldn't be drinking rum,' that's what I'd tell my children." Pascuala began to cry as she talked about two of her daughters who had died, both in the past year.

"It's been a year. It's been a year since two of my children died. The last one died during Holy Week. The two died almost together. They died fifteen days apart. They were already big. I tried to kill myself drinking rum. I lost myself drinking rum. I only have three children now. This is my son here. One boy. Two girls. But there were nine, nine, nine. Now they're gone."

I bought sodas for Pascuala and the rest of the women and children. We sat together quietly drinking our sodas while Carmela and I waited for the bus. On the ride back to Chenalhó I couldn't stop thinking about Pascuala, how a mother could bear watching two children die in the same month.

In the following weeks I would see Pascuala from time to time. Once she was walking down the road, drunk, carrying her machete. She welcomed me like a long-lost friend and asked me to come to her house. When I stopped by later that afternoon Pascuala and her husband Mariano were lying down on crudely constructed wood planks in their tiny one-room house. Pascuala could barely lift her head to greet me. She told me they were both sick and that I should come back another time.

The next time I stopped at her house Pascuala, Mariano, and their eldest son Javier, were eating tortillas and cooked greens. Pascuala told me to come in while Mariano and Javier kept eating. No one offered me a wood block to sit on, so I crouched near the door. I asked Pascuala if we could talk sometime, that I had more questions I wanted to ask her. I told her I would bring some beans when I came. We set a tentative date.

While conducting my survey I found two young Pedrano couples who welcomed me into my homes and helped me with my interviews. One of the couples, Mónica and Bernabé, had lived in San Cristóbal for a while and were worldlier than most Pedranos. However, Mónica preferred living

This drawing was made by Catarina, a seven-year-old Pedrana. The youngster had stopped by Mónica's store while I was making beaded necklaces to trade with women. When Catarina asked me for a necklace I told her I would make her one in exchange for a drawing of a drunk woman. She agreed to the exchange and immediately sat down on Mónica's porch ready to draw. I gave her a piece of paper and a marking pen while she conferred with her little sister. "What does a drunk woman look like? What does a drunk woman do?" they asked each other. The little sister thought, and then said, "Make her crying." Catarina nodded in agreement and carefully but confidently drew this picture. Catarina and her sister seemed pleased with the finished drawing. For me it was as truthful a representation of a drunk Pedrana as any word picture I could draw.

in a hamlet where she could grow her own corn and raise chickens, and run a small store out of their house. Bernabé taught at a nearby hamlet school where he often had to stay the night. Although Bernabé was a heavy drinker in their first years of marriage, he hadn't drunk for several years except on special holidays.

The day that Pascuala and I had set to talk, Mónica agreed to come with me to help with the interview. Pascuala was sober when we arrived and seemed open to talking. We explained that I would ask Pascuala questions and then if I didn't understand her answers Mónica would help me. As with Angélika, I began with Pascuala's childhood.

"Can you tell us how it was when you were little?"

"I didn't do anything. My mother just ordered me and said, 'Grind corn, make tortillas.' That's all she said to me. Then I said to her, 'O.K.' I obeyed her and I made tortillas and I also ground corn. My mother told me to sweep the house. 'I'm going to go to work. Stay here and sweep the house,' she would say. 'O.K.,' I would say. And I would stay and sweep the house. That's what I did. That's all."

"Did your mother drink rum?"

"Yes, my mother drank rum. She went out with my father to get drunk. I stayed to grind, as you see my little daughter grinding now. When I finished grinding I began to sweep the house. I was carrying my little brother on my back. When I finished I went looking for my mother so my little brother could nurse. That's all."

"Did your father hit you when you were little?"

"Ah, yes. He hit me. Because at times I didn't grind corn. I didn't grind because I was little, and also I was carrying my little brother when my mother got drunk. Then sometimes I didn't have the tortillas ready when my parents returned from drinking rum. Then they hit me with a bull-whip or rawhide."

"Did your mother hit you?"

"Just my father hit me. My mother didn't hit me."

"How many brothers and sisters do you have?"

"Ah, I have three brothers and also two little sisters."

"Did you cry a lot in your parents' house?"

"I cried. I cried a lot. My brothers hit me, too. They hit me as they still didn't have wives. I took care of them. They were a lot of brothers to take care of."

"Did you drink rum when you were little?"

"No, I never drank rum. When I began to drink I had two daughters."

"Why did you start to drink?"

"I started to drink because my child died. My first daughter died.

When she died she was already five and a half years old. When she died I felt very bad because she was very obedient. She swept the house very well. She ground corn very well. She made tortillas well. She always fixed everything up. There was nothing she didn't want to do, my little daughter. . . . She always did the things that had to be done. If we had beans she would put them on to cook. If I needed someone to watch things, she would do it. That's why when she died I began to drink. I felt terrible. It would have been better had I died. When my daughter died I would say: 'Let me die. Let me die.' And then I began to drink. . . . Now if my daughter had grown, then I wouldn't have drunk. When she was little I didn't drink. It was because of her death that I began to drink rum."

"Do you remember what you did the first time you drank, how you felt? Was it bad for you or what did you feel?"

"Ah, I felt very bad when I drank the first time."

"Why?"

"My head began to ache. The pain in my head was like from rabies. I really got drunk. Also my stomach hurt and it wouldn't let me eat. And then I got very sad, because my daughter had died. When I got drunk I hadn't eaten. There was never any food. I just cried. Then that made my stomach even worse."

"The second time?"

"It didn't do anything to me."

"Then the third time were you used to it?"

"I had gotten used to it. It didn't do anything to me anymore. My head didn't ache anymore. My stomach didn't hurt anymore. Nothing bothered me. I ate well. I feel well when I'm drunk. I don't feel bad in my stomach anymore. No more."

"Did you get married according to tradition?"

"Yes, yes. My husband went to my parents to ask for me. He gave my parents one garrafón of rum. But only my parents drank it. I didn't drink it. He gave *guineos* [small bananas], pineapples, bread, meat. That was all that he gave."

"How old were you when you married?"

"I was eleven when I got married. And I was fifteen when my first child was born. We lived with my parents for nine years. It was better because my husband didn't have a father. Also, my father was like my husband's father and my mother was like his mother, because my husband was very little when his parents died."

"Did he [your husband] hit you?"

"Yes, he hit me."

"Why did he hit you?"

"My father made him drink rum and he got drunk. But my husband was very young, the size of my son. He was little. I was afraid of my husband when he got drunk. My husband hit me a lot and I cried. I didn't want to drink and that's why I didn't drink rum."

"And now when you both get drunk does your husband hit you?"

"Ah, not now."

I asked Pascuala how it was between her and her husband when they drank. She said that they didn't argue and that they stayed away from people who drank and picked fights. According to Pascuala, when Mariano passed out in Chenalhó on a market day she waited for him and he did the same for her when she passed out. Pascuala's description of their relationship reminded me of an older couple in Chenalhó who were well known for their drinking and their peaceful union. Pedranos claimed that this couple drank together in their house daily and at fiestas, but never raised their voices to each other, except in song.

"Do you drink when you go to the plantation?"

"I don't drink. I only drink here in my village. I can't drink on the plantation because it makes me embarrassed. It makes me ashamed. You see, it's a different place there. My people aren't there."

"You didn't have the desire in your heart to drink when you came back from the plantation?"

"Only when my brothers made me drink, because my brothers drink, too. They oblige me to drink. They give it to me and then I drink it."

"Then do you begin to buy it too?"

"I begin to buy it too."

". . . I would like to know how your dreams are. Do your dreams help you sometimes? Do you have some good dreams or some bad dreams?"

"All my dreams are bad."

"Can you give me an example of a bad dream?"

"O.K. One time they [demons] bothered me in my dreams. When I was pregnant they hit me in a dream. With that I got sick. I couldn't get up. Sickness always comes from my dreams. Sometimes they rob my hens. They cover my eyes or my face so that they can rob me. Then they carry my hens away and leave my face covered. But the hens stand for my children and soon after my children get sick."

"Do you understand what your dreams mean?"

"Yes, I understand what they're trying to say. 'It's better to offer your candles,' they say. 'With that you'll be well, because you suffered a lot when your daughters died,' they told me. 'It's better to offer your candles and with that your children will grow.' They tell me constantly, 'Offer your candles, so your son has a better life. May you do it. May you do it,' they say. They show me this consistently in my dreams."

"Can one stop drinking through dreams?"

"One can't. One can't."

"Have you dreamt that someone says to you, 'Don't drink rum. It's better to give it up. Leave it in peace.'?"

"No. No. But, when I wanted to join the Presbyterians, that was my plan, she [the Virgin Mary/Mother of the Sky] told me in my dream that she didn't want me to. She said,

"'Why are you going to do that? Where are you going? Hurry up and find a little rum. Go find it. I'm going to drink a bottle to calm my heart's thirst [for anger], because of what you're planning to do,' she said to me. She gave me money to buy the rum, but that woman was angry when she gave it to me. I took the money and went to find some rum and then we drank it together. 'Only we will drink it,' she said. She had a good grasp of my shoulders and she held me and shook me hard. 'I'm going to see that you behave, because I don't want you changing your religion,' she told me. 'I don't want you going to another side,' she said. 'I only want you to be here,' she told me. When she said this to me she held me tight. That's all she told me. And with that I couldn't give up rum, I mean with this dream."

"And hasn't anyone told you to give up rum in your dreams?"

"Nobody tells me to give up rum in my dreams. They only tell me this when I don't drink: 'Why don't you drink? Are you with the Presbyterians now and that's why now you don't want to drink rum?' That's what they say to me. Nothing more."

"You don't want to give it up? You aren't sick from drinking rum?"

"If I don't drink rum for three or four weeks I get sick. I don't feel like eating. I don't feel like drinking water. I don't feel like working. I don't feel like bringing firewood. I don't feel like doing anything. Now if I drink rum and get drunk for about three days, then afterwards I eat well. Like ten tortillas. And also I take three gourds of corn gruel."

Quite unexpectedly, Pascuala began to question me. No Pedrano had ever interviewed me pointedly about a personal subject, except Antonia, and she only rarely. Most Pedranos asked me about my eating habits and how much things cost in my country, and of course, where my husband was, but few had asked me much more about my life. Rightly, Pascuala wanted to know about my drinking.

"Do you drink rum now?" Pascuala asked.

"I drink wine. I don't like beer and rum, but I like chicha."

"You like chicha."

"Yes, I drink a little, no more. When I drink I feel very content. But when I drink too much I feel sad."

"You feel sad."

"I just drink a little. Only a little, as I haven't had problems with rum like my husband. Before, my husband drank a lot. He didn't behave well. Even after he gave up rum he scolded me and there were many problems. But now my husband doesn't drink."

"What did you give him to drink so that now he doesn't drink?"

"He went to a hospital, to a clinic. But in the clinic there isn't any medicine. Only prayers and his dreams. And also he went with a group called 'Alcoholics Anonymous.' This is a group of people who have given up rum and who help each other. Now I feel very content with my husband."

"Yes, then, because he doesn't get drunk any more. I've thought like that, too, that I would get better if I found medicine [a way to get well, restore balance] and I could give up rum that way. I want to give it up, too, if I could. But it's just that I can't give it up. One can't give up rum. If I could give it up I would leave rum. Then I would be better off. . . . But I don't find it. I'm already tired of looking for it and asking."

Perhaps because of her interest in listening to me even in my poor Tzotzil, or because I felt drawn to her, I wanted to help Pascuala, to encourage her to keep looking for a cure for her drinking. With Mónica's help I tried to encourage Pascuala to look for help in her people's prayers. Pascuala shook her head.

"But, I'm tired. I asked, but Our Lord didn't give me results. I got nothing from that. We're still poor. We can't buy our clothes. I went to pray but I can't give it up. I went crying and I carried my candles but I couldn't give rum up with that."

I suggested to Pascuala that maybe the prayers didn't work because she didn't go with her whole heart.

"It could be. But I went with my whole heart, when I went to ask for my situation to be better, so I could buy our clothes. I went with my whole heart. With my whole heart. Also my mother always prays for me. But nothing happens."

"What did your mother say in her prayer?"

"She said that she felt sorry that we were very poor and that I can't buy our clothes and that we don't have skirts, that my son doesn't have shirts, that we don't have anything to eat, that we can't buy beans, that we can't buy meat. That's what my mother said, but I couldn't give it up with that, no. Now my mother is tired of praying."

After our first talks I kept trying to help Pascuala stop drinking; I thought that with encouragement she could overcome her ambivalence about giving up rum. Pascuala and I went to Chenalhó and spoke to a shaman who agreed to pray for her. Pascuala's mother and I provided bus fare back and forth to Chenalhó and I agreed to buy rum and candles for the prayers. Unfortunately, or so it seemed to me at the time, my efforts to help Pascuala failed when I got hepatitis and didn't return to Chenalhó for about a month. Although Pascuala went through with a couple of the prayers, she ran out of money for candles and bus fare, the shaman got angry when I didn't show up and Mariano said he didn't want Pascuala going to town so often. Pascuala told me that she wasn't impressed with the shaman, who happened to be a follower of Catholic Action. The shaman invoked ideas about the immorality of drinking in her prayers and insisted on couples getting healed together. The first idea seemed to offend Pascuala. Although the second fit traditional ideas about gender relations, nevertheless, perhaps because Mariano didn't want to quit drinking, Pascuala knew that without consensus between them the prayers had to fail.

Talking with Mónica, I also learned more about Pascuala's drinking history. Mónica and others told me that it wasn't true that Pascuala only started drinking after her children died. She had begun to drink long before she married. Her parents and brothers were known drinkers. Mónica had heard that Pascuala suffered terribly at her brothers' hands. Once, one story went, Pascuala's older brother hung her from a tree because she had been talking to a boy. These stories supported my impression that Pascuala had started drinking long before her two daughters died and her fifteen-year-old son, Javier, was born. Javier seemed bright, but his features didn't look normal for Pedranos. His unusually low nasal bridge, short nose, and the overall appearance of his eyes looked like photographs I had seen of children with fetal alcohol syndrome. I asked Mónica if she had noticed something strange about Javier's face. She said she had, and that Pedranos say children are born with a "crooked face" like Javier's, or don't learn things fast, because their parents drank too much before the child was born. Later another Pedrano said the reason is that when parents drink their blood becomes contaminated, contaminating the child's blood, as well. Whether or not Javier has fetal alcohol syndrome his people seem to attribute his problem to both parents' blood, not just the mother's.[2]

When I came back to Chenalhó a year later, I found Pascuala walking down the road with her machete, sober. She said she hadn't drunk for quite some time and asked me to come visit. When I did later that day I found Pascuala stirring corn gruel, drunk. Two of Pascuala's brothers were standing by the door, another man was passed out on the floor, and Mariano was covered with a blanket waiting for a shaman to come to cure him.

Javier knelt over a bottle of rum serving cups to his mother and uncles at their request. Although I had never seen Javier embarrassed at his parents' drinking, now, doing his drunk mother's bidding, he seemed more like a resigned child of an alcoholic than an obedient son. Pascuala's brothers told me they came to visit Pascuala because she knows how to drink. They said that many times in the past she had quit drinking, but she always started back again. I left Pascuala this last time angry that her brothers had so much influence over her and that, except for her mother and perhaps her children, she had no source of support if she decided to stop drinking.

Besides Pascuala and Mariano, the only notoriously heavy drinking couple in the hamlet were Mónica's in-laws, Bartolo and Otelia. Since they lived next door to Mónica, I had ample opportunity to observe their relationship. Mónica said that her in-laws drank as often as they could find rum. Although they were both shamans, they were too debilitated from drinking to travel far for curings. Bartolo was still strong enough to work in others' fields and at times neighbors solicited his help, offering him rum in return. With gifts of rum, earnings from his labor, cash advances on Bartolo's wages, and borrowing, Bartolo and Otelia managed to survive and support their drinking habits.

Otelia and Bartolo had both been married once before. Their spouses died around the same time and, soon after, Bartolo and Otelia began to talk. Otelia said she would come and make Bartolo's tortillas. She left her children with an aunt, only taking her youngest boy, Antonio, to live with Bartolo. Antonio had been following his mother around to curings since he was able to walk. At about seven he started drinking. Once when he was around ten years old he got drunk and scared Mónica's eight-year-old daughter by chasing her into her house and pleading with her to take care of him. Then he threw himself on Mónica's bed where he thrashed and wailed until Mónica and others could restrain him.

Mónica describes her in-laws' relationship as "a game." Bartolo calls Otelia a worthless drunk. She calls him a crazy man. He says, "I can have another wife who doesn't drink, who fixes the house, sweeps, bathes, and cooks. Go with your son. Nobody wants you." One night after Bartolo had been sober for about three months Otelia called him a Presbyterian, a Catechist, and a stupid, worthless man, and tried to bully him into drinking again. He called her a whore and threatened to kill her. She said if he didn't drink he could go to shit.

One morning when I arrived at Mónica's she informed me that her in-laws had been drinking for a couple of days and were on a binge. After non-stop drinking throughout the day, by seven that night Bartolo was screaming at Otelia and threatening her with a machete. When Mónica and I arrived at their house Otelia had managed to wrest the machete from Bartolo, who seemed too drunk to do much damage. Mónica took the machete from Otelia and scolded her in-laws, telling them to stop yelling and hitting each other. Then we took the other machete and left. Mónica hadn't grown up with heavy drinking in her home and wasn't used to the fighting that went on between her in-laws. Bernabé often had to stay at his school overnight, leaving Mónica alone to deal with his parents. She tended to stay out of their way, unless she thought that one of them might hurt the other. One time she ran to Otelia's defense when she lay half-naked after Bartolo had kicked her skirt off. Other days when her in-laws left to go drinking, Mónica would go into their house and remove the machetes in case they came home drunk. Occasionally Otelia sought refuge in Mónica's house, but when she left to stay with a son in another hamlet Bartolo was too ashamed to come to Mónica for food. Although she sometimes regretted not being able to use her in-laws as babysitters as they were not reliable, Mónica seemed content taking care of herself, her children, her store, her fields, and her animals.

One afternoon when Otelia was sober Mónica helped me interview her about her life. We sat in Mónica's yard drinking sodas, as her chickens and children chased each other between our chairs. As in other interviews, I asked Otelia to start with her childhood. She told me that her parents had made chicha and were shamans. While accompanying her parents during healings, Otelia learned to drink chicha. It wasn't until she served her first cargo as *me' kapitan* (the counterpart to *kapitan,* captain; they are the second most important set of officials in all fiestas except Carnival) in a fiesta that Otelia began to drink rum. I asked her what her drinking was like when she was married to her first husband.

"We didn't drink a lot of rum. I never went out to look for rum. But my first man didn't live a long time. He died on me very young. . . . But I never forgot rum. I always drank, until I married the second time. Then I gave up rum. When I was pregnant with one of my sons I didn't drink. One year and a half I didn't drink rum. I drank when we did a curing ceremony, but I vomited a lot. That's why I gave up rum. Then I began to drink again. I can't say that I'm a good person, because I drank too much when I was growing up."

"How did you learn to pray?"

"I learned to pray with my second husband. We learned how to pray a little, to cure people, the children of the Gods. I was the first one to learn the prayer. God gave it to me in my dream. I dreamt about the same time I was thinking about joining the Presbyterians. I had been thinking of going with those who listen to the word of God. But I dreamt, 'Now, don't do that. That's what's making my children the way they are now. They're not doing well, as you see. They don't use even one candle. . . . They don't talk to God anymore.' That's what an old man and an old woman [totil me'il] told me in my dream. Then they gave me some herbs and some pine branches. The pine branches were very big. They represented candles. Also, they gave me a hunk of corn gruel and that represented incense. 'It's better for you to have this. This is what you should pay attention to. You will learn this. Take the gourd for your incense,' they told me."

"Did you drink rum in prayers?"

"Yes, I drank. I drank. I drank because I made an offering of rum in order to cure. That's how we pray in all the places I've gone. . . . It began with our ancestors. And it's what we dream, too. They [the Gods] gave me rum in my dream. 'You will use the contents of this gourd your whole life,' that's what they told me. It [rum] was in a green flask. I saw it well. Like the one over there. 'Let this be yours forever,' they said to me. 'Bring us some bottles.' Then they emptied the bottles of rum into my flask and said, 'Don't ever abandon in your heart what we've brought you.' That's how it was in my dream. That's how I learned to pray. It doesn't come to us just any way, only in our hearts."

"Do you get sick from drinking rum?"

"No. No. I never got sick on account of rum. I only got sick from illnesses. Rum never gives me high blood pressure."

"How do you feel from drinking rum?"

"We enter into darkness. We don't know where we're going on account of rum. Truthfully it brings us to this. That's how it is. It's very bad. We get into trouble because of rum. We scold each other, like my husband. That's how we are now. We commit crimes on account of rum, because rum is the Devil's. It's very bad."

"What happens to your soul when you're drunk?"

"You forget everything. The soul is paralyzed and that's why you don't realize that your soul has been committing a crime for hours. Your spirit leaves you and goes very far."

"Are there many people whose bodies are hurt by rum?"

"Ah, many. But it's much worse still where you go. Where there's money, they spend it all on rum. Rum has also hurt me. I couldn't get up. I couldn't eat anymore from drinking. The demon makes me drink, I think."

"When you are sober do you dream that you are drunk?"

"Ah, yes, [I get drunk] once in a while when they give me rum in my dream. At times I don't drink it because it's bad, but at times I drink it.

'Drink now what you know how to drink,' the demons tell me. 'You are demons and Satan,' I say in my heart. It seems that it's on the earth, or it seems that they are our family. But it's them [the demons] deceiving our spirit. They are demons with black faces. It's the very Devil.

"At times they give me a bottle or they put rum in front of me. The cups or bottles are there in a circle; they [the demons] leave them in front of their eyes and their presence. That's how it is in my dream. They want to make us disheartened. This is no good. Our hens don't grow, or we can't find meat. It's because of spiritual envy. That's how spiritual envy bothers us. That's how it is.

"When they give us rum to drink, they want us to return an equal amount. When we can drink we return the drink. Also when they invite us to a good meal of turkey, chicken, beef, or pork and they bring us a heaping plate, they oblige us to return it. All these things are works of the demon, even though those who are giving us things to eat look like our family. That's how I always dream.

"When we return it [the rum or food] then we restore the balance. Now we can have our hens back. We can blind the envious ones. That's what they say. If we accept, for example, a cup or a bottle in our hands, in our dreams, in our spirits, in our souls, in our lives, if they give it to us before their eyes, then we return it [saying], 'With my cup, with my bottle.' That's what we say when we cure. That's what we say when we offer rum. Three candles of twenty pesos each are for envy and two *cuartas* [small bottles] of rum. That's what we need to cure envy in the spirit. Because we'll get sick if we don't give a bottle. That's why we need rum.

"That's why we can't find medicine for this type of illness. That's why I haven't been able to cure myself. . . . The demons deceive us a lot, especially me because I drink a lot. Our spirit tricks us a lot. It gives us everything, but in our dreams. I believe that's what they did to me, why I was touched. It was the work of the envious ones. I believe that it's the Devil who walks with me. . . ."

"Can you stop drinking through dreams?"

"You can only give it up if you want to give it up. If you go to ask for help in the churches, then you can give it up. But now I drink very little because I'm sick. Now I drink very little. I hardly ever get drunk. I never get sick from drinking."

"Do you cry a lot?"

"Yes, I cry a lot. When my first child and my first husband died, I cried a lot and I fell on the ground. I didn't feel like eating. I couldn't eat. My husband didn't scold me or get angry. If I had corn gruel, I prepared it for him and I felt content and I drank my gourd of corn gruel, too. I was used to that. And I can't forget it. One doesn't forget [loved ones]. I suffered a lot from their deaths. When my husband died I couldn't sleep. I dreamt that he was there, or that we were eating together.

"I drank a lot of rum. It's that I felt so alone then. My husband told me, 'You'll drink alone when I'm dead. For me it's better that you don't marry another man when the day comes that I have to leave you.'

"That's why I drink. These things don't pass from me. . . . It's very bad when someone gets sick or when someone dies on us. It was the same when my son died. I nearly died from sorrow. He was still a small boy. He was a fine boy. I cried a lot when my first son died. . . . Later I got sick. I wanted to die. 'It's better for me to die, too, now that my son and my son's father have died.' That's what I said."

Awkward in handling grief and in making transitions in Tzotzil, abruptly I changed the subject.

"What things does your husband do when he's very drunk?"

"Nothing, he just hits me. He was very bad when we got married. From the beginning he has always yelled at me. . . . My present husband drinks a lot. We both drink a lot. . . . Sometimes we drink for ten days straight. My daughter-in-law and son have seen us. It's been very bad. It doesn't matter to my husband if he throws you out. You have to be very afraid of him. He has always been jealous. Once he gave me some whippings. He gave me two dozen thrashings. It made me afraid to see my body. It was black on account of the thrashings. Then I was going to leave him. I was going to forget him because he made me very angry. That's the way it still is. . . ."

"How do you feel when your husband comes home drunk?"

"Ah, when I'm not drunk, I'm afraid. I feel like running and hiding, because I've seen how men are when they're bad. My husband was very bad before. He always ran me out with a machete and a stick. Then I stayed outside for the night. That's what happened to me before. That's why I'm afraid. . . .

"But my husband drinks a lot because his heart wants it that way. When he gets up in the morning he looks for all the bottles and he sucks on them until he gets the last drop. When he doesn't find any he goes out looking for it. That's how he gets up every day. Although we don't have money he borrows it and pays with his work. If he doesn't borrow it we suffer a lot. He cries a lot when his stomach hurts and it gives him diarrhea. . . . That's how it is now. That's why my husband isn't drinking now."

Mónica explained that it'd been a month since Bartolo drank rum, and he was taking vitamins that his son in Tuxtla gave him.

"What is the most important thing to you on earth? Is to drink the best thing for you?"

"Well, I would like not to drink, to give it up. Just that. That would be better. But it's just that I can't give it up. When I see that someone has a bottle of rum in his hands, it doesn't make me feel like drinking, but if they tell me, 'Drink!' then I know that I'll warm myself a lot. Then I'll drink a lot and feel very content. I don't know how to drink alone. But if someone invites me, it seems that I can leave my tortillas behind. Rum is very delicious. Truthfully, it's very delicious."

I wanted to know if Otelia knew "I am a drunk woman, I am a drunk girl" or any other songs or stories. I asked Mónica to read a published song-prayer by a Chamula woman to her mother-in-law to see if it would remind Otelia of similar songs, prayers or stories. In contrast to the words to "I am a drunk woman, I am a drunk girl" the words of the Chamula song-prayer, "I am a woman my woman" are self-affirming and proud. They speak of a woman who is confident of her ability to work and be supported by the spirit world (Jiménez López and Past 1987: 37):

> I am woman my woman
> I am girl my girl
> I am woman the woman
> I am girl the girl.
>
> I know how to work
> my leg works
> my hand works.
> I am girl my girl
> I am woman my woman.
>
> You made me woman
> You gave me woman
> woman of the flowers
> mother of the sky.

Otelia laughed as she listened to the words of the song-prayer, as did Mónica reading it. Later I asked Mónica why the song-prayer made them laugh.

"Because the woman is very confident, capable of many things. My mother-in-law was ashamed because she doesn't know how to weave and because the woman's song-prayer is like a celebration of her life."

Otelia said she didn't recognize this song-prayer or know any other stories. "I'm a woman of the mountain," she told me.

A few weeks later I happened to walk by Otelia's house when she was on a binge. She called me into her kitchen, where she was drinking with Bartolo, Pascuala, and Mariano. Javier was sitting with his parents, not drinking. I sat down on a wood block next to Pascuala, who held a glass of rum but didn't take a drink, perhaps out of respect for our last talk. Pascuala and Mariano seemed sober, in contrast to Otelia and Bartolo, who had been drinking for about eight days, Mónica told me later. Although I was on my way to another house, Otelia wouldn't let me go. Pascuala, Mariano, Javier, and I were Otelia's and Bartolo's audience for over an hour as they jabbed each other with insults and got drunker and drunker. Although Bartolo offered us cups of rum, he drank directly out of the bottle, and seemed more interested in his own thirst than in decorum.

Uncomfortable with the verbal abuse and fearing that Bartolo might reach for a machete again, I tried to take some control by asking Otelia to sing for me.

"Otelia, would you sing 'I am a drunk woman, I am a drunk girl'?"

"O.K. But you'll have to pay me a little."

"Yes, she'll have to pay!" Bartolo broke in.

"Sit down and be quiet!" Otelia scolded him. "She'll pay. She always comes and takes pictures or gives beans or whatever."

Pascuala nodded.

Tossing another cup of rum down her throat, then wrapping her arms around her middle as if to wind herself up, Otelia began to sing. Even Bartolo kept silent as Otelia's body became a metronome and her voice an echo from a deep well of pain.

I am a drunk woman
I am a drunk girl
Yes, yes.
Yes, I am a woman

I don't have a father
I am a drunk woman
I am a drunk girl.
That's the way it is,
that's the way it is.

I am going, girl,
I am going, mother,
I'm really going, yes.

I'm on my way to worth-
    lessness,
I'm on my way to death,
I'm a woman, yes,
I'm leaving, yes.

I'm a woman alone,
I'm a girl alone,
I'm a woman completely
    alone,
I'm a girl completely alone . . .

Otelia woman I am,
Otelia girl I am, so it is.

I'm not grieving in my heart
because I will always be but a
　woman,
because I will always be but a
　girl.
Carry me away,
take me to a far away place,
so I may go, yes,
so I may leave, yes,
so I may get out of this, yes.

It's not my fault,
It's not my crime,
because I'm a woman alone,
because I'm a girl alone,
only this, I said . . .

I'm going for good,
I'm going with the shit.
Let my father kill me,
Let my mother kill me.

I also have a son,
I also have a son.
I have a relative,
I have kin, yes . . .

I'm living near my dear
　daughter-in-law,
My poor, dear daughter-in-
　law cares about me.

This one [Bartolo] is very
　pitiful,
poor old man,
poor thing,
He's pitiful . . .
Let him keep going on in
　his stupid way.
Let him go once and for all.

Yesterday he said,
"Be gone with you!
Get out of here!"

This is how I got sick.
This is how I am meeting
　death.

I can go to the plantation.
I have relatives,
I have brothers and sisters.

Although Otelia had started her song with spirit, as her words got more personal her lips quivered and she began to cry.

My head hurts me,
my heart hurts me,
because he told me this
　yesterday,

"It's no good your being
　here.

Another woman will come.
Another girl will come,"
poor Bartolo told me.

It hit me hard.
It offended me.

When Otelia finished singing no one spoke. Pascuala, Mariano, and Javier sat without moving. Unsure of what to do, I waited for someone to say something. Soon Bartolo remembered his anger and started to scold Otelia again. But Otelia didn't strike back. Her song seemed to have taken her deep into herself and far away from us. I wanted to get far away myself, but didn't want to feel like a voyeur or robber who snatches something private and runs with it. Eventually I left for Mónica's house, hoping that with Pascuala and her family still there and Mónica and I next door, we could help Otelia if Bartolo started to hit her.

7 *Water of Hope, Water of Sorrow*
A Processual Framework on Drinking

Angélika, Mónica, Pascuala, and Otelia brought me face-to-face with some contradictions in Pedranos' lives, and contrasts between their people and mine. In doing so they highlighted several issues which connect to drinking, gender, and community cross-culturally. Problems, boundaries, control, and narrative are four important ones.

Angélika, Pascuala, and Otelia told me about their problems because I asked. If I hadn't, they would have probably kept these experiences to themselves. Most Pedranos don't talk about everyday pain and suffering and don't label these "problems." When I asked Angélika if she had problems when she was growing up she replied, "That's just the way it was. We were like that." In response to my questions about what Bartolo did when drinking, Otelia said, "Nothing. He just hits me." Nevertheless, in song-prayers and in their responses to my questions, women spoke about their pain and problems. Pedranos generally value a stoic attitude toward personal problems. However, that doesn't mean they like the things that vex them, or if given the chance to vent their hurt, they won't do so. But whether women stay silent, sing out, or talk to someone, they know that pain and problems are the stuff of life.[1]

K'op, the Tzotzil word for both problem and prayer, recalls rum's dialectical role in both causing and healing imbalances. Pedranos use "problem" to describe situations where men and women don't fulfill their work obligations to their households and community, and scold and/or hit their spouses, children, or other Pedranos. Women openly describe ways men abuse them or their children as a result of drinking: scolding or criticizing them, being excessively jealous, accusing them of adultery, taking up with other women, hitting them and their children, not working enough in the milpa, and not providing them with corn, beans, and some cash. Clearly, Otelia, Bartolo, Mariano, Victorio, and Pascuala have problems with drinking; they don't fulfill their work obligations at times and are often consumed in their own pain and suffering.

Pedranas' approach to problems seems to militate against blaming themselves when things go wrong and being absorbed in their own pain or suffering. Unlike American women and Ladinas, who often try to fix things, Pedranas generally accept what others do as the way things are, God's will, and often reserve judgment, waiting for the consequences of the person's actions. While Pedranos don't hold a person responsible for his actions while drunk, since his soul has left him and he can't think clearly, they do hold him responsible for his actions, overall. In crises they evaluate the total situation they are in with the person, rather than the person, and make decisions that will serve the majority.

In some ways this attitude resembles attitudes American family members take when they subscribe to the disease concept of alcoholism. Accepting that "their alcoholic" is sick, they realize that she will continue to act irrationally until she emotionally accepts the fact of that sickness and looks for help to heal herself.

The subsistence economy and relatively strict sexual division of labor in Pedrano households creates clear boundaries which seem to militate against enabling and co-dependency. Each household member is aware of her importance to the household and is relatively clear about boundaries between the sexes and generations. Women who are doing their work, like Angélika and Mónica, see the boundaries between themselves and others clearly. Despite the abuse Angélika has suffered and the challenge she faces living with an alcoholic, she seems cheerful, not resigned. Whatever Victorio does to her, Angélika goes on with her work, taking time out to laugh at herself and others. She is proud of her accomplishments and confident of her ability to carry out demanding work.

Pedranos say that the best way to live is to take care of one's own work and self and let others take care of theirs. Because everyone knows what is expected, it's clear when someone is neglecting his work or abusing his family, and most women don't try to make up another reality. No Pedrana with whom I talked tried to protect a loved one's drinking. Even if they tried, I doubt that family members could keep drunken behavior secret. Although banana trees and hilly topography hide houses from view, people living in hamlets know a lot about their neighbors' business. They know even more about each other in Chenalhó. When Pedranos hear a far-off child cry, they know who the child is and what punishment the parents are meting out, or if the parent is drunk and hitting the child unfairly. When a man and woman are arguing, people assume one or both are drunk.

Close contact with extended family members also makes secrecy difficult. Even when living alone with their husbands, women maintain frequent contact with both parents and in-laws. Both sets of parents keep tabs on young couples, and when drinking becomes a problem it doesn't come as a surprise to anyone, except perhaps to the problem drinker. If an abusive husband is brazen enough to blame his wife and send her back to her parents, her parents don't blame her and she does not blame herself, because she didn't choose her husband. However, sometimes a man's relatives will blame his wife, accepting his definition of why his marriage did not work out.

Leaving one's spouse creates a crisis, but kinfolk usually support women who leave abusive husbands. Most women know they can find places with their parents, married children, or married siblings, as Angélika did the first time she left Victorio, and as Otelia has done at times. Older women are even less likely to put up with abusive husbands than younger women are, as their married children often live with them or they can find a home with a married child, making their husband less critical to their children's survival and their own. Sometimes there is nowhere for abused Pedranas of any age to go and as American women often do, they will stay with abusive husbands or parents. Otelia and Bartolo seem enmeshed in each others' compulsions, although she talks about leaving him. That none of her daughters had married yet may have influenced Angélika not to leave Victorio, but I do not think that economic factors feature as strongly as emotional and spiritual ones in Angélika's decisions.

Control—my tendency to personalize it, Pedranos' to collectivize it— became pivotal to my understanding of Pedranas' relation to alcohol. Looking back over my life from their vantage point, it seemed like a doomed struggle to control myself and my environment. Growing up started with believing that I could control many things, then little by little realizing that I could not, and eventually oscillating between accepting and fighting this awareness.

Although Pedranas struggle with some of the same issues of enmeshment and control that American women face, they don't begin life believing they can control everything. They learn to control their tools well, but everything else (people, prices, weather, future events) they embrace with mixed wonder and fear. They know the difference between tools and community norms, which they can control, and other people and destiny, which they cannot.

Pedranos say that one can never know how another person feels, nor how he will act, so it is useless to be preoccupied with others. Pedranos seem to have found a way of separating themselves emotionally from others, a task that many Americans learn for the first time in self-help groups for families of alcoholics like Alanon. Americans call this attitude "detachment." Detachment in the United States follows from a sense of separate selves and involves acting as if each person is only responsible for his or her own feelings, attitudes, and destiny. Pedranos' ideas of detachment involve a balance between personal responsibility and responsibility for the well-being of the whole community. Independence, and freedom from obligations to others, seems to scare most Pedranos. In contrast, "dependency" often carries a negative connotation in the United States, as it does in Mexico. Ladino men view dependence as demeaning, fit only for women and children. Ladinas often see dependence on men as making them vulnerable. However, recovering alcoholics and their families in both the United States and Mexico distinguish between unhealthy dependencies such as on alcohol or a co-dependent spouse, and healthy ones, such as on Alcoholics Anonymous or Alanon (Alcoholics Anonymous 1987).

There seems to be a striking similarity between attitudes toward "letting-go" of things one cannot control that Pedranos learn from birth, and those Americans learn for the first time in twelve-step programs. For Americans the experience of "letting-go" is a personal and often revelatory experience. It contrasts with denial, the compulsive refusal to accept an unpleasant reality (Dentan 1988: 876). Its effects are described in the literature of Alcoholics Anonymous and Alanon, as well as in some literature on conversion. Unfortunately, as Dentan (ibid.: 870) suggests in his discussion of "letting-go" among Senoi-Semais, horticulturalists of the West Malaysian hills, the language may be difficult for audiences of scholarly papers to take seriously:

> Letting-go occurs, gradually or all at once, after a prolonged period of stress, what anthropologists used to refer to as a "state of cultural distortion," Christians as "being sunk in sin," and AA as the "bottom." Letting-go renders the individual open to a radically changed way of life, often radically different from what went before but usually involving self-control, refusal to try to control others, a rejection of worrying about whether one's plans will succeed and an acknowledgement of personal powerlessness and insignificance.[2]

At times Pedranos, like Americans, do try to control other people or destiny. Angélika resorts to scolding Victorio, and Mónica scolds her in-laws, in an effort to get them to stop drinking. Other times Angélika and Pascuala's mother pray to the saints to make Victorio and Pascuala stop. Although it was probably not her main incentive, Angélika may have heard the saints encourage her to take cargos in part to provide an acceptable context for, and some control over, Victorio's drinking. She also knew that Victorio would have to cut down on his drinking during the year or more before the fiesta in order to save the money they needed to serve their cargo.

Pedranos seem to walk a fine line between being able to control their own drinking and others' controlling their drinking, due in large part to the reciprocity inherent in the offer of a drink. Waking or dreaming, Pedranos say that one should accept the offer of a drink. When fulfilling their obligations to their households and communities, Pedranos often describe their drinking as contributing to an overall feeling of contentment. Even Otelia seems to have kept her drinking under control when she served a religious cargo with her first husband. However, Otelia describes a darker side of the obligation to drink when speaking of the Devil who makes her drink. For women like Pascuala, the Devil often comes in real life in the loving and not-so-loving form of their own husbands and brothers.

Although control is a problem for men, they do not have to deal with women's control over their lives. In contrast women must face all the forms of control men face plus men's control over various aspects of their lives, including drinking. Patriarchal tendencies in Pedrano society shape a woman's and her kinsmen's drinking in different ways. However, in general, women drink like their kinsmen. Judging by Pascuala and Otelia, Pedranas whose male kin drink a lot and oblige them to drink run the risk of drinking a lot. Otelia indicates that each of her husbands set the tone for her drinking while she was with them. Pascuala's drinking seems to mirror her husband's, and when she is with her brothers she seems to match them in amount and style of drinking. These women's drinking histories corroborate research findings which indicate that American women's drinking resembles that of their husbands, siblings, or close friends (Wilsnack, Wilsnack and Klassen 1984).

However, Pedranas who leave their communities and their kinsmen's control can be susceptible to problem drinking as well. Indigenous women undergoing mestizoization experience alcohol problems like women who challenge male dominance in the United States.[3]

Changes in roles and power relationships throughout the life cycle affect the amount of control men have over a woman's drinking. For many Pedranas the end of childbearing marks a time when their power and influence are increasing. As grandmothers, shamans, midwives, veteran weavers, and cargo holders, women exercise considerable power. While drinking in their cargos as shamans, midwives, and cargo holders is their right, Pedranos generally associate drinking with the heat of advanced age and say older women's drinking is often not problematic. Except for Pascuala, who was still young, the only Pedranas I met dependent on alcohol were older women who had served or were still serving cargos as shamans or religious leaders.[4]

Pedranas' varied roles throughout their lives seem to give them some protection against problem drinking.[5] From their first roles as daughters and apprentice weavers to their last as grandmothers and cargo holders, Pedranas balance several demanding roles at once. Most Pedranas value their varied roles, and losing one or more can be difficult for them. Since Pedranas bear many children, losing one child rarely makes a woman lose her identity as a mother, but women feel the loss of a child deeply. The high child mortality rate in Highland Chiapas means that most women lose at least one child and many women lose several. Rather than getting used to the pain, most women seem to layer one painful loss on top of another. Children's deaths chip away at a mother's identity. Although Pascuala started drinking before her children died, she repeatedly mentions their deaths to explain why she drinks. The deaths of Otelia's children undoubtedly contribute to her drinking, as well. In her song Otelia stresses that she still has children, sons, and a daughter-in-law. Of all the things they can't control, Pedranas rebel most against not being able to keep their children alive. In their resistance to this ultimate injustice, they may turn to anything that might give their children a longer life.

Giving up one's cargo after successfully fulfilling it is another way Pedranas may feel they have lost control or become less valuable as a result of no longer holding a particular position which others value, a condition social psychologists call "role deprivation." However, through their cargo service Pedranos acquire heat, and this continues to give them value in their own and others' eyes. Angélika mourned the loss of her cargo, but she went on with her life. Victorio, in contrast, couldn't seem to function well outside of a cargo. His world fell apart immediately after the Feast of St. Peter, and he only started to put it back together when he began curing again.

Grieving and depression are two expressions of loss of control which I struggled to untangle while doing fieldwork. The distinction between depression and grieving became important to me as I tried to deal with discrepancies between my overall impression of the social and emotional environment in Chenalhó and others' accounts. Many Ladino doctors and some anthropologists report widespread depression in Indigenous communities. In contrast, I would not describe the social environment in Chenalhó as depressed. The few households I lived in and the many I visited were full of laughter and joking, even when they contained problem drinkers. The sustained, tender contact between family members in households was punctuated by intense and awe-inspiring meetings between other Pedranos and the Gods at fiestas. In cooperative work women search for new ways to improve their own and others' lives. The balance Pedranos create between household and community relations seems to bring them stability and hope in spite of considerable physical and social stress.

Pedranos do recognize depression. They describe men and women who don't eat, cry often, can't work, and have bad dreams as depressed. Otelia and Pascuala seem to be depressed. Both women, but especially Otelia, expressed low self-esteem and couldn't sleep or eat at times. When a woman is sober Pedrano values seem to militate against depression. When a man is sober they seem to encourage him to respect women's work and position. However, habitually drunk Pedranos degrade women. Drunken or depressed women in turn are less able to assert their worth when men try to put them down. Otelia, and to a lesser extent Pascuala, seem to have given in to rum and the men in their lives.

While Otelia's and Pascuala's stories seem consistent with several findings about control issues and American women problem drinkers, my perceptions about Angélika and women's relation to others' drinking do not fit my society's ideas about alcoholic families and "co-dependency." I attribute the lack of fit to some important differences between how Pedranos and Americans view control.

Meeting Angélika when she was in a powerful position no doubt influenced my positive evaluation of her and her situation vis-à-vis control. The image of Angélika standing in her ceremonial blouse holding a bottle of rum reverently in front of her lasted as long as I knew her. Despite Victorio's compulsive drinking, Angélika never seemed powerless to me. When Victorio did not fulfill his duties I saw her draw on her personal strengths, her work selling chicha, her children's support, and service to the saints. Selling chicha beside her daughters she joked and laughed, while continually exploring ways to improve their lives. In reflective moments she talked openly about her feelings. Although I questioned if I was accepting Angélika's actions at face value, I was convinced that, whether or not they were based on myths, through them Angélika was living with some measure of dignity and hope.

I hesitate to use "enabling" to describe Angélika's behavior. Enabling in American households usually involves futile efforts to keep things under control and personal adjustments that few recognize, least of all family members involved. In such households the alcoholic is frequently the hub around which everyone revolves. When he or she moves, everyone else moves. While Angélika may have been upset at times by her husband's actions, I did not see Victorio as pivotal to her or her children's lives.

I also did not see the shame, secrecy, and denial reported for enabling family members.

Similarly, I hesitate to depict Angélika as a "co-dependent," that is, a person who because of her relationship with an alcoholic has become out of touch with herself and is tempted to deny and lie about her situation, the same way that alcoholics do (Schaef 1987). Although this description fits compulsive drinkers like Otelia, Bartolo, and Pascuala, it does not fit as well for non-drinkers like Angélika and Mónica. Even though these women live in daily contact with an alcoholic, they seem in touch with their own lives. Angélika continues to evaluate her life and look for direction through the collective awareness of her people, expressed in dreams, prayer, and service to the Gods and saints. Mónica turns to more household-centered strategies, like raising her children and keeping her store running smoothly, to balance her own and others' needs.

Another important understanding all four women gave me was that the religious or collective justifications Pedranos offer for adjustments to problem drinking work for them. These explanations work for them through various narrative forms, including prayer, dreams, song, and metaphor. Through these forms Pedranos express their feelings, cope with hardships, and heal themselves of drinking problems. For example, to stop her own problem drinking Angélika sought direction from powerful invisible beings in dreams and prayer. Although Angélika serves rum in the fiestas in which she officiates, respecting its sacred power all the while, in her dreams the Mother of the Sky and God tell her that when she and her people drink too much, rum rises to the sky and makes the heavens reek. They have told Angélika clearly that if she and her people cannot drink rum respectfully, then it is better for them to give it up. The cutoff point for these powerful beings and Angélika seems to be when people put rum in the place of everyday necessities, like food, clothing, and self-respect.

While in Western terms Angélika's coping and healing strategies may be "unconscious," she would be more likely to explain them in spiritual or communal terms. "The saints told me to do it; I had to do it for my people," were replies she gave to my questions about why she took a particular path. Angélika sees her own recovery from problem drinking and Victorio's periodic excessive drinking and violent behavior as enmeshed in a long history of service to her people and her family that they share. This service, based on cargos, is the measuring stick for her life. Without it her life would lose much of its meaning and purpose. When Victorio acts as if alcohol is more important than the Gods or his family, the saints and other invisible beings remain at the center of Angélika's life.

While Angélika cured herself through prayer and dreams and continues to use them to reinforce her relationship to her community and the Gods, Otelia and Pascuala make of their dreams and prayer elegant defense mechanisms to support their drinking. In stark contrast to Angélika's account, Pascuala states that the Moon-Virgin comes in her dreams to keep her from joining the Presbyterians and putting an end to her drinking. She depicts the Moon-Virgin/Mother of the Sky as an angry mother scolding a disobedient daughter. As the errant daughter Pascuala lets her "mother" bring her back into conformity and into the secure world that rum creates for her.

Otelia's invisible advisors are an older couple and Satan or the demons. Otelia says that before she became a shaman, an older man and woman, probably totil me'il or God and the Virgin Mary, brought her rum, poured it into a gourd, and told her that the gourd would be hers forever. Now that she is no longer healing, Otelia does not need rum, but she interprets the prophesy that rum will always be with her to justify her continued drinking. The powerful beings who visit her in dreams today are not benevolent beings, but demons. And rather than limiting the amount they give her to one gourd, they set many bottles before her and keep emptying them into her cup. For Otelia, the invisible advisors no longer bring her rum as an accoutrement of service to her people. Instead, they deceive her into drinking herself sick with their unending supply of rum. Her dreams allow Otelia to rationalize her inability to stop drinking.

While the demons keep her drinking, Otelia copes with the consequences of her own and her husband's drinking through song. The most striking thing about Otelia's improvisation of "I am a drunk woman, I am a drunk girl" is the loneliness. While Pedranos collectivize much of their experience, they seem to see grief and compulsive drinking as unshareable. When women are both grieving and drinking, like Otelia and Pascuala, they are utterly alone. While grief makes all Pedranos feel alone for a time, they eventually return to the comfort that dependence on others brings. Drinking, traditionally a communalizing experience for Pedranos, helps them return to feelings of belonging.

Otelia and Pascuala, however, seem to have replaced a healthy dependence on others with an unhealthy dependence on rum. In phrases such as "I am on my way to worthlessness" and "I am going with shit," Otelia reveals just how little self-worth she has. Later she makes a desperate call for help, "Carry me away, take me to a far away place, that I may get out of this." Otelia's self-abnegation and call for help is a haunting reminder of the extent to which Pedranas have internalized oppression and the unfair burden that they bear in their communities and in the larger society. Even though Pedranos value complementarity and collectivity in their communities, they often play these out at women's expense. This is nowhere more apparent than in the discrepancy between Pedrano admonitions about expressing anger and women's testimonies of the abuse they have endured at the hands of drunken parents and husbands.

Within traditions, song-prayers seem to be the only acceptable vehicle through which women can publically verbalize what they feel and think. Pedranos give drunk women permission to sing. Although men often sing while drunk in fiestas, they do not use song as a forum to express their personal views and feelings. In contrast, Americans and Ladinos say it is disgusting for women to display their emotions when drunk, while they give permission to drunk men to sing songs. At such times men may sing bawdy group songs, or sorrowful solos about the same subjects Pedranas take up in song, i.e., feeling alone, or being abandoned by an unfaithful spouse or a deceased loved one, etc. But unlike Pedranas, they do not often sing about their spiritual power or relationships with divine beings.

Pedranas' song-prayers resonate throughout households and Pedrano consciousness and embarrass everyone but the women singing. While husbands say their wives' songs are drunken babble, when listening to a woman sing they lower their heads, as if accused. Children giggle when asked about their mothers' song-prayers, but when no one listens to their questions or fulfills their needs they, too, sing to get attention. When questioned about their own songs women don't seem ashamed. They seem to appreciate that their drunken songs make public stories of pain and powerlessness which are not theirs alone, but belong to their people.

In their chosen narrative forms women don't express the kind of anger or outrage one might expect from great suffering, but I believe that these forms enable them to release their feelings and/or begin to heal themselves in the context of their traditions, which mean so much to them. Like angry Americans who opt to throw a dish or hit a pillow instead of another person, Pedranas make a chopping motion in the air at the end of their songs, an aggressive action which allows them to strike out in anger without actually hurting anyone.[6] In song passages where they speak of the Gods as parents and protectors, women affirm that they are not alone or abandoned, even if kin have died or left them. They state that they have a secure place in the collective whole and that spiritual beings empower them.

Otelia's song-prayer also speaks about the life-cyle and mortality. Otelia told me that she used to sing "I am a drunk woman, I am a drunk girl" with her parents during *sk'in ch'ulelal* (Feast of the Souls). While Pedranos flock to Chenalhó during other fiestas, during the Feast of the Souls on November 1st and 2d they stay in their hamlets, visiting cemeteries and homes of relatives and neighbors. Women prepare altars of rum, food, flowers, and incense, gifts to their ancestors' souls, which later living relatives and neighbors will eat. At their relatives' gravesides they drink, weep, and sing while groups of men play stringed instruments. With its focus on kinship bonds and life-cycle changes (e.g., alternating between "girl" and "woman"), the song seems especially suited to this fiesta. As Otelia says,

> I am a woman who has to die
> I am a girl who has to die, yes.

Otelia, Angélika, and Pascuala seek surcease in song, prayer, dreams, and sometimes the bottle. But in spite of grief from losing children or from

Altar for the Day of the Dead in Antonia's house, October 31, 1987. Antonia loaded the table she normally uses to store food and cooking utensils with beef, flowers, candles, bananas, oranges, peanuts, sodas, shrimps, and corn and bean tamales. Then she placed two chairs before the altar to welcome deceased relatives' souls.

not being sufficiently loved and appreciated by parents or spouses, each woman in her own way underscores her people's regard for depending on each other, for parents caring for children's souls, for spouses complementing each other.

My interviews with Angélika, Otelia, and Pascuala convinced me that the schematic approaches that social scientists and health professionals use to describe problem drinkers and their families in my society often scant the power of narrative and the importance of community. The tests and diagnostic criteria we use to determine who has a drinking problem seem to show only what people lack, not the powers they may have. Through prayer, dreams, and song, Pedranas define their experiences with drinking as well as find ways to deal with its damaging effects on their own and others' lives. While Pedranas are concerned about aberrant behavior, especially how a parent's behavior affects a child or how a witch could harm them, they seem just as concerned about dysfunction in the institutions of their society. In contrast, the stress on psychological and social characteristics of American alcohol users obscures the role of American institutions in alcoholism, especially in women (Marsh, Colten, and Tucker 1982).

In my efforts to recognize the powers Pedranos have and to deal with contradictions between ritual and non-ritual drinking, I came to see drinking within a social and political framework. Such narrative forms as Otelia's song-prayer, in which she started out confidently within the context of her traditions, i.e., a standard tune familiar to all Pedranos, and eventually moved to expressing her personal pain, led me to see drinking processually. It seemed important to understand why Pedranos and other Indigenous groups in Highland Chiapas start drinking in the first place and how their drinking changes, rather than focus solely on the outcome of their drinking.[7]

Whether in a single drinking event or over the course of their lives, Pedranos usually begin drinking in service to their families or communities, with relatively strict rules governing drinking order and comportment. Otelia began drinking while accompanying her parents at healing ceremonies. Angélika used rum to solicit help for her cargos and to offer her helpers during the fiestas at which she officiated. Both before and during the fiesta rum was important to heat the bodies and souls of all participants so that they would feel like serving each other and their Gods. Accepting rum in dreams may herald a cargo or bring illness or good fortune. In shamanic healing ceremonies, drinking returns the gift of rum that evil or good invisible beings offer in dreams, thus restoring balance between visible and invisible beings. In healings and fiestas drinking forges bonds of reciprocity between mortals, Gods, and fellow Pedranos. It temporarily erases fear of uncontrollable visible and invisible others, who, while they are drinking or acknowledging a gift of rum, are lowering their defenses, too. (Cf. Lomnitz 1969 for Mapuche of Chile.) While drinking in ritual settings all parties are in the same mental state and no one has an upper hand. While the Gods and saints consume their gifts of rum, incense, candles, and flowers they, too, are content. Although at times even in this context drinking becomes excessive, as long as no one is aggressive it is an accepted avenue through which Pedranos can feel unified with each other and their Gods.

However, when fulfilling their service and opening up to the essence of a flowery universe, Pedranos sometimes go overboard. With too many cups of rum fear may return along with other repressed feelings about a hard life or unresolved interpersonal conflicts. Some Pedranos seize this culturally appropriate time and other informal times to air their feelings of anguish, anger, despair, and grief. Especially when they are drinking compulsively and grieving deeply, the full weight of both their own and their people's losses comes down upon Pedranos. In these moments even alcohol cannot take away their pain. However, integrated as it is into Pedrano traditions, at this and other times alcohol mediates tremendous tension that until recently Pedranos have not had the power to translate into more effective forms of resistance. Nevertheless, Pedranos' efforts to sanctify rum and keep it within bounds are poignant reminders that they have never been able to make it work for them as they have their Native Gods.

Despite the reality that Pedranos develop dependencies on alcohol just as Americans do, Pedranos' concepts of self and community provide them with a solid base upon which to devise strategies to deal with compulsive drinking, without turning to outside institutions. I believe that most Pedranos see their selves in relation to their own and others' drinking problems, as described in systems theory (Bateson 1971). Although Bateson geared his theory toward explaining why some people in Western society become alcoholic and others do not, the theory illuminates how Pedranos construe experience and how their epistemology can help problem drinkers in their society restore balance.

Bateson describes two types of relational styles—symmetrical and complementary—through which people or groups experience being a part of a higher system or power. In the former style, both parties respond with the same behavior, like the arms race or an ice skating duet (ibid.: 9). In the latter each party responds with a different, but complementary, kind of behavior. Each supplies lacks or needs; together they make up the whole.

The symmetrical state, which embodies relations of opposition and competition, is an acceptable occidental epistemology. Alcoholics, however, have trouble making it work for them because they also extend this style to their conceptions of self. Internalizing the symmetrical state obliges alcoholics to polarize their selves and their compulsion to drink. The way out of this tense state is to drink, for through drinking alcoholics find a shortcut to complementarity, to a sense of wholeness.[8] But as their drinking escalates, alcoholics find their relationships to real and fictitious others and forces polarized to an intolerable degree. Deterioration progresses until they realize that their drinking is a system they cannot control.

Before alcoholics take paths of recovery they face a double bind—the need to choose between two punishing alternatives, to continue to drink and die, or to stop drinking and live without release. If they let the double bind take them down to what AA calls "the bottom," there they may experience an involuntary change in their deep unconscious epistemology. Many alcoholics say this is a spiritual experience, which springs the trap and makes the double bind irrelevant (ibid.: 14). In this position alcoholics begin to experience their selves as parts of larger fields of informational pathways, no longer polarized nor delimited by bodies and minds.

Like recovering alcoholics in AA, Pedranos recognize that their survival depends upon integrating themselves into a larger system and living humbly under the protection of powers stronger than themselves. Traditional Pedranos raise their children to "make their souls arrive" within a framework of "letting-go" and relating in a complementary way in the world. Children learn that spouses and generations complement each other, mortals and Gods complement each other, and that it takes a long time for one's soul to arrive.

This perspective, I believe, makes sober Pedranos less likely than Americans and Ladinos to delude themselves into thinking they alone can control their own or others' drinking. Traditional Pedranos have not developed the view that their selves are separate from unconscious processes nor that the need to drink daily is a distinct behavioral system. Since "alcoholism" and the opposition of mind to matter do not exist for Pedranos, they do not give "alcoholism" a life of its own and therefore do not see it as a force outside of their "selves" which they must resist.

Some Pedranos seem more likely to take on an integrational style in which they see themselves in competition with external events, forces, and other Pedranos. Although most Pedranos lose young children and often have just finished grieving for one when another dies, Angélika, Otelia, and Pascuala and their husbands seem to have experienced an inordinate amount of economic and emotional deprivation during their childhoods, stemming from parental or sibling abuse and early deaths of parents. Later stresses and losses, such as marital conflict and the deaths of children and spouses, have added to their grief. Although alcohol has aggravated these losses, it has also offered a short cut back to community, to a sense of their part in the larger whole. Surrendering to rum makes sense for these Pedranos and many others, as rum is endowed with sacred power. Nevertheless, for Otelia, Bartolo, Pascuala, and Mariano, rum has become more important than the larger system it serves, and the complementarity they experience is short-lived. Their fellow Pedranos agree that these people's relation to alcohol has superseded their oligations to their families and community.

Of the drinkers discussed in this chapter, only Angélika has realized how her past drinking threatened the traditions which connect her to her family and her higher system. Through dreams and prayer she healed herself. I regret that I failed to ask Angélika what happened to make her "hit bottom," and what it would take for her to leave Victorio to "hit bottom." It seems that hitting bottom for Pedranos is just as dramatic as for Americans. The transformative power of this experience for Pedranos seems to lie in loneliness, the pain of separation from others which is so difficult for Pedranos to bear, rather than in a kind of awakening, such as Americans often report experiencing. Women put abusive men in this position when they leave them to go to parents or a brother or sister. Knowing that they have safe places to go where they are usually welcome enables women to act on their feelings and in their best interests. Leaving also communicates clearly to a man to what depths he has fallen, for now there is no one to make his tortillas or beans, to share his life. Men, in contrast, cannot put women in this position as easily, as most women know how to work in the field or can buy their own corn and beans with earnings from selling their labor or artisan products. However, for both men and women, hitting bottom seems to involve being unable to survive in the complementary way the ancestors dictate. Living alone, unable to rely on his wife and daughters, Victorio has nearly hit bottom, but through his curing work he clings to a sense of belonging to something larger than himself and doesn't have to make a drastic change in his personal epistemology.

Once a Pedrano has hit bottom and begins to climb up, the journey seems to be easier than for Americans. I believe the difference lies in Pedrano collective values and the central tenet of humility before higher powers to which they subscribe.

While "letting-go" and waiting for direction from the Gods strengthens Pedranos when they confront problem drinking, when caught up in their own or others' drunken pride the Gods will not hear their prayers, and dreams are always bad. All Traditional Pedranos know how to make prayer and dreams work for them. But these resources will not work if they see only the malevolent face of the Gods in dreams or they expect the Gods to do all the work when they pray, like Otelia and Pascuala. Traditional Pedranos say that to make prayer work, one must approach the invisible powers humbly. But they add, one's heart must want to change and one must wait patiently.

8 "Beneath God's flowery hands and feet"
Shamans' Cures for Problem Drinking

Drip down drop by drop
    and come, my Lord.
Now let it be soon, my Lord,
    now let it be quick, my Lord.

Early one evening after I had been living with Antonia for about four months, I heard Domingo praying in Tzotzil in the sleeping house. Curious, I walked by the half-open door to see him kneeling at the back of the house in front of a row of white candles. Several sweet gum boughs formed a protective wall behind the candles. At Domingo's left, fingers of smoke drifted up to the ceiling from a pottery incense burner. Domingo's humbled body and husky speech spelled urgency and fear. Many nights I had fallen asleep listening to Antonia and Domingo praying, but this prayer was different. On other occasions Antonia and Domingo also prayed rapidly and knelt humbly, but they did not change their tone of voice nor sing their prayers as Domingo was doing now. The other prayers had passages of Spanish, too. This prayer was all Tzotzil and contained many words I did not know.

I asked Antonia what was going on, why Domingo was praying this way. Antonia told me what I feared—that Domingo was asking God and the saints to keep his family safe from harm that envious neighbors were wishing on them. I knew that neighbors had been talking about my enriching Antonia and Domingo. When I pressed her Antonia told me some of the rumors that were circulating. In a particularly creative one, Antonia and I were manufacturing money. Although even Antonia was amazed at the ridiculousness of this rumor, after recalling the afternoon a neighbor woman came to visit I understood how the rumor might have begun. That afternoon I was writing in my notebook with a technical pen. Antonia,

Domingo, and the boys were used to looking at my pen and all had tried it out at least once. Antonia suspected that the woman, who had probably never seen such a pen and did not know how money is made, thought it might be an instrument to make money, and so the rumor started.

Although we weren't materializing money, I was paying Antonia for room, board, and for teaching me her language. I was also buying weavings from Antonia and fellow cooperative members and helping them expand their markets in the United States. I understood how Antonia's neighbor had only to exercise her imagination a little to conclude that we were making money.

But rumors are one thing. It is another to leave one's house in the night to go to a cave in the Earth Lord's domain with candles, rum, and incense in order to sell your neighbor's soul. I had read that a witch's soul will roll over three times before a cross and transform itself into a *nagual,* usually a domestic four-footed animal, and in this form devour his victim's soul (Laughlin 1988:7).[1]

Domingo did not tell me that he thought an envious neighbor had prayed for evil in a cave somewhere, but he was worried enough to take action. His humble prayer in the sleeping house was his effort to blind that neighbor's vision, forefending the fulfilment of the malevolence.

Before the night Domingo prayed against envy I had not come face to face with its power in Pedrano social life. Now, I began to be more attentive to relationships between Pedranos and to think more about how my presence in their home was affecting Antonia and Domingo. Even accidents, like burning Felipe with hot water, took on new meaning. Perhaps they were not random, but manifestations of malice. I was clumsier than usual the morning I spilled hot water from my coffee pot into the ashes, burning Felipe's leg. Steam and smoke swirled around us and we couldn't see who was hurt until Felipe's scream shot out above the other children's. Antonia ran to the corner of the house and began scraping the skin of a squash to make a salve for Felipe's leg. As she applied the salve to his burn I held him by his shoulders and tried to comfort him.

Now envy was no longer just an interesting aspect of Pedrano ideas about illness and social relations. It was an evaluation of my presence. My actions, both real and imagined, changed life in Antonia and Domingo's household and community. Pedranos make changes without outsiders' help, and without attributing them to witchcraft. But like all visible and invisible beings, I was capable of good and evil, and like all Ladinos and foreigners I could set Indigenous people against each other. No one knew if I would bring good or bad fortune or how I would bring it. And everyone, even those who knew me well, could not completely trust me. Antonia told me why it was hard for her and others to believe that I could not hurt them:

"Those who doubt you, what you say, may see your actions are good, or hear you say you want to help us, but they can't see what you do or say when you go back to your country. We don't know what things are like there, what you are capable of in your powerful country. Even if you don't change there, you might hurt us without wanting to."

I told Antonia and Domingo that I would leave if they felt that my presence was endangering them or their children beyond a level they could live with. Knowing that I had hurt and could still hurt her family, either by myself or as a pawn in others' hands, made daily life harder for Antonia, but she kept her sense of humor. She usually laughed off the innocuous rumors while Domingo prayed to counteract the effects of the more dangerous ones. Lacking Antonia's capacity to laugh things off, I often felt remorse. Still, during my first year my ego was just strong enough to let me believe that I had something to offer Antonia directly and her people indirectly that could balance out the dangers of fraternizing with me. As my understanding of the complexity of Pedranos' lives deepened, I became more dubious that I had something to offer them. When I returned in 1988, I tried living with different families, not wanting to burden Antonia and Domingo further and hoping to know different households.

As my understanding of envy grew it was easier to understand why Antonia hesitated to introduce me to people. Going door to door with me would have only publicized that an outsider was living with her and Domingo and enriching them through her resources. "All the neighbors know you are here, but if they don't see you they might forget about you," Antonia said.

Although she did not go out with me often, Antonia was quick to recommend people whom I could look up on my own. When it came to learning about envy, prayer, and drinking problems Antonia suggested some healers who could help, but she added that one need not be a shaman to pray against envy or to ask God's help to stop drinking, and that neither witnesses nor rum were necessary. Most Pedranos treat their own or family members' drinking problems through prayer, dreams, and herbal remedies without calling on a shaman. But for major problems Pedranos usually seek counsel from well-known shamans, knowing that these specialists will do everything within their power to cure them, including descending into the underworld to rescue their souls from subterranean forces of evil.

If I wanted to know how experts dealt with envy, Antonia suggested I talk with her father's sister's husband, Armando. She said that he might be willing to explain how to give up drinking, as well as pray for someone close who has a drinking problem. Many Pedranos came to Armando for help, she said, because of his reputation as a wise and experienced shaman. I had met Armando at the Fiesta of San Nicolás, and since then I had heard of his work with OMIECH, the Organization of Indigenous Doctors of Chiapas, but I never knew that he was related to Antonia. Knowing that Antonia was circumspect about recommendations, I trusted that a Pedrano shaman would not find it disrespectful or presumptuous if I asked him to use his healing practices for my people. I looked Armando up and we made a date to talk. When I arrived on the appointed day Armando's wife told me that he had gone to a meeting in San Cristóbal. The next time he was at a meeting again. I had begun to accept that every task I undertook in Chenalhó took three tries.

On my third try I found Armando at home. We greeted each other, and it seemed as if he was free to pray. Seconds after I arrived a Pedrano came to the door asking for Armando. The man told Armando that a family member was sick and needed his help. While I was admiring a weaving of one of Armando's daughters, Armando and the man left. Realizing that they had gone, I asked Armando's wife when she thought he would be back, and if I should wait. She said that he would be back soon and that I should sit down and wait. I waited what seemed an interminably long time. Finally I decided that the meetings in San Cristóbal, and now this, were Armando's way of refusing my request. I was offended and left the house, telling Armando's wife that I wouldn't need Armando's services. She seemed amused. I wasn't.

On the way out of town I passed the church and decided to look inside. I figured that Armando and the man would have finished their first prayer in the Chapel of Holy Cross, and would now be praying in the Church of St. Peter, the correct sequence for prayers. I left the light of the town square and stepped just inside the door of the candlelit church. I thought I might see Armando and the man kneeling at the altar, bowing before their candles and incense, but I didn't expect to be moved by the sight of them. Their white tunics, belted at the waist, glowed like two signal lights on dark water. Armando's voice drifted back to me in a stream of deep, sonorous tones. Suddenly it made a great difference to me that they were believers and I was not. I was ashamed.

In those moments I began to understand that to talk to powerful beings in sacred places in Chenalhó, one must humble oneself at God's altar. Pedranos kneel beneath God's "flowery face," under the rain of drops from his "flowery feet and hands" because he demands and rewards patience, something of which I had relatively little, by Pedrano standards. After that day I no longer held so tight to the belief that my repeated trips to town, the mere fact that I had made it all the way to Chenalhó, Chiapas, should demonstrate my sincerity and let me line up for a shaman's services along with other Pedranos. Still, I continued struggling to accept that what really mattered to Pedranos and their powerful beings was that once in their presence I would wait patiently and come back again and again. And that I would go to the end of the line.

By putting me off, whether intentionally or not, Armando did for me what many shamans do for their clients. He educated my soul, humbling it before the powerful beings. He also taught me about Pedrano souls. Although Armando did not demonstrate how he advocates through prayer for sick souls, he did agree to an interview. During our interview Armando told me in Spanish how he used to drink during healings and at other times. While he was passed out his soul would wander off and get into trouble. He gave up rum through prayer many years before, and now only blows it on afflicted body parts or sprinkles it over pine branches and candles during healings. Armando told me that he had received his cargo to organize shamans into a regional organization, and later an international one, through a dream. Later in an interview with a United States journalist, Armando said that a jaguar came to him in a dream and kissed him, telling him they would live together and give each other strength to heal people.[2] Armando listened to my pulse to show how Pedranos discern the cause of an illness. He remarked how strong my heart was, and told me I would live long. Then, in Tzotzil, he described how people get sick.

"You have one soul here right now. But you have another. When you have fallen asleep, when sleep has seized you, your soul leaves you and goes walking around. It goes through the streets, into houses, wherever it wants. Also, it can go to places where spirits are, that is in the low places. Now, when it runs into a friend they talk together. They give each other a soda, a tortilla, or a piece of meat. But your soul gets burned by the food, as if it got burned from eating food in broad daylight. But this is deception. It is the evil and coldness of the Devil.[3] He always attacks the spirit. It makes us sick in our soul. . . . Suddenly some part of our body hurts us and we feel as if we were beaten. Our head also aches. We have a lot of rheumatism from bad air. . . . When we realize what has happened, we just go to someone who knows how to cure, who knows how to pulse. The reason for the consultation is to see if one is sick in the soul, if there was witchcraft. It is through taking a person's pulse that we know what is deceiving our soul. It could be that they gave the soul a soda, or they shot it with a gun, or they struck it with a machete, or they hit it somewhere in the street, or they ran over it with some car, or they killed it in the dream. . . . But this is curable. One knows everything through pulsing, and with this one can tell if the illness is only in the soul. One can present oneself [in prayer] and lay out one's candles. And when one already knows the problem, one asks Our Father that he calm our body, that he soothe it, that he make it better through God's blessings and with the [help of] the Holy Mother who is in heaven. Because [we pray] to Our Father and also to all the angels and all the Gods. God sees everything, although we don't listen to what he says. We don't listen to him when he speaks. . . . That's why we burn a candle. There are different candles, some are yellow, some are white, some are multicolored. I put down thirteen, ten candles depending on whether I ask for help for illnesses from which one dies rapidly or for little illnesses of the soul. If the illness is a great illness of the soul I put out a candle of five hundred pesos, and six candles of twenty pesos and a soda and a little rum. The rum is only for blowing over the candles. I don't drink it. I only use it to blind the Devil's eyes."

Describing sickness, Armando draws a fluid boundary between physical and psychological disease, as well as between visible and dreamed worlds. Traditional Pedranos say that sickness, in the form of envy, usually comes in dreams, *vayichil,* and that illness brings one closer to death. Thus, illness and death share the same word, *chamel.* Pedranos don't always know if it is a malevolent or benevolent being who has come to them in a dream, or whether they have come to rebuke or rescue them. What matters is that a powerful presence has come into their bodies, bringing either good or evil. As their illness progresses, Highlanders realize the meaning of their dreams and what may have happened to their souls. "Elasticity" in dream logic and "the generous time span allowed for a dream's prophesy to unfold" reinforce the prophetic value of dreams (Laughlin 1988: 10).

Traditionalists recognize two complementary souls, the *ch'ulel* (the inner soul), and the *vayhel* (the outer animal spirit-companion, or alter ego). A baby vayhel is born at the same time a human baby is born. Both animal and baby grow at the same rate, their fates forever joined. In ideal conditions a vayhel lives in the safety of a corral tended by totil me'il, the father/mother ancestor/protector, the power of good in humans. Pedranos say that long ago there was no need for shamans, because totil me'il took care of people's souls. In those times there was no soul loss. If people got sick, instead of reciting long prayers beseeching help from totil me'il and a host of other Maya deities and Catholic saints, they simply prayed to totil me'il saying, "Please heal me."

As Armando describes, while people sleep or are passed out their animal spirit companions wander, courting danger to themselves and others.

Any physical or social problem befalling themselves or relatives tells Pedranos that the vayhel has gotten out of the corral and in its wanderings has encountered an evil force, perhaps a nagual. Now an abnormality exists in both visible and invisible social and moral orders which they or a shaman must normalize.

Even many members of Catholic Action, like Antonia and Domingo, respect the power of dreams, Traditional prayers, and the two-soul concept in treating illness. Most Pedranos say that only prayer and dreams can reveal the state of one's soul, which one must know to treat disease. Since Pedranos say that illness is punishment for wrongdoing, a cure must discover the offense in the invisible world and redress it (Arias 1973: 50). Discovery and redress usually require the aid of a shaman who knows how to deal with the invisible world. A general rule when someone falls sick is to find a shaman to diagnose the illness through pulsing, and then go through the proper prayers to counteract the envy or redress the wrong that brought the illness.

Besides dreams, pulsing is an important diagnostic tool. Pedrano shamans say that they don't actually hear blood; instead they feel it, if it is high, or low, ascending, descending, jumping, turning, or stopping. Like the person whose body it occupies, blood walks, and in that way keeps itself hot. If blood stands still it becomes cold, and death follows. Although the heart, like a furnace, warms the blood, the blood keeps stoking the heart. Drinking too much rum can overheat the blood and burn the heart.[4]

Once a shaman has diagnosed a problem, he may massage, give steam baths and herbal remedies, induce vomiting, let blood, blow or spray rum on a patient, suck or kiss a patient's head or hands with salt and water, "seize" an illness by passing eggs or branches over a patient's body, and sacrifice a hen or rooster in exchange for a person's lost soul: but never without prayer. In curing prayers Traditional Pedranos offer rum to all the invisible beings dwelling on the earth and in heaven in a number of ways: they may sprinkle or blow it at the feet of saints' statues, or over candles and pine boughs used in curings. They may blow it on wounds. And they may drink it, in curative doses and as a symbol of reverence for the powerful beings. But with or without rum, prayer remains the basic treatment for emotional and physical disease, the principal weapon in the battlefield of dreams.

Although I had been observing shamans from a distance and had come to understand that Pedranos see compulsive drinking as a disease of the soul, I still had not secured a prayer for one of my friends or family. I wanted the spiritual help for two friends, Kate and Joe. While I was in the field Joe was struggling with sobriety, and Kate with facing her own problems instead of preoccupying herself with Joe's. In one of her letters Kate asked me to pray for her and Joe "in whatever way you pray."

Reina offered to introduce me to some shamans she knew who could pray for Kate and Joe. I had found that after discussing with Antonia whatever it was I wanted to know about, then I could go to Reina and her family for help in finding people who knew something about it. (In addition to our fear of envy, Antonia had too much work at home and for her co-op to go around introducing me to people.) In contrast, although the women in Reina's household were busy, they shared the work, and were not weavers or involved in a cooperative. At any given time at least one of them was usually free to accompany me on a visit.

All of the shamans Reina and her family recommended were women, and heavy drinkers now or in the past. Magdalena, for example, lived in town, drank moderately, and might be willing to pray, for a fee. Her hand was badly burned from falling into the fire once when she was a child, but she still made bread and cooking pots, as well as being a shaman.

Then there was Manuela, another shaman from town, who was also a midwife. She belonged to "Jnet'um," a midwives' group of OMIECH, and was friendly with Ladino doctors in Chenalhó. Recently she had become a follower of Catholic Action. Although she drank in the past, now she did not use rum in her prayers or drink alcohol otherwise.

And there was Juana. Juana stayed for weeks at a time in San Cristóbal, curing Ladinos. When in Chenalhó, she was often drunk. Reina said she had heard that Juana prayed for God to kill her husband after he left her for another woman. Juana's husband did get sick and died soon after; but, Reina added, only God knew if it was Juana's prayer that killed him.

Magdalena

Magdalena was making bread when Pancha and I came to her door. She eyed us uneasily as we stood outside the door waiting to be asked to come in. Although we'd made arrangements to talk, Magdalena said that she didn't have time to talk now because we'd arrived a little late. (By our calculations we were early).

Pancha told her that I would pay her for her time, and she smiled and said, "Come." We offered her rolls we'd brought. She made coffee and gave us some of her rolls. Several of Magdalena's ten children listened as we talked, and Pancha translated when needed.

Magdalena said she drank a lot in her first years of marriage, but stopped after about five years. From then on when someone offered her a drink she tried "doing the action," but people were insistent, and eventually she settled on accepting just one cup. Now she drinks only one cup and never gets drunk or sick from drinking.

"Magdalena, how did you learn to pray?"

"I was eleven years old when I learned to pray. Now I'm thirty-six, very old. I have ten children. But, it seems that I'm O.K., not one of my children has died. My husband went with the Evangelists; a long time ago I threw him out. But it's only been two days since he left this time. He took two of his sons and left. I stayed here in my house because I don't want to learn anything [about Evangelical religion]. I want to learn from above, in the church, in the earth, from the angels. That's what I want to learn. I want to talk in the forest, I don't want to go [to the Evangelical Temple] . . . "

"Did you learn to pray in your dreams?"

"Yes, in my dreams."

"How?"

"He told me, 'Well, what do you want to do? What do you want to learn? Because your heart is thinking a lot,' he said. 'Ah, nothing,' I said. 'I just want to learn to pray,' I told him. 'Good,' he said. 'Is it really true that you want to learn to pray? That's fine,' he said. 'We're going to put down your rum,' he said. He gave me a cuarta (beer bottle) of rum. He put down a plant. He put down a candle. That's how I learned."[5]

"Do your dreams help you with problems?"

"Yes, when I offer the candles it gets better. Then I don't dream. [In our dreams] we see horses, cows, pigs, mules, dogs, snakes, caterpillars, worms, earthworms. We see everything. That's why we go to inform [God] in the church. Then we don't see anything. If these kinds of dreams continue, then we'll get sick. Our bones ache, our head, everything [aches]."

"Do you understand what your dreams mean or do you have to ask someone?"

"Yes, I ask about the meaning. I ask a man. It seems that he's a man, but he's God. He has hair like your hair [light brown]. But I dream very well. I don't know how to dream bad dreams. I make the sign of the cross three times. I go on my knees, 'Ah, I've come,' I say, 'Father,' I say. I kneel. 'Ah, you've come, my daughter. Ah, poor thing,' he says. 'It will be O.K.' he says. 'Well, what illness do I have?' I ask. 'I have these dreams. I see horses, I see snakes. I see cats. I see dogs. I see everything. Could it be that someone is doing this to me?' I ask. 'No one [is doing it],' he says. 'It's envy, ' he says. 'It's envy. Lay down your candle, the way you do with your candles. Don't eat breakfast,' he says.

"That's my dream. I fast for nine days. When I fast I offer a chicken, my exchange for my soul, and those who drink offer a bottle of rum."

"What use does rum serve in prayers?"

"It's not important that we use rum. Well, this is how we do it: we offer our flowers and we put down our candles and we sprinkle the rum. Because if we sprinkle rum the blood warms up. Rum counteracts demons. It's to blind their sight. . . . It's to frighten the demon and make him go away. Well, Father God who is in the skies doesn't do anything. It's only the demon who wants to eat people. That's why the shaman blows rum on the sick person, to make the demon go away, to make him stay behind us. He always wants to eat us. The demon is in the midst of people. That's why rum is always at the side of the flowers. Then if the sick person drinks rum, the Devil doesn't like it because it makes the person's flesh stink and he doesn't want to eat him.

"Truthfully, the shaman doesn't know what rum is for. He just says Our Father wants it. But Our Father in heaven doesn't want rum. He doesn't know how to drink rum. Only the Devil drinks rum. And also people. . . . We also gather people together with rum and we heat ourselves so that heat enters our faces and also our blood. That's the way Our Father wants it."

"And incense, what use does that serve?"

"It's Our Father's food. It's for the saints. You can mention ten or fifteen, or if you want twenty-five saints, but you need a little incense for each one. And it's also for Our Father."

"What kind of medicine do you use and what kinds of illnesses do you cure?"

"For the sickness *ak'bil ch'ulelal* we use a stick of *zorro* root [*Petiveria allaceae L.*], tobacco, garlic, pepper, and cloves.[6] I don't use branches. I only use branches when it's a cure with many flowers. That is for people whose souls have been rejected by their parents who raise them, those whose guardians don't care about them, those who aren't in the embrace of the Gods. . . . For this we do a very big healing. We must bathe the sick person. Also, I put flowers in an arc and [I put down] nine candles, nine palm branches, nine orchids, and nine branches of shrubs called *tilil* [rapanea] and *konkon* [cavendishia]. The bath [healing] is a bucket of heated medicines with four witnesses. Also they [the witnesses] have to fast and bring the herbs and a very healthy chicken or rooster, and nine candles. That's the way we do it. . . . I do this two times. Each time I sweep over the person with herbs and flowers. If you could come and see it and you had someone who could take photos, it's very pretty. I sing, too. . . . When I finish singing we bathe the sick person with the cooked medicines so that the sickness leaves. We also bathe the witnesses and they carry the sick person to his bed. After he has gone to bed I have to wait a little bit before measuring out the four cuartas of rum. After I serve the rum, it's over. The other bottle of rum stays [is for Magdalena to keep]. I put the candles in rows. I ask Our Father another time. [7]

"My deceased father and grandmother always cured with medicinal herbs. I learned from them. We drank one cuartita of rum. I copy and learn from other shamans. Some have very short branches. In contrast, mine are quite tall. If the person is tall, you need tall herbs and flowers. I search for flowers that are one meter tall."

"What does ak'bil ch'ulelal cure?"

"One encounters it [the illness] when we go somewhere, like San Cristóbal or Tuxtla, in whatever place, or in the hamlet. The sickness comes rapidly. The heart or the stomach hurts. We have diarrhea. We're dizzy. We swell up. We can't do anything any more. . . . If a man drinks and he complains that his stomach hurts, this is envy. That's why his stomach doesn't want rum. But the envy obliges him to drink. A shaman can cure this. I can cure this."

"What do you do when someone asks your help to stop drinking?"

"Well, I ask him what he wants. If he drinks too much, let's say. Then I will say, 'You can't fill up on this. You'll commit a crime. Also you'll look for enemies. Now, if you want, we'll put down your candles. Also we'll put down your flowers in the church. It's O.K., now,' I'll tell him. They become very relieved. 'Well, tell me how much you're going to collect so I can give it of my own free will,' they say, like you say."

"How are you now? Does your heart or your stomach hurt?"

"I feel a little bad. . . . I cough all the time. My face aches. . . . Well, truthfully I have my husband, but he doesn't give me money, not even a piece of cloth for a skirt. We Indigenous women need our blouses, our skirts, our belts, and our shawls. We need it all. He doesn't give me these things, even though he has money. He sells rum and he has a record player. He takes it into the town square and with that he earns 10,000 pesos, at times 15,000 or 20,000 pesos. But he keeps it all. I take care of myself. He doesn't give me his money. I look after all my children. That's why

I have the right to go where I want. I go to a hamlet and sell something. That's how I take care of myself by myself. Well, that's why it's very difficult. I'm sick, but still I give it all I have because my food and what I give to my children doesn't come from anywhere else. . . ."

"How do you make money?"

"Well, I don't earn much. I make bread, I sell pitchers and pots, that's all. And also they give me a little for my prayers."

When I asked Magdalena if she would pray for Kate and Joe, she hesitated. From what Magdalena had told me about her husband, her tattered clothing and her childrens', her household seemed to be very poor. I wondered if Magdalena saw my request for a prayer as a chance to make some money and was deciding how much she could ask for. Finally, Magdalena said that she would need to pray twenty-four times for my friends. The fee for the whole package would be 20,000 pesos. I looked at Pancha for help in explaining to Magdalena that I didn't want that many prayers. Pancha explained that although I did want to help my friends, I was thinking of just one or two prayers. Reluctantly, Magdalena agreed to pray just one prayer, a "sample," we called it. We arranged to meet at seven A.M. on Christmas Eve and that I would pay her 3,000 pesos. She told me to bring three white candles.

At seven A.M. on Christmas Eve in 1988 I waited in front of the church, sipping a glass of hot atole that one of the vendors sold me. Tonight women would dance to the music of pre-Hispanic water whistles before the manger of the Christ child, the only ceremony each year in which women dance, I was told. But this morning was like any other, a couple of women selling atole in the market, a few hung-over policemen sweeping up debris from yesterday's market. Magdalena appeared, to my relief, walking out of the morning mist toward the church, holding her shawl over her mouth and nose. We greeted each other and entered the church where other shamans and their clients were in various stages of their prayers. Magdalena gently set each candle into drops of hot wax on a board in front of us. Then she knelt, brushed the hair from her face and began:

> Now, I come beneath your feet, my Lord,
> and beneath your hands, my Lord,
> before your flowery presence,
> before your flowery face, my Lord,
> up there, there where your throne is, my Lord,
>   [God's hands and feet are his altar]
>
> for your son whom you bought,
> for your son for whom you paid,

for him, before your flowery presence,
before your flowery face, my Lord . . .
I come on my knees,
I come bending low to the ground, my Lord,
and with that let my sin be forgotten,
and also let him forget, my Lord.

Let him be humbled.
Let me bow down before you.
Let him be bound to you, my Lord,
in his mind and in his heart, my Lord.

Please then, my Lord,
don't let him give in to his desires.
Don't let his heart dwell on rum, my Lord,
on your cup, my Lord,
on your bottle, my Lord,
on beer, too, my Lord,
on *Tecate*, my Lord,
    [a commercial brand of beer]
and on *Presidente* rum, my Lord,
    [a commercial brand of rum]
on pox and on *nich pox*, my Lord.
    [strong rum]

Even though it may be delicious to him, my Lord,
even though it may be so sweet to him, my Lord,
even though it may seem good to him, my Lord,
rum is what makes us sick, too, my Lord.
Well, it's what brings us death, my Lord.

It's no good, my Lord.
It's no good at all, my Lord.
Your first cup of your first pitcher,
it's the only thing you gave us.
That's the only way you wanted it.
Before your flowery presence,
before your flowery face, my Lord.

Only you look at him, only you, my Lord.
Please, stand up tall, too.
Draw near, and encircle him.
Stand firm.

Come close to him.
Before his flesh,
before his body, my Lord,
please, do it for me, my Lord.

Let it be erased from his mind.
Let it be erased from his heart, my Lord . . .

Let him change his drink then, my Lord.
He can't continue like this, my Lord,

before your flowery presence,
before your flowery face, my Lord,
flowery God, flowery Ladino . . .

. . . Let his mind be moved, my Lord.
Let his heart be moved, too, my Lord.
Let his blood pressure rise too, my Lord,
and let him have stomach pain, too, my Lord,
    [so he'll know rum is bad]
if it can be done, my Lord,
if that's possible for you, my Lord . . .

That's how I am here, sitting humbly,
with my face to the ground . . . my Lord,
Father in Chix te'tik, my Lord . . .
    [a hamlet of Chenalhó]
Father in St. Paul,
    [Chalchihuitan, a neighboring township]
Father in Los Chorros,
    [a colony of Chenalhó]
Father in Yaxal Jemel, my Lord . . .
    [a hamlet of Chenalhó]
Mother Catherine, my Lord,
Mother who are in Pantelhó, my Lord . . .
    [a neighboring township]

Deny it to me then, my Lord . . .
Help me give it up, my Lord.
Let him give it up once and for all.
Let him leave your home in order to do this.
    [possibly = "hit bottom"]
Let it remain beneath your feet.

Let it remain beneath your hands, my Lord,
that which was your first cup,
that which was your first pitcher, my Lord,
the drops from your feet,
the drops from your hands,
here before your flowery presence,
here before your flowery face, my Lord . . .

[Magdalena asks my "brother's" name. I reply, "Joe."]

Listen then, my Lord,
here before your flowery presence,
here before your flowery face, then, my Lord.
I leave him beneath your feet.
I leave him beneath your hands, my Lord,
the faraway man,
the faraway Ladino, my Lord.
He comes from the United States, my Lord, this Joe . . .

Well, my Lord, before your flowery face,
before your flowery eyes, too, my Lord.
Do me this great favor then, my Lord.
Grant me your mind.
Grant me your heart, my Lord.
Grant me your flesh.
Grant me your body.
Grant me your goodness.
Grant me your love, my Lord.
That's how it is, my Lord.

Help me give it up, my Lord.
Help me forget it, my Lord,
the drops of your feet,
the drops from your hands, my Lord.

. . . Help him give it up.
Help him forget it, my Lord . . .

That's all.
I come kneeling.
I come kissing.
I come bowing beneath your feet,
beneath your hands, my Lord,

before your flowery presence,
before your flowery face . . .

. . . So it is also to my Holy Mother Mary,
there in the sky,
here within the earth, my Lord,
before your flowery presence,
before your flowery face, my Lord . . .
flowery God, my flowery Ladino Lord.

Although I didn't find someone to transcribe Magdalena's prayer until months later, I told Antonia and others what had happened and what I had understood. From my description of the time and setting Antonia had her doubts about the prayer's effectiveness. She said that for the prayer to work we would have had to go to the church early, about four A.M., and we would have had to go to both the Chapel of Holy Cross on the hill and the big Church of St. Peter in town. Still, something apparently happened to Kate and Joe around the time Magdalena prayed. When I returned to the States Kate told me that she had felt a change over the Christmas holiday, that it had been a turning point for her and Joe.

Manuela

When I was trying to learn about prayer and drinking problems another friend was on my mind. Carly, sixteen when I saw her last, had been experimenting with drugs and alcohol since she was fourteen. I asked Manuela to pray for her.

The day on which Manuela agreed to pray for Carly she led me first to the Chapel of Holy Cross. Manuela stopped at the chapel door to catch her breath, gathered her shawl around her, bowed her head, and began to pray:

Through the sign of the Holy Cross
free us from our enemy, my Lord, our God.
In the name of The Father,
The Son and The Holy Ghost, amen.

I followed Manuela into the chapel, where she paused just inside the door to make the sign of the cross. After greeting another woman shaman, Manuela set down our three candles and told me to light them. Kneeling before the candles and holding Carly's photo like an offering, Manuela continued her prayer:

. . . I have something to say to you.
I have something to take up with you, my Lord . . .
for your daughter,
for your daughter whom you bought,
for your daughter whom you bought
with your blood, my Lord,
flowery God, Jesus Christ, my Lord.

Look, how she is, my Lord.
She indulges herself.
She makes herself owner, too, my Lord,
of your first cup,
of your first pitcher,
of your first portion, flowery Lord.

Perhaps it's because of some envy, my Lord,
or perhaps it's because of some anger, my Lord . . .

Because of it she can no longer buy clothes;
she can no longer buy her chile;
she can no longer buy her salt;
she can no longer buy what she needs.
She can no longer buy things that serve
her well-being then, my Lord,
before your flowery presence,
before your flowery face, my Lord.

Well, this abandoned one makes me pity her, my Lord.
Look how she is then, my Lord.
Let her flesh become strong.
Let her body become strong too, my Lord . . .

She's just a child, my Lord,
to be using rum and becoming the owner of it,
of your first cup,
of your first pitcher,
of your first portion, my Lord . . .

Don't let them be like food, or soda.
They don't serve her well-being
nor for her upbringing.
Don't let this poor Christian shame herself
by passing out in some street or path, my Lord . . .

But as rum is bought, my Lord,
where she drinks it
they don't just give it to her.
        [possibly = money lenders may loan money, but they sell rum]
They don't give it to her to help her . . .

It can't be that the demons make her do it, my Lord,
before your flowery presence,
before your flowery face, my Lord,
before your flowery presence,
before your face . . .

. . . Thus it is written in your Bible.
Thus it is in the scripture,
that we mustn't drink a lot of rum, my Lord.

That's what you said in your story.
That's what you said in your talk, my Lord, flowery God,
that's what you said in your book, flowery Father,
Jesus Christ, Father who art in heaven, my Lord.

"Respect yourselves, you can't use rum.
You can't take possession of rum,"
that's what you said, my Lord.

For this reason, my Lord,
here, put a part of it for me in her mouth
and in her lips, my Lord.
        [reduce the amount she is drinking]
Grant her your healing power, my Lord . . .
there in distant mountains, my Lord,
there in distant lands, my Lord . . .

Let her be educated well about your first pitcher,
        [learn rum's traditional role]
your first portion, my Lord,
flowery Jesus Christ, my Lord . . .

You are the only savior, my Lord.
You cured the lame.
You cured the blind.
You cured the leper . . .

There they deceive her, my Lord,
they are demons who are at work in her life . . .

Satan tricks her.
There the bottles of rum are lined up, my Lord,
and he is there with them, my Lord.

Now cast rum out of her mind for me there, my Lord.
Cast it out of her heart for me, my Lord.
She can't be always lying down,[8]
nor continue with drinking then, my Lord.

For this reason do me the favor, my Lord.
Let her mind turn around.
Let her demons be defeated
and let her be re-born, my Lord.

Let her get back on the good path,
because she has been lost, my Lord,
flowery God, flowery Ladino,
great God, Jesus Christ, my Lord . . .

Grant her a heart capable of everything, my Lord.
Let her work in her house.
     [let her have enough food or money not to have to work on a
     plantation]
Let her work in her home.
If she has a stone, my Lord;
if she has money, my Lord . . .

Let her buy something to eat.
Let her buy bread.
Let her buy soup.
Let her buy beef.
Let her buy whatever,
whatever she eats there in her land, my Lord . . .

Let her know how to keep it.
Let her know how to value it, my Lord,
if she has stone, my Lord,
if she has money, my Lord . . .

How does one earn stone, then?
How does one find money, my Lord?

Well, it's not easy to find your blessings, my Lord.
It takes a lot out of us to look for it, my Lord . . .

She will obtain it if she moves her feet, my Lord,
    [hard work, sobriety = reward]
if she moves her hands, my Lord,
then she finds your blessings, my Lord.

Do me the favor now, my Lord.
That's why, thou who standest erect:
Throw out the demon!
Throw out the Devil,
from her mind,
from her heart.

So, too, if she hears some music somewhere,
or hears something,
don't let her go.
Don't let her follow it . . .
    [possibly, keep her in line with traditional values]

This is why I come,
kneeling with my face to the ground,
beneath your feet, my Lord,
and under your hands, my Lord,
under your shadow, my Lord . . .
Holy Mother Mary, Mother Rosario . . .

Look at me, my Lord,
at your daughter.
Send me your healing strength.
Lower it to me.
Let your strength fall and send your power
to your poor Carly, my Lord,
flowery God, Jesus Christ, my Lord . . .

Manuela turned to me as we were leaving the church and said,
"You have to give a little alms, like a peso. It's for your gift to Our Father Jesus Christ and Our Heavenly Father. And also the mayordomos sweep the mud up that we bring in with our feet. It's also for them. They need a little."

I gave the caretaker a few pesos. On our way down the hill to St. Peter's Church where Manuela prayed a second time, I asked her how many more prayers we would need and if she had stopped drinking through prayer. She replied,

"Ah, Cristina, yes. You have to come another time. You have to come three times. Wait, we'll say it well. . . . It's been a while since I gave up rum. I said to Our Father: 'I'm very poor. I'm practically naked. I don't have clothes. I don't have skirts. I can't buy chile or salt. It [rum] is not my food.' But I thought about it, that I'm poor for a reason. I gave the trago and chicha seller my money so that *he* could have good clothes while I was naked and poor. This is the truth."

Juana

"Ah, the first time Holy Cross came to me in my dream I was a little girl, only seven.

" 'Look, you,' he said.

" 'You are going to take your little gourd.

" 'You are going to take your corn gruel.

" 'You are going to take your net bag.

" 'You are going to take your candles.

" 'You are going to take your pine boughs.

" 'You are going to take your rum.'

" 'It's O.K.,' I said, 'I'm going to take them.'

" 'But you aren't ready yet,' he said.

" 'It's O.K.,' I said, even though I didn't know how to heal. I was very bold. My heart was very strong before.

"Holy Cross came to me in my dreams three times. The last time it left words in my hand.

" 'Look in your hand.'

"I looked in my hands. It was Tzotzil. Although I couldn't read, it was as if the words of the prayers were recorded in my heart, like the words on your tape recorder. My heart couldn't forget them."

Seven-year-old Juana was ready. Secretly she had been mixing water and wild tobacco, imitating shamans when they mix rum and tobacco for a curative drink. She used water because she had no money to buy rum. Behind the house, out of her mother's sight, she prayed over gourds of her mixture and gulped them down. She felt high, as if the water were rum. She vomited, but kept on praying and drinking.

A year later Juana's mother became sick. Her father ignored Juana's offer to cure her mother, but finally, after several shamans had failed, he let her try. Using her mixtures Juana prayed over her mother and healed her. Her mother was afraid, did not want her daughter to heal, fearing she might pray for evil instead of good. Juana's mother was a weaver and wanted her daughter to weave, but Juana did not like counting threads. She preferred dreaming. Juana went to her grandfather about her dreams, and he told her:

"Yes, granddaughter, you are going to pray. You are going to heal. You are going to earn your food and clothes. You are going to take your cargo."

The old man knew that a shaman's life is hard, but he could see that Juana was determined. He led her up the hill to the Chapel of Holy Cross and there in front of her three candles he beseeched Holy Cross, the other saints, and God to teach Juana well, to keep her from suffering unduly and to give her a good husband to help her.

Juana and I were both forty-two when we met. She looked fifty-five or sixty, so ravaged by rum was her face, but Juana insisted she was forty-two. Juana's cheeks were drained and lined, her eyes yellowy-pink. She often shook as she moved. In Juana I met my first seriously addicted Pedrana, and the signs were unmistakable. Her grandfather's hopes and her mother's fears had come true. Juana had married, but her husband died suddenly after leaving her for another woman. With a finger to her lips, Juana told me that she had prayed for God to kill him, and a year and a half after he left her, he died. About seven years after her husband died Juana began to drink a lot, outside of her healing work. She would drink in bed alone, sometimes going on binges that lasted several days. Her children had to go to neighbors for their food. They would throw out her bottles when they found them. Sometimes when an older relative scolded her she felt ashamed of herself and stopped drinking for a while. But her periods of sobriety never lasted long.

Over the years Juana developed a clientele in San Cristóbal, as well as in Chenalhó, her native township. Praying for Ladinos, who paid her well, let her buy her own corn, beans, and clothes. Juana never wore Pedranas' clothes, preferring instead the store-bought dresses and shawls of Ladinas. She made sure that her children learned Spanish and spoke a mixture of Spanish and Tzotzil at home. Although on the surface Juana looked and sounded more like a Ladina than a Pedrana, she prayed from the heart of a Traditional woman. Her prayers were ardent and long, and each time she prayed she gave up some of her life force.

Rum and healing were Juana's reasons for living. They reinforced each other and gave her life purpose. That rum was devastating her body and straining her relationships was not important to her. To drink and to heal were.

The only time I managed to record Juana sober I heard Juana as she may have sounded before she began to drink compulsively. Although she was edgy throughout, probably thinking about the bottle she had hidden somewhere in the house where she was staying, her words drew pictures of Juana's many faces. I heard the strange but determined child who learned to heal despite her mother's resistance, the mother who got the best possible godfather for her son (Padre Miguel, the priest in Chenalhó), the shaman who had earned both Mestizos' and Pedranos' respect, and fear, and the adept "stranger handler" who was now adding an American to her list of contacts. Juana, like rum itself, mediated between worlds. With rum her constant companion, she swung back and forth between Native and non-Native worlds and the visible and invisible realms.

People in liminal roles can be intense and unpredictable. Juana's behavior should not have surprised me. But maybe because the first shamans I met limited their use of rum, being with Juana was intense and confusing for me. I sensed that it was also hard for Juana to be with me at times, although she laughed and joked even in the midst of her prayers. Juana took me as close as I got to the invisible realm of Pedrano cosmology. I brought her as close as she had been to the strange world of *"el norte."* Escaping, Juana to her bottle of rum in the outhouse, me to my cup of coffee in my room, was the way we usually parted.

Once when Juana was drunk I tried to record the story of how she received her cargo at age seven. My translation of part of her story opens this section. Another time I asked Juana if she knew "I am a drunk woman, I am a drunk girl." Juana moved immediately from talking to singing. Although self-critical and somewhat contradictory, Juana's song-prayer also affirms her spiritual power and close relationship with God.

> I am a drunk woman,
> I am a drunk girl,
> It's better that I am not [drunk],
> because they just hit me on account of rum,
> they just yell at me.

> I am a drunk woman,
> I am a drunk girl, my Lord.
> See how I am, my Lord, Manuel.
> You bought me.
> I don't belong to anyone else.
> Look, I have a house.
> I have a home.
> It's O.K., tzina la, tzina la, la, la, la, girl.

> Because I am drunk,
> because I drink rum, look how I am.

Look how I am, my Lord Jesus, María,
Look how I am, my godmother Virgin.

There is my father,
there is the one who prays for me.
There is Manuel [Jesus].
There is Hilario in his house.

It's O.K. that you laugh at me.
    [Juana laughs; I am not laughing.]
It's a shame.
It's a pity, my child, my offspring.
One is my son,
one is my daughter.

Look how I am before your flowery face.
Look how I am before your flowery presence.
My head is sober.
My heart is sober.

Although Juana's drunken Spanish and Tzotzil words were important, they were difficult to transcribe, translate, and interpret. Eventually, I decided that Juana could best inform me through Tzotzil in prayer, for that was where her words were clearest and most powerful, as she demonstrated and others confirmed.

Magdalena's prayer for Kate and Joe had been brief. Knowing that most Pedrano prayers are long, I decided to ask Juana for another prayer for Kate and Joe. This time I had a photo of Kate and a shirt of Joe's, if Juana wanted them. She said we would use the photo. She also said that we needed pitch-pine branches, incense, three bottles of rum, and nine candles. All but the pine branches I could buy in the market.[9] Juana insisted that we go together to her sister's house in a Chamula colony on the outskirts of San Cristóbal where we could cut branches to just the right size.

The morning we set off—Juana, her twenty-year-old son Rogelio, Reina, Daniel, and I—the fields around San Cristóbal were spotted with pools of rainwater, but we were like children on a Saturday outing as we made our way across them. Juana was as sober as I ever saw her that morning, as she searched for herbs to use in her curings. Some of their names, she could tell me, some she had forgotten.

When we reached what had once been Juana's sister's house, it was abandoned. An older Ladina came out of her house and said that Juana's sister had moved to another colony down the road. I watched as Juana shifted into her Ladina mode, admiring the large pears that filled a basket by the woman's chair. She asked if we might buy some. Following Juana's lead I bought several. Eyeing a few pitch pines near the side of the road, Juana asked the woman,

"You wouldn't know who might be the owner of these little trees by the side of the road?"

"Ah, yes, those trees. Well, they aren't mine. They belong to the man who lives across the road."

"It's that we need some for a curing. Just twelve tips."

"I'll send my granddaughter to ask if you can have some branches."

I watched as the little girl made her way through the field to where the man was working. The man glanced our way, went into his house for his machete and ladder and in a short time we had our branches.

Not far down the road we found Juana's sister's house. Rosita came to the door of her scrapboard house slowly, bent over with pain. When she saw her sister so weak and drained, Juana helped Rosita to a chair in the yard and began questioning her. Pain spilled across Rosita's face as she talked. Gradually the litany of physical and emotional abuse she had suffered drew Juana in. Speaking in Spanish, the two women spit out one painful memory after another. There was the time the woman with whom Rosita lived after their mother died hung her from a tree because she had misbehaved. Then there was the time their father had killed his brother in a drunken rage. Now Rosita's husband, Salvador, a Chamula, was drinking too much, hitting her and not providing for her and their seven children. Juana told Rosita that all the abuse she had suffered since childhood had brought on her present illness.

Juana led her sister to her bed and greeted Salvador, who had appeared while the women were talking and crying. Salvador asked Juana to pray for Rosita. Juana told him to go buy a bottle of rum and some tobacco. He left immediately and returned within a few minutes with tobacco and a bottle of tequila, the only liquor he could find, he told Juana apologetically. Tequila would do, she said. Juana asked Salvador for a gourd, a clove of garlic, cloves, and some pepper. While he collected the ingredients she requested, Juana carried a chair to the backyard. Once seated she poured two cups of tequila into a plastic bowl and then the other ingredients. By that time I realized that Juana was going to pray over the mixture, as she had done for her mother when she was a child, and for fellow Pedranos countless times since. Elbows resting on her knees, arms extended in front of her, Juana cradled her bowl in her hands as she prayed for the powerful beings to bless its contents. At one point she and Salvador paused to drink a cup of tequila, and then another cup after she finished praying. Now the mixture was *ilbilal pox*, blessed rum.[10] Rosita would drink it and the next day Juana would return to pray for her. I knew that Juana was planning to go back to Chenalhó soon. She told me that those plans were off now, as she had found her sister and her sister needed her.

On our walk back to town I asked Juana if she still wanted to pray for Kate and Joe after the emotional reunion with her sister. She told me to come back later that afternoon for a prayer, the first of six that she would pray for Kate and Joe. She specified what each prayer would be for, as Rogelio helped me jot them down in my little notebook. The first, *mu xa xi' ilin smalale,* would keep Kate's husband calm and not angry. The second, *il k'op ch'ulelal,* was a prayer to counteract spiritual envy, in case someone was guarding envy in his heart and wishing harm to come to either Kate or Joe. The third, *muk' ta ch'ulelal,* was for a great spiritual envy. The fourth, *komel ch'ulelal,* was to cure fright that Kate or Joe had incurred during their waking hours or in dreams. The fifth, *tuch' bil ora,* was to counter a prayer that witches pray in order to shorten someone's life span. The last prayer, *ixtambil ta ch'ulelal,* literally badly-placed spirit, was another prayer to counteract a witch's prayer. The whole series Juana called *metz ch'ulelal.*

Once back at her eldest son's room, where she was staying while in San Cristóbal, Juana made a fire with a few pieces of charcoal in an old washbucket and began to set up the altar. First she propped six branches of pitch pine against the wall and set two bottles of soda at either end. In front of the pine branches, between two soda bottles (I had asked Juana if I could substitute soda for some rum), she placed the bottle of rum. In front of the branches she stuck nine short white candles on a board. Then she placed a pellet of incense in her burner and lit it. As an afterthought, Juana took Kate's photo and leaned it against a bottle of soda.

With our drinking and conversational breaks, Juana's first prayer took over an hour to complete. Juana moved easily back and forth between the urgent intensity of her prayer and casual banter with Reina and me. Getting progressively drunker seemed to facilitate that movement.

Just before beginning her prayer Juana asked me one more time exactly what I wanted her to pray for. I explained that I wanted her to pray for God to give Kate strength to make the right decision about her marriage, because her husband had a drinking problem. Juana asked me if Kate had any children. When I replied, "one," she seemed convinced that it would be best for Kate to leave Joe.

Juana began:

> Flowery Ladino, now Father, my Lord,
> Apostle, now Father Santa Cruz,

Mother, holy Lady Mary.
I come on my knees.
I come bending low,
now in their flesh,
now in their body,
now in your flowery countenance,
now in your flowery presence.

After acknowledging her arrival, Juana continued calling up the saints and God, urging them to make it quick and soon. She told God to leave his heavenly station and drip down, drop by drop, to Kate and Joe. Early in the prayer Juana sprinkled two cups of rum and one of soda on the branches. With each bottle she made a circle over the cloud of incense, sanctifying its contents. At one point she gave me Kate's photo and removed a framed saint's photo from a plastic bag that she kept on her altar. This she circled over the incense as she had the bottle. Three times during her prayer Juana stopped to drink, once alone, the other times with Reina and me. Each time Juana drank first, then Reina, then I.

As Juana prayed in a rapid stream of Tzotzil, I didn't understand much of what she said. Still, I understood enough to be impressed by the urgency and compassion with which she approached the Gods on behalf of two mortals she had never met. Repetition, perhaps more than rhythm and tone, contributed to the urgency.

After translating Juana's prayer, the direction of her petition became clearer to me. Its basic outline goes:

Leave there and come.
Drip down from there and come, my Lord, [god = rum]
now in the body,
now in the flesh,
of your daughter, Kate, my Lord. . . .
Put it in Kate's mind.
Put it in her heart,
if she must leave her husband,
if she must leave her companion, my Lord. . . .

Stand up and come, my Lord.[11]
Look and see what condition Joe is in,
there in the United States.

Let him leave his wife, my Lord.
Let him leave his companion.

Let him look for another.
Let him go with her.
Let him go with her on a straight path.
Show him where he can find a good woman,

Show him where to find a fine young woman, my Lord.

That's why I come on my knees before you,
why I come bent low, my Lord. . . .
Let him be there with his head lowered, my Lord,
humbled, my Lord, this Joe. . . .
Let him follow in the footsteps of his foremother.
Let him follow his roots and his origin . . .

. . . Let him be transformed into a dog.
Let him be transformed into a pig.
Let him be transformed into a horse.
Let him be transformed into a cow.
Let him be transformed into a sheep.
Let him be transformed into a deer.
Let him be transformed into a bear.
Let him be transformed into a black bear, my Lord.
Let him be transformed into a he-mule, my Lord.
Let him see how he is.
In that way, too, blind his eyes . . .
Transformed as a pig let him see his wife, his companion. . . .

Juana urged me to drink. She said that if I didn't drink the rum or carried it away in a bottle, the prayer wouldn't have the desired effect. I drank one cup. The other cups I sipped and gave back to Juana or to Reina. We also drank the three bottles of soda, cup by cup.

Let her leave her husband.
Let him be erased from her mind.
Let him be erased from her heart,
with six branches,
six branches brought from the mountain.

It's not good that he goes on ahead, my Lord,
with envy and problems,
with the furious ones,
the resentful ones.
        [possibly furious and resentful ones = drunkards and/or witches]

Let their eyes be blinded.
    [prevent them from bringing harm]
Blind their presence, too . . .

Show him the path he must take.
Let him see the way he is. . . .
Show him how low he has fallen.
Let him take the way of the lowly ones. . . .

Now with Kate,
may she be set free, my Lord.
Let her look [for another husband].
Put it in her head, my Lord,
that she must act.
It is a pity,
that he does nothing but drink rum,
that he does nothing but drink chicha,
that it is just sickness,
that it just stinks,
that he can't do anything,
that he can't get better. . . .

Let the moment arrive, my Lord.
Let the day arrive, my Lord . . .
my father Apostle, my father Holy Cross,
my mother great woman, Jesus.

Let my words be carried
in the air and clouds.
Let the encouragement of my mouth,
the encouragement of my lips,
be carried on the clouds, my Lord. . . .

Juana asked me if Joe hit Kate. I told her I didn't think so. She pushed me, as if she couldn't believe that Joe didn't hit Kate. I finally went along with Juana and said, "He may hit her a little, but I don't think so."

Her mind and heart are bothered, my Lord . . .
He scolds her.
He hits her.
But it shouldn't be like this,
before your flowery countenance. . . .

I returned the following Sunday for the second prayer with two bottles of soda and a chicken. Juana was already drunk when I arrived. Her two sons watched silently as Juana moved around the house, refusing to engage with anything or anyone until prayer focused her.

Juana sprinkled a shot glass of soda around the candles and began.

> But, you shouldn't listen to his words.
> Don't let Joe's words carry weight.

> I have brought his cup for him.
>   [rum = offering and possibly symbol of giving up control of rum]
> I have brought his bottle for him, too. . . .

Juana motioned for Reina to give her the hen. Earlier she explained that I would stand in for Kate and Joe, and the hen would be the *k'exol* (substitute) for Kate's and Joe's souls.[12] I sat on a chair facing the altar as Juana rubbed the chicken over my head, back, chest, shoulders, and down each of my arms. Then, with a snapping sound that I heard often in Highland Chiapas, but never got used to, she broke the hen's neck. Reina prepared and cooked the chicken as Juana continued:

> This Joe, now, God, Jesus Christ,
> this is his substitute,
> before your flowery countenance,
> before your flowery presence.

> Also, Kate, my Lord. . . .
> Mother, great woman, great woman
> who has brought us into the world,
> great woman who has formed us . . .
> stand firm and come
> into the body, into the flesh,
> of your daughter. . . .

> In Buffalo, this land is.
> It is before your flowery countenance.
> It is before your flowery presence, my Lord,
> holy land, holy sky, holy spring,
> holy angel, holy hills, holy angels. . . .

Juana ended her prayer abruptly. I suspected that she had been on a drinking binge in which her sons and I were interfering. We ate our ritual meal of chicken, broth, tortillas, and coffee, tensely.[13] Realizing that I should go but feeling that I would lose Juana when I did, I asked her if we could pray two prayers each day over the next few days to speed up the process. She assured me that there was still plenty of time, as she wouldn't be going to Chenalhó for at least three more weeks because she was curing her sister.

I didn't see Juana again while I was doing fieldwork. I came down with hepatitis soon after the last prayer, and could not follow through with many of my plans. When I was well, I went looking for her in Chenalhó and San Cristóbal. I had several chats with her children, mostly about their futile efforts to control their mother's drinking, but the remaining prayers went unsaid. I told Juana's children, who seemed quite mestizoized, about Alanon and Alcoholics Anonymous. But none of us thought Juana would go to AA, and I doubt that her children went to Alanon. I left Chiapas afraid that if Juana kept drinking as she had been, she would not live much longer and I would never see her again.

The first weeks of translating Juana's prayer back in Buffalo were confusing, like my time with Juana. I doubted that I could make sense of her prayer, as I wondered how to make sense of her life. I remembered how drunk she had been while praying, but I felt strongly that she had been in control in both prayers, that she had had a plan. With help over several months, I began to see the outlines of what I think Juana envisioned in her prayers.

The careful way Juana went back and forth between Kate and Joe and female and male powerful beings, calling up a representative from one sex, then the other, reflects the emphasis on complementarity and interdependence which shapes Pedrano daily life. Although I had asked Juana to pray mainly for Kate, as Magdalena had focused on Joe, Juana chose to deal with Kate's problem within the context of her relationship to Joe. Juana treated Kate's and Joe's problems as intertwined, but needing to be unwound and rewound in another way with different partners. While I wanted Juana to be free to pray for an outcome she thought best, I was hoping that she would pray for Kate and Joe to stay together. But Juana did not share my concern about keeping them together, especially when she heard that they had only one child. She seemed to think that Joe had already broken their bond and that no repair was possible, only re-pairing with different partners. By asking for another partner for Joe once he sobered up, Juana also stressed the reciprocal rights spouses have as long as they treat each other respectfully and take their responsibilties seriously.

More than Magdalena and Manuela, Juana suggests a matrilineal bias in her prayer. In commanding God to send Joe to his mother, to his foremother, she is sending Joe to his mother's lineage to find his roots and his strength, not to his father's. This command contradicts the patrilineal bent of Pedrano society, but affirms the control that Pedranos say parents have over opposite-sexed children's souls. Although Juana's relationship with her own mother was distant, she asks God to validate the importance of the mother's line for sons.

Juana seems to be asking God to create a more just world for Kate by not heeding Joe's drunken pleas, and instead hearing Kate's wish to be free. Juana doesn't speak about Kate leaving Joe, even though Pedranas are free to leave abusive spouses. She may be giving Joe this responsibility because she sees him as the one who needs to change, not Kate. Freedom for Kate in Juana's prayer is life with a new, responsible man.

In her prayer Juana acknowledges that the Gods have both good and evil powers. She cleverly combines these by transforming Joe into various animals which are both humble beings and spirit companions of witches. Turning Joe into a pig may have been Juana's imitation of Jesus when he turned his older brothers into pigs before ascending into heaven and becoming Our Father, Sun. At first I thought that Juana was giving Joe power to hurt others because she identified with his obsession with alcohol, and wanted him to triumph over people who didn't want him to drink. Usually only powerful shamans can transform themselves into naguals. As both a powerful shaman and a reputed witch, Juana knows that in the form of a nagual Joe can feel powerful, too. But, she also knows that Joe has to push through darkness, overcome his demons before he can get well. I believe that Juana has some fun with her prayer, but that her main objective is to humble Joe and free Kate. She therefore puts Joe in a battlefield, but not without weapons. She gives him a new spouse and a new identity with which to overcome his adversaries. From this position Kate can see Joe humbled (her revenge), God can come and support him (his duty), and Joe can reevaluate his life and "get back on the good road" (his responsibility).

In Alcoholics Anonymous terms Juana knows Joe has to "hit bottom." One Pedrano counterpart to a spiritual bottom seems to be the "low road" or "the road of the lowly ones." With these phrases Juana could be referring to the underworld where demons live. Juana's request for God to "drip down drop by drop" reflects her people's association between rum and God, as well as ancient Maya ideas about Sun's daily journey and its association with sacred substances, including blood, incense, and intoxicating beverages.

Ancient Maya inscriptions (see Chapter 2) depict Sun's setting as a journey down the World Tree via its sap (blood) to the underworld. Each night Sun descends into darkness, only to climb back to renew the world each morning. Juana could be setting the stage for God to take Joe with him as he drips down the tree of life on a journey of spiritual renewal. To help God and Joe on their way, Juana sprinkles drops of rum (blood) on pine boughs as if she were watering a tree, and wafts clouds of incense (from smoldering tree sap) over a saint's picture.

From many things she says in her prayer, it is clear that Juana identified with Joe's struggle. Although she wants Joe humbled, she doesn't want him to suffer too much. She wants him to be happy on whatever corner he may be, and to have an attractive, devoted partner. While recovering alcoholics in the United States often say that one must be alone at the bottom, it is typically Pedrano to pray that a person hitting bottom have a good partner to support him there, but not necessarily the same partner that he was with on his way to the bottom. It's possible, too, that Juana never imagines Joe's getting sober, just cutting down his consumption to an acceptable level, as Manuela advocated for Carly. But at points Juana reveals her own suffering and seems to want to humble herself, and Joe, so that they can both heal, even if that means abstinence:

> Look how great is my weariness,
> my weakness, my Lord . . .
>
> . . . Go to see it for me, my Lord,
> go in order to cure me of it, my Lord. . . .

Shamans must continue to humble themselves as go-betweens with the Gods, but these passages and other parts of her prayer could be Juana's efforts to heal herself by counter-transference, i.e., by identifying with her client. Although Juana's overall purpose was to help Kate and Joe, on another level I think that she was also sketching a scenario for a prototypical "good life," how her own life might have gone had she found a supportive partner, as her grandfather had prayed, or had she not gotten caught up in the thicket of envy on the road below, as her mother had feared. I think that she also tried hard to see the best realistic options for Joe in the United States, a faraway land that she could only imagine. Nevetheless, by speaking of the United States and by asking God to humble Joe in the form of a black bear, an exotic animal which lives in this country, Juana demonstrated her knowledge of foreign worlds from which anthropologists come, perhaps believing that God would be impressed. I was.

Although rum may be eroding her mental and emotional capacities, I believe that Juana will hold tight to her ability to heal and commit witchcraft until the end. The intensity with which she guards envy and resentment in her own life feeds into the central role envy plays in her work as a shaman and as a witch.

After a year of translating and analyzing prayers, I returned to Chenalhó for the Feast of St. Peter. On my agenda was finding out how Juana was doing, and asking Magdalena and Manuela for permission to leave cassette copies and transcriptions of their prayers in the library of "The House of Culture" in Chenalhó. I hoped that young Pedranos might listen to the prayers and be encouraged to respect their people's traditions.

Although I never found Magdalena, Manuela and I ran into each other when I was strolling around town, and she gave me permission to put her prayers in the House of Culture. Working my way through the crowds in the market, I found Reina's atole stand. Reina updated me on her family and several other people, including Juana. She said that Juana had stopped drinking about eight months before. When I asked where I could find her, Reina pointed to a stall directly across from hers, where Juana's frail but determined face peered from behind a table of trinkets.

Juana was indeed sober. She pulled a chair out for me and said,

"You've come. Sit down."

I told Juana how good she looked. I asked her how she had stopped drinking, and she told me that God had helped her. I expected to hear that, but when I asked how he had helped her, Juana surprised me by explaining that God told her someone was forcing her to drink. Juana explained that a Ladina who used to sell rum to her had prayed that Juana would drink herself to death. Juana said that the woman put something in her bottle before she sold it to her.[14]

"But how did you stop, Juana?"

"I prayed to God to reverse the curse, so that the woman would start drinking too much. Now I have stopped and she is drinking herself sick."

Remembering Juana's struggle with envy and her penchant for witchcraft, it struck me as logical that she might stop drinking through witchcraft. Juana added that now she was curing with sodas, and that sodas could be as powerful as rum.

I returned once more to Chenalhó after that visit. I didn't find Juana that time, but I talked to Rogelio who told me that his mother was back to drinking again, and that she was very sick.

Juana has a lot invested in her identity as a witch and a heavy drinker. Like some women accused of witchcraft in the Middle Ages in Europe, Juana seems to have made a covenant with Holy Cross and rum in an effort to gain power in a society in which she is relatively powerless. But when it comes to helping a suffering Pedrano, I believe that Juana can just as quickly pull out of her soul her ancestor's healing power. Living with one foot in both Indigenous and Ladino worlds, Juana has maximized her options for healing, witchcraft, and drinking.

At the time each of the three shamans prayed, in a rapid stream of Tzotzil, I did not understand much of what they said. Still, I understood enough to be impressed by the urgency and compassion with which they approached the powerful beings on behalf of three mortals whom they had never met. Perhaps in part because their words were antiquated and obscure, I sensed something deeply rooted in their prayers. As Gossen described (1974: 215) and now I could hear, Tzotzil-Maya prayer is "linguistic essence," its form far removed from ordinary speech.

K'op, Tzotzil for prayer, involves talk between humans and invisible beings. Repetition stands out in Tzotzil-Maya prayers, as it does in conversations between Pedranos. Pedranos say that repeating words heats them up, making them powerful enough to move people, God, or other powerful beings to action. Like rows of identical symbols on clothing and the annual cycle of saints' feasts, couplets in prayer, following on each others' heels, command the powerful beings to come and see what is happening to their children. With intoxication, repetition becomes even easier to achieve and to tolerate. Pedranos say that as they get more drunk, their words become more powerful, as long as they can still remember them.

More is definitely better in Tzotzil-Maya prayer. Nevertheless, Pedranos tire of the same phrases. Shamans often show their cleverness and skill by using parallelisms, varying one or two words in repetitive couplets, chipping away at the outer crust of ritual language.

> Let him follow in the footsteps of his foremother.
> Let him follow his roots and his origin . . .
>
> (Juana's prayer)

Although repetition is an aid in getting the powerful beings to pay attention to their words, shamans also follow specific steps to assure their prayers' success. One of the first steps they take, and repeat throughout their prayers, is to call up the powerful beings. Unless called upon, the Gods are generally indifferent to humans. As Magdalena suggested, Pedranos will call up as many saints as they care to, or have incense for. They evoke their own patron saints or patron saints from neighboring townships. Occasionally Pedranos give a name to a saint, not knowing if it actually exists. Shamans often subsume divine entities under "My Lord," which can stand for God, Jesus Christ, the Virgin Mary, any or all of the saints and the Maya spirits and ancestral Gods, such as totil me'il. At points in their prayers each shaman also refers to God as "my Ladino Lord," although that may not mean that they equate God with Ladinos. Even though Magdalena mentioned that the Lord has light brown hair like mine, she may have been identifying the Lord with Sun, another light-colored deity and a powerful Maya God. While Pedranos do see light skin and hair as markers of non-Indigenous people, they also identify light-colored with things divine. The Virgin Mary's counterpart, lakes, are light-colored (see Chapter 10). Some Pedranos say that St. Peter comes to them in dreams as a big white man. But many women say that the Virgin Mary comes to them in dreams dressed both as an Indigenous woman and as a Ladina.

While calling up the Gods a shaman must convince the powerful beings of her humility and her client's:

> That's why I come on my knees before you, my Lord,
> why I come bent low, my Lord . . .
> . . . Let him be there with his head lowered, my Lord,
> humbled, my Lord, this Joe.
>
> (Juana's prayer)

Bowing beneath God's feet and hands and asking God to let their clients remain beneath his feet and hands, all three shamans try to ensure that their clients will come into a respectful relation to rum, as rum, too, is always beneath God's hands and feet, dripping down in the form of his good works. God's feet and hands, from which rum drips, are his altar. This is where Pedranos must stand to receive his blessing:

> Now I come beneath your feet, my Lord,
> and beneath your hands, my Lord,[15]
> before your flowery presence,
> before your flowery face, my Lord,
> up there, there where your throne is, my Lord . . .
>
> (Magdalena's prayer)

Each shaman in her own way speaks about God's sending his presence in the form of rum from the drops of his hands and feet. Coming to humans in this way, rum is the distillation of God's bounty and blessing:

> Drip down from there and come, my Lord.
> now in her body, my Lord,
> now in her flesh, my Lord,
> in your daughter, Kate, my Lord.
>
> (Juana's prayer)

Repeatedly, all three shamans ask God to come near to or into the body and flesh of their clients, not into their souls or spirit. While bodies and souls are equally important to Pedranos, bodies must do their work in the visible world they never leave. Humans bear the burden of living on the earth principally through their *sbek'tal* (bodies) and their *stakupal* (flesh)

(Arias 1973: 45). Souls, in contrast, make a round trip from the invisible to the visible world. While in the visible world, they are only sojourners in bodies.

Gradually, as each shaman gains courage and her words become heated, she begins to ask for the specific help she or her client needs:

> That's why, thou who standest erect:
> Throw out the demon!
> Throw out the Devil,
> from her mind,
> from her heart.

(Manuela's prayer)

Throughout their prayers the three shamans repeat, profusely, specific ritual words and phrases. One of the most important of these is *nichimal, florido* in Spanish, "flowery" in English (Gossen 1974). Pedranos use nichimal most often as an adjective, but sometimes as a noun. It derives from the way Tzotzil-Maya peoples crown all sacred things with flowers and branches, just as ancient Maya Gods and rulers adorned the World Tree with their blood, and as the Christian God sacrificed his son on the cross, spilling drops of his blood/good works/rum. Pedranos express the idea of a flowery universe when they decorate caves, crosses, and the doors of the homes of caretakers of the church, and also when they weave flowers sprouting from the head of Holy Cross on the border of their blouses. Classic Maya Gods were wondrous creatures who traveled via the World Tree from one invisible realm to another. Few contemporary Pedranos have ever seen depictions of these Gods, but their ancestors have carried forward the spirit of these ancient Gods in prayer imagery and weaving designs. Even though Pedranos rethought their Maya Gods in relation to the anthropomorphic Christian God and Catholic saints, they never severed their Gods from:

> the first flower,
> the first leaf,
> the drops from the leaf of a tree.

(ritual language for rum)[16]

In their prayers the three shamans stress that God owns rum. They recall that God gave Pedranos everything, serving them in the amounts he thought appropriate and prescribing how Pedranos should consume them. All three shamans seem to say that when drinkers take possession of rum, they trespass on God's territory and try to be like Gods. Only by beseeching God to take back control of rum, by putting alcohol-dependent people be-

neath God's feet and hands, can shamans help people stop drinking compulsively. One diagnostic feature of drinking problems for Pedranos seems
to be that drinkers act as if they, not God, own rum, and thus start serving
up their own portions, ignoring the social and spiritual drinking order.

> She's just a child, my Lord,
> to be using rum and becoming the owner of it, . . .
>
> (Manuela's prayer)

While accepting one's portion in any Traditional Pedrano gathering is
important, Pedranos do not focus on possession. In fact, possessing rum
and other sacred substances is what gets Pedranos in trouble. Shamans
should remind people of their rightful portion of God's gifts, and remind
them that God knows that their egotism created the imbalance which
shamans are trying to correct. In the repetition of the portions in which
God gave rum, shamans seem to say that God gave a model to follow that
still works.

> Your first cup of your first pitcher,
> it's the only thing you gave us.
> That's the only way you wanted it . . .
>
> (Magdalena's prayer)

Shamans frequently go back and forth in prayer, creating a kind of dialectic unity between themselves and their clients, as Juana exemplified so
skillfully. At various points in their prayers they may stand in for their
clients, and sometimes they may ask for help for themselves, as when
Magdalena says,

> Deny it to me then, my Lord.
> Take it away from me, my Lord.

Magdalena stands in for the person needing help, at the same time accepting that she is in a position to receive help should God grant it. She is
God's vehicle through which he can send his power.

Manuela and Juana mention envy and anger as possible causes of
drinking problems.

> Perhaps it's because of some envy, my Lord,
> or perhaps it's because of some anger, my Lord.
>
> (Manuela's prayer)

In Manuela's second prayer she lines up rum alongside Satan, deceit,
and demons, recalling Otelia's description of how the Devil uses rum to
trick us.

Thus, my Lord, drive the demon out of her mind and out of her heart.
It can't be that she is lined up.
It can't be that her flesh,
her body is hanging,
    [possibly, like meat that the demons will eat]
and that she is deceived,
where the demons carried her, my Lord . . .

At several points in her prayers Manuela speaks about the inequality between those who have stone/money, and those who do not. In dreams and stories Pedranos tell of how people can receive money magically from the earth. Sometimes they find it miraculously under a stone; other times they receive it from Earth Lord, or as a reward for helping a wounded snake (Earth Lord's daughter).[17] Manuela's references to money also reflect her people's awareness of the great effort it takes to survive in the market economy, and the folly of wasting hard-earned money on rum. Manuela's affiliation with Catholic Action has no doubt influenced her critique of rum, which rests on balancing material and spiritual considerations. When Manuela gave up rum it seems that she took stock of her life, comparing herself with those around her who didn't drink and were better off than her. She saw the money lenders and rum sellers walking around in their nice boots, while she went barefoot:

He, yes, now he is walking,
creaking in his new boots.

At Catholic Action meetings Manuela joins fellow Pedranos in ana-lyzing the unjust economic relations with which they have to contend, and the examples Christ gave them of how to live according to God's plan. Drawing on her knowledge of the New Testament, she compares the battles humans wage to survive with Christ's passion and good works on Earth.

Manuela is not unusual in Chenalhó in successfully combining Tradi-tional beliefs and practices about prayer with Catholic Action beliefs and practices.[18] I found much flexibility in Chenalhó, perhaps due in part to Padre Miguel, the progressive priest who has lived in Chenalhó for about twenty-five years. The kind of prohibition that is described for other parts of Mesoamerica I found only among Protestants, and even then some of them turned to shamans when they were on their deathbeds.

Traditional Pedranos say that only *j'iloletik* (shamans) have the strength of heart and mind to command the powerful beings to come and help mortals, to take on the charge of confronting envy and defeating it. When shamans approach the Gods sober, both they and rum become blessed and beloved. Rum enables an experienced shaman to speak authoritatively and at length. When she drinks it or sprinkles it on pine boughs, it counteracts the drink a witch took when praying for evil. Blowing it on a wound, break, or bite, she blows the hurt into the world and starts the healing process.

Even when the problem they take up with their Gods is drinking, shamans continue to respect rum's traditional role in healing, whether they choose to drink it down, sprinkle it on pine boughs, or offer soda in its place. The resulting changes they make in ritual language and practice resonate throughout Tzotzil-Maya society, connecting ancient with new elements of life. In prayer, shamans both reaffirm what the ancestors have ordained and express their views about a range of personal and community concerns. Prayers often reflect a shaman's experiences and what she considers worth talking about to God. When a shaman prays to help herself or someone else stop abusing alcohol her prayer is her analysis, in ritual language, of her and others' relation to rum.

Of all the heavy drinkers whose behavior hurts their families, shamans are most likely to escape reproof because their work and service to their Gods and their people require them to drink. Some shamans, like Juana, find in alcohol a solace from painful lives and a means to seek revenge. They risk developing a relationship with alcohol that supersedes all others and shortens their lives. Even shamans who do not seek solace in rum may drink enough rum, over years of healing, that they develop a dependency that threatens their emotional and physical well-being.

Rum, whether received in dreams or awake, heats a drinker and encourages fear, resentment, and envy to grow, if a person harbors these in her heart. But in the act of healing, their drinking serves to counter others' resentment that causes illness. As witches, shamans threaten the tenuous calm that Pedranos create, but as healers they reinforce Pedrano identity and solidarity. The complicated passages in Juana's prayers and confused chapters of her life reflect the contradictions and complementarity between good and evil and Maya and Spanish beliefs, which Pedranos carefully manipulate in healing and witchcraft. While heavy drinking and witchcraft feed into each other in ways that may be destructive for individuals and their families, they support traditional ideas about social relations and disease.

Although Magdalena and Manuela demonstrate that shamans do not have to drink in prayer for the Gods to hear them, Pedranos say that alcohol helps people express the way they see things. Rum heats and empowers their words. Drinking on one level has been a way to validate both men's and women's power. Women's spiritual power becomes especially evident in the drinking order of prayer. In other rituals where both men and women are present men always drink before women; but during curings no man present can drink before the shaman.

Today in Chenalhó older women and younger women who are shamans can drink without reprobation, at least from Traditionalists. In the first case advanced heat (authority) and fewer child care responsibilities give an older woman the right to drink. In the latter case, a younger woman's work justifies drinking. Attitudes about drinking in relation to beliefs about healing recall pre-Hispanic injunctions against drinking which were based more on age and class than on sex.

All three shamans I interviewed were elders by Pedrano standards. All of the women have had relatively unstable marriages, and seemed to prefer the greater freedom that their single lives afforded. All mentioned being able to support themselves, and going where and when they wanted to without having to consider someone else. All knew the pros and cons of drinking too much rum, but only Manuela substituted soda for rum in her curings. All spoke authoritatively to the invisible beings, assessing situations as they saw them.

Men and women shamans are careful to call up powerful beings of both sexes in prayer. At every curing, as well as at every act of witchcraft, totil me'il, father/mother ancestor/protector, are present. Women as female mortal extensions of totil me'il wield their power in the realm of prayer, dreams, and religious cargos. Although only male shamans pray at sacred places for the whole township three times a year, and only men hold public offices, older Pedranas pray along with their male counterparts for the whole township at each fiesta. Most Pedranos say that a woman shaman is as powerful as a man, and a woman's dream, especially the dream of a young virgin, can change the course of events in her community.

Women shamans in Chenalhó generally support traditional roles and concentrate on the areas in which they have power, healing social and physical ills among fellow Pedranos. Although women's power is limited in the realm of formal politics, the power Pedranas have in spiritual life is a reservoir of personal and communal strength that has helped sustain their people through centuries of oppression. While prayer and dreams reflect vulnerability and the ubiquity of envy, through these vehicles women shamans seize their personal power, enabling themselves and others to act independently and inventively. The complex, and often oblique role of prayer, gives women a framework in which to integrate their own visions of social justice with traditional ideas about social and spiritual complementarity.

A lot is at stake for Pedranos in maintaining control over their traditional ways of healing themselves and their communities. Prayer remains the most important strategy for dealing with social and physical ills in Chenalhó. It is both personal and communal. In the latter context it articulates with more recognizably political Pedrano analyses of their relation to powerful entities in their lives, the Gods, rum, witches, Ladinos, and Gringos. Prayer is an important way in which Pedranos carry forth rum's sacred legacy, recognize women's spiritual equality with men, and celebrate the complementarity between men and women and Gods and mortals. Recited with or without rum, prayers demonstrate in their form, content and purpose much of what is powerful and healing in native beliefs in Mesoamerica today. They are intelligent and creative ways Indigenous men and women work together to deal with social problems.

9

"It's time to change"

Mestizoization and Drinking

It's time to change
It's time to change
Dear Reina
It's time.

While Angélika and her daughters helped me make contacts to learn about healing, they taught me about mestizoization, the process whereby Indigenous people take on aspects of Ladino social life, including speaking Spanish, dressing in Ladino clothes, and working in occupations outside agriculture. One by one Reina, Pancha, and Josefina left Chenalhó to pursue personal aims, then came back again. Except for the short time Reina spent with her first child's grandparents, she stayed at home with her mother, where they shared household work and chicha production and sales. Pancha was a maid in San Cristóbal for a while, then quit, explaining that her employer didn't pay her enough. After a few months back in Chenalhó she had an affair with a married man, a town official, and eventually gave birth to their child. At fifteen Josefina talked to men often and without shame. She talked to the bus driver, to her teachers, and to the boys at school. They came to her house to buy chicha, and sometimes they stopped her on trails and teased her.

Unlike her sisters, Josefina never wore traditional clothes. She often sported jewelry, sometimes gifts from boyfriends. As Josefina moved further from tradition, Victorio and Alejandro fumed over their bottles of rum. Angélika reminded Josefina of her household duties, but when she forgot them Angélika didn't scold her harshly. She seemed proud that Josefina was in secondary school, and never complained to me about her.

Fifteen-year-old girls rarely travel farther than Chenalhó. Josefina often went to meet the bus that passes through Chenalhó six times a day.

Sometimes as I was getting off Josefina stood nearby waiting to talk to the bus driver's helper, usually a young mestizoized man. When she wasn't talking she gazed up at the windows steamy with the breath of Ladino couples. Josefina took it all in, both Indigenous and Ladino worlds, and decided that she wanted to be on the bus. When she could wheedle some money out of her parents to go to San Cristóbal she sat next to the bus driver on an upside-down crate. On the windshield above her head, next to a picture of the Virgin Mary, was a placard with two of the bus driver's favorite sayings:

"The woman and the guitar belong to whoever plays them."
"The mare must have a virgin's belly, a married woman's breasts, and a widow's rump."

Eventually Josefina remained in San Cristóbal. She found work in a dress shop and stayed in a rooming house. She seemed content taking weekend trips home to see her mother and sisters, showing off a new dress each time. Pancha and Reina, with children of their own, remained with their mother. While I watched Victorio vacillate between periods of drunkenness and sobriety, Angélika's household seemed to look more and more like the matrifocal households typical of Ladinas in Chenalhó. Although I continued to resist labeling Angélika an "enabler," more and more she became the emotional mainstay of her family. Whether at home, in the fields, at church, or in the market selling chicha, Angélika was there for both her family and her community. Pedranas do not usually accept the sole responsibility for monitoring the emotional tone of households, nor for upholding family honor. But as Victorio's drinking continued, Angélika seemed to take on this responsibility more and more.

Rumors about Angélika's daughters never stopped while I was in Chenalhó. It seemed that everywhere I went people talked about Reina and her sisters. One particularly cruel rumor said that one day when Reina was selling chicha in the market, she ladled up a pair of her panties. (A Mestizo saying goes that if a woman wants to control a man she simmers her panties in his soup.) When I asked Antonia why people were so cruel to Reina, she said,

"When girls don't get married people say they only want to sleep with men, that they're lazy and don't want to do the work that wives should do."

Although Antonia is critical of women who don't follow traditions, at Reina's invitation she came to see her a couple of days after her second child, Daniel, was born. Reina seemed to want Antonia's advice. Antonia listened as Reina, weeping, explained her situation. Antonia didn't tell her what to do, but later told me that it was for the best that Reina accepted her in-laws' invitation. Having one child without a husband is easier to fix than having two, she said. Perhaps Antonia thought that as long as the grandparents of her first child were willing to accept Daniel, Reina should consider herself fortunate and go with them.

During the fiesta I didn't know what others thought of Reina, and was surprised when Domingo got angry at Antonia for visiting her and at me for helping her give birth. Like Victorio and Alejandro, Domingo wanted Reina to pay for her sins. Domingo and I had our first serious disagreement over Reina. He quoted the Bible verses that served him, I quoted the ones that served me.

"In the Bible it says that men and women should marry and be faithful to each other."

"But Domingo, do you remember what Jesus did when people were stoning a prostitute? He made them put their stones down and he said, 'If there is someone out there who hasn't sinned, you cast the first stone.'"

Antonia just sat there like someone enjoying a tennis match. Domingo tried to elicit my sympathy for Victorio. He described the pitiful state he had found him in the day before, walking around town in torn dirty clothes. I pointed out that he had been beating his wife and children and was drunk most of the time, so his daughters felt justified in not taking care of him. Domingo conceded that Victorio had been drinking a lot, but he had stopped and now, Domingo said, Victorio's daughters should take care of him. Domingo eventually left Antonia and me to our work. I didn't feel like working. I wanted to know what Antonia was thinking.

"Antonia, do you see my point?"

"Yes, I understand what you're saying, that it isn't fair to blame only Reina. The men are also to blame. But Reina didn't show her parents respect, by having two children without marrying. Giving herself to men, she isn't respecting herself either."

Antonia defends fidelity and obedience to parents and husbands. This conviction serves her in a marriage based on an economic partnership, not romantic love. But through many years of trying to make their partnership work, Antonia has grown to love Domingo. Like Angélika, Antonia justifies her relationship in religious or collective terms. She says that she prayed to God to send her a good partner. With Domingo's legacy of heavy drinking, there have been hard times, but even in these times she believes that things will work out if she follows the ways of her ancestors. In speaking about her *"destino"* (destiny) Antonia seems neutral, neither saying that it imprisons her, nor that it fulfills her dreams. Her attitude of "we'll wait and see" seems to be a healthy response to changes that mestizoization and women's increasing importance as cash providers is bringing to households and communities.

Living on the margins of Ladino society and selling rum and chicha, it is difficult for women like Angélika's daughters to fit into traditional expectations about women. While Pedranos consider making and selling chicha honorable work, many women also sell rum at the same time. The drinking that goes on at houses where rum and chicha are both available is often disrespectful and violent. Although Angélika and her daughters usually go on with their work at a distance from the men who come to their house to buy and drink, drunk men try to talk to them, and in so doing break through the code of respectful behavior between the sexes. Tradition states that marriageable girls should not speak to eligible men. For this reason most chicha sellers are married women. Angélika's daughters are exceptions.

I knew how much Reina and her mother and father depended on selling chicha to support themselves, but I wondered if Angélika could not have found some other way of making money, just to reduce the amount of alcohol drunk on her premises. As it turned out, Reina took matters into her own hands. She began talking with relatives and friends who sold atole about production costs and potential profits. Then she borrowed money and invested in a big metal pot. The weekend after I saw her walking down the street swinging her new metal pot, she was ladling up atole in the market. By changing from chicha to atole Reina may have confirmed accusations that she was no longer behaving like a traditional woman (Pedranas do not normally sell atole, nor wear underwear), but she avoids dealing with drunks and says that she makes about as much as she made from chicha, about 5,000 pesos a weekend in 1987. Like married couples living with parents, Reina kept her earnings from chicha and now atole separate, using it to clothe herself and her children. But when her mother needed her, she helped make and sell chicha for the family.

Amidst hostile gossip Reina kept on struggling to keep her dignity and support her children. At times I thought she ought to step back into line with traditions in order to be protected by the system in which women like Antonia had married and now negotiated new, hopefully stronger positions. But no respectable man came to petition for Reina, and she wouldn't take just any man. She said that she didn't want an old husband (over twenty-seven), or one who drank a lot. Popular opinon had it that she should be glad if a widower would have her.[1] She had passed up her chances to marry a young man who would pay her parents well (i.e., he would give them a sizeable amount of money in addition to gifts) for her youth and virginity.

I was never clear if the man who fathered Daniel had raped Reina. While Angélika and her daughters protect each other when strange men stay around to drink chicha, the girls told me of many times they were alone when men became aggressive when drunk. I don't know if they told their mother about these times, but I suspect they did. Several Pedranas in hamlets said that unmarried girls tell their parents of inappropriate behavior by any man, kin or non-kin, without shame. Still, many factors are involved in a girl's decision to tell, even in hamlets and especially about kinsmen. Although she expects to be believed, a girl may fear that her accusation will disrupt her household. In the cases I heard of involving incest between stepfathers and stepdaughters, and sex between brothers and sisters-in-law, even mothers who believe their daughters do not usually send the offending men away. Instead they send unmarried daughters to live with relatives and married daughters to live with their husbands or in-laws. I wondered how ready girls, fearing separation and pain, would be to tell of abuse.

Reina implied that she had loved Rafaela's father. It seems that he made some overtures to marry her, but never followed through. It crossed my mind that maybe Reina resisted marriage in order to get back at her father for his treatment of her and her mother and sisters, by denying him the bride price and respect that is his due. I wondered if perhaps she just wanted what she could get at the moment—attention, sex, or a gift. Perhaps she only wanted babies, and did not expect more from men, like some Mestizas I had met.

When Daniel was about a year old, just when I had decided that Reina wanted to remain single, she took a rare trip to San Cristóbal. Before leaving Reina confided to me that the older relative in whose house she would be staying had a son who was a teacher. Once in town she confessed that she was leaving town to avoid an eighteen-year-old man who wanted to marry her. The young man had come to her house with his parents and a case of sodas to ask to marry Reina, but she didn't want him. For one thing he was too young. For the other, he once kicked her in the shins when he got drunk in her yard.

A teacher, in contrast to a youngster prone to drunkenness, is a good catch. As Pedranos say, a salaried person gets paid even if he doesn't work. This man was especially desirable being young, handsome, light-skinned, and not a heavy drinker. Reina's plans didn't work in San Cristóbal. On the bus ride back to Chenalhó, her head lowered over Daniel's sleeping body, she barely spoke.

Watching Angélika and her daughters deal with living on the boundary between two worlds, I was struck by the contradiction between Indigenous women's strengths and their subordinate status. Irrespective of Angélika's ability to stay in touch with herself, the abuse she and her daughters suffered contradicted the code of respectful behavior the ancestors had prescribed.

The abuse also contradicted what I had seen in Antonia's and most Pedrano households that I had come to know. It contradicted how I felt, so much safer in the hills of Chenalhó than in the streets of Buffalo. Despite what Angélika had told me, I couldn't help seeing Pedrano households as less disordered and violent than most Ladino or American households. Watching Pedranas laugh and help each other around the fire in their households and in fiestas, I didn't see depressed women or women with "well-developed defenses." I saw women who know the healing power of ritual and community, and the difference between what they can and cannot change.

Nevertheless, I came to accept the "deviant" label for Angélika's family, even though I blamed Victorio's behavior, while Pedranos tended to

I asked several young Pedranos to draw how they think their lives will look when they are in their early twenties. The Pedrana, fifteen or sixteen years old, who drew this picture, grew up in a hamlet but attends secondary school in Chenalhó, and only visits her parents on weekends. The heavy Ladino cast to her drawing may reflect her expectations of what I wanted her to draw, or the strength of Ladino influences in her life. That she changed the name of her prospective husband from Antonio, a common Pedrano name, to Fidelino, a Ladino name, reflects her efforts to make her drawing as Ladino as possible. Her caption reads: "This is where Fidelino lives with his woman. First they were girlfriend and boyfriend. Later they got married and went to live in Fidelino's house."

blame Angélika's daughters' promiscuity. Pedranos said things like: "What the girls are doing is no good. They are giving themselves to men." The forcefulness of people's criticism made me wonder if it was a defense against the threat that Angélika's daughters presented. The girls were a constant reminder of the push and pull of Mestizo society, the pros and cons of Pedrano and Mestizo values, the contradictions between them. That Reina was able to rebound from hurtful slander and use it to reevaluate her relation to both societies, speaks to women's resilience and strength. Yet the abuse and punishment that single women like Reina suffered seemed to be of a different order than the abuse married women suffered. In part this difference seemed to stem from unmarried women's marginalization in relation to the dominant institutions of their society. It also seemed to relate to Pedranos' association of these women with the interface between Ladino and Indigenous societies.

While Pedranos stress respect between the sexes, generations, and between mortals and the Gods, Ladinos place their highest value on respect for private property and family honor. Women play a pivotal role in this system, for claims to legitimacy rest on their virginity, proper marriage, and chastity. In contrast, Pedranos say that both men's and women's virginity is important to family honor. However, in Pedranos' concern over losing their traditions they unfairly criticize women who choose not to marry, like Angélika's daughters, and women who are breaking new ground as spokeswomen for their communities, like Antonia. Antonia accepted her cargo as a cooperative leader after she married, when her traditional roles as mother and wife and the cargo institution could protect her. Angélika's daughters deviated from the norm by having children without marrying, and were not protected by their society's institutions. Like an increasing number of young women, they say they would rather raise their children with a family member than risk living with a man who drinks and might make their lives difficult, not to mention make them poorer. While some young women in this position move to San Cristóbal to find work, Angélika and her daughters have relied on each other to co-mother the children, make chicha and atole, and sell it in the marketplace. When Reina returned to Chenalhó after her abortive attempt to marry and find work, she seemed relieved to be home again. Even with intermittent abuse, in Chenalhó she has a house, land, and people who love her.

Victorio and Alejandro have had more contact with machismo than Pedranos in remote hamlets, and they seem to have accepted the idea that women uphold their family honor. Like many of their Mestizo counterparts, they *"andan donde quieren"* (go where they want). But Victorio is there for the important rituals of his cargos and to cure his people. Alejandro says that he doesn't drink in bars in the city, because it is often violent there and if you are a stranger nobody will defend you. But he drinks daily in bars and at his house when he comes to visit Chenalhó. Perhaps because he is still single and often drinks with Mestizos, who generally accept young men's drunkenness, both Mestizos and Pedranos find his antics amusing and do not criticize him.

In general, it seems that as Pedrano society comes to look more like Ladino society, problems with alcohol and domestic violence increase. Indigenous men who when sober are clear about their own and others' rights and responsibilities in households, and the importance of maintaining a balance within their communities, when drunk often disregard others' rights, forget their responsibilities to their families and communities, and get caught up in contests of power with other Pedranos over land or women.

When they are on the defensive Pedranos also get into power struggles with Ladino men and mestizoized Indigenous people. Such a power struggle occurred in Domingo's hamlet a few months after the Feast of St. Peter. The husband of a young Pedrana accused her of sexual relations with the hamlet schoolteacher, a mestizoized Pedrano known for having several "wives" and drinking heavily. Estela, the young woman, fled to her parents' house while her husband took the problem to the hamlet *agente* (the president of the hamlet). Although a teacher abusing young women is nothing new, the men of the hamlet decided to take a stand this time. Antonia and I sat around the fire night after night waiting for Domingo to return from all-night meetings at the schoolhouse, where the hamlet men put both Estela and Lorenzo, the teacher, on trial. Lorenzo belonged to the Vanguardistas, a faction of teachers opposed to the Democráticos, a faction that most campesinos supported. In effect, the men were putting on trial Vanguardistas and the Mestizo interests they represented. When a group of teachers from another hamlet and the area inspector, also a Vanguardista, tried to pass in their car, the men put a chain in the road and put the inspector in jail saying that he, too, violated women.

Domingo told us that hamlet police went to arrest Estela at her parent's home and brought her, tied in ropes, to the schoolhouse. There they put her in one room and Lorenzo in another. Domingo played a central role, along with a leading Protestant, in cross-examining the schoolteacher. Lorenzo defied the men, telling them they had no rights to try him and he wasn't afraid of them.

One man replied,

"What you're doing is no good. We're all Pedranos and yet you do this to us. . . . You go around violating people. . . . We built this house for you, and now you bring women into it. What good is it to us if you teachers know how to read, when all you do is go around bothering women? All you do is steal our women. If we go around hitting our wives, it's you teachers who are to blame."

The men then brought in Estela.

"Is it true that you had relations with the man, that you accepted him, knowing you had a husband?"

"It's true. He dragged me into his room. He sat me down on the bed and he took my son and laid him down on the bed. Then he lay down. After that he began to violate me," she said.

"And you obeyed him?"

"Yes, I accepted. Maybe the Devil made me do it."

Estela stayed in the teacher's room five hours. The length of time she stayed convinced the men that she had been a willing partner.

The men decided that Lorenzo had to pay a fine of a half million pesos, part to the husband and part to the community. They said that he must have that much money because he has two wives, one at the school and one in San Cristóbal, and he is an employee of the government.

During the affair, which lasted several months, the men sent Estela to her parents, with only the clothes on her back and without her two-year-old child. Lorenzo stayed in San Cristóbal. He offered to pay Estela's parents her bride price, but he refused to pay the huge fine the men demanded. After much debate the men decided they had to do something that would show the teachers they meant business. They closed the school for a month. Lorenzo took the case to the Ministerio Público in San Cristóbal and several of the men involved, including Domingo, had to go to San Cristóbal to settle the matter. Eventually Estela's husband regretted raising the issue. Estela came to ask him to take her back. Her breasts were aching, she said, and she missed her child. He took her back. The men had spent a considerable sum of money on bus fare back and forth to San Cristóbal, and eventually had to reopen the school.

I knew Lorenzo. Most times I saw him in Chenalhó or on the bus he was drunk, but when he wasn't he talked with me about his work and was polite. Once when he was drunk he asked me to stay with him and be his wife. Another time he kept trying to put his arm around me and when I pushed him away, he hit me repeatedly on the shoulder to get my attention. Drinking clearly helped Lorenzo vent his machismo.

The strength of the men's response to this affair surprised Antonia and her neighbors. At the waterhole women voiced fears that if Lorenzo had to pay a huge fine he would find one of their men alone someday and kill him. Word spread that Estela's mother defended her daughter and scolded her son-in-law for the problems she said he was causing.[2]

Domingo and his friends knew that Lorenzo had been one of them when he was a child, but going away to San Cristóbal and becoming a teacher had made Lorenzo a Ladino to them. Jacinto Arias, another Pedrano who left his community to study outside, wrote a master's thesis at Catholic University in the early 1970s in which he discusses the fate of many young teachers (1973: 91):

> Drinking for many of them has become the main escape from their "self," which inevitably asks the universal question, "Who am I?" This question causes constant pain to such transitional people, so that most prefer avoiding to answer it. Loneliness is a common existential experience for these people who have abandoned the at least partially meaningful things which they used to fill their "self" some time in the past. An example of what is meant can be found in the so-called "hippies." These people have abandoned what their parents deemed valuable but they have not found something else that can satisfy their dreams, ideals and expectations. This creates an experience of emptiness in their being, which could be the reason that many of them stick to drugs. A very similar phenomenon has happened to the Highlander teachers; they have run away from their traditional culture but they have not found something else that could feed their beings. Once the Maya 'numinous' was meaningful to them and could feed their existence, but now this 'numinous' is no longer attractive because it has lost its meaning. They have felt drawn to the Ladino ways but they have not been able to assimilate them.[3]

Although young women caught up in this change can develop drinking problems, it is more common for women to suffer from the drinking problems and abuse of mestizoized boyfriends and husbands. Rosa, Juana's daughter, lives in Chenalhó and is married to a teacher. Like her mother, Rosa prefers Ladina clothes and speaks Spanish well. Rosa says her mother made her childhood miserable, scolding and beating her. Although her father defended her, Rosa went to live with her godmother. At twenty-four years of age, Rosa has given birth to eight children. She can barely keep them clothed or fed since her husband drinks up most of his paycheck. Like many Indigenous teachers who work in distant hamlets or townships, Rosa's husband stays overnight at the school and comes home on weekends. But often he doesn't come home until the weekend is half over.

"On Friday he goes to San Cristóbal to collect his pay. I tell him to take one of the children with him to buy their shoes or pants. He says, 'No, I'm just going on a quick trip and I'll be back.' But he stays in San Cristóbal drinking. When he wakes up on Saturday it's too late to buy his bus ticket back to Chenalhó. When afternoon comes he isn't here and there's no money. When he finally comes home, he doesn't have any money. He spends about 120,000 to 140,000 pesos on rum. This happens to other women, too.

"When he drinks he gets crazy. He hits me. But I stay with him because I have my children. Now he says he wants another wife. He says that when he finishes his classes he's hungry, and he has to make his own fire and he burns his hands cooking his own food. I tell him, 'If you go and don't give me anything, how am I going to survive?'"

Many Indigenous teachers have two "wives"—the original wife they visit on weekends and another "wife" they live with in the community where they teach—for at least a part of their career. Sometimes men leave their first wives in favor of the second wife, who meets their needs on a daily basis. First wives like Rosa fear their husbands will strand them without support, while they put up with drunken abuse.

Verónica, Carmela's mother, is also married to a man trained as a teacher. When I met Verónica, her husband, Ernesto, had recently left a teaching job and was working in the town hall. That Ernesto had a drinking problem, no one, Ladino or Pedrano, disputed. Ernesto often drank his midday meal, and by night he would pass out and be unable to go to work the next day. But when Ernesto was sober he was enthusiastic about life and appreciated his family.

One day after Ernesto had left for the town hall I asked Verónica about her marriage and her husband's drinking. The pressing issue for Verónica that day was that Ernesto was getting drunk a lot and accusing her of having an affair. But in fact it was he who had had an affair, with Verónica's sister. Ernesto had two children with his sister-in-law. But Verónica wanted to stay married to her husband.

In the past Verónica followed Ernesto wherever he went to try to find work as a teacher. She bore his drunkenness and jealous accusations. They went to many hamlets and other townships where Ernesto taught. No doubt, his drinking played some part in their having to change jobs frequently. Eventually Verónica got tired of picking up all the time. Their two oldest girls were starting school, and when Ernesto took a job teaching in a distant town Verónica wouldn't go with him, even though he begged her. She stayed at home taking care of their milpa, children, chickens, and pigs.

At the school Ernesto kept drinking. Once he fell into an arroyo when he was drunk and hit his head. According to Verónica a relative told him:

"Look, Ernesto. You're pitiful. You drink too much. Believe in God. It's better. That's how you can stop drinking."

Ernesto invited the elders of the Presbyterian church to his house to talk. Verónica gave them food and atole. Ernesto told Verónica that he wanted to accept the word of God, and then asked her and their oldest daughters if they wanted to also. Verónica and her daughters said they wanted to join, too. Soon after the whole family began worshiping in the Presbyterian church on the hill above Chenalhó.

But changing his religion wasn't enough to help Ernesto stop drinking. He began to drink again. He took a teaching job and kept his drinking under control for a while. While teaching he earned enough to serve a religious cargo with Verónica. On weekend visits to his family, Verónica and he would prepare for their cargo, visiting kin and neighbors to borrow things they needed for the fiesta. Only once during this time did Ernesto hit Verónica when he was drunk.

Although Verónica was proud of Ernesto's education, she would have preferred that he work in the milpa and be poor, in order to have stability in their lives.

"We have land in the hamlet where my husband was born, and I go there to cut coffee, but I have to go with just my daughter because Ernesto is drinking in the marketplace. At my in-laws' house I cry, 'It's like I don't have a husband. It would have been better if I'd never married,' I say to them. 'I would have been better off alone,' I say."

For a while Ernesto took up weaving women's skirt lengths (typically Ladino men's work). He sold some of his land in his parent's hamlet and bought his own foot loom. But he began to drink again, and eventually he sold the loom to pay his debts. Then he told Verónica he wanted to leave the Presbyterians and go back with the Catechists. But Verónica didn't want to go back to Catholic Action, the group they had joined before becoming Presbyterians. She told me, "People who pay attention to the saints will be lost. They'll be punished. There's only one God."

But Ernesto joined the Catechists despite Verónica's decision to remain Presbyterian. And he began to drink again. Then for nine months he gave up rum, but he started to drink again.

"After he finishes listening to the word of God in church he goes out into the market and begins to drink. He gets angry and hits me with a leather strap. He pulls my hair. He scolds me. He just fights. . . . His heart is no good. 'Get out of here. Go,' he says, scolding me. 'This is my house now,' he says. I go hide somewhere on the mountain or I go into milpas or sometimes I shut myself in my house.

"'I don't want to go because I don't have a problem,' I say. 'If I'm the one with the problem I'll leave. . . . If I had had relations with another man you would have the right to say that, but I don't have a problem,' I said.

"That's why my children get sad. We cry and get sick. I don't know what we're going to do. Three times I threw him in jail to keep him from scolding and hitting me. He tore my clothes and pulled my blouse.

"When he drank in the past I would go without my shawl into the streets, to my sister's house. If I looked sad my parents would say, 'You should leave him. You look unhappy,' my parents would say. 'Why do you love this man who runs around with other women?' they say. But I love my husband. I only want one husband. I don't want to divorce. My four children will be sad. They get along with their father.

"That's why there's still a problem. I'm not happy. But what can I do?"

Violence toward women in Ladino and Indigenous communities is pervasive (Garza Caligaris and Ruiz Ortiz 1992; Rosenbaum 1993: 52–55). While many Ladinos and Pedranos would like to blame alcohol for jealousy, envy, and violence, the roots of these problems lie in an interplay of economic and social relations. The statistical association between drinking and violence cross-culturally is overwhelming, yet causal connections are unclear. In colonized areas of the world, part of the violence which sometimes follows heavy drinking may be connected to Indigenous peoples imitating the invaders or conforming to invaders' stereotypes of them (Dentan 1992: 241). Given alcohol's perceived disinhibitory function, it both relieves men of feeling responsible for their violent behavior, and allows family members to excuse them, based on the belief that it was the alcohol that made them do it. Room (cited in Nero 1990: 85) notes that alcohol is a useful explanation, particularly where relations of domination are changing. Dentan (1992: 241) sums up our received wisdom on the subject of alcohol and violence: ". . . while drinking may not be sufficient to produce drunken violence, it potentiates the expression of violence along stress lines already present even in a peaceable society. Thus introducing alcohol works against peace."[4]

The stresslines along which alcohol facilitates violence toward women in Chenalhó are women's growing participation in the cash economy and an overall breakdown of traditional conceptions of community and alcohol's role in expressions of those. In general, it seems that as Pedrano society comes to look more like Ladino society—fragmented, competitive, with many different ideas of how one can drink and act when drunk— problems with alcohol and domestic violence have intensified. When drunk, Pedranos often imitate Ladinos. Part of their imitation involves speaking Spanish and being focused on dominating women.[5]

Although Pedranos have bought into machismo to varying degrees and struggle with rapid economic change, their strong collective institutions still protect women to a greater extent than Ladinas' institutions protect them. Women like Rosa, who live in the *cabecera* (head village) and whose husbands are Mestizos, seem especially vulnerable. When they are victims of domestic or other violence, these women may appeal to the courts, which are dominated by men, but this is often their only support. More traditional women also use the court system, but as a backup to the support they receive from within their traditions. For example, young women will even complain to parents or in-laws if their husbands try to make them do something sexual that they don't like, like sleeping together nude. If complaining doesn't resolve the problem, the two sets of in-laws try to work it out. If they can't, both families take the problem to the authorities. While the court system in Mexico and the United States has traditionally treated spousal abuse as a domestic problem, the Pedrano court treats it as a community problem. For example, many women say that they have as much right to file complaints against husbands who get drunk and beat them or force them to have sex, as they do against strangers who might do the same thing. Ladinas and mestizoized Indigenous women living in urban centers like San Cristóbal have fewer options. Although the fabric of social reponsibility in Indigenous communities tears at times, it is fashioned to protect Indigenous women from abuses that Ladinas, who live in an individually oriented society, must endure.[6]

Machismo and alcohol have affected Pedranos' social relations, but Pedranos have resisted absorbing Ladino ideas about women and alcohol completely into their culture. I believe that Indigenous men, and to a lesser extent women, pick and choose between Mestizo and Indigenous ideas depending upon the situations they are in. As we have seen, in their rituals Indigenous people imbue alcohol with a sacred power that is absent in Ladino society. As for ideas about women, it seems likely that since the Spanish invasion, Highland Maya men have used the prerogatives that contact with male-biased Hispanic culture afforded them to bolster up their egos and courage, and support whatever male bias existed in their society before Spanish influence. However, two factors seem to have kept Indigenous men from buying wholesale into the Ladino ideas about drinking and the Mestizo myth of women's subordination. These are economic interdependence between the sexes, and a view of spiritual strength as a collective rather than an individual achievement.

10 "For ye are bought with a price"
Traditions, Religions, and Drinking

Traditionalists

For a long time I had been wanting to talk to Humberto, an elder who had held several cargos and knew many stories. Whenever I asked about appearances of the Mother of the Sky/Our Mother or the Moon-Virgin, people mentioned Humberto. They said that he could tell me stories of when the Mother of the Sky appeared to Pedranos in dreams or in the form of lakes, ordering them to hold fiestas in her honor and to get their drinking under control. One such dream had come to a Pedrano in the mid-1970s, just at the time when Protestant groups and Catholic Action were gaining strength. My efforts to find this Pedrano failed, but José, an older Pedrano friend who often came to my rescue, told me not to fear: I would not have to leave Chenalhó without hearing the story from someone who knew it well, his uncle, Humberto.

As usual it took three tries to find Humberto at home and free to talk. The day José and I finally talked with him, we found Humberto planting spruce trees on the hill above his house. At first I thought that Humberto wouldn't be able to talk, but a soft drizzle had started and it seemed that he might stop working. Humberto greeted us and said he would talk to us after finishing his work and chatting with his nephew. The nephew, Cristóbal, and his young son had arrived just before us. Like a dog circling, Cristóbal broached the subject on his mind. He had heard about a landslide on the radio, and wanted his uncle's opinion on what this might portend. Humberto kept digging at the dark soil while Cristóbal probed for some reassurance that such a disaster couldn't happen in Chenalhó.

"It's good that nothing like that has happened here yet. We haven't experienced any strong tremors or landslides here. Not yet. Uncle, could it be because we still worship Our Father, because he's still in our hearts, because that's the way it was with our ancestors?"

The Church of St. Peter drawn by Francisco Gómez Pérez.

"Look, this apostle St. Peter in the church, in reality he doesn't speak to us. He's made of wood. But his image went up to heaven and he guides us from there. We still worship him. We still celebrate his masses. We ask his blessing to prevent famine, or tremors, or a strong storm, or other bad things. We praise the apostle because that's our tradition."

"Yes, it is."

"But things are changing. We don't all believe the same. Now there are other religions, many religions. We don't know which one to join, which one is best. But as for me, I feel content with what I have, and I'm going to stay with that. That's how I was raised. Also I've realized that we all have a little bad in us, we all sin."

The conversation between Humberto and his nephew was typical of many talks which took place in fields, on paths, and at hearthside when I was in Chenalhó. In all times, but especially in times as full of change as these, young Pedranos look to their elders for their perspective on the meaning of events. Even José, who at fifty was no youngster, had agreed to come with me to talk with Humberto in part because he knew he would learn something important, something that might help him understand some of the changes in his community.

Mentioning the landslide, Cristóbal was probably alluding to appearances of the Mother of the Sky which Pedranos still associate with heavy rains, landslides, and lakes forming. He undoubtedly connected the landslide with failure on the part of the community where it occurred to follow the traditions, necessitating divine intervention.

In spite of their commitment to traditions, Pedranos accept change and uncontrollable events as a constant in their lives. Berger (1979) suggests that peasants experience change intensely, due primarily to their capacity for observation and their economic situation. Pedranos talk constantly about small and great changes in weather and land, and what meaning these portend. As producers of their own food and also as buyers and sellers in the market, Pedranos note every economic change for the worse, however small. A slightly reduced yield in the corn crop one year, combined with a rise in the price of corn, can mean that a family who runs out of corn in the last months before the next harvest may suffer hunger, illness, even death.

As José knew, and I discovered, Humberto had been keeping close watch of events transforming his community and had much to say about them. The day we came to visit, Humberto told us some stories and traditions from the past and how these relate to his own and his people's vision of the future. Specifically he told us about the origin and purpose of rum, his own drinking, the growth of Protestantism, and what he knew of appearances of the Moon-Virgin in Highland Chiapas.

About his own drinking, Humberto said that he no longer drank because a doctor had told him it was affecting his heart. Although he drank a lot over the years, Humberto said he never drank much when serving his many cargos. Before taking his cargos he would put down his candles and ask Our Father, "Please, my Lord, put rum to one side, take rum away from me. Don't let me shame myself through rum."

Of all the topics on which he spoke, Humberto was most animated when talking about Our Mother and the spread of Protestantism. A key factor affecting Humberto's faith in the Mother of the Sky seemed to be his wife's recovery from a serious illness several years back. When his efforts to heal his wife failed, Humberto went to a place where a fellow Pedrano said he had seen Our Mother. The man called Our Mother "Holy Mother Ann," and said that she had left a cross below the ground. Humberto placed his candles on the spot where the cross was supposedly buried and prayed to Mother Ann to heal his wife. Humberto's wife recovered quickly, and he still visits this place to ask the Virgin's blessing.

Although I asked Humberto to talk specifically about the dream from the 1970s, he told me he had to start at the beginning, the first time Our Mother appeared in Highland Chiapas in a part of Tenejapa called Matzam.

"They say that she was a person, or rather that she converted herself into a person. My parents told me that she was a woman from Tenejapa, and that she and her husband had a child. The child didn't talk, but she wouldn't stop crying. She wanted water, just water. Her parents didn't know why. They went to the river and when the child cried, she said 'suyil.' Each time they went to the river she cried strangely, saying, 'suyil, suyil.' For this reason her mother called her Suyil.

"One day Suyil went to bathe herself with her mother. The child was seated on the edge of the lake, and when her mother was distracted she went crawling into the lake. 'My child has disappeared!' her mother cried. Her mother didn't know where the child was in the lake. She had seen her fall into the lake out of the corner of her eye, but she couldn't run fast enough to grab her.

"A little over an hour after she threw herself into the lake, the child suddenly appeared. When she came out of the lake she said to her mother,

'Don't be sad, because I've come to stay here. Don't cry any more. I will stay here forever.' 'That's good,' said her mother, who had calmed down from crying, because now she had the spirit to live."

As the child grew the lake also grew, until it was huge. Humberto didn't remember how many years Our Mother stayed at this place; he only said that she stayed there a long time and then came to Chenalhó.

"Over the years the Tenejapanecos stopped respecting Our Mother in this place. So she changed her place. When she left there was a great rainstorm, with much wind and flooding. She flooded a quantity of land like what one uses to plant forty ears of corn, more than a half hectare. Finally, in a place below Taki U'kum in hot country, she stopped flowing and formed a great lake."

During this time many Pedranos had dreams in which they saw Our Mother at her new home in Chenalhó.

"When the elders saw that Our Mother had come here, they went to advise the authorities. In the past, as you know, there was a lot of respect.

"'Our Mother has come,' they said. 'They say that she's Our Mother who was in Tenejapa who has come to our land,' the people said. 'Now that Our Mother is here, what do you think?' they asked. The elders replied, 'We'll take care of her. We have to take care of her now that she belongs to us. We'll worship her. We'll make a cross and a crown for her. We'll offer candles and ask for her blessing.' 'That's good,' the people said.

"So, long ago the authorities attended masses at the lake. But they didn't dress the same as the rest of the authorities. They wore black woolen cloaks. They carried scarves and good walking sticks, like they use in fiestas. They dressed in a place called 'They Dress with Flags.' That's a hill. They wanted everyone to be dressed before arriving at the place where Our Mother is. So, on arriving they were dressed in flags. Then the authorities sat in a row and women helpers put out food. That's how it was when my father went there. They had these masses for a long time. The Virgin stayed there a long time."

Dream accounts and stories of Our Mother/the Moon-Virgin in Highland Chiapas demonstrate repeatedly that when Traditionalists perceive a threat to their traditions they begin to dream of "Our Mother," a maternal ancestor/protector counterpart to "Our Father." Pedranos sometimes unite Our Mother and Our Father in totil me'il. They also refer to Our Mother as the Virgin Mary and Our Father as St. Joseph, Mary's husband. Often they see Our Mother's presence in dramatic changes in the weather or the land. In the mid-1970s the threat was the growing rate of conversion to Catholic Action and various Protestant groups. While Protestants had been proselytizing since the 1950s, the Catholic Action movement was just beginning, and it was making Traditionalists nervous. They saw more and more Bibles in net bags and people entering the church, not to kneel in prayer to the saints, but to sit in pews to listen to fellow Pedranos talk about "the word of God." Although Bishop Samuel Ruiz and the religious working with him in Highland Chiapas intended Catholic Action to encourage Pedranos to be proud of their Native traditions and to analyze the origins of their oppression, Traditionalists didn't see this. They saw instead the outward signs of yet another invasion. Combined with Protestant proselytizing, this new movement seemed to be more than they could bear and still retain their identity as a people. Most Traditional men agreed with Humberto. As long as they were content with what they had, and since it seemed that Protestants and Catechists also sinned, a known Devil was better than an unknown one.

Although the first fiesta to the Virgin lasted around sixty years, eventually the lake dried up and people began to say that the Virgin was discontent. In 1974 the Virgin and San José (possibly totil me'il), appeared in a dream to Ruíz Paloma, a past regidor. The Virgin was indeed discontent. Although she said to him, "I will always come here. I will always be here," she admonished Pedranos for their disrespectful drinking and their refusal to contribute to fiestas. She told Ruíz Paloma that his people weren't honoring her when they were lying in the streets drunk. She no longer heard their prayers, and her breasts were drying up. It was a shame, she said, because the land was rich. But if her breasts dried up she couldn't feed her children. On the subject of Protestant and Catholic Action converts she said that they should cooperate in Traditional fiestas. As for alcohol, she explicitly requested that there be no alcohol at the fiesta in her honor. Soda would do.

News of Ruíz Paloma's dream spread, and Indigenous people from all over Highland Chiapas came to place crosses and candles on the banks of the lake where the Virgin had once been. Humberto took his family there, too. They left a cross. Many Highlanders reported dreams or visions in which the Virgin spoke to them in the following years. Women from each hamlet in Chenalhó wove garments with which they dressed the crosses. Weavers also made a garment for the Virgin, which they placed in a gourd and threw into the lake. During fiestas the authorities came with musicians who brought their cornets, flutes, and drums. While usually authorities are the only ones who dance in fiestas, in this fiesta everyone danced, down to the youngest children. At these fiestas Ruíz and his wife officiated like an alperes and me' alperes. Ruíz recounted his dream, and a few older women also sang a special song-prayer to the Virgin. The women had adapted their song from one that women sang in Tenejapa when the Virgin was there. Women sang their song at masses on the lake and in Ruíz' home. *And* they *were not* drunk when they sang.

Between 1974 and 1977 Ruíz continued to report dreams in which the Virgin spoke to him. In one report she told him that Pedranos should build a church in her honor. In another she said that she needed god-daughters, a few young women to accompany her in her fiestas and to assist Ruíz' wife. Pedranos began to suspect these later dreams, especially the request for goddaughters. Rumor went that Ruíz had an affair with one of the goddaughters who had come to live in his household. From then on many Pedranos doubted everything Ruíz had said from the beginning. A rumor started that the Virgin had risen, as the lake was now just a marsh. People stopped going to visit the lake, and the fiestas ended. Although Humberto said his cross must still be there, he expressed the received wisdom of his people, "It seems that the messenger ruined the message."

On the subject of Protestantism, Humberto expressed sentiments I heard often from Traditionalists. "They just live because they live" sums up their major criticism of Protestants. Traditionalists and many Catechists maintain that by refusing to offer gifts to powerful invisible beings in fiestas and healing ceremonies, Protestants reject the ancestors' belief that life becomes possible *only* through reciprocal relations between Gods and mortals. As with his account of Our Mother, Humberto told me that in order to talk about Protestants he had to start with the time before they came, when his people were united.

"Before there was only one belief among the people. In *cooperación* (the monetary contribution Pedrano households make to major fiestas and masses held in hills throughout the township three times a year), in public works, and in everything we did we were united. People who have other religions now, were our friends in making the fiestas in the past. If the authorities called the pasados to the pueblo, they all came. When they received orders to collect money for the masses, or a message to pass on to their people, they went back to their hamlets to collect the money or to give the message to the president of their hamlet. But little by little, some people stopped obeying the orders and separated from us.

"The one who began this story, I mean this Presbyterian religion, was Miguel Maxe. He had gone to a plantation where he worked for a long time. There he walked around the plantation and met a Ladino. I don't know if he was a Mestizo or a Gringo. They talked and the man told him about the gospel. Miguel listened to what the Ladino said.

"'What I believe in is really good. It's the Bible, the only book of Our Father Jesus Christ.'

" 'Is this really true?' Miguel asked.

" 'Yes, it's true,' the Ladino said. 'If you accept it, everything will be good. If you don't accept it, you'll die.'

"Then Miguel Maxe began to read the Bible, and he liked it. He put a marker on the place where it talks about the fire, that we'll go there if we aren't perfect.

"Eventually he came back to Ch'ibtik. When he arrived he began to talk to the people who had saints in boxes.[1] 'Listen, those boxes and your saints, they're good for nothing. Put them away. What I've found is better. It's the word of Our Father. He's the only Father who was sent to us. That's what they told me on the plantation. I'm studying the word of Our Lord Jesus Christ. It's not just someone's talk. It's written down, here in this book,' Miguel Maxe said.

" 'Could it be true?' the owners of the boxes asked.

" 'Yes, it's true,' Miguel replied.

" 'It's really true? Then for once and for all I'm going to shut up the saint in the box,' one of the saint's owners said. 'It's better to learn what it says in the Bible,' he said. 'Our apostle, our saints in the church, they're not good for anything any more. They're just wood, made by hand. But this book, Our Father gave it to us.'

"Well, that's how it happened with the first Presbyterians, how a few of our people abandoned their saints and began to read the Bible. From Ch'ibtik the new Presbyterians carried their message to relatives in Pechiquil. . . . Now many more have entered that religion and their numbers keep growing. They publish the Bible in great quantities and they distribute it from house to house, deceiving those who can't read, those who are sick.

" 'Look,' they say. 'Now you have the Bible. Look at it. It's the very word of God. There's no other. It came from God's very own hands. Now all you need to do is study the word of God Our Father. If you study the word you'll be strong. You'll never die if you believe in this. It's better to accept the word of God.'

"They also say, 'You shouldn't drink rum anymore; you shouldn't do anything bad.' And they say, 'This father you make masses for, he's not Our Father. You shouldn't give money to worship him. We must dedicate ourselves to studying the word of Our Father.'"

Humberto's final comment on Presbyterians was that Miguel Maxe, the man who first brought the Bible to Chenalhó, eventually abandoned the Bible and went back to the traditions. According to Humberto, Miguel served several traditional cargos after that. (See Appendix C for a history of Protestantism from written accounts.)

Protestants

And he said unto me, Write: for these words are true and faithful.

Revelation 21: 5

"In my dream I was perched on a leaf. I didn't weigh anything. I saw something hanging from the sky, a cable, like a cable of light. I had it in my hands. Someone talked to me, but I didn't know where he came from.

"'Mateo! Come down to earth this minute. Go tell your companions to talk with God right away. Tell them to finish with everything that they see on the earth. Let the hour come. Let them see everything that comes to pass in heaven. Go tell your friends.'

"I didn't see where the voice came from. I just held the cord in my hands. But suddenly I came down to earth. Here I was on the ground and I did what he told me. I began to call all my friends to action. I got all the men and women together. They were crowded together here. Then I said,

"'Cry out, all of you, men, women. It's better to talk to God. Let everything that you can see here on earth come to an end. Let the hour arrive when we're going to see what will come to pass there in heaven. Let the day draw near. Let everything be finished now.'

"'It's no good. It's nothing but fear; it's nothing but sadness; it's nothing but weeping, here on earth. It's no good.'

"When I said this I kneeled down and talked to God. I began to cry. It was very bad. I made my companions feel sorry for me. I said,

"'All that will come to pass here on earth is fear, weeping, sadness. That's all you will see, my companions. You haven't seen yet what is going to come to pass in heaven.'

"At about 12:20 A.M. I woke up and couldn't go back to sleep. I felt sorry in my heart for my companions. I felt serene. I got out of bed quickly. I began to talk to God, because I felt serene. I began to write on a paper everything that he told me. I have it written down right here. I felt content. Serene.

"That's how the Holy Spirit speaks. The Holy Spirit is very beautiful. It gives us serenity in our hearts. If our heart is very empty and the day passes this way, it's because you forget to talk to God the whole day. But, now you feel delivered into the hands of God. That's how I pass the night. That's how I wake up. You feel serene in your heart." (See Appendix D.)

The coffee in my cup had cooled as Mateo, a respected Protestant elder, finished an account of one of his dreams. Since seven A.M., when I arrived at his house, Mateo had drawn his family and me into the invisible world of his dreams. I had come to ask Mateo about his conversion to the

Presbyterian faith and his past drinking. Mateo politely responded to my questions, but became animated when recounting his dreams. Since Mateo's dreams seemed to be an important influence in his life, I asked him if one can quit drinking through dreams.

"No, it doesn't stick. It doesn't last. As for me, when I didn't believe in the Lord, I drank a lot of rum. But even when I began to listen to the word of God I didn't give up all my bad habits. I still drank. I still hit my wife. I believed in God, but I still ran my wife out of the house. I still looked around for other women. But eventually I accepted the Lord.

"There are two forms to listen to the word of God. First it enters through your ears and goes out. It doesn't enter your heart. It doesn't stay in your heart. But eventually the word of God came into my heart and I believed. Yes. Then it wasn't through hearing that I believed. Not until I truly believed that the Lord was my savior could I quit. That's how I gave up rum. Rum stayed behind me. But it took a while doing it that way. It took many years."

The morning darkness had lifted and the schoolteacher's appearance in the doorway told us that the day was upon us. The schoolteacher, who had come by for a visit before classes, brought us back to the pressing matter in the visible realm, the upcoming presidential election and cooperación. While cooperación had always been an issue for Protestants, until this election Traditional authorities had not pushed the issue if they refused to cooperate. During my first year of fieldwork, I heard little about cooperación. Instead the focus of community conflict was alcohol sales and use. The percentage of Protestants in the township population has been growing, however, until they now make up, by their own estimate, about a third of the township population. Each conversion diminishes the number of people who bear the burden of cooperación. Seeing these events as focal points of unity and important to cultural survival, the current political and religious authorities are forcing Protestants to cooperate. In 1988 Protestants did not agree among themselves how to respond. Some said if they give into cooperación, Traditionalists will demand more, for example that they also serve cargos. Others said that if they cooperate now, when Traditionalists demand more later they can always say, "We did what you asked, but we can't do more." The stronger group in 1988 were those who did not want to cooperate.[2]

Like all community concerns, cooperación and prohibition are closely related issues, although Pedranos draw their lines differently over each. In the struggle over alcohol control, Catechists and Protestants have found common cause. Although Protestants say sobriety is not a prerequisite for membership, once a person has joined, fellow parishioners help him see that alcohol goes against God's word (if the person hasn't already accepted this). On the community level, Protestants advocate prohibition. While most Catechists don't say that rum is evil, as Protestants do, they say strict controls are important. Many Catechists would prefer prohibition. Meanwhile Traditionalists, influenced by rum sellers, religious cargo holders, and often their own compulsive habits, look the other way at infringements of rules regarding alcohol sales and use.

In contrast, over cooperación Catechists have more in common with their Traditionalist brothers and sisters. Both groups say fiestas are an integral part of Pedrano social life and necessary for the prosperity of their community. Although Catechists express more ambivalence than Traditionalists about rum, they share Traditionalists' reverence for all components of fiestas, from rum to candles to skyrockets to statues of the saints. Protestants, in contrast, say that rum is only one of many Catholic and Traditional symbols spelling fear, poverty, ignorance, and ungodliness. According to the Bible verses Protestants quote, offerings of food, rum, and incense to saints' statues are idol worship and the Devil's work (1 Corinthians 10:27–31):

> If any of them that believe not bid you to a feast, and ye be disposed to go; whatsoever is set before you, eat, asking no question for conscience sake. But if any man say unto you, This is offered in sacrifice unto idols, eat not for his sake that shewed it, and for conscience sake: for the earth is the Lord's, and the fullness thereof.

Protestants seem to find justification in the Bible for freedom from a traditional system of personal restrictions and communal obligations which are not only idolatrous, but costly and time consuming. Seeing feasts for Catholic saints and Maya ancestor Gods as idol worship, Protestants no longer serve religious cargos nor assist cargo holders in fiestas. They have also stopped offering feasts at the graves of deceased relatives on November 1st, and their relatives' souls are not welcome back at their homes the following day to eat and drink rum, atole, tamales, meat, and other foods.[3]

Protestants also say that their religion releases them from the fear they felt when they believed in Traditional ideas about illness and healing. While missionaries tell Indigenous pastors, "You are like shamans to your people," pastors and believers reject traditional healers and healing, calling shamans "witches." Although Protestant elders like Mateo find power and direction in their dreams, Protestants generally say dreams are bad. Some say they pray to God to help them stop dreaming, and their prayers work.

In rejecting traditional ideas about collective and personal well-being, Protestants pass on a very different idea of living to their children. In some all-Protestant hamlets young children have never seen a healing ceremony or a traditional mass in the hills. Protestants seem to have substituted personal salvation through one God, Jesus Christ, for the idea of collective salvation through perpetuation of traditions and ancestors' souls. This departure strikes at the base of traditional Pedrano identity. Since the Spanish invasion, Pedrano saints' fiestas and masses in the hills have served to both identify their communities and to perpetuate them. The idea of collective salvation has endured (Wasserstrom 1983: 77):

> Individual salvation, far too precarious an idea in those years of early death and sudden flight, remained in their minds strictly a Spanish notion. Among the Indians, men and women might attain salvation only if their villages outlived individual members, only if their descendents lit candles for them and wept over their graves on the Day of the Dead. As for their souls, these became absorbed into that collective soul commonly called "our ancestors." To the memory of these righteous forebears—who, as Christ had promised, would one day rise again and live for a thousand years—and to the village saints, native men and women addressed their prayers and lamentations. For had not the Fathers told them that the souls of good Christians live forever at God's right hand? Inspired by the idea of communal survival, then, they surrounded their *pueblos* with shrines and crosses. Beyond these limits, they seemed to say, lies a hostile world, a world of *ladinos* and untamed beasts. Inside, they declared, our ancestors watch and wait, ready to speak on our behalf when the Day of Judgement arrives.

In addition to promoting personal salvation, Protestants set themselves apart by stressing private capital accumulation.[4] Protestants say their new prosperity is due to improved living conditions made possible by saving their money, rather than spending it on rum, candles, and chickens for healing ceremonies, or on lavish outlays of liquor, food, and other ingredients at traditional fiestas. Although not a separate economic class, Protestants create more prosperous enclaves in existing communities, or "new" communities in hamlets in which almost 100% of the population has converted. Within these communities Protestants no longer need non-believers' acceptance. Protestants often develop supportive relationships, attested to by provisions of medicine, food, or money for needy families, and a fund of corn for widows in at least one Pedrano hamlet. Several communities have successfully organized to improve services, such as water and roads. Perhaps more than any other outside group, Protestant missionaries have focused on relieving immediate pain and suffering in Indigenous communities. Non-believers say that Protestants hold out resources as bait to attract needy people to their religion. Once inside the fold, if a new-comer wants to leave, Protestants withdraw their support, leaving the person worse off than before. They add that rather than concern themselves with improving life in the here and now for the majority of the people, they just take care of their own and wait for the ladder to come down from heaven so they can climb up to "life eternal." Protestants maintain that pursuing life eternal is not irrelevant to daily survival, but consistent with living a peaceful and productive life on earth. As one daily expression of "life eternal" they offer improved dealings with others. Protestants say that once they convert they stop doing offensive things that they used to do, like swear, drink too much, and hit family members.

At the time I talked with Mateo I knew that teachers in hamlet and cabecera schools were courting the Protestant vote, assuring Protestants that their candidate, a teacher, wouldn't force them to cooperate if elected, and would help them improve community services. The Cardenist party supported teachers. Most Catechists and Traditionalists had joined forces to back a *campesino* president, expressing their dissatisfaction with the twenty year legacy of teachers representing them. In doing so they drew stronger lines between themselves and Protestants. Traditionalists were pressing the issue of cooperación, maintaining that although some Protes-tants had not been cooperating for nearly thirty years, it was time to show their solidarity with their pueblo by starting to cooperate again. Before leaving Mateo's house that day, I took the opportunity to ask him how he felt about the election.

"We have an agreement with the teachers because their intentions are to help those who believe in the word of God. The teachers know the laws. They know how to read. Those of us who believe in the word of God choose people who are educated, those who know how to read, those who are wise, those who know the content of the law. The campesinos, those who are in the Democratic party, ORIACH, they don't know how to read. They don't respect the content of the law. They say that the law isn't good for anything. They say that it's only the law of the Ladino authorities. But their candidate is giving orders, saying that the suffering for those who be-lieve in the word of God is going to start. Although religion is free, accord-ing to Article 24 [of the Mexican Constitution], the campesino candidate says the law is no good because it's a Ladino law. And campesinos should-n't follow it because they're Indigenous people. I'm not happy about the Democratic followers. Their work's no good. It's the Devil's. My people don't know which way to go. It seems that there is no candidate. It wasn't like this before. Before if we had already chosen a candidate, he would stay and all the people would unite behind him, even if there were two factions."

I took my leave while Mateo and the teacher continued talking. Later, when translating two other dreams that Mateo had told me that morning, I heard Mateo express a different interpretation of community conflict than the one he expounded in the teacher's presence. This interpretation combined traditional belief about dreams as guides in daily life with Biblical prophecy in the book of Revelation and premillenialism.

"Just a week ago I had a dream. I saw something in the sky. Something exploded. But when it exploded I felt serene in my heart. 'What's that?' I asked. In a little bit I saw something on fire in the sky. It shone. The sky was red. It was cloudless, but only a small part. I could hardly see. My friends were very afraid. They didn't talk. Someone was crying. But I began to shout, 'If you're sad, come! Come with me. If you're sad come with me!' I was shouting. And they came with me."

Another time after waking up from a dream in which he spoke with God Mateo felt very content, as if at last he understood what was happening.

" 'How will this happen?' I asked. Now the two thousand years is going to end, the pact that God made. Now it's ready to be fulfilled. Signs are coming in the sky and on earth. The people are turning into each other's enemies. They've begun the persecution. All who believe in God will be expelled. Everyone will be beaten. Everyone will be delivered into the hands of the authorities. The hour will arrive, the signs that God is coming now, the signs that everything he has said will happen. That's why I believe this way in my heart. I saw this in my dreams."

The campesino candidate won the 1988 election by a very narrow margin, much to the Protestants' dismay. Judging by the almost clear split—Protestants backing the teachers' candidate and Traditionalists and Catechists joining forces behind the campesino candidate—it seemed that Protestants now constituted almost half of the population. Although they lost the election, Protestants were a growing constituency with a fair number of their people in public offices and a specific agenda which threatened the very concept of community that Traditionalists and Catechists held.

While Protestants differ in their positions on cooperación and ideas about community, on drinking they agree. To drink at all is folly, they say, because the reason they drank in the past was to get drunk. (Alcoholics Anonymous asserts that alcoholism means never being able to control one's drinking the way normal people, "social drinkers," do. It's the state of alcoholics, not their past, which renders them incompetent to drink.) Protestants who drank in the past say they sought spiritual power in rum. Those who converted first to Catholic Action, then later to a Protestant religion, say that they were fooling themselves thinking they could still drink a few times a year. If they drink often enough they might start believing that drinking brings them power. With conversion, Protestants say they find spiritual power in living as Jesus Christ did, that is, not speaking bad words, showing compassion, and not doing anything to hurt others knowingly. Serenity comes to those who follow Christ's example, Mateo says.

Presbyterian pastors differ from more fundamentalist pastors in not focusing as much on taboos, like drinking. Recognizing that the Bible doesn't say that alcohol is evil in itself they prefer to say, "Those of us in this faith agree not to drink," rather than "You can't drink if you want to be one of us." If a newcomer drinks after converting, his or her fellow Presbyterians will say something like "He hasn't become one of us yet."[5] Usually they try to entice obdurate drinkers back into the fold, as Verónica describes pastors doing for Ernesto. Two Pentecostal Ladino missionaries told me that they forbid members who have returned to drinking from speaking at services, but not from listening. (Recovering alcoholics in AA meetings in San Cristóbal take a similar approach to drunks who come to their meetings.) In the missionaries' words, "the brothers or sisters take the person's voice away."

Protestants who successfully give up drinking say they do so through putting alcohol into God's hands, where they put everything else that bothers them. If a person gives up rum in this way, it becomes God's burden, not his. Praying to God to take their burden, and believing that he will, seems to be enough to bring the serenity and sobriety that Mateo describes. Protestants say that people who cannot seem to keep from drinking have not let God's word enter their heart. When they listen, God's word just goes through their ears and out, as Mateo says it was for him before he truly believed. Listening so that God's word stays requires faith and time.

While Mateo gave generously of his thoughts about drinking and co-operación, it was Verónica who gave me an understanding of what issues women stress and why women convert. Verónica was my only Protestant friend. Verónica was open with her thoughts, especially the advantages of Protestantism over Traditionalism and Catholic Action. One morning while she was finishing making tortillas I asked her to tell me why she had changed her religion.

"When I got married I was with the Catechists, but that didn't make my husband stop drinking. Eventually I stopped listening to the word of

God in the church because the Padre still drinks rum and beer. . . . A young Pedrano who got married in Chenalhó served a lot of beer at his wedding, and the Padre and the Catechists drank. The Padre tells people who get married, 'If you only drink a cup of rum or a few beers at the wedding, you aren't sinners. Just one cup isn't a sin. It's not a sin to smoke cigarettes either,' he says.

". . . The Presbyterians are better. . . . [They say] 'You don't have to drink rum. God doesn't want us to drink rum. Beer makes us crazy. Cigarettes are no good. If you want to believe in the word of God, give up everything. If you get angry a lot, talk to God. If you talk every day you won't get angry any more. You won't dream a lot,' they say. 'To give it all up your heart has to be big. But when you listen to the word of God you get a little healthier. . . .'

"We don't want to pray in the church, like the priest does. We'll lose our way if we worship the saints whose images are there. We don't respect them. We respect just one, he who came to extinguish our sins on the cross. . . . That's how we want it, so we'll be well. Although the Bible is the same in both places [Catholic Action and Protestants] and I sing the same in both, it's better with the Presbyterians. We look for eternal life. We listen to the word of God. In the middle of the word of God we put together the offering, a gift to God, we call it. Then we sing. We talk to God. We don't give candles any more like the Catechists do. The Catechists still ask shamans to pray. Praying is no good because it requires rum. Whether it's a man or woman shaman, they'll scold us if we don't have rum."

After his most recent drinking relapse Ernesto joined a more fundamentalist Protestant group. Verónica wanted to stay with the Presbyterians, but Ernesto convinced her to go with him. Their daughters decided to stay with the Presbyterians. That was their right, Verónica said. Verónica and Ernesto joined the church and were baptized in the San Pedro River.

"When Ernesto enters the church the people feel happy because there's another man who has given up rum. 'Thanks to our Lord, Ernesto has come,' they say. 'Poor man,' they say. 'He's a drunk. He scolds his woman and his children. He doesn't have money. If he had money he could fix up his house. He could get electricity. It's better for him to talk to God. . . .'

"If my husband drinks rum or if he hits me after he leaves the church, then when he goes back the next time they'll look at him and say, 'You got drunk. We're going to straighten things out.' If he asks for forgiveness, they tell him to come in and learn about the word of God."

Many women convert to Protestant groups, often before their husbands do, for the alcohol-free social world these groups offer. In large part this trend seems to stem from women's pivotal role in monitoring household resources and family health. Testimonies of Protestant women in the household survey I conducted convinced me that when people do not have basics, such as food, health care, and shelter, they may join groups that show them ways to reduce their own and their children's suffering, even if this means abandoning valued traditions. Keeping their children from dying is a strong incentive for women to convert to Protestant groups. Indigenous women, who have learned not to expect help from anyone, hear that Protestants provide health care and assistance in family crises. Some women have converted because Protestants gave them patent medicines which healed them or their children, convincing them that the Protestant God can heal. Of the women I knew who had sick or dying children, most were willing to try anything to save their children from suffering. But most said they had to have their husband's permission to seek a non-traditional doctor.[6] In health care men are more conservative than women. Since rum is an integral part of healings and more men are shamans than women, men's conservative attitudes toward health seem to be aspects of their defending rum's role in traditions, their importance as shamans, and possibly their own alcohol dependence. Protestants' greater openness to non-Indigenous medicine attracts women whose husbands' conservatism and vested interests hurt them or their children. Although women put up with most forms of male dominance, over matters of health care many women resist strongly. Converting is a way to subvert men's authority.

Some women who converted before their husbands told me they did so in part to encourage their husbands to stop drinking, but once in the new religion what made them stay were new, more respectful ways of relating to fellow Pedranos and God. And they added, unless a man's heart wants to change, joining a religion will not make him stop drinking. While Traditional society gives women support if they want to leave abusive spouses, some women do not have safe places to go. Protestants may open their homes to such women.

Whether or not their husbands lead or follow them into the new religion, through converting many women acted on their own and their children's behalf. While scholars and even their own people depict peasant women as bulwarks of tradition, Pedranas demonstrate that they make swift, radical changes when they perceive a threat to what they hold dear.

Women benefit from conversion in material ways and in the short run, but some changes Protestants are making in traditional gender relations may not necessarily benefit their daughters and granddaughters in the future. In their formal roles Protestants seem to limit women's possibilities. During services women take offering on the women's side of church, one woman prays out loud, and several women sing in choruses, but no women fill cargos as deacons or pastors. Wives assist husbands who are deacons and pastors, much as couples serve traditional cargos, but women have no voice in decision making and do not represent their people in public meetings.

Protestants also make changes in courtship and marriage. They advocate shortening bride service to a few months, in contrast to the one or two years Traditionalists and Catholic Action followers favor. Protestants say that a shorter bride service enables young couples to become independent sooner and therefore able to progress faster, materially. In contrast, Traditionalists say that longer bride service enables young couples to grow slowly into manhood and womanhood within the context of extended households. Although I did not study the effects of shortened bride service, it seems possible that this and other changes toward greater independence could isolate young women from supportive relations with kin, and encourage more focus on self and less on community.

Catholic Action

> We know that struggling against alcohol doesn't solve all our problems, but it is important because when people give up rum this gives birth to *conscientización* [consciousness-raising] and organizing.
>
> From article on "alcoholism" in *Nuestra Palabra* ("Our Word"), a newsletter of ACCH (Informaciones de la Amistad Campesina Chiapaneca), a peasant organization popular among many Catholic Action followers. February 1988.

Acción Católica (Catholic Action) began in Highland Chiapas in the early 1960s under the direction of Vatican II and Bishop Samuel Ruiz García. Today over seven thousand Indigenous men and women lay leaders, assisted by nuns and priests, organize their communities into small groups which identify and study the sources of their economic exploitation and political oppression, and develop strategies to confront these.

"Don Samuel," as religious workers affectionately call him, is the spiritual leader of Catholic Action in Highland Chiapas. His followers—Catholic priests, religious and lay workers—say he is carrying the same spirit that Bartolomé de Las Casas carried almost five hundred years ago, when he recast the role of salvation from saving "heathens" to establishing social justice. As the thirty-sixth successor to Las Casas' historic See in Chiapas, Ruíz confronts more subtle, but no less oppressive, mechanisms of domination.

Not long after I arrived in Chenalhó I stayed with Antonia's parents when she and Domingo went to be confirmed by Bishop Ruíz in Yav Teklum,

From article on "alcoholism" in Nuestra Palabra, *February 1988. Illustration reads (On left) "To your health! Uuuuff! I have a cough." (On right) "To your health! Yes! It doesn't matter to us if we drink. The money is mine."*

a nearby hamlet. Knowing that Bishop Ruiz encourages fiestas, music, and expressions of strong ethnic identity in Indigenous communities, I wanted to know how he would perform the confirmation. While there are priests in Highland Chiapas who still give the Mass with their backs to parishioners, Antonia said that Bishop Ruiz not only faced them, but didn't perform the Mass in the church. So many Pedranos had come to Yav Teklum to be confirmed that they spilled out of the church onto the road leading out of the village. Bishop Ruiz conducted the Mass outside, in front of the church, wearing traditional Pedrano clothing.

The night of the confirmation Antonia and Domingo stayed in Yav Teklum, Antonia in one house with women, Domingo in another with men. Before going to sleep they sang songs. I had heard these songs many nights and mornings around their fire. Later I heard Verónica's daughters singing similar songs around their fire. Singing and playing instruments together is an important part of accepting any new religion in Highland Chiapas.

Laying the groundwork for Catholic Action in Latin America in the 1950s, liberation theologians and practitioners realized that people are moved as much by pleasure as by duty. Although at first they were worried about the focus on saints and rituals in native communities and the lack of concern for the ethical demands of love (Berryman 1987: 69), as their understanding of poor people's lives deepened, they began to see popular religion as understandable responses to poverty and domination.

Liberation theologians worked out their ideas during the 1960s and 1970s while revolution spread throughout Latin America. Amidst death and destruction liberation theologians developed a theology of life, as opposed to a theology of death, which they said capitalism embodied (ibid.: 102). Liberation theologians pointed to the hypocrisy of the United States' selecting torture and murder as the only worthy human rights issues, while most Latin Americans suffered the constant abuses of hunger, unemployment, and inadequate shelter.

Catholic Action religious workers say they "accompany" Indigenous people in their struggle rather than direct them. Nuns and priests find in native practices values and practices that they hold dear, for example patience, faith, and sacrifice. They study native languages and try to break down the traditionally hierarchical relationships between Indigenous people and religious workers.

In classes and meetings Catholic Action workers lead followers to see Jesus Christ as another powerful invisible being to whom they can pray for guidance and whose life they can study for wisdom about their struggle for justice. Catechists relate events in Jesus' life to their people's history, as they do their ancestors' stories to their memories. They worry less about chronology and more about understanding. Treating Jesus' parables and stories like signs and symbols from their ancestors, they learn to see Jesus' love and commitment as they do the enduring support they receive from totil me'il. For example, in a meeting in which Catechists identified cooperación as their most pressing problem, the sisters suggested they study the following verse (1 Corinthians 1:10):

> Now I beseech you, brethren, by the name of our Lord Jesus Christ,
> that ye all speak the same thing, and that there be no divisions
> among you, but that ye be perfectly joined together in the same
> mind and in the same judgement.

After one of the Catechists read the verse aloud, people began to offer their analyses. The sisters asked, "What does God's word say to us? What does God want us to do? How can this help us deal with our community problems?" One of the sisters asked the Catechists what they had in common with Traditionalists and Protestants. Various men offered language, clothing, etc. Eventually a man said that they were all campesinos, that they all raised their own food. One of the sisters suggested that although Pedranos were having trouble resolving their religious differences, they could work together on the premise that they are all poor campesinos.

Meanwhile, each group could be strong in its own faith and respect the other groups' faith since, until all Pedranos are free of oppression, none are.

In case of doubts or questions the Catechists or sisters might go back to the text, then back again to Pedranos' experience. Liberation theologians call this analytical method the "hermeneutic circle" (ibid.: 61).

Like anthropologists who speak of "dialoguing" with communities they study, liberation theologians speak of "dialoguing with the poor." Before Catholic Action, priests, nuns, and Indigenous people did not engage in any dialogue. In fact, in a particular ritual each group might be thinking something quite different. To a great extent Indigenous people are still thinking differently than priests in Highland Chiapas, but they have begun to dialogue with priests and Catholic sisters, whom they call "Madres" (Mothers).

Madres seem more successful than priests in listening to Indigenous people and in breaking down the hierarchy of the Catholic church. Although based in San Cristóbal, Madres spend weeks at a time in Indigenous communities meeting with lay workers to discuss community concerns. The times I saw Madres at work in Catechist meetings, remote hospitals, and Guatemalan refugee camps, I saw them listen carefully to Indigenous people's concerns and ideas. They seemed committed to helping them probe the wisdom their people already have. When priests cannot make it to meetings, Madres are there, to talk about whatever problems people might have. Madres put women's agenda within an overall economic and political liberation context, much as they do within their own religious communities. In their own communities Madres may have developed a more feminist critique of male dominance, but in their work with Indigenous people they do not address more radical implications of feminist theology. They do however confront the grosser manifestations of machismo and advocate greater respect for women in Indigenous communities and in the larger society. For example, at a planning meeting for a workshop to train Indigenous men in health care, some men brought up the problem of finding someone to cook for them while they were in San Cristóbal for the training. One of the Madres suggested they start learning how to cook their own food. While on the subject the Madres told all men present that when they come home from the milpa, before resting it would be a good idea to see if their wives need help with housework or child care, as their wives have also been working all day.

Although Pedranos know that Madres have not borne children and do not have husbands, they seem to have more confidence in the Madres' than the priests' capacity to understand their problems. Catholic Action followers see Madres as caring people, always ready to help them or their children. In their teams these women share work responsibilities like kinswomen in Pedrano households. Their relationships with priests are complementary, much like relationships between Pedrano spouses. Some Pedranos speculate that priests and sisters have sexual relationships. Although the loving attitude that Madres take with Pedranos is maternal in tone, generally, they do not look down on them; from the interactions I observed they treat Pedranos as intelligent people with valuable traditions meriting respect, and problems deserving immediate attention.

Besides the Madres, Pedranos also have close relations with Padre Miguel, the priest in Chenalhó. Making up my fieldwork schedule, I had planned to talk to Padre Miguel during my first month. Before meeting Antonia I lacked confidence that I could find a way into Pedranos' lives and views without help from some non-Pedrano go-betweens. Fortunately, I did not talk to Padre Miguel until after I had started learning from Pedranos. From Pedranos I learned that they had developed a sound critique of rum, based on their own and their ancestors' ideas, ideas they had learned from studying Christ's life, and from experiences of other townships with prohibition. As it turned out I began to rely so fully on Pedranos' analyses that I did not speak with Padre Miguel or other non-Indigenous people in depth about their views. From brief conversations with Padre Miguel I understood that he considered education the only effective way to deal with rum, and he believed that having strong families, Pedranos had the resources to handle it this way. I agreed with Padre Miguel on one level, but on another level Pedranos seemed to be telling me that education wasn't strong enough to counteract the appeal of rum. As one Catechist put it,

"Padre Miguel says if Satan enters one's soul a person will commit sins, with or without rum. It's true what he says, but maybe he thinks when we criticize rum that we think rum is the only evil thing. The Padre can't know how we think. He doesn't have a wife or children. He doesn't work the land. He can't know how campesinos like us live. He can't know how a woman suffers when her husband drinks too much and hits her and yells at her. The issue for us when we criticize rum is exploitation and injustice toward women. Everyone knows women and children who suffer from hunger, lack of clothing, or medicine because their husbands or fathers drink too much and don't handle their money right. Just down the road there's a woman who doesn't have any clothes and other things she needs because her husband drinks too much."

What seems to distance many Pedranas from Padre Miguel is not so much his important position and gender, but his unmarried status and his acceptance of drinking. Although Padre Miguel is a godfather to some Pedrano children, he is not a true father and a husband. Pedranos told me,

"Priests don't work the land and don't have families to support. They eat good meals and can even get drunk, without anyone telling them that they shouldn't. They have cars and can take off to faraway places for months at a time." They probably said the same things about me, and I had not shown a shred of the commitment to them that Padre Miguel had. At first I felt bad for Padre Miguel, since he was one of the first people who had supported Pedranos in their struggles for social justice. A truer man of God I had never seen, I told myself. But the facts remained. Padre Miguel was not a campesino, nor a family man.

At one of the Cathechist meetings in 1987 when rum was a central concern, Cathechists reported that Padre Miguel advised them not to get embroiled in the question of prohibition. Padre Miguel's words on this occasion did not fit with what Catechists had heard about the consequences of heavy drinking in their classes, or what they had seen with their own eyes. One man replied,

"Well, that's fine, Padre Miguel. But then why do you give us courses in rum, if afterwards you say that it's no good for us to get involved in controlling rum? You taught us about all aspects of rum in the courses. But now that we are publicizing our position, you say that it's not good to get involved. Why did you tell us this about rum in the course if you thought that we shouldn't get involved? That's just games."

Catechists don't need Padre Miguel's permission to conduct their affairs the way they see fit, but they would like his blessing. They recognize that he has sacrificed dearly on their behalf and that he loves their land and traditions. Given increasing conflict between religious groups, Catechists desire consensus within their own group, to be united in their hearts.

Followers of Catholic Action struggle to reconcile the contradictions they find between the church's teaching and their own experience. Antonia stressed that, although it is only her opinion, she thinks Pedranos need the Bible in addition to their traditions because they have lost some of the faith their ancestors had. Long ago the ancestors had strong ideas about God that, like the Bible, taught their people how to live in all times. But over the years Pedranos failed to remember the ancestors' stories and songs, and now they no longer know how to go on in a "good way."

One day Antonia looked up from her weaving and broached the subject of the Padre and prohibition.

"Why doesn't Padre Miguel let us try to prohibit rum, and then we'll deal with the problems as they come up? We don't have to end up like Mitontik. One reason they still drink a lot in Mitontik is because Chamula is near by and they can easily get rum there. In Chenalhó it's much harder to get rum when one runs out."

Prohibition appeals to Catholic Action followers, who see rum sales and consumption as part of an overall economic system which exploits and divides them. A February 14, 1988, issue of "Nuestra Palabra" listed conflict over alcohol as one of several related issues facing campesinos. Other issues included: lack of land, unjust wages, low price of campesinos' production, high price of factory merchandise, takeovers of presidencies, assassinations of fellow campesinos, and problems of Guatemalan refugees. Catholic Action followers do not advocate prohibition for narrowly moralistic reasons. They have looked at power relations in their communities and have decided that rum sellers and political leaders only care about what will make them rich and powerful, not what will benefit campesinos. For Catholic Action followers, legislation directed toward "prohibition as temperance"[7] would be a statement to powerful outsiders that Pedranos control their own affairs.

Catholic Action, with its social action agenda yet respect for traditional dialectical notions of Gods and rum, seems to appeal to Pedranos who are willing to live with contradiction and difference. Followers must balance independent thinking with the body of knowledge their ancestors passed on. For guidance they have their beloved saints, and Jesus, who suffered for the world and seems to understand their suffering in not such a different time and place (Berryman 1987).

Protestants generally advocate personal solutions to "the alcohol problem," saying that if one listens to the word of God one will no longer want to drink. Protestants do not approve of organizing against rum as Catholic Action followers have, i.e., in meetings and through legislation. But some Protestants support Catholic Action positions, and within their communities Protestants have de facto prohibition. In 1988 while they were allied with teachers, who are often heavy drinkers, Protestants no doubt felt restricted in openly supporting prohibition.

While individuals have tools to heal themselves of problem drinking, as a group Pedranos disagree on the tools or structures with which to heal the deep wounds social and economic inequality have inflicted. But despite their differences, Pedranos have been able to live relatively peacefully.[8]

Many factors seem to facilitate tolerance of dissension and a democratic attitude in Chenalhó. Due in part to Ladino presence in the cabecera, which has made it as much an economic as a spiritual center, spiritual power seems to be more decentralized in Chenalhó than it is in Chamula, where the cabecera has no Ladinos and the church is a powerful unifying symbol. Pedranos identify strongly with their hamlets and colonies. Many hamlets have their own Catholic and Protestant chapels as well as schools. In contrast to Chamulas and Zinacantecos, Pedranos have not developed a powerful cadre of leading political figures. Pedranos tend to choose their leaders for humility. During the time I was in Chenalhó Pedranos left decisions over issues like rum control and cooperación "pending," that is they kept analyzing them. They left room for Protestants to say "Only God can make us cooperate," and for Traditionalists to say "Only God can take rum away." In similar situations, powerful leaders in Chamula and Zinacantán might have forced a decision on both rum sales and cooperación, irrespective of God's wishes.

11 "Today we say: Enough!"[1]
New Voices, New Collective Action

"I'm telling the truth; you have no shame, you rat," one woman said. "It's your fault that my husband and I are separated," another woman said.

"Look, my son hit me. My son gets drunk, too. It's your fault that my son and my husband hit me. You're to blame! You're nice and fat because your stomach is full of shit. But it's from my money that you're fat, from my son's and my husband's sweat. I haven't been able to buy any clothes. I haven't been able to buy our food. I'm the one who has to buy our food when they're passing their drinks around. How can I pay for clothes? How can I pay for the things we need?"

Two women speaking out at a meeting on rum
in the community Yav Teklum, 1988

For the first time in Pedrano memory women are speaking in public forums about their people's problems. The women who took the microphone at the large gathering in Yav Teklum did not mince words. Before the rum sellers, the town officials, and family and friends they blamed rum sellers and corrupt officials for their suffering.

Some men reportedly cringed at the women's words. These were strong words, and rum sellers were known to become angry and sometimes retaliatory when their interests were thwarted. But in part through women's testimonies and analyses, many hamlets throughout Chenalhó legislated stricter controls for alcohol sales and use. Several hamlets restricted permission to sell rum to leaders of religious fiestas, enabling them to raise the money needed to buy supplies their cargos required. Others restricted rum sales to weekends and certain hours, and some predominantly Protestant hamlets went dry.[2]

Chamula women vendors selling weavings in front of the former Convent of Santo Domingo, San Cristóbal de Las Casas.

After I heard about the meeting in Yav Teklum I tried to find the women who had spoken there. Due to various obstacles, I never interviewed a woman from the Yav Teklum group. But I did interview one woman from another hamlet who had organized women a couple of years before. Petra was a follower of Catholic Action at the time she organized women to speak out about drinking problems. We talked one day after service in the Catholic chapel in her hamlet.

"In the past I had a lot of problems. My husband drank a lot. It was very difficult when my husband drank. He spent all our money. I couldn't buy our clothes or food. That's why I started to organize the women.

"I got ten or fifteen women together. The women accepted my idea. We talked with the agente in our hamlet.

"'If you want, we can prohibit rum. Because we're suffering. Our husbands get drunk,' I told him.

"'I don't know,' the agente said.

"'But why don't you know? It's your responsibility to settle problems,' I said.

"'I don't know, I don't know how to justify it.'

"'Why do we want to prohibit rum? It's because it's very bad when my husband drinks a lot. Because he hits me and yells at me and does all kinds of bad things. That's the way it is with all the women; they're suffering. Their husbands hit them. That's why rum isn't any good.'

"Although we women got together, we couldn't win. The agente didn't pay any attention to what we said, and rum wasn't prohibited. We felt like prohibiting rum. We could have. But that's what happened at that time.

"Later my husband got a little bit of reason back and he gave up rum. That was about four years ago. But other women are still suffering.

"'Why can't we try another time to prohibit rum?' the women asked me. 'Let's talk to the agente. . . .'

"'We'll go and talk to the president,' the agente said.

"But it never happened that we went to talk to the president. And again the agente didn't pay any attention.

"That's how it ended up, because I don't know how to speak Spanish. If I had known how to speak Spanish, I could have gone to talk to the governor. . . .

". . . That's why we have problems with rum. Rum is still available. I want it to be prohibited. But the agentes here are very stubborn. Half want to prohibit rum, half don't want to. . . . We don't know how to be free. We're blocked."

Women's participation in the prohibition movement in Chenalhó is an important aspect of their experience with changes in drinking and gender relations. These incipient efforts seem to have much in common with women's experiences in prohibition movements in other small-scale homogeneous societies. In Truk, where rapid change is also occurring, women have been organizing since the 1970s to control alcohol sales and use (Marshall and Marshall 1990). Trukese women learned their organizing skills in Protestant churches. In Chenalhó women are learning organizing skills in Catholic Action. In Catholic Action meetings women learn that alcohol is not the cause of all their problems, but they see efforts to control its use as a starting point for reevaluating traditions and relationships.

Antonia and the women who spoke up at Yav Teklum are making connections between their personal troubles and social issues and developing a more assertive and independent interpersonal style in the process. Some young women take well to this style, and in so doing find a personal voice. But they also risk individuating themselves from fellow Pedranos, a risk many Pedranos find too frightening to face. Women who follow Catholic Action walk an especially difficult path. Women hold ritual cargos, participate in decision making, and speak in services. At each meeting a man and woman, not married to each other, co-facilitate discussions. These new public roles for women have led to gossip and criticism. Critics say that working relationships between men and women who are not related only lead to promiscuity or adulterous liaisons.

The last year of my fieldwork in Chenalhó, 1988, Antonia dubbed the year of much rain and community problems. Antonia was concerned that even God might think her proud for confronting problems among fellow Pedranos, that perhaps a good Pedrana would not stir up trouble. But her Catechist training had encouraged her to confront exploitation and injustice, and she was not going to back down now. Summing up the conflict she confronted during this time, Antonia said,

"For example, if I want to put behind me something that's not so good about our traditions, the Traditionalists say, 'What she's doing is no good.' But if I want to act on something good in the traditions the religious ones will say, 'Ah, she's still doing things according to the traditions. She doesn't believe in the word of God.' This is how the two ways collide."

Indigenous women in Highland Chiapas have not had a voice in the public arena since before the Spanish invasion. Beginning in the 1970s Catholic Action and the cooperative movement have given women a context in which to speak out about domestic concerns, such as health, shelter, and compulsive drinking. Many Indigenous women are speaking out for the first time, moving out of their confinement in the more private sphere of the household. But like Latin American women of all classes and races, most Indigenous women in Highland Chiapas reject movements to organize that threaten their identities as mothers and wives (Safa 1988).

Women seem to be gaining strength to speak from the pivotal positions they occupy, in their households as well as in traditional ideology. From within the context of their household-based roles, and prescribed rules about appropriate behavior and men's and women's responsibilities to each other, Pedranas know when someone is not doing his or her part. When their husbands are pulling their weight, despite the limitations patriarchy places on them, Pedranas seem content with their positions and reluctant to lose the complementary relations through which they and their husbands support their families and their Gods. But when drinking keeps their husbands from doing their part, Pedranas are not so ready to accept the restrictions their patriarchal society places on them. Pedranas see how alcohol tends to dissolve the self-restraints a good Pedrano husband or father has internalized and erodes his sense of responsibility. As women say, "Alcohol makes people crazy." Unlike American women who are often confused about their duties and responsibilities and are ready to blame themselves when things fall apart, Pedranas know who is to blame when they have problems—heavy drinkers (usually husbands, fathers, and stepfathers) and rum sellers. The former they do not say are bad people, just temporarily out of balance, crazy. The latter, however, they equate with the Devil himself.[3]

Pedranos justify women's role in controlling rum because of their household-based authority. However, while these roles give women authority to speak out about threats to household functioning, something besides their economic roles also supports their right to speak. Important symbolic associations Traditional Pedranos make between women, Earth, fertility, coldness, Moon/Mother of the Sky, water, lakes, and the number three may be influencing Traditionalists to accept women's participation in public decisions about rum.

Women's roles as mothers and perpetuators of the group seem to be as strong today as they have ever been in Indigenous communities in Highland Chiapas. Summarizing women's roles in seventeenth and eighteenth century revitalization movements and their continued importance in symbolizing essential "Chamulaness," Rosenbaum (1993) demonstrates the importance of the association Chamulas make between women and the earth, personified in Earth Lord's Daughter. To Chamulas, yajval banumil represents wealth and well-being (ibid.: 185). Being cold and close to the cold earth, women have power to subdue or counteract hot things, such as rum.

Pedranos also associate women with Moon, water, and lakes. In dreams and visions the Mother of the Sky often reminds Pedranos about the basics of life, e.g., not to substitute rum for food and "good drinks." In the recent revitalization movement in which Traditional Pedranos associated the formation of a lake with the arrival of the Mother of the Sky, women had important roles in the fiesta in her honor. Seeing the Mother of the Sky in the form of a lake, Pedranos could have interpreted her coming to be an assertion that water is prior to everything else, including rum. When Pedranos offer rum to request a favor they often say, "Take my water." (Zinacantecos say "Take my cold water," Laughlin, personal communication.) But interpreting the Mother of the Sky as a God of all times, Ruíz Paloma said that she came to urge Pedranos to use sodas, tastier than water and less damaging than rum. While it seems that she could have just as well told Pedranos to use chicha, a more traditional drink than sodas, Ruíz reported that she wanted Pedranos to offer her soda, slightly more expensive than chicha, and therefore closer to rum in the weight of sacrifice required to provide it. By the 1970s soda was becoming a functional equivalent of rum in many communities in Highland Chiapas.

Today in Chenalhó three, not four (men's number), comes up frequently in Traditional beliefs and in strategies to control rum. For example, the symbolic core of households is the hearth and the three stones that create it. Here women transform corn into tortillas, through which all Pedranos receive physical and spiritual nourishment. Whether in their roles as household managers, ritual specialists, or emissaries of the Mother of the Sky, women repeatedly maintain that rum is not food, that one cannot expect it to do what food does, i.e., feed the personal and collective soul. In their adherence to traditions Pedranas seem to be saying that one cannot let rum be a substitute for all that Pedranos hold dear, including their households, communities, and Gods. Other associations with the number three include the three visitation dreams required for a person to become a shaman, and the three cup limit in ritual drinking settings. In the latter instance, filling oneself with three cups of rum seems to bring one to a threshold. At this point one is heated enough to unite with other people and the Gods. Those who go beyond this threshold may not go out of bounds with their drinking, but they cannot get any closer to each other and their Gods than they were at the three cup point. In terms of strategies to control rum, Pedranos have created several customary patterns, including drinking only three times a year at the three major fiestas.

My analysis of women's symbolic power and importance in Chenalhó parallels Rosenbaum's findings for Chamula women. Rosenbaum locates Chamula women's power in a "combination of their symbolic endowment as the regenerative power of the Earth and the social group, their role as exemplars of traditional culture, and their position as central actors in the community's structures of prestige and power" (ibid.: 186). Rosenbaum's study of Chamula and mine of Chenalhó demonstrate the important roles women play in articulating spiritual and worldly realms, as well as in economic relations. Our studies are similar to findings about women in other non-Western societies (e.g., Bell 1983 on Aboriginal women). Aboriginal women showed Bell that they share guardianship of religious law with their kinsmen. In their separate rituals focused on love, land, and health, women help people and land to "grow up" and stay in harmony together.

In addition to symbolic areas of power, women's growing participation in the cash economy and greater involvement in the external labor market is giving them leverage in their communities. Men know that they need their wives' contributions to support their households, and that their wives do not have to put up indefinitely with unjust treatment. However, changes in men's productive roles, including their decreasing capacity to support their families off the land and their increasing dependence on wage labor, seem to offset benefits for women. Men often become jealous of their wives' productive capacity and more public role in community affairs.

On a return trip to Chiapas in 1989, an unannounced visit I made to Antonia and Domingo gave me some insight into tensions that Antonia's increasing economic importance to their family through her weaving is creating in their household. I realized immediately upon arriving that I was interrupting an argument. Antonia's agitated movements, Domingo's lowered head, created a tension I wasn't used to feeling in their home. When I asked what was wrong, Antonia explained that the president of Chenalhó had asked her to help unify the cooperatives, but she was too busy to take on more responsibilities and Domingo resented her increasing involvement outside of their home. Antonia was frustrated because she could not move on in her life without an agreement with Domingo about their respective responsibilities. To Antonia's relief, she and Domingo began to work out an agreement the day the president of Chenalhó came to find Antonia to take her to San Cristóbal to meet with a lawyer to discuss unifying the cooperatives. Domingo had to concede that Antonia's cargo was as important to their survival, possibly more important, than his cargo as a Catechist. Over the years Domingo has become a strong supporter of Antonia in her role as a cooperative leader.[4]

In addition to weaving cooperatives, there is also a writers' cooperative, Sna Jtz'ibajom, in San Cristóbal de Las Casas. Three of its ten members are women (Laughlin 1991). Two of the women, Petu' Krus Krus from Zinacantán and Chavela Jvaris Ch'ix from Aguacatenango, have become the first Indigenous woman playwrights of Mexico. While the men's works focus on traditional folk tales, the women's dramas depict contemporary life.

The last scene of Jvaris Ch'ix' play treats alcoholism, and Krus Krus' play is about the story of a young woman whose father dies of drinking and whose stepfather intimidates her until she kills him.

Protestant Chamula women, expelled from their ancestral lands, have created informal support groups in the sixteen settlements making up the *cinturón de miseria* (belt of misery) around San Cristóbal. In these groups women strategize better ways to sell their crafts to tourists and gain the economic independence which enables them to live apart from abusive or irresponsible husbands (O'Brian 1994; Sullivan 1992). Sullivan (ibid.: 39) reports that while men welcome their wives' incomes, they may resent their wives' pressures on them to contribute financially and to take over more household work. Some husbands relapse into drinking, renounce their new religion, and return to Chamula. Nevertheless, Sullivan argues that Chamula women vendors are proud of their ethnic roots at the same time as they pick and choose among aspects of Ladino culture (ibid.).

Recently Indigenous women migrants from various townships have found common cause with Ladinas in organizations headquartered in San Cristóbal. One organization, El Grupo de Mujeres de San Cristóbal (The Women's Group of San Cristóbal), started in 1989, focuses on reducing violence against women. The group provides legal assistance, medical aid, and emotional support to women, and attempts to raise women's awareness of their rights and their communities' awareness of their needs.

While membership in cooperatives or informal support groups brings more money into women's families and gives them a framework in which to organize together and with their kinsmen, participation also brings problems and risks. The most pressing problems cooperative members face are being unable to rely upon a steady income, and risking envy from their neighbors and tension in their households. As Antonia's and Domingo's struggle illustrates, marital tension is an inevitable consequence at this time. Men and women are no longer clear about what others expect of them. Women, like Antonia and Petu', are breaking new ground. The changes in their lives that collective work is bringing require them to carefully balance their new economic independence and broader influence with traditional expectations about women. Antonia may not be so willing to comply with traditional expectations if Domingo resents or challenges her new roles. Petu' has already stood up against her family's accusations that she is a prostitute. Ironically she states, "It is more acceptable for me to be a servant than an actress" (Laughlin 1991: 89). In Chamula, where women have been economically independent for a longer time, some couples are making the kinds of adjustments necessary to keep their unions complementary, and therefore more or less traditional. When women first be-

came involved in sales to tourists, their husbands accused them of being
"women of the street," or destroyed their work (Komes Peres 1990). As
women's financial contributions became more important to family survival
and as more women became involved in artisan production, couples began
to resolve some of their conflicts. For example, Chamula men now take a
more active role by acting as Spanish-speaking "go-betweens" and security guards for their wives on trips to San Cristóbal, and they carry their
wives' products with them to sell when they go looking for work (Rus
1990). However, in Amatenango del Valle, although men and women
worked out similar compromises, as women replaced men in the market
men became fearful and resorted to violent repression (Nash 1993).[5]

Speaking in public and taking leadership roles in Latin American
communities requires courage. Political leaders often use women for their
own purposes, pulling them out of traditional roles and then plunking
them back into them at a whim, or making promises that they don't keep,
just to placate women. However, township-wide recognition of Antonia's
efforts to represent women weavers, and the Chiapas government's decision to award the Chiapas prize for literature in 1992 to an Indigenous
man and woman, the woman being Petu', demonstrate how recognition of
women's concerns by political leaders on township and state levels can le-
gitimate Indigenous women in the eyes of their husbands, as well as native
culture in the eyes of outsiders.

While women's growing independence is creating tension for Pedranos, Antonia and others continually reminded me that the most pressing
issues for Indigenous men and women continue to be grinding poverty
and assaults on native traditions. Until recent times Pedranos have preferred to pull together in household units, strengthening kinship relations
and collective values in their efforts to deal with these problems. Anyone
who chose to work independently was an anomaly and a threat to the tenuous balance. Women who go it alone have posed a greater threat than
men, as women's household-based work has usually kept them closer to
home, and in touch with their household needs and resources. Men, who
often have to work away from home to supplement the family's income,
have had a lot invested in controlling women's movement.[6]

My observations and feelings about Pedranas' lives and what scholars
have written about women in Mesoamerica suggest redefining concepts
like "patriarchy" and "oppression" in terms relevant to Indigenous women's
lives. Although no patriarchy allows women to act freely, the kind of patriarchy I saw in Chenalhó makes men and women partners in most aspects of life, not just those necessary for survival. Other researchers in

Mesoamerican communities have noted a similar stress on the importance of women's work and interdependence between the sexes in daily life. Where before researchers studying Mesoamerican societies had seen only male dominance (e.g., see Rothstein 1983, for discussion of Lewis' research in Tepotzlán, 1963, and Beals' research in Cherán 1946), some have seen cooperation between the sexes (e.g., Elmendorf 1976; Rosenbaum 1993; Rothstein 1983) and a "responsible" patriarchy in which, although men have privileges, they value strong family bonds and providing for their wives and children (Maynard 1963).

At the same time as women assert their importance in Highland Chiapas patriarchies, men perpetuate symbolic and social constructs which undermine women's power and autonomy by depicting them as highly charged sexual beings needing to be either controlled or protected (Rosenbaum 1993). Restrictions on women's freedom, such as arranged marriages, punishment for premarital sex, illegitimacy, or adultery do suggest that women have less domestic power and autonomy than men, however Bossen (1983) argues that some restrictions, like arranged marriages, affect boys as well, and that life-cycle changes also shape restrictions for both sexes.[7]

While recognition of women's strengths and importance has begun, researchers coming from Western societies in which addictions have torn the fabric of interpersonal relations and in which media refer to relations between men and women as "the battle between the sexes," are still struggling to balance the strengths and weaknesses of different gender systems and to conceptualize them from within the experience of the women and men who create them. In their efforts to understand interdependence in marital unions in subsistence economies, early feminist ethnographers developed a "separate spheres" framework through which they portrayed women enjoying relative equality with men by ruling the domestic realm (e.g., Chiñas 1973). Some scholars suggest that Latin American women place themselves in this sphere to benefit from the positive association between women's subordinate position and the Virgin Mary's suffering. Critics of this argument say that combining isolation within the domestic sphere with the emulation of the Virgin rationalizes women's powerlessness as it condones men's superiority (Nash 1989, cited in Ehlers 1991: 3).

The "separate spheres" framework, and the complementary ideal that Indigenous peoples such as Pedranos hold, do encourage respect for women's roles and traditional values. However, these ideas risk marginalizing women in analyses of social relations (Rapp 1979). They also risk obscuring how men keep women out of public office or unfairly punish single women or women who don't fit into traditional roles, like Angélika's daughters. When Pedranas decide not to marry, their contributions to family and community, albeit complementary in many respects, do not gain them the respect that married women receive. In fact these women may become fair game for both Ladinos and Indigenous men. However, in another way complementarity between the sexes may be an accommodation Pedranos have made to encroaching machismo. Holding forth this ideal of gender relations seems to have allowed Pedranos to continue asserting traditional ideas of relative equality in all relations, even though women were not equal in all respects to men in Maya state societies and became subordinated to men as time went on.

While men have used complementarity to defend their interests, asserting its importance can also give women power. For example, when complementarity breaks down in the marriage bond, as when men drink too much, everyone is aware of what has happened and women are justified in leaving husbands and in depriving them of their share of household resources. For both men and women in Chenalhó, complementarity continues to be a measuring stick of relationships.

Increasing independence of both sexes is becoming an issue for Pedranos, as for traditional societies undergoing modernization worldwide. In Chenalhó more and more young people are leaving their communities in search of education and work. More women are becoming sole supports of themselves and their children by selling artisan and agricultural products. Young, single women stand at the center of these changes. Their kin, their parents, and Ladinos often prevent them from acting freely. From Ladino school administrators to parents, to daughters, everyone has different ideas on how young women should behave. Recently a trend not to marry at all or delay marriage is evident in communities closer to San Cristóbal or the Pan-American Highway (Collier 1990; Nash 1993). By 1989 Pedranos were noting a trend in Chenalhó for couples who eloped to delay a visit to the girl's parents until they had seen the agente. The agente negotiated a bride price acceptable to the girl's parents, dismissing the many visits and gifts of food, rum, and sodas which bind two families together and create a network of support for young couples. This network has been especially important to young women when their husbands have not treated them well. Another important catalyst for change has been paving the thirty-seven-kilometer-long dirt road between Chenalhó and San Cristóbal. Beginning in 1992, young Pedranos have been able to go to San Cristóbal and return easily in one day (if they have the bus fare), thus increasing their awareness of options for staying single and living in Ladino society.

While schooling can give girls opportunities to develop themselves in new ways, increasing their status and power, leaving their families to enter high school in Chenalhó or San Cristóbal often means that girls must work as servants in Ladinos' homes to pay their room, board, and school expenses. Although many Ladinos treat young servants well, others exploit them and treat them cruelly. Watching young Pedranas look for work, schooling, or relationships in San Cristóbal, I felt torn. It seems that this generation of young women will have to struggle to keep open a window of hope for greater justice and equality, while finding ways to defend themselves against backlash from both Ladinos and Indigenous men.[8]

Although life will continue to be hard for Pedranas, I do not think that Pedranas would say the most important thing about their lives is that they are oppressed by men. Admittedly, strategies such as Angélika and her daughters have adopted are ways of coping that enable them to live at the boundary between two social orders, often unappreciated and disrespected. Yet, during my time in Chenalhó, Pedranas taught me to take women's concerns out of a Western framework of individual rights and put them into their framework of community and cultural survival.

Throughout this book I have stressed the rewards of women's participation in the collective experience of their culture, because I believe that Pedranas are integrated into a whole, with an economic and spiritual base, which the "developed" world's focus on individual rights can't replace. In doing so I don't want to condone or minimize the abuse women suffer and have suffered at the hands of their kinsmen, as well as Ladinos. The question I would pose is: Can Pedranas "raise their consciousness" of their own oppression and work to end it in a way that does not entail a move toward individual rights and an end to their communal traditions?[9]

12 Conclusion

... Tarova lifting her face uncertainly toward me, stood for the enduring debt that I would take away, the knowledge which was impossible to share, that between those mountains, among the grasses of the valley, and under the bright envelopment of this sky I had felt a sudden and interior flowering like the compensation of grace, absolving me of my inadequacies and renewing my own existence in the lives of others.

Kenneth Read on fieldwork with Gahukus
in New Guinea (1965: 210–211)

Over the year and a half I was in Chenalhó, Pedranos opened me up to new understandings of community and drinking, much as Gahukus awakened Kenneth Read. Such is our privilege as anthropologists to be reborn in the lives of others.

Doing fieldwork in Chenalhó I came to understand Pedranos' ideas about community and drinking from within the context of their rituals. In both public and household rituals Pedranos convey their faith that the universe constantly renews itself. When Shamans ask "flowery God" to send the drops (blood/water/rum/healing power) from his hands and feet to their people, they evoke Sun's journey of renewal via the blood (sap) of the World Tree to the underworld and back. Symbols women weave into ritual and daily clothing perpetuate their ancestors' belief in a fruitful universe while they make of their own and others' bodies a universe in flower (Morris 1988).

From this symbolic perspective, ritual drinking to intoxication, but not to the point of passing out, appeared to me as one way Pedranos try to connect an interior opening-up within themselves to an exterior flowering in the universe. Drinking in service to their Gods empowers individual drinkers, unites the group, and carries on ancestral values and beliefs.

To understand a different way of living, I tried to see drinking from this traditional perspective. I felt that I could not do otherwise, so strong was my sense that in the respectful and tender codes guiding relations between people and their Gods, Pedranos have a foundation for a well-balanced society.

In households unaffected by problem drinking, I was impressed by the way Pedranos express their dependence on each other. Beyond fulfilling work obligations, family members laugh often, touch unintentionally, and take great comfort in being together. In the public realm Pedranos demonstrate their difference from more individually oriented peoples through focusing on the aspect of their lives that has distinguished them as distinct peoples—their public rituals. In these rituals I saw Pedranos perpetuate values and a learning experience different from that of Ladinos and Americans. Through the hard work of memorizing petitions and prayers and in carrying out time-honored traditions, cargo holders demonstrate their talents and worth to themselves, their Gods, other Pedranos, and outsiders.

While I felt obligated to understand the sacred foundation Pedrano elders have laid, I also saw much casual drinking and disregard for traditions among young men and some young women. Pedranos' rituals of renewal demand obedience to strict rules and a commitment to the group. Elders have been able to make their rituals with alcohol work for them because they have integrated these rituals into a whole that sustains their people and that they in turn sustain though ritual obligations. Pedrano elders still work tirelessly to sustain their vision of wholeness, but for centuries ritual supports alone have not been enough to keep problem drinking at bay. Deepening economic inequalities involving alcohol as a medium of exploitation, and the rapid pace of social change in the Highlands, put more and more men and women of all ages and traditions at risk for dependency on alcohol. Evaluating gender relations and alcohol's contradictory roles in Chenalhó, I do not want to ignore the historical position of Pedranos in the broader society and how drinking within the framework of fiestas may defend compulsive behaviors and privileged positions. On the negative side, commitment to traditions may be a blind adherence to a way of doing things that has lost its meaning and destroys people. From this perspective, the association of rum with God's flowery hands, face, and feet, and dreams in which the Mother of the Sky forbids a person to stop drinking, are elegant forms of denial or accommodation which enable Pedranos to live with some measure of dignity, yet numb themselves to painful truths.

In view of rum's contradictions, Pedranos have taken different perspectives. Some Pedranos focus on rum's sacred role, its connection to God. They hold tenaciously to the view that rum and chicha are integral to communal rituals. Others, especially women and Protestants, focus on rum's bad side, saying it comes from the Devil. They report that drunk husbands and parents beat women and children and spend precious money on rum. Even elders who respect rum's ritual role say that their ancestors didn't drink to the point of passing out when they conducted rituals, and that they didn't tolerate violence or disrespect. Elders in Highland Guatemalan communities also report that their ancestors believed passing out in rituals was disrespectful to the Gods (Victor Montejo, personal communication). Besides problems resulting from excessive drinking in fiestas, most Pedranos say it is not good that more young men and women are drinking just for pleasure, not with their parents in household or communal rituals. And everyone knows someone who drinks too much, so that it causes him or her physical harm.

Conversion to Protestant groups, and to some extent involvement in Catholic Action, provide social worlds without alcohol, in effect new social identities. However, Traditionalists say that what is wrong with Protestants and Catholic Action members is that they don't follow the path the ancestors walked. Specifically this means that Protestants no longer serve ritual cargos; they no longer visit sacred places in the township to leave offerings of rum to the earth; they no longer garnish graves with yellow marigolds on the Day of the Dead; nor decorate altars with candles, flowers, meat, and tamales. Rather than dedicate themselves to renewal on Earth, Traditionalists say that Protestants wait for rebirth in heaven. However, perhaps in part to retain a connection to the idea of renewal, some older Protestants have transferred Traditional rituals to Protestant ones. Although Protestant elders like Mateo keep alive a wisdom about integrating new ideas into old ones, when elders are gone young people often forget what they have seen, and no longer value how their ancestors resisted centuries of external and internal pressures to divide them.

While they focus on life eternal, Protestants also offer a way to improve one's life in the here and now, e.g., quit drinking, raise one's standard of living, and improve one's health. More and more women are joining Protestant groups as ways to a better life and more control over their children's future. And many are staying with these religions even when their husbands return to the traditions (Sullivan 1991).

Were Protestants not missionizing in Highland Chiapas, probably many more people would be materially a lot worse off. Protestant missionaries have been some of the only outsiders willing to help when Indigenous people needed shelter, food, clothing, and medicine. But in the long run I believe that Protestant groups undermine traditional Pedrano values of community and service. While Protestant converts may lose their fear of invisible beings and become more autonomous and less fatalistic, they lose their people's connection to powerful forces of good, such as totil me'il.

No one knows how Indigenous people might have responded to continued economic and political oppression had missionaries not stepped in. In light of their responses since the Spanish invasion, it seems likely that Indigenous people would have eventually redirected their skills of accommodation, integration, and analysis, which many use to convert, to make changes stemming more directly from their common traditions. For Pedranos I believe that these changes would have had to embody their ideas about power, service, reciprocity, humility, complementarity, narrative, and justice. If these ideas and the structures that support them can survive, Pedranos may still have a chance to act together to solve their problems. This seems to be the direction Catholic Action is encouraging Pedranos to take.

Besides responding to rum's contradictory roles on the level of beliefs, Pedranos also respond on the level of social action. Whereas in the past Pedranas did not speak out about their problems, today they are speaking out about alcohol. They state clearly that Ladinos and rum sellers have used and still use rum as a devastatingly effective tool to dominate them and their husbands. In recognition of rum's role in their subjugation, Pedranos are turning to social action to revitalize their communities. La acción, Catholic Action, cooperatives, prohibition movements, rules regulating sales and consumption, and the substitution of sodas for rum in some rituals exemplify ways Indigenous people are responding to rum's contradictory roles throughout the Highlands.

By the end of my fieldwork in Chenalhó I had come to see drinking as one element in an ideology of service to the Gods in which who serves whom, when, where, how much, in what way, and for how long, seems more resistant to change than *what* Pedranos serve. By the 1970s soda had become the functional equivalent of rum in many Highland communities. Many Pedranos say their rituals are just as powerful with soda as they are with rum. In all likelihood, substituting sodas or tightening controls of alcohol sales or prohibition will be hardest for Traditional Pedranos, whose whole idea of what it means to be human is connected to ritual drinking. However, prohibition in neighboring townships doesn't seem to deter Traditionalists there from drinking; they just come to Chenalhó or Chamula to drink.

Strategies for Pedranos who want to moderate their drinking include drinking at only major fiestas, or confining drinking to curing ceremonies only. From their reports and those of relatives these Pedranos have been living peacefully and productively this way for many years. Another strategy for women who want to control their own or others' drinking has been to join collectives that transcend religious differences and offer them a means to confront economic exploitation. The cooperative movement has given women a context in which to speak out about domestic concerns, such as water, health, shelter, adultery, problem drinking, and domestic violence. In cooperatives women are beginning to reevaluate the heavy burden of service to households and communities that they bear. Just as American women found it necessary to balance service to others with their obligations to themselves, Pedranas are asserting their rights to change inequalities they see that their kinsmen do not, or prefer not to acknowledge. But in doing so many Pedranas are concerned about losing their obligation to serve their communities. While Pedranas worry about their own and their children's survival, group survival also concerns them. Cooperatives seem to nurture both Pedranas' growing feelings of self-worth and continued commitment to communal values.

Describing the ways Pedranos experience drinking and deal with its problems, I have tried to portray healing from drinking problems as most successful when it draws on their cultural traditions. Preserving the power of their traditions and healing strategies has become a pivotal concern for some Pedranos, in the face of outside efforts to make them change. This is why I have devoted much of this book to contextualizing traditions surrounding alcohol within the total fabric of Pedrano society, past and present. As Magdalena said in her prayer for Kate and Joe, "That's how power comes, my Lord."

Power for Pedranos, and any people with strong traditions, seems to come through keeping sacred/powerful substances, objects, and experiences in their proper time and place, as definitions of those dimensions change. Although intoxication was a part of ancient ideas about community, as hard as Pedranos tried to imbue rum with the sacred qualities of ancient substances, they could not make it work for them as they had so many other Spanish symbols. They could never quite contain its power in the proper time and place. Pedranos' struggle with rum's contradictory roles demonstrates just how important it is to view their efforts to restore balance on personal and communal levels from historical and holistic perspectives. While individual Pedranos can pay a heavy price for an alcohol-centered life, Pedranos' communal rituals with rum provide a structural base for reevaluating rum's negative aspects and for acting in new ways.

Like Indigenous peoples throughout the world, Pedranos struggle on a daily basis to resolve contradictions between their Native beliefs and those of the "modern" world. Pedranas showed me that both their problems and solutions arise from their embeddedness in a social, spiritual, and economic whole with deep and strong roots. It is ironic and sad that while affluent Westerners struggle to reconnect to each other and our traditions—to feel a sense of wholeness—we encourage "underdeveloped" people to become like us.

In their roles as mothers, wives, healers, and community organizers, women in Native American societies skillfully mediate between old and new. One event in particular, and a small gesture at the end of it, crystallized my awareness of how creatively Pedranas do this. It was a weaving competition at Antonia's house in 1987.

The women had just finished scattering pine needles on the ground and hanging the last weavings on clotheslines when the representatives from the cooperative store in San Cristóbal came over the hill. One man in the party, with a long, blond ponytail and T-shirt depicting a Maya glyph, seemed to step out of another time and place. But as he walked onto the sacred space of pine needles, the women greeted him like an old friend. I felt that I was seeing an old friend, too, as Walter (Chip) Morris had been one of the first people I met in Highland Chiapas. Chip came to Highland Chiapas in the early 1970s, learned Tzotzil, and began to help Indigenous women organize themselves into cooperatives. Since that time Chip keeps coming back, and women respect him for his commitment.

The competition was lively, made more so by the women's delight at being able to joke with Chip in Tzotzil. At one point Chip gave the group a gift of money from the cooperative store to use as they saw fit, saying, "You can even use it to buy rum if you want." Although weavers still serve rum in competitions, Chip knew that the women in Antonia's cooperative were changing traditions. He made the women laugh, while assuring them that he respected their right to control their work and lives. After Chip and the other representatives awarded prizes for the best weavings, they ate the meal the women had prepared. Later, after they left, the women ate and talked about the competition. They critiqued every aspect, from decisions about prizes to what they would do with the money for their group. As they were finishing their food, María got up to serve the sodas that the guests had not drunk. She set the remaining bottles on the pine needles in the middle of the gathering of women. Then she appointed a younger

woman to serve. She gave the drink pourer a little ceramic pitcl
Antonia had bought the week before at the market. The drink
walked around the circle serving each woman pitchers of soda until all the
bottles were finished. Rather than helping themselves, the women followed their people's tradition of distributing their resources equally and
ceremonially. They reminded me that whether Pedranos are serving rum
or soda, what matters is community.

IN MEMORY OF THE MARTYRS OF ACTEAL

DECEMBER 22, 1997

María Capote Pérez
Martha Capote Pérez
Marcela Capote Ruiz
Marcela Capote Vázquez
Graciela Gómez Hernández
Guadalupe Gómez Hernández
Roselia Gómez Hernández
Daniel Gómez Pérez
Juana Gómez Pérez
Lorenzo Gómez Pérez
Sebastián Gómez Pérez
María Gómez Ruiz
Paulina Hernández Vázquez
Susana Jiménez Pérez
María Luna Méndez
Catarina Luna Pérez
Juan Carlos Luna Pérez
Marcela Luna Ruiz
Juana Luna Vázquez
Lucía Méndez Capote
Vicente Méndez Capote
Margarita Méndez Paciencia
Manuela Paciencia Moreno

Miguel Pérez Jiménez
Alejandro Pérez Luna
Juana Pérez Luna
Silvia Pérez Luna
María Pérez Oyalte
Juana Pérez Pérez
Rosa Pérez Pérez
Ignacio Pukuj Luna
Marcela Pukuj Luna
Loida Ruiz Gómez
Manuel Sántiz Culebra
Alonso Vázquez Gómez
Victorio Vázquez Gómez
Antonia Vázquez Luna
Juana Vázquez Luna
Margarita Vázquez Luna
Rosa Vázquez Luna
Verónica Vázquez Luna
Antonia Vázquez Pérez
Josefa Vázquez Pérez
Marcela Vázquez Pérez
Micaela Vázquez Pérez

Epilogue

But we ask you, Lord,
when they travel on the road,
take care of us,
the women,
that nothing happens on the road,
in the van. . . .

I am crossing my hands,
and kneeling,
to ask your blessing on everyone
who is present,
and most importantly on the women.

The story of the women artisans, Lord,
we ask you to put it in the middle of your hand,
of your document,
of your book,
that they be in the middle, Lord.[1]

The shaman knelt on a bed of pine needles before twenty-four candles and asked God to protect the twenty-four people gathered around him. His prayer opened a weaving competition on June 27th, 1998. The importance of prayer in Pedranos' lives has not diminished since the late 1980s when I conducted research for this book. However, the subjects that shamans take up with God have changed. This shaman's prayer refers to dangers on the road and to the centrality of women's cash earnings and support networks to his people's survival. He speaks of a world that a decade ago Pedranos could have only seen in dreams.

As I write this epilogue, military and paramilitary troop movements make life in Chenalhó harder than anyone can remember. Danger of harassment and physical assault increases the risks of traveling, both from home to fields and to and from San Cristóbal. Threat of violence increases the hardships of tending and harvesting crops that Pedranos depend upon for food. Over ten thousand Pedranos (one third of the township) live in internal refugee camps, unable to return to their homes or tend their fields.

What has happened in Chenalhó that tanks now thunder over Earth, that cornfields lie untended? How have Pedranos been able to make sense of such disrespect? As this book documents, during the 1980s Pedranos worked patiently together to solve their problems with alcohol and other issues; they preferred to leave disagreements pending until reconciliation could be reached.

Despite this legacy, time after time government representatives have disrupted Pedranos' search for their own solutions. The military's presence today in Chenalhó is a stark expression of this history of disrespect. Government officials maintain that the military is in Chenalhó to restore peace. Yet, analysis of aggression by paramilitaries reveals that their acts are not the product of local dynamics, but of concerted efforts by the government (i.e., the Partido Revolucionario Institucional, or PRI) and the Mexican military to serve their own political interests by manipulating stress-lines between Pedranos.

While forced change has caused much suffering, cooperative and peaceful organizing has brought welcome changes. For the past few decades Pedranos have been transforming daily life to serve their own interests by creating democratic organizations. These organizations draw their strength from local relationships to the land and the ancestors, and their effectiveness depends on the face-to-face interaction through which people construct and affirm their identities. Before the Zapatista uprising Pedranos in these organizations remained relatively isolated from other indigenous people in similar organizations. They were as surprised as I was when a group of indigenous men and women calling themselves the Zapatista Army of National Liberation (EZLN) rose up in rebellion on January 1, 1994. Although they needed time to make sense of the uprising, many Pedranos eventually embraced the Zapatista cause as their own. Today approximately one half of Chenalhó's population are sympathetic to the Zapatista agenda and belong to what Pedranos call "civil society."[2]

In light of these dramatic changes, how are women faring? Specifically, what are they saying about themselves, alcohol, and their communities? The past decade of observing Pedranas struggle to gain greater control over their lives has deepened my resolve not to neglect or disrespect their own descriptions and analyses of alcohol and community. This epilogue owes much to analyses Antonia has given me and insights I have acquired from assisting two women's cooperatives she helped form. Throughout the time I have known her, by way of her community involvements Antonia has been teaching me about her people's search for greater control. Antonia's story illustrates women's deep consciousness of place and change and highlights the complex, layered roles they play as producers of knowledge and as people of action in their communities and beyond.[3]

> We can look for our own food. We know how to seek it. We are searching. Our mind, our struggle, our imagination, we have these. We know what to do.
>
> —Antonia

In 1987 when I lived with Antonia and Domingo, they were absorbed in reflecting on the teachings of Jesus as members of the Word of God. They were passionate about social change and became involved in a coffee and weaving cooperative and helped run a cooperative general store. All of this work was in addition to the heavy workloads the couple carried as subsistence farmers. Complicating their increased work were Domingo's headaches, which were so debilitating that he often spent whole days in bed. Many mornings Antonia was forced to send Felipe, Sebastian, and Rodrigo (the baby in 1987) to the fields to work without their father's help.

During these years, Antonia fulfilled many roles, including mother, wife, daughter, sister, farmer, weaver, household manager, co-op representative, and Catholic organizer. Antonia's compassion for Domingo's suffering complicated her growing awareness that her workload was more than double his. In meetings with other Word of God members Antonia considered how carrying a heavier workload than Domingo, even when he wasn't sick, was connected to a gender ideology that privileged men. She also reflected on how unjust it was that her children worked in the fields while Ladinos' children "had birthday parties," as she put it.

Over the course of my annual visits with Antonia, I saw material suffering take its toll on her. The fall of world coffee prices in 1989 combined with the effects of the government's structural adjustment policies deepened poverty in Chenalhó (Tanski and Eber n.d.a). Political conflicts intensified, as more and more Pedranos resisted the policies of the PRI. When I visited her in 1993, Antonia told me that she had stopped going to the chapel on Sunday and that she didn't pray much, either. She blamed her lack of time and energy on increasing childcare and co-op demands. In addition, she said she felt alone among her kinswomen in her struggle for justice. At this time Antonia's fourth son, Augustín, was five years old and Antonia was pregnant with another child. She confided to me that she felt so desperate about finding a way to feed the new baby that she considered giving it away. But she didn't and Serena was born.

On January 3, 1994, three days after the Zapatista uprising, Antonia gave birth to Guadalupe, her sixth child. Despite one more mouth to feed, that month was a turning point for Antonia. I didn't go to Chiapas in 1994, but I received letters from Antonia in which she told me how she felt about the uprising:

> I am very content that there are people called Zapatistas. Because I didn't know how we could struggle to make the government hear us. For years only the Catholics went to San Cristóbal or Tuxtla to march. And the government didn't pay any attention to us . . . It's been two years since I went to Tuxtla to march with thousands of people. We came together in Chiapa de Corzo. Walking by foot from there we arrived in Tuxtla. It was really hot and I was carrying my Serena. But the government only treated us like animals, like monkeys, like flies that fill up the streets . . . I don't complain to the government any more. It doesn't understand anything. It treats us like animals. But it is more animal than we are.

In early 1994 Antonia became a Zapatista. Today being a Zapatista is her most important identity, although she remains committed to her other identities, as well. Antonia says she will always be a Catholic; she calls her work in the Zapatista base "a holy struggle" and compares this work to that of the early Christians, like St. Peter and St. John.[4] She remains devoted to working with other women in cooperatives, including two new cooperatives she helped form: Mujeres Marginadas (Marginalized Women), a bakery cooperative that women in her Zapatista base started, and Mujeres Por La Dignidad (Women for Dignity), a weaving cooperative composed of Zapatista supporters from four townships.

Antonia experiences the most conflict between her identities as a Zapatista and as a mother and wife. In accordance with the EZLN's women's law,[5] Zapatista bases elect equal numbers of male and female leaders. This requirement has done much to promote women's participation in the political affairs of their communities. Yet, women are hard-pressed to find the time and energy to fill leadership roles. The women in Antonia's base decided that only single women could serve as base representatives because married women had too many duties to take on this extra work. The women said that it would have been good if a husband had offered to take over some of his wife's work in order for her to be a representative, but no man did. Faced with the contradictions between rhetoric and the facts of their lives, women have turned their energies to creating grassroots economic initiatives. Women's weaving, baking, and agricultural cooperatives create social spaces in which to reconcile contradictions between the Zapatistas' agenda and women's own understandings of themselves. Also, in these groups women often earn the only cash their households and bases have.[6]

While Antonia had to decline the nomination to represent her support base, Domingo took on the role of representative. Domingo's cargo and Antonia's responsibilities have meant that their children experience added stress and work harder than ever. Sebastian seemed to gain strength from the challenge. In addition to working long hours in the fields, he took up weaving. He also attends weekly Zapatista base meetings with his parents. In contrast, Felipe has had a harder time.

Felipe was embarking on manhood when his parents became involved in the Zapatista movement. At first he attended base meetings with his parents, but he preferred to hang out in the headtown with van drivers. Felipe was attracted to these young men who drink, drive fast, have many girlfriends, and use Spanish instead of Tzotzil. He wanted to learn to drive and make a living like these men. Felipe would return home for periods of time, often repentant. At one point he even served as a sentry for the support base. Huddled under a blanket at the lookout on the mountain above his parents' house, he kept watch for paramilitary troops.

In recent years Antonia has often expressed feeling torn between her desire to see Felipe find personal happiness and her fear for his soul if he leaves behind his family, their traditions, and the land. Antonia recognizes that the new paths that young people are taking in education and employment may contribute to their families and communities something of value not available within traditional knowledge and experience. However, she also sees that these young people frequently disrespect their elders, get caught up in heavy drinking, and forget the traditions. Antonia's fears were compounded in the mid 1990s by the recruitment of alienated young Pedrano men into paramilitaries. In the support base parents try to protect their children from this kind of cooptation by giving children over 13 an opportunity to offer their opinions.

Approximately 165 men, women, and teenagers (about a third of Antonia's hamlet's population) belong to the Zapatista support base Antonia helped form. Base members meet weekly to discuss the Zapatistas' agenda for change, define their problems in relation to that agenda, and seek solutions according to their own experiences and cultures. Members come from the three major religious groups, although only a handful of Protestants belong. Protestants joining Zapatista bases represents a shift from the 1980s when they were reluctant to organize for social change.

In the summer of 1995 Zapatista support bases in Chenalhó joined the movement throughout Chiapas to form autonomous townships.[7] Describing this decision, Antonia explained,

> We want to be clean. It's necessary to be separate, well separated. It's necessary to break away in order to be free to form ourselves, to offer our own opinions that come from within our groups. We don't want to be a part of it [the PRI government] anymore.

The formation of an autonomous township with parallel functions to the official PRI-dominated government provoked a split in Chenalhó between civil society and supporters of the PRI. Most of Antonia's relatives sympathized with the aims of the autonomous government, but they did not back it or join Zapatista support groups, mostly because of the commitment and risk this entailed. Some joined Sociedad Civil Las Abejas (Civil Society the Bees), a group of Catholics dedicated to nonviolent resistance that formed in 1993 in Chenalhó. Others remained independent, although critical of the PRI.

The violence in Chenalhó that began in 1995 and continues today is a result of the threat that communities with large bases of support for the Zapatistas pose to the state and federal governments. Constrained by their truce with the EZLN, the Mexican military works through paramilitaries to repress alternatives to the PRI (Global Exchange, 1998). The state and federal governments' support and maintenance of paramilitaries is one component in the low-intensity war in Chiapas. During 1997 more and more members of civil society—and even PRI supporters—had to choose between fleeing for their lives or assisting paramilitaries to oppress their fellow Pedranos. By the end of the year the numbers of Pedranos in internal refugee camps in and around Polhó, the center of the autonomous township, reached almost one third of the township's population.

Despite efforts to restore peace in Chenalhó, the unthinkable occurred on December 22, 1997, in Acteal. On that day nine men, twenty-one women, and fifteen children were massacred by the paramilitary group The Red Mask. The shooting started at 11:30 A.M. while people were praying in the chapel and lasted until 4:30 in the afternoon. Army personnel standing on a hill above Acteal witnessed the shooting but did nothing to stop it. It is a tragic irony that the forty-five Pedranos killed belonged to Las Abejas, the civil society group committed to a nonviolent approach to conflict.[8]

Although Antonia didn't lose any relatives or friends in the massacre, she was deeply saddened by it. In the aftermath of the massacre Antonia summed up daily life in Chenalhó as, "One moment happiness, the next sadness." She said happiness comes while working with others to create a new life; sadness takes over when people die for this desire.

> The struggle is my glass of water.

Domingo used this phrase in 1997 to tell me why he is a Zapatista. Listening to his account I was reminded of associations in Chenalhó of water with drops of moisture from the leaves of the World Tree or from God's (Jesus') hands and feet. I also remembered the story Domingo told in 1987 about how he stopped drinking through a dream in which St. Peter gave him a cargo to make balls of incense from the sap (blood) of the sweet gum tree (see pages 52–55).

These associations and talks with Domingo and others in Zapatista and Las Abejas support bases suggest a sense of calling and sacrifice entailed in belonging to these groups. Much as the World Tree, Sun/Jesus, the early Christians, and ancestral mothers/fathers sacrificed water, blood, and rum to sustain a balanced and just universe, civil society members sacrifice their time, resources, and even their lives to restore justice and balance in their communities.

For Domingo, being a Zapatista is integrated into the cargo he received to be a catechist when he stopped drinking. Like this cargo, serving his people as a representative of a Zapatista base satisfies Domingo's thirst for coherence and justice. Much more fulfilling and long-lasting than a cup of rum, the holy struggle is a form of reciprocity between Zapatista supporters and the spiritual forces. In this struggle, these Pedranos build the social capital to defend themselves against their opponents, much as shamans blind the eyes of the evil ones by sprinkling drops of rum on pine boughs.

Today more Pedranos draw upon local understandings of alcohol as "water of sorrow" than in the past. Zapatistas and Las Abejas de-emphasize alcohol's dialectical qualities and show less tolerance for ambivalence. Even among supporters of the status quo it has become increasingly acceptable over the past decade to substitute sodas and use *la acción* (the action) for rum in all rituals.

Gaining control over alcohol has become a symbol of the larger effort of Pedranos in civil society to obtain greater control over their lives. To help me understand the symbolic importance of controlling alcohol, Antonia explained that in their holy struggle it is important not to drink because when people drink they desecrate the passage over Earth. Pedranos in civil society substitute soda for rum in all ceremonies to guard against such disrespectful behavior. Although soda is a symbol of things Ladino, these people say that soda is more acceptable because it does not distort people's perceptions nor make them crazy.

Zapatistas and Las Abejas maintain that prohibition is necessary to reconstitute Pedranos as a people and restructure Chenalhó along more pluralistic lines. Their positions on alcohol show a change from the 1980s view of prohibition as temperance to prohibition in a stricter sense. For example, one early morning in spring of 1996 several men in Antonia's support base stretched a cloth sign across the entrance to their hamlet proclaiming: "All alcoholic beverages and drugs are prohibited here. Anyone found growing, selling, or consuming these will be thrown out." Angry neighbors who were not Zapatista sympathizers tore down the banner only a few hours after it was raised.

At the same time as they prohibit alcohol, Zapatista base members redirect themselves and their fellow Pedranos to other symbols of solidarity, such as their native language, new rituals with soda instead of rum, and the clothing that women brocade with symbols encoding the Tzotzil-Maya cosmology. This refocusing is part of a revitalization project aimed at cleansing Chenalhó of symbols of Ladino domination, such as jail, rum, the Spanish language, and machismo (Eber n.d.). The revitalization movement in Chenalhó today recalls previous movements during which Indigenous people reconnected to a sense of themselves as the true Christians.

Denying alcohol's power as a linchpin in Pedranos' interwoven sense of self, community, and symbolic universe appears problematic considering the revitalization movement's focus on restoring connections to valued symbols. Unlike soda, rum is a multivocal symbol relevant within and linking together many realms of social life. Alternative ideologies, such as Protestantism and The Word of God, have tried with mixed success to contain alcohol while anchoring the dialectic between Pedrano core symbols and Christian ones. Their less than impressive record with alcohol seems to be a factor influencing Zapatista and Las Abejas members to take more politically motivated positions.

Civil society's rejection of alcohol makes sense in respect to the devastating experience that Pedranos have had with it. But at times the rhetoric coming from civil society seems to convey that if Pedranos will only do away with alcohol and the PRI, oppression will end. Invoking a sense of shared suffering in the face of the "bad government" may be comforting, but it contradicts local knowledge about the multidimensionality of experience. It contradicts Pedranos' awareness that all are capable of abuse, of failing to respect others, at any moment that they stop attending to their behavior. Pedranos are keenly aware that it takes each person, working hard every day, in order to bring individual souls inside bodies and to keep societies balanced. They know that they can never stop working on their individual comportment without risking harm to themselves or others. Despite the Zapatista women's law, women know all too well how kinsmen can benefit from the persistent ideology that women are subordinate to men. And Pedranos of both sexes have only to look at the crimes committed by some of their own people, who forgot ideas about souls and joined paramilitaries for the promise of power and material rewards.

In light of these local understandings, the harsh punishments used in Zapatista bases for problem drinkers represent a change from Pedranos' previous reluctance to force their will on others. Like the catechists before them, Zapatistas maintain that people continue drinking because they are not yet conscious of their own oppression. However, in contrast to past positions, base members show little tolerance for drinkers who refuse to become conscious of their oppression. For example, if base members find out that one of their members has been drinking, the *agente*, the principal representative of a base, and his two assistants will counsel the person. After the third counseling session, if the person continues drinking two young men appointed from the base bring the person to the agente's house where they tie him to a tree for several hours.

With its focus on providing Western biomedicines and health care to Indigenous people, the Zapatista health agenda also contradicts core Pedrano ideas about human relations. Although Pedranos in civil society still use the services of shamans, the Zapatista agenda does not try to raise awareness in the broader society about shamans' roles and their knowledge of plants used in Indigenous healing practices. In 1997 Domingo surprised me by recommending AA for people who want to stop drinking.

In the current fervor of reflection about who they are and what their community should be like, women in cooperatives skillfully adapt valued traditions to their contemporary experiences. True to the promise they showed in the 1980s, women's cooperatives are providing contexts for their members to carry on culturally nuanced reflections about identity and cultural survival. In co-ops, women combine symbolic expressions of their identities, such as hand-woven clothing, with materially based statements about how hard it is to be human and how even harder it is to be a member of civil society.

In their discussions women in co-ops and in other civil society groups make strong statements about which traditions serve their interests and which should be abandoned. The traditions that women in Antonia's base say they want to preserve are those that women direct to serve their own and their household's needs—for example weaving ancestral clothing and welcoming back the ancestors on Days of the Dead.

Drinking is at the top of the list of the "bad" traditions that women want to abolish (Eber 2000; Tanski and Eber n.d.a). Women say that drinking is not a tradition that their ancestors entrusted them to carry on, but a practice that they came to either accept or tolerate over time. At least in public discourse, men agree.

Despite rejecting alcohol, women in civil society are aware of its power as a multivocal and multivalent symbol representing and linking divergent values and practices. They recognize its historical role in maintaining reciprocal relations between human beings and between people and spiritual beings. But their concern for preserving justice and reciprocity overrides these considerations.

Women seem well positioned to create and develop new symbols for their communities in light of their expanded roles as wage earners and political organizers. In their cooperatives women propose more respectful symbols of reciprocity than alcohol, while establishing new more reciprocal relations in fair trade and international peace and justice networks (Eber 2000). In all their relationships, women in civil society are wary of being incorporated into a global community of consumers who have lost their connections to ancestral lands and traditions (Tanski and Eber n.d.a).

I originally ended this book with the word "community." While much has changed in Chenalhó, Pedranos continue to articulate the material, social, and moral dimensions of their lives in order to keep the local group—however definitions of that group may change—as their key social referent. For the most part, Pedranos' search for justice remains rooted in an awareness of being an integral part of something beyond themselves that is ordained by God and the ancestors, yet contingent upon individuals' daily actions and interactions. This understanding strongly informs the criteria and calculations with which Pedranos shape and reshape their social arrangements and relations to alcohol.

Within this framework of community and communal rights, Pedranos are carving a space for individual rights. When I wrote this book I did not anticipate how individual and communal rights could coincide in a more inclusive, nondichotomous conception. Antonia and other women in civil society have shown how this is possible by simultaneously demanding rights for themselves as individuals, as women, and as members of a community.

In the late 1980s I was struck by the eloquence and power of shamans' words in prayer. At the dawn of the twenty-first century, the words that stand out for their passion and power are those of women in civil society speaking of their collective work. Both forms of discourse emanate from an awareness that people need something beyond their individual selves to endure the work of being human. Prayer and collective struggle put into practice the belief that social welfare and development depend upon cooperation between humans and the spiritual forces. In contrast to alcohol, which when abused leads to alienation, prayer and collective work foster connection.

In the fragment of prayer that opens this epilogue, the shaman describes a road ahead that is full of danger. He reminds us that despite the rewards and protection of collective work, Pedranos in civil society, especially women, are highly vulnerable. Women in civil society face a male-dominated, alcohol-influenced agenda promoted by well-funded opponents of democratic change. The threat posed by these men and their agenda, combined with Pedranos' painful and protracted struggle with rum, may best explain civil society's view of prohibition as a necessary step toward liberation.

Christine Eber
Las Palomas, New Mexico
December 1999

Appendix A

Traditional Pedrano Gods

Traditional Pedranos use "God" to refer to a range of Catholic and Maya deities, including Earth, totil me'il , Sun, Sun's Father, Moon, lakes, the Virgin Mary, Corn, Corn's Mother, Tobacco, and the Catholic saints. Traditionalists are especially devoted to Earth, *totik* (Sun/Our Father), *me' tik* (Moon/Our Mother), and *totil me'il* (totil glosses as "father," me'il as "mother," and together they gloss as "ancestors"). In dream accounts and prayer Pedranos depict Sun and Moon as complementary and equally powerful. Sun, identified with maleness/Jesus/God, and Moon, linked to femaleness and the Virgin Mary, often become one in dreams. Moon may also reveal herself in lakes that form after storms. Totil me'il is an evocation of male/female and good/bad dualities which characterized ancient Maya Gods (Thompson 1970).

While generalized Earth is female, various angels, or sacred places, assume a male aspect. Earth Lord is one of these. When Pedranos speak of Earth Lord, it is often in stories about receiving money from Earth or being required to serve Earth Lord in a manner similar to the obsequious ways Pedranos have had to serve Ladinos. Pedranos also say that Earth Lord is Rain God, or Lord of mountains, and that he guards the corrals where animal soul counterparts to humans' souls live. However, Pedranos also say that totil me'il guards animal spirit companions. In their alternating use of Earth Lord and totil me'il Pedranos play out vividly the dialectic between Christian and Maya beliefs.

In Chenalhó saints are like Gods. Pedranos associate St. Peter, the patron saint of Chenalhó, with Sun and maleness, and usually describe him as a Ladino. St. Peter often appears in dreams, as does Holy Cross, whom Pedranos say is an extension of omniscient Earth and more powerful than either St. Peter or the Virgin Mary. Holy Cross appears to Pedranos most often as a man, but at times as a woman. Some say that s/he alone comes to shamans in dreams to give them the power to heal. Holy Cross takes the form of a holy tree, serving for Pedranos as the ancient ceiba, "World Tree," served for ancient Mayas.

Appendix B

Non-Traditional Healing in Chenalhó

Many Pedranos go to health clinics if their illnesses prove resistant to prayer, but they generally keep contact with a shaman once they begin medications. Even some Protestant Pedranos turn to shamans when they are gravely ill or dying, although Protestants say that traditional prayers are expensive pagan rituals requiring rum.

Several kinds of non-traditional healers work informally with traditional shamans, herbalists, bone-setters, and midwives, and provide important services for their communities. "Health Promoters" are Pedranos who receive training in programs offered by a religious group or a government agency, and then set up private dispensaries or drugstores in their local hamlets. The Padre in Chenalhó keeps many medicines in his house and either sells them cheaply or gives them away. Several Ladinos in Chenalhó center sell medicines from their homes and give out medical advice. A few Ladina midwives serve Indigenous women.

Professional, organized, and certified healers in the township of Chenalhó or nearby, include doctors and other health promoters affiliated with various state and national organizations. The two clinics operating in Chenalhó in the late 1980s were a clinic run by the Cultural Mission, a government development agency, and the Centro del Salud (the Health Center), run by the Secretaría de Salud, Jurisdicción Sanitaria II (Secretary of Health). The National Indigenous Institute closed its clinic when it withdrew its resident staff from Chenalhó in 1988, although it was operating during my first year of fieldwork. Other organizations such as DIF (Desarollo Integral Familiar, "Family Development Agency"), the National Institute of Nutrition, and other state and government nutrition projects conduct periodic health surveys, vaccination programs, and miscellaneous informational programs. In 1988 a nurse at a clinic in La Misíon Cultural (the Cultural Mission) in Chenalhó tried to start an Alcoholics Anonymous group, but backed down when rum sellers and town officials worked against it. AA is successful in urban areas in Mexico, such as San Cristóbal, but there are few groups in Indigenous communities.

Most non-traditional doctors staffing clinics in Indigenous communities are there to fulfill the mandatory one or two year term of service in rural areas. They are usually not from Highland Chiapas and do not speak Tzotzil. They are also responsible for time-consuming documentation, which often takes priority over treating people. Although Indigenous nurses from local communities usually work closely with doctors, women are often reluctant to trust either doctors or nurses, especially male ones. Usually they only go to the latter in emergencies.

Despite clinics, pamphlets, and radio programs which broadcast health tips in Tzotzil, Indigenous people must have bus fare or walk long distances to visit clinics, be willing to deal with an alien environment and language once there, be literate to read instructional pamphlets, and have a radio and money to keep batteries in it in order to hear informational programs. Even when someone makes use of these resources, positive results aren't always forthcoming. For example, even if Pedranos boil water at home, while working in their fields they drink whatever water is available. Most importantly, Pedranos have little money to buy the foods that doctors and radio programs say their children need. If a hen produces eggs, a woman will often sell them to have a fund of cash rather than feed them to her children, even if the cash she earns eventually pays for medicine or a clinic visit to cure a problem better nutrition might have prevented.

Through the National Indigenous Institute and the National Institute of Nutrition I had the privilege of meeting some exceptionally committed doctors who are collaborating with Indigenous healers. These doctors understand that trust in care providers, faith in traditions, and the support of kin and one's community are important factors in treating problem drinking and other illnesses in Indigenous communities. OMIECH, the Organization of Indigenous Doctors of Chiapas, and a relatively new sub-group, Jnet'um (Midwives), resulted from collaboration between Indigenous and non-Indigenous doctors.

The relationships Indigenous and non-Indigenous healers are developing are critical to Indigenous people's efforts to control their own health and healing. In 1990 the Chiapas legislature passed a health law requiring shamans and other traditional healers in Indigenous communities to take a course in modern medicine and secure a state license. Sebastian Luna, the leader of OMIECH, summed up the wisdom of his people: "People die because they don't have good water, food and work, not because the healer treats them" (*Los Angeles Times* February 12, 1991).

Appendix C

Brief History of Presbyterianism in Chenalhó

(based on written sources)

Protestants first came to Mexico during the war between the United States and Mexico in 1846, when the United States found Protestant influence useful in undermining Mexican resistance to U.S. imperialism (Pérez Pérez 1991). In 1902 a group of North American Presbyterians based themselves in Tabasco, eventually sending missionaries to Chiapas. The first Presbyterians arrived in Chenalhó in 1953. In 1965 followers built their first chapel. Today there are 30 Protestant chapels in Chenalhó.

Protestant evangelical goals, such as literacy, modernization, and Western health programs, mesh well with government goals and do not tax government funds (Gossen 1989: 223). Protestants pose little threat to national assimilationist policies; they encourage Indigenous people to look for sources of their problems in personal shortcomings and cultural inadequacies, and solutions in transforming individual psyches. By the 1950s Presbyterians were working throughout Mexico with the full support of the Mexican government.

Presbyterians pose a threat to non-Protestants in Indigenous communities in Highland Chiapas by refusing to pay cooperación, fulfill cargos, or buy alcohol, an important source of revenue for cargo holders. As Presbyterians' numbers grew and their refusal to participate in communal celebrations became more of an issue, Traditionalists in Chenalhó began to threaten them. In 1957 a Traditionalist assassinated a Presbyterian man, and was incarcerated ten years for his crime. Despite warnings from authorities in San Cristóbal, in 1965 Traditionalists attempted, unsuccessfully, to expel Presbyterians, blaming them for hunger and suffering (Pérez Pérez 1991).

Needing outside support and guidance in their new religion, two Pedrano Presbyterians made contact with Kenneth Weathers, an American missionary with the Summer Institute of Linguistics. Weathers offered to translate into Tzotzil verses of the Bible, which he reproduced in pamphlets to be distributed among Pedranos. Eventually he arranged for Pedrano children who had finished sixth grade to go to Ixtapa, Chiapas, for a course of two and a half years, during which they learned to translate Spanish into Tzotzil. He continued to guide Pedranos in Bible study as well as instruct them in personal hygiene and nutrition until Mariana Cowan replaced him in 1974. Until she left in 1980, Cowan dedicated herself to translating the Bible and setting up a clinic in Pechiquil. Vern (René) and Carla Sterk and Al (Alonso) Schreuder currently offer guidance to Pedrano pastors and deacons from their base, the Bible Institute, in San Cristóbal.

Appendix D

Revelation 21:3-8

(King James Version; the biblical verses to which
Mateo refers in his dream account in Chapter 10.)

And I heard a great voice out of heaven saying,
Behold, the tabernacle of God is with men,
and he will dwell with them,
and they shall be his people,
and God himself shall be with them, and be their God.
And God shall wipe away all tears from their eyes;
and there shall be no more death, neither sorrow, nor
crying, neither shall there be any more pain:
for the former things are passed away.

And he that sat upon the throne said,
Behold, I make all things new.
And he said unto me,
Write: for these words are true and faithful.
And he said unto me, It is done.
I am Alpha and Omega, the beginning and the end.
I will give unto him that is a thirst
of the fountain of the water of life freely.
He that overcometh shall inherit all things;
and I will be his God, and he shall be my son.
But the fearful, and unbelieving, and the abominable,
and murderers, and whoremongers, and sorcerers,
and idolaters, and all liars,
shall have their part in the lake
which burneth with fire and brimstone:
which is the second death.

Notes

Preface

1. For critiques of reflexive approaches see Clifford and Marcus 1986, Marcus and Fischer 1986, and Ruby and Myerhoff 1982. For critiques of male bias in anthropological research and writing and discussions of the foundation feminist scholars have laid for contemporary ethnography in the postmodern era see di Leonardo 1991, Harstock 1987, and Mascia-Lees, Sharpe, and Cohen 1989. For an example of foregrounding the voices of non-Western peoples see Calvo et al. 1989.

1. Frameworks and Methods

1. Burkhart's (1992: 23–54) study of the significance of Aztec women's "home front" chores, which complemented their husbands' activities on the front lines of battle, demonstrates the value of domestic work to Aztec society.

2. Feminist anthropologists are continually reworking the major frameworks summarized in this chapter. For a historical overview of the changes they have made and are making see di Leonardo 1991. One of the strengths of feminist anthropology is that its practitioners have been committed to an ever-widening dialogue.

3. See Behar's (1993) life history of Esperanza, a Mexican flower seller. I share Behar's concern with not depicting Latin American women as passive victims. However, while Behar uses Esperanza's story to illustrate personal survival strategies, I use Pedranas' individual stories to tell a collective story.

4. See MacAndrew and Edgerton 1969: 100–164 for citations from colonists about native North Americans, and Chapter 2 below for citations about drinking in Mexico.

5. As drinking became more and more widespread in Indigenous societies in the Americas in the 1970s and 1980s, many Indigenous communities took steps to control it, with dramatic results. For example, the Alkali Lake Band, a Shuswap band from British Columbia, made a dramatic transformation from nearly universal alcoholism before the 1970s to 95% sobriety in the 1990s (Alkali Lake Indian Band 1985). The Ontario Native Women's Association report (1989) on drinking and domestic violence in Indigenous communities, discusses the success of "Healing Circles" that Native women are forming throughout Canada to heal themselves and their families' of problems from alcohol and domestic violence. Indigenous programs for preventing and treating alcoholism stress strengthening communities, providing education for children in their native languages,

increasing employment opportunities for men and women, and returning to the conception of life as a circle connecting physical, spiritual and emotional worlds (e.g. LaDue 1991).

6.   The literature on drinking and gender differences in diverse ethnic groups within the United States is burgeoning. While studies of Hispanic women's drinking (Caetano 1987) indicate that overall they abstain or drink infrequently, recent research among Mexican American women indicates that drinking is highly variable and depends on generational status, acculturation level, social class and place of residence (Mora and Gilbert 1991: 47).

7.   My parents raised me in a small mid-Michigan town where the Presbyterian Church and the college in which my father taught were focal points of my early life. Drinking and drinkers were not part of my growing up, although I liked to hear stories of my maternal grandfather's experiences as a wine steward in a Chicago hotel.

8.   I chose to illustrate this book rather than use photographs because sketches seem suited to capture the fluidity and tentativeness of social life and identities that fieldwork makes so clear. Through sketches I hope to give generations to come a sense that Pedranos and I are every bit as vulnerable and vital as they are, that all of us at all times continually sketch our own and others' identities, erasing some parts, adding others, until we die.

2. The Time of Suffering

1.   "From the Conquest to the Revolution and even decades beyond, 'history' was for the Zinacantecs what they defined in a sixteenth-century dictionary as 'the book of suffering, the book of hardship'—famines and epidemics, tributes and taxes, servitude and destitution" (Laughlin 1988: 2).

To summarize changes in drinking and gender throughout this "book of suffering," I use accounts of Central Mexico and Yucatán because knowledge of these areas before and after the Spanish invasion is more complete than that of Highland Chiapas. Several chroniclers from these areas translated Native books and wrote lengthy accounts of Indigenous peoples' traditions (e.g. Sahagún, Motolinía, Zorita, and Landa). While chronicles and archival materials exist for Highland Chiapas, these provide a much more limited picture of life in this area. (See Calnek 1988 for a reconstruction of pre-Hispanic and colonial periods in Highland Chiapas and a critical analysis of available sources). Despite regional variation, archaeological evidence and ethnohistorical studies suggest that Indigenous peoples of Mesoamerica had similar social systems before the Spanish invasion (Gossen 1986b).

2.   See Rosenbaum 1996 for an overview of the pre-Hispanic gender system in Mesoamerica and Nash 1978 and Leacock and Nash 1977 for changes Aztec elites instituted. Leacock and Nash suggest European chroniclers of native cosmologies in Mesoamerica exaggerated tendencies toward hierarchy and male dominance in accordance with Christian-Judaic traditions.

3.   Jellinek (1977) suggests that in various places and times as people realized alcohol's powerful effects on them, they put alcohol in the place of water or milk, as the ritual symbol par excellence. When accepting rum or chicha in rituals Pedranos frequently refer to it as "your water." In rituals with rum the people of Amatenango del Valle refer to rum as "the washings of the legs and of the arms of our saint and leader Jesus Christ, the great master holy Jesus Christ, Santiago, Santa Lucía" (Nash 1985: 209, 191–192).

4.   See Paredes (1975: 1146) for the complete story. The story, which describes Mayahuel's transformation into a tree, is similar to ancient and modern stories of the Maya goddess Xtabai (Landa 1941; Eber 1991: 549) and contemporary Chamula stories

about *xpak'in te'* (ibid.: 550; Rosenbaum 1993: 77–79, 200–225). These stories depict women who inhabit the forests and entice men into sex and drunkenness.

5. See Navarette-Pellicer 1988: 87–91 for a more full discussion of rum production at this time.

6. See MacLeod 1973: 73–74, 94, 140 for a discussion of these and more abuses. Chiapas Indigenous people no longer drink cacao, except occasionally at baptismal meals.

7. According to the Polanco Census of 1778 there were 2,500 whites in Chiapas, in a total population of 64,000. Besides Indigenous people this population also included 5,000 Negroes and Mulattos and 5,000 Mestizos (Trens 1957). The population of Chenalhó totalled 288 married men and women, 35 widows, 28 widowers, 210 girls, and 331 boys, a total of 892 "souls," according to the census.

8. See Taylor 1979: 85 for the role drinking played in court cases involving men's physical abuse of wives or lovers in an Oaxacan village and in Central Mexican villages during the colonial era.

9. Sun and Moon were the most important deities of ancient Mayas. Ixchel/Moon was Sun's wife and the Goddess of the earth, weaving, childbirth, and maize. Due to her infidelity to Sun (Thompson 1954: 227–228) and her erratic character, following the monthly cycle of the female menses (Kintz 1990; Schele and Miller 1986: 153), Mayas were ambivalent about Ixchel. Rosenbaum (1993: 67–94) traces this ambivalence to the present day.

10. See Rosenbaum (1993: 22–26) and Gossen and Leventhal (1993) for women's roles and symbolic importance during revitalization movements in Highland Chiapas.

11. The recent rebellion in Highland Chiapas in January 1994 bears a strong resemblance to earlier rebellions. Like their colonial compatriots, the young men and women of the Zapatista National Liberation Army rose up in desperation over ongoing land seizures, deepening poverty, and human rights abuses. Time and space constraints prevented a more thorough treatment of the rebellion, which occurred while this book was in press.

12. Ricardo Pozas'(1962) ethnological recreation of the life of a Chamula man living in the mid-1900s and B. Traven's (1971) "jungle novels," which he wrote in the 1930s, evoke the misery of debt peonage and plantation work.

13. I am indebted to Jan Rus (1994) for his most recent analysis of economic and political change in Highland Chiapas, on which I have based much of this brief overview of Ladino/Native relations since the 1930s. See also Crump 1987 for a discussion of Ladino and Native monopolies on rum. Crump (ibid.: 248) suggests an analogy between the role sodas are playing in Highland Chiapas with the role tea played vis-à-vis gin in all classes in England at the turn of the nineteenth century.

14. See Breedlove and Laughlin 1993: 242–243 for stories about *moy* from Zinacantàn.

3. I Have Come

1. See Gossen (1986a) for an in depth analysis of Carnival in Chamula, and Bricker (1973 and 1981) for analyses of Carnival in Chamula, Chenalhó, and Zinacantán.

2. See Arias 1985: 69–70, Bricker 1973, Rosenbaum 1993: 75–76, and Blaffer 1972 for a comparison of the Blackman figure in Highland rituals. The Blackman also comes to life in stories told around home fires and in dramatic productions of Sna Jtz'ibajom, a Tzotzil-Tzeltal writing and theatre cooperative.

3. Mayas give the name *pom* to balls of incense made from copal (Nahuatl *copalli*, incense), the fragrant resin from copalquahuitl conifers, especially the hard translucent

fragrant resin from the burseraceous *Protium copal* (e.g., Gates 1978: 161). The sap of the sweet gum, *Liquidámbar styraciflua,* is resinous, fragrant, and copious in Central America and is the preferred incense in Chenalhó.

4. Cf. *alisiles,* alféreces' attendants in Amatenango del Valle, who watch to see that alféreces do not get too drunk to perform (Nash 1985: 208).

5. Cf. the role of liquor in Tarahumara culture. Living in dispersed family groups, Tarahumaras retreat at the sight of outsiders. To ease embarrassment in large gatherings they use liquor (Bennett and Zingg 1937, cited in Nash 1985: 223).

6. Many Ladinos in Highland Chiapas use *Indio/India* (Indian) and its patronizing diminutive form, *Indito/Indita,* to refer to Indigenous people. These terms contrast sharply with *Indígena,* a respectful term Indigenous people use to stress their native roots and to distinguish themselves from non-Natives.

7. *La acción* is the expression for holding a cup of rum or chicha to one's mouth without drinking; sipping a little from the cup; or drinking only one cup. La acción allows Pedranos to participate in drinking events without compromising their decision to abstain or limit their drinking.

8. Like Alcoholics Anonymous members, Pedranos use "pride" both to refer to feelings about accomplishments and to refer to "an obsessive acceptance of a challenge, a repudiation of the proposition 'I cannot'" (Bateson 1971: 8).

9. Pedranos say that one should accept *cargos,* work on behalf of one's community. Traditional cargos include service as shamans, midwives, musicians, caretakers of the church, leaders of fiestas, weavers of festival garments, and officers in hamlet and township government. Catholic Action members and some Protestant church members also say their roles as catechists, ministers, deacons and musicians are "cargos." With the growing cooperative movement women are now taking on non-traditional political cargos as leaders of cooperatives (See Chapter 11).

4. Making One's Soul Arrive

1. Arias takes this story from the Popol Vuj, written after the Spanish invasion by scribes of the K'iche' Maya nation in Guatemala (Tedlock 1985). Arias states that Pedrano stories are similar to those in the Popul Vuj, although names and places vary.

2. In a 1988 census I conducted with adult women in a hamlet of forty-five households, nineteen women reported that at least one member had gone to work on a plantation at least once in the past year.

3. Fifteen women had lost no children, however this may have been due to their young ages. Eleven were under thirty years of age. Information is lacking for three women.

4. Dentan (1988: 121–123) describes a similar belief about soul loss among Semai, a West Malaysian people. Like Pedranos, Semai say that the precipitating event is a startling stimulus. Classic symptoms for both groups include anemia, diarrhea, pallor, fever, and listlessness. Roundworm burdens are heavy in Semai settlements, as they are in Highland Chiapas. Dentan notes that soul loss and roundworm burdens share the same symptoms.

5. The bride petition in Chenalhó is called *joyol.* (Cf. Laughlin's [1963], Collier's [1968] and Rosenbaum's [1993: 89–120] descriptions of *jak'ol,* the courtship and marriage petition in Zinacantán and Chamula.) While today some Pedrano suitors only give their in-laws money, or money in addition to food, Pedranos still encourage young men to give food gifts, since when their in-laws eat these it cements the bond in a way money cannot (cf. J. Haviland and L. Haviland 1979: 326 for the role of gifts in Zinacantán.) Of

all the consumable gifts, *chayem uts 'alal*, the four bottles of rum a Pedrano boy offers his prospective in-laws at the final visit of his bride petition, is the most binding. Even so, it is becoming increasingly common for non-drinkers, especially boys who follow Catholic Action, to give cases of soda instead of rum.

6.   Pedranos conceive of the life cycle as beginning in a cold state and ending in heat. As Pedranos mature they become hotter, until finally in old age their heat is considerable. Pedranos increase their heat through bearing children, serving cargos, or healing fellow Pedranos. Pedranos stress that heat, like heart size, increases with age and service to the community, for both sexes.

7.   In the three-hamlet area where I conducted my research the first year, I was only aware of two unmarried men. One was seeking a second wife after his first wife had died. The other was a drunk whose wife had left him. He had no house and no one to cook his food. He was the only person in the hamlet who had broken into houses to steal food.

8.   In their household rituals, Pedranos stabilize family life and teach children their place in their households and community. Wolin and Bennett (1984) have found that American children living in "ritually protected families," i.e., households in which family members do not let an alcoholic disrupt the most important family rituals, are less likely to have problems with drinking in adulthood than children living in households where family members let an alcoholic disrupt their family rituals.

5. "Before God's flowery face"

1.   Indigenous men in various Highland communities say that women, through their coldness and closeness to powerful Earth, can endanger men (Rosenbaum 1993: 69–70). For example, Pedranos say that by stepping over a man's food a woman can cool it, and by extension his virility. Women can cool or "tame" objects associated with male heat, for example bulls (Guiteras-Holmes 1961: 55) and guns (Bricker 1973: 10).

2.   Pedranos refer to the banquet of beef and bean tamales for Carnival as "the sacred victim, the sacred banquet, the contents of the table, the contents of the altar cloth" (Arias 1985: 161).Pedranos also refer to pigs as "older brothers of Our Lord," remembering Jesus' final revenge before ascending into heaven.

3.   Cf. Farriss' (1984: 322) description of fiesta meals of colonial Mayas as "a kind of communion, an offering of food to the divinities made and shared by the community through their civil-religious leaders."

4.   The flags Angélika refers to are the flags of Santiago that the regidores wave over her head in the oath of office. She may have seen them in her dream, or anticipates seeing them when she has the cargo.

5.   Cf. Mauss' (1954) discussion of gift exchange as a total social phenomenon in which gifts charge ordinary indebtedness with emotional and communal content.

6.   As with most substances, men usually share cigarettes, passing them around so that each man can take a drag. In contrast to moy, wild tobacco, Pedranos do not see tobacco rolled up in the form of cigarettes as sacred.

7.   Cf. with the social isolation Lakota abstainers experience. Lakotas will say to a fellow Lakota who doesn't want to accept a drink (Medicine 1983): "I didn't know you're such a *wasichu* [white person]."

8.   See Morris (1987) for an analysis of symbolism in a ceremonial blouse from Santa María Magdalenas Aldama, a semi-independent community in Chenalhó.

9.   An inscription on a carved limestone panel at Palenque, a Classic site in lowland Chiapas, indicates that ancient Mayas used the same word, "k'exol," to signify someone's

replacement (Schele and Miller 1986: 275, 276). Even today Pedranos refer to a child named after a father or mother as his or her "k'exol."

10. Of twenty-eight incoming and outgoing standard bearer's wives in thirteen fiestas in 1988, on only two occasions did cargo holders drink rum. Each occasion was a talk that the incoming and outgoing women have about fiesta expenses. At the other talks both cargo holders made la acción and carried their rum home.

11. Until recently few scholars of Mesoamerican societies have treated women's ritual roles at length. See Rosenbaum (1993: 147–175) for a discussion of Chamula women's roles in cargos and a comparison of these with other analyses of women's ritual roles in Mesoamerican communities including Linn (1976), Mathews (1985), and Stephen (1991). These studies demonstrate the authority women obtain when their ritual service links them directly to the supernatural beings that represent their communities.

6. "Now I am going like a branch and its leaves"

1. To lose a net bag for Pedranos is as much a matter of identification as economics. When Pedranos lose net bags they also lose a piece of their identity, as Pedrano bags are unique, like their clothes. Net bags are time consuming to make and Pedranos are loathe to lose them.

2. While I didn't study children carefully for signs of FAS, I rarely saw a Pedrano child with noticeable features associated with this syndrome (See Dorris 1989: 150 for photographs of children with FAS). Proscriptions against women drinking heavily until they are middle-aged might keep the incidence of FAS low in Chenalhó. Except for a drink at fiestas or curings, during their childbearing and rearing years, few women drink daily or compulsively.

7. Water of Hope, Water of Sorrow

1. In their study of problem drinking Siverts et al. (1973) asked if some people drank too much and did themselves harm. They found the answer startling. Some men widowed late in life drank themselves to death. Otherwise there was no problem (Carter Wilson, personal communication).

2. Both Pedranos and Semais have experienced powerlessness against dominant others, slave raiders for Semais and Ladinos for Pedranos. Semais developed a sense that appearances deceive, that even when things seem safe they may not be (Dentan 1988: 870). Powerlessness was a collective historical experience for both Semais and Pedranos which obviates experiencing powerlessness personally in order to "let go" (ibid.: 876).

3. See Eber 1991: 460–464 for portraits of mestizoized women teachers who drink heavily.

4. Cf. findings of the Mexican National Health Survey which indicate that worrisome drinking in women is highest among divorced and widowed women and among women between sixty and sixty-nine years (Solache-Alcaraz et al. 1990).

5. Studies of American women indicate that women who have multiple roles may have lower rates of alcoholism than women who do not have multiple roles (Wilsnack, Wilsnack, and Klassen 1986).

6. AA's ways of dealing with anger are similar to Pedranos'. AA emphasizes "letting-go" of anger, keeping things simple, and dealing with feelings "one day at a time." These programs recognize that healing is a life-long process best undertaken in a community of fellow sufferers.

7. In a special issue on alcoholism of a Mexican journal, *Nueva Antropología* (New Anthropology) (1988) the authors also take a processual view of alcohol use. They propose situating an individual's alcohol dependence within the overall productive, social, and ideological contexts of alcohol use (ibid.: 4).

8. A move from sobriety into intoxication seems to be a step from symmetry into complementarity cross-culturally. Ethnographic studies of alcohol and other drug use world-wide illustrate that transcendence has been and is still an important goal (Jellinek 1977). It is a rare ethnography about a Latin American people which does not at least mention drug use, often in connection with transcendence (See Eber 1991: 562 for list of some ethnographies).

8. "Beneath God's flowery hands and feet"

1. In addition to sending their nagual, witches in Highland Chiapas may also sell their victims' souls, inject victims with foreign objects, send illness in the air, or harm by contagion or through evil eye. The first and last ways are the most common in Chenalhó. (See Adams and Rubel 1967: 336 for regional variations.)

2. The cleverest shamans, who often have more than an ordinary amount of ego but must use it in service to their people, are usually the only people with jaguar souls. Indigenous people in Highland Chiapas also associate coyote souls with shamans. Both animals are clever, as shamans must be. However, some Chamulas say that drunkards can have jaguar souls and wife beaters coyote souls (Linn 1989: 261).

3. Extreme temperature states are dangerous to Pedranos, especially children. Traditional Pedranos say that the Devil's illness is cold in contrast to rum which is hot. Since rum is hot it has power to counteract the coldness of the Devil. Other dangerously hot states are anger, annoyance, and sleep (Arias in Guiteras-Holmes 1961: 213). Parents protect young children from the coldness of the Devil and dead people, the temporary heat of pregnant women, and the extreme heat of past cargo holders or shamans. Generally Pedranos use cold foods and drinks to treat hot illnesses and hot foods and drinks for cold ones; however, the central concern for Pedrano healers remains determining the condition of the soul. (See Tedlock 1987 for ways K'iche' Maya shamans and laiety apply hot-cold symbolism.)

4. Nash (1967: 133) calls pulsing a kind of exploratory "sociopsy" comparable to biopsy in modern medicine. Shamans in the Tzeltal community Nash studied say that witches leave their signatures in the blood of victims. By pressing her thumb on a patient's wrist a shaman speaks to her patient, causing him to reveal his fears about his social relations.

5. Most shamans receive their cargos in dreams. Rum offered by the Gods in dreams can symbolize one's calling. The powerful beings measure it out in specific quantities and give the healer possession of it for healing. See Laughlin 1976: 7–9 for a list of Zinacantec dream motifs and their interpretations.

6. *Ch'ulelal* is any sickness or injury that comes in dreams. (See Hilario's dream in chapter 4 and Eber 1991: 475–476 for specific types of ch'ulelal.)

7. Pedranos say that common childhood illnesses, like fever and diarrhea, may result from both parents fighting, one of the parents getting drunk and abusing the other or the child, or from one or both parents failing to appreciate their child. A father's drunken anger is perhaps the commonest cause of a child's sickness. (See Eber 1991: 482 for *ta stot ta sme,* a common Pedrano prayer to counteract effects of abusing rum. See Holland 1963 and Fabrega and Silver 1973 for illnesses whose etiology involves witchcraft and drinking.)

8.   Manuela equates a sober lifestyle with standing up. As long as one's feet and hands are moving, one's blood is warm. In contrast, sleeping or passed out one is cold and vulnerable to sickness. Manuela may also be urging Carly to follow the Lord's example as he rises from a squatting, sitting position to a standing position of healing power.

9.   The person or persons soliciting prayer are responsible for supplying rum and other elements. The quantity of rum may range from one to three bottles. Shamans can substitute soda for rum, but most will offer at least one bottle of rum, sprinkling it over branches and around candles if they do not want to drink it. Other elements of prayer include candles, incense, soda, chickens, floral wreaths, saints' pictures, articles of clothing, and boughs from *Liquidambar styraciflua,* the "sweet gum tree." Shamans commonly use three, six, seven, nine, and thirteen candles. Classic Maya conceived of the heavens as composed of thirteen layers and the underworld as composed of nine (Thompson 1970: 195). Most shamans whom I consulted about prayers to stop drinking told me they use three candles. After finishing their prayers, shamans often let their candles burn down so that they will keep feeding the powerful beings. For some prayers shamans tell clients to light a *veladora* (a short thick candle), and keep it lit day and night as a symbol of their life force. Smoke from balls of incense is also food for spiritual beings. Some say that one must offer one ball for each saint called up in prayer. Sweet gum boughs upright in the ground symbolize a person's soul. Branch size depends on time of day of prayer, client's stature, and type of illness.

10.   *Ilbilal pox* is a combination of rum and other ingredients which shamans ask God to bless and then give to sick people. (*Poxil,* the Tzotzil word for "medicine," unites *schi'il,* "total or mixture of various ingredients," with *pox* "rum." Pedranos say that their ancestors used to drink chicha and rum to cure various illnesses. Today Pedranos still use rum in numerous curative drinks. To make ilbilal pox shamans mix from one to three cups of rum in a gourd with pepper, cloves, *pilico* or *sik'olal* (forms of commercial tobacco), *moy* (wild tobacco), and *axux* (garlic). After praying over the contents, asking God to bless it, they give it to the sick person to drink. (See Eber 1991: 479–483 for recipe for ilbilal pox, and other remedies using rum).

11.   Commanding the powerful beings to get up and send their healing power, Pedranos say, "rise, get up, stand up tall" and "stand firm." They assume that God is sitting, like Sun before it begins to rise or as it sets. In order to see the faraway places where his children are and to heal them, God moves into a standing position.

12.   Chickens are *k'exol* (substitutes) for clients' souls in prayer (Arias in Guiteras-Holmes 1961: 174). Shamans sweep live chickens over the bodies of their clients in prayer, absorbing the illness into the chicken. Pedranos also use k'exol to refer to human substitutes in ritual office and children who bear the same name as their parent. A human k'exol is always the same sex, while some shamans say that the substitute for a woman's soul must be a hen and for a man's, a rooster.

13.   After curings everyone present eats. Eating and drinking together, shaman, witnesses, and family members reaffirm bonds of reciprocity with each other and the Gods, thus counteracting the solitary drinking and eating of those who distance themselves from fellow Pedranos and their beneficent beings (e.g., witches, some Protestants, and mestizoized Pedranos living in San Cristóbal). Linn (1989: 261) suggests that eating alone may be a metaphor for the capacity to live without constant spiritual supervision.

14.   A popular strategy among Ladinas who want their husbands to stop drinking is to secretly put medicine in their husbands' drinks that makes them sick. They hope that eventually their husbands will decide that they are getting sick because their bodies can no longer take liquor.

15.   "I am beneath thy feet, beneath thy hands" is a commonly repeated phrase in Q'eqchi' Maya prayers from Guatemala (Abigail E. Adams, personal communication).

16.   See Laughlin 1993b: 104 for poetic associations Zinacantecos make between plants, the Gods, and rum.

17.   Laughlin (1988: 8) compares Earth Lord with the Faustian devil, bestower of both treasure and death. Food and drink consumed in dreams ". . . are products of the netherworld, transferring their subterranean chill to the dreamer's body" (ibid.: 9).

18.   Cf. dialectical complementarity between shamans and Catholic Action converts in Momostenango, a Highland Maya community in Guatemala (Tedlock 1986).

9. "It's time to change"

1.   Women who marry after twenty-five usually marry widowers or divorced men. (Most girls marry when they are between fourteen to sixteen years of age).

2.   See Rosenbaum's (1993: 55–61) discussion of Chamula men's and women's extramarital affairs, and community reactions to men's pursuit of second wives.

3.   See Eber 1991: 460–464 for portraits of women teachers who drink heavily.

4.   In her study of drunkenness and domestic violence in the Republic of Palau, Caroline Islands, Nero (1990) argues that Palauans play out the stresses of economic and social change in their marital relationships. As in Chenalhó, women's increased power as wage earners is threatening their spouses. Nero suggests that while traditional Palauan society afforded women high status, and wife-beating was not accepted, today Palauans seem to excuse such behavior when perpetrators are drunk. Since Palauans first learned to produce alcoholic beverages during the Japanese occupation of the Islands in 1914, it seems that both drinking and violence, especially domestic, have increased.

5.   When drunk, Pedrano men tend to imitate Ladino men. For example, many Pedranos who know Spanish but only use it when they have to will speak Spanish when drunk. Similarly, Harvey (1988) notes that drunkenness encourages Quechua speakers to use Spanish, opening the door to new forms of discourse through which they confront the contradictions and ambiguities of their lives.

6.   See Rosenbaum 1993: 174–175, 178 for a discussion of gender ideology and women in the Chamula court.

10. "For ye are bought with a price"

1.   *Me' santo* (mother of the saint), is a box containing an image or picture of a saint or a stone that a Pedrano claims to have found in a sacred place in the earth. Consultations involve placing an offering of rum, candles, or money beside the box, then addressing the box with one's problem. Sometimes the saint "talks" by tapping on the box; other times petitioners or owners hear the saint "talking."

2.   Dialogue between Traditionalists and followers of various Protestant groups and Catholic Action continued in local meetings, and at the township level, during the year and a half I was in Chenalhó. (See Eber 1991: 369–374 for excerpts from the transcription of a township-wide gathering in October 1988 on "Justice and Tradition" organized by the *Instituto Nacional Indigenísta*.)

3.   Protestants hold their own feasts, often at the same time as traditional ones. Protestant feasts are alcohol-free.

4.   Weber (1958) argued that the Calvinist doctrine, which stresses hard work and moral virtue, facilitates productive capitalism. See Kearney 1970, Nash 1960, Watanabe

1992, and Goldin and Metz 1991 for their studies of conversion and connections with alcoholism and social change in Mexico and Guatemala.

5. I am grateful to Vern (René) Sterk and Carla Sterk for information on Protestant pastors' ideas about drinking.

6. Although women seek shamans for more serious problems and take care of minor illnesses themselves, if they want to go to a clinic their husbands sometimes veto their wishes. At times a husbands' last words mean that a child suffers or dies (Eber 1991: 254–255).

7. Marshall and Marshall (1990: 147) suggest that "prohibition" is a misnomer because it does not prevent people from drinking. They suggest that what prohibition does often accomplish is more temperate behavior expressed in either reduced drinking or in reduced social disruption and violence associated with drinking, or both.

8. The potential for different groups to coexist in Chenalhó seems unique among neighboring Highland townships. In Chamula, for example, conflict between religious groups over rum sales and traditions reached a peak in the early 1970s. It ended in Traditional Chamula political leaders expelling thousands of Protestant Chamulas from their land, at gunpoint. About 20,000 Chamulas have been expelled since 1974. Some *expulsados* (expelled people) founded evangelical communities around San Cristóbal; others live in squatter settlements (Rosenbaum 1993: 179–184; Gossen 1989: 217–229).

11. "Today we say: Enough!"

1. This phrase was the cry of the Zapatista National Liberation Army on January 1, 1994, when it launched an armed rebellion in several Highland Chiapas towns. I use the Zapatistas' cry to frame this discussion of Pedranas' new ways of speaking and collective actions because it describes the tenor of women's growing resistance to accepting domination by powerful outsiders.

2. In 1988, at a township-wide meeting, authorities agreed that rum sellers could keep selling rum while paying a tax. However, they limited sales to two days of the week, Saturday and Sunday, from six A.M. to four P.M. Rum sellers who went ten or fifteen minutes beyond the deadline would go to jail for five hours. Repeat offenders would go to jail for twelve hours and pay a 5,000 peso fine. The third time they would lose their right to sell.

3. Patriarchies, such as Pedranas live in, can become crucial organizing issues for women outside the intelligentsia. Alcohol was the focal point of patriarchal domination in two successful women's organizations in the United States in the nineteenth century, the Women's Christian Temperance Movement and the Anti-Saloon League. These organizations radicalized women to the extent that they challenged male prerogatives, such as getting drunk. Men's mockery of the WCTU and the Anti-Saloon League reflects just how threatened they were by these movements. Ten years ago in Mexico, Chatino women from Santiago Yaitepec, Oaxaca, began a movement to prohibit drinking which is still in effect. Women's temperance movements need reassessment, and Indigenous women's movements in Mexico need further study. I am grateful to Robert Dentan for pointing out to me the connections between Pedranas' organizing experiences around problem drinking and those of women in different kinds of patriarchies.

4. The group which Antonia represents had its beginnings in Sna Jolobil, one of the oldest and largest of the cooperatives in Highland Chiapas. Since 1988, when there were four weaving cooperatives in Chenalhó, cooperatives have proliferated. Before

weaving cooperatives developed in the 1960s and 1970s the only outlets available to Indigenous women were direct sales to tourists, or sales to Ladinos whose shops lined the streets of San Cristóbal. Then and now Ladinos rarely pay weavers what their work is worth, and often make large profits. Cooperatives provide Indigenous people the potential to resist economic exploitation (Eber and Rosenbaum 1993).

5.   While tension is increasing in Chenalhó, it has always been more intense in communities like Amatenango (Nash 1993) and Chamula (Rosenbaum 1993; Rus 1990, 1994). This difference may be due to a combination of factors, including a class of powerful men in Chamula and women's greater access in both Chamula and Amatenango to non-traditional markets. (See Nash 1993: 127–129 for the story of a young woman who was murdered because of her artisan activities.)

6.   D. Rus and J. Rus (personal communication) add that Chamula women may take a lot of abuse before leaving their husbands. They suggest that women reflect on beatings by drunk husbands, recently returned from plantation work, in the context of their shared struggle to survive in a hostile and fragile world. The Ruses suggest that with plantation work less plentiful in recent years, women may be less willing to put up with their kinsmen's drunken abuse.

7.   For discussions of the complexities of Mesoamerican women's productive roles see Bennholdt-Thomsen 1993; Bossen 1984; Chiñas 1973; Ehlers 1990, 1991; Nash 1993; Rothstein 1983; Rus 1990; Stephen 1991; and Young 1982.

8.   See Garza Caligaris and Ruiz Ortiz 1992, Juárez Ch'ix and de la Cruz Cruz 1992, and Freyermuth Enciso and Fernández Guerrero 1993 for personal testimonies of single Indigenous women living in and around San Cristóbal. Studies of Native American women in the United States and Canada who move away from their communities indicate that they appear to be at higher risk for developing drinking problems (LaDue 1991).

9.   I am grateful to Elizabeth Kennedy for helping me toward an understanding of Indigenous women that respects their integration in a whole with an economic and spiritual base which the individual rights focus of American feminism cannot replace.

Epilogue

1.   Cristóbal Ruíz Arias provided the Spanish translation of this Tzotzil prayer for inclusion in the film *Chiapas: Prayer for the Weavers,* produced by Judith Gleason (New York: Filmmaker's Library, 1998.) The English translation is mine.

2.   I use the term "civil society" to refer to those Pedranos who oppose the domination of the Revolutionary Institutional Party (PRI).

3.   I am grateful to Jennifer Abassi for her insights on the importance of local-level research to convey women's agency. Since the Zapatista uprising we have been able to read the words of many Indigenous people from diverse localities. For example, see Freyermuth n.d.; Gutiérrez Pérez 1998; Hernández Castillo et al. 1998; Ortiz 2000; Pérez Tzu 1995, 1999; and Rovira 1997. For additional insights from Antonia, see Eber 1998, 1999; for insights from Mónica, see Eber 1998.

4.   Since the uprising many Catholics working for social justice have been persecuted and several priests have been deported. On February 15, 1997, Michel Chanteau, Padre Miguel, was deported to France after 32 years of service in Chenalhó. His expulsion came several months after Jacinto Arias Cruz, township mayor at the time, threatened Chanteau's life. For background on The Preferential Option for the Poor in Chiapas

(known in Chenalhó as The Word of God and as Liberation Theology in other parts of the world) see MacEoin 1995; the web page of the Diocese of San Cristóbal de las Casas, http://www.laneta.apc.org/curiasc; and Chanteau 1999.

5.   The EZLN's Women's Law has ten points (*Doble Jornada*, February 7, 1994). In 1997 women in Antonia's base received from EZLN representatives an expanded agenda of thirty-four points regarding women's rights. See Eber 1999 for a discussion of women's views and projects in Antonia's support base.

6.   For discussions of women's economic strategies, including cooperatives, see O'Brian 1997; Rovira 1997; and Tanski and Eber, n.d.a and n.d.b. For discussions of women's participation in public life see Garza n.d.; Harvey and Halverson forthcoming; Hernández Castillo 1998; Rojas 1994; Rovira 1997; and Stephen 1996. See Kovic and Eber n.d. for a collection of works about women in the struggle for peace and social justice.

7.   For a historical survey of relations between Pedranos and the state see Garza and Hernández Castillo 1998, and Eber n.d. For a broader discussion of the reordering of native society in Chiapas before and after the uprising see Collier and Quaratiello 1999; Harvey 1998; Nash 1995; Rus 1995; and Rus et al. n.d.

8.   For background on Las Abejas see Hidalgo 1998. For accounts of events leading up to and after the massacre at Acteal see Arriaga et al. 1998; Aubry and Inda 1998; Centro de Derechos Humanos Fray Bartolomé de Las Casas 1998; and Marín 1998b. Hernández Castillo et al. 1998 and Speed n.d. provide women-centered analyses of the effects of the low-intensity war. For a discussion of the Mexican military's part in forming and maintaining paramilitaries see Marín 1998a.

Glossary

la acción: making the motion of drinking a cup of rum without actually drinking it. (Sp.)

Acción Católica: Catholic Action; the grassroots movement of Liberation Theology in Highland Chiapas. (Sp.)

alperes: standard bearer of fiestas. (Tz.)

atole: a hot rice drink or a variety of hot corn-based drinks made for special occasions. (Sp.) Tz. *ul.*

cabecera: head village and administrative and economic center of a *municipio* or township. (Sp.)

campesino: a person who works the land, a peasant. (Sp.)

cargo: work on behalf of one's community, literally burden or weight. (Sp.) Tzotzil distinguishes between *abtel patan* (work for the community), such as is done by a *regidor* (councilman), and *nichimal abtel* (work for the Gods), such as is done by the *me' alperes* (madam standard bearer).

Catechist: a Catholic Action lay leader.

chicha: fermented sugar cane juice. (Sp.) Tz. *yakil vo'* (literally, "confused water").

cooperación: the monetary contribution each household donates for three annual community masses in the hills. (Sp.)

copal: a resin from the sweet gum tree, shaped into balls, hardened and burned for ritual purposes. Tz. *pom.*

cuarta: small beer, Coke, or Pepsi bottle. (Sp.)

enganche: system of labor contracting for coffee plantations or logging camps; literally "hooking". (Sp.)

Evangelico: a Presbyterian or any Protestant. (Sp.)

k'exol: change of religious or political office, the one to whom one gives an office. (Tz.)

k'op: prayer, word, problem. (Tz.)

Ladino: a term which Pedranos often use interchangeably with Mestizo to denote non-Indigenous people living in Mexico.

Madre: a Catholic nun, "Mother." (Sp.)

matz': uncooked maize dough, mixed with water for a drink. Also called *uchu mo'*. (Tz.)

me': mother; a female marker. (Tz.) *me'* precedes the titles of all female ritual roles, e.g., *me' alperes*. (See *alperes*)

Mesoamerica: an area approximately from the Panuca-Lerma drainage north of Mexico City through Central America to east of the Ulua River and Lake Yojoa in Honduras, where Aztec and Maya civilizations flourished before the Spanish invasion.

milpa: corn and bean field. (Sp.) Tz. *chob.*

moy: a mixture of ground wild tobacco (Tz. *vako'*, Sp. *bobo tabaco*, L. *Nicotiana tabacum*) and unslaked lime used as a talisman. (Tz.)

nagual: a person who transforms himself into an animal to harm others. (Tz.; variant is *naval.*)

nichimal: flowery. (Tz.) Glosses include: "sacred" (Arias 1985), "beautiful" (Laughlin 1975), and "pretty" (Holland 1963).

pasado/a: a man or woman who has held important religious or political cargos. (Sp.) Tz. *pasaro/a.*

paxyon: passion; the name of the highest officials of Carnival. (Tz.; pl. *paxyonetik.*) From Sp. *pasión.*

Pedrano/a: a Tzotzil-speaking man or woman born and raised in San Pedro Chenalhó. (Sp.)

peso: basic unit of Mexican currency. (Sp.) In 1987 1,000 pesos equaled about one U.S. dollar.

pox: term for medicine, and rum made from distilled sugar cane juice. (Tz.) Sp. *aguardiente.*

poxil: medicine. (Tz.) *Poxil* unites *pox* (rum) with *schi'il* (total or mixture of various ingredients).

pulque: a fermented drink made from maguey; Nahuatl *octli. pulquería* a shop selling pulque. (Sp.)

San Cristóbal de Las Casas: the urban center of Highland Chiapas, about 25 air miles from Chenalhó. (Sp.) Tz. *jobel* (thatch grass).

San Pedro Chenalhó: one of the eighteen Tzotzil-speaking *municipios* (the Mexican political division below the state comparable to townships) in Highland Chiapas, Mexico. (Sp.)

semet: the round clay or metal griddle for baking tortillas. (Tz.) Sp. *comal.*

tortilla: a very thin, unleavened maize pancake. (Sp.) Tz. *vaj.*

totil me'il: the father/mother ancestor/protectors. (Tz.)

Tzotzil: one of the four languages (Tzeltal, Tojolobal and Chol being the other three) spoken by Mayas in Chiapas.

vixin: sister. (Tz.)

world tree, ceiba, silk-cotton tree, "God-tree," Tz. *mojan*, L. *Ceiba pentandra:* To ancient Mayas, who called it *yaxche*, the ceiba was the fifth world direction (up and down).

References

Adams, R. H., and A. J. Rubel
1967　Sickness and Social Relations. In *Handbook of Middle American Indians*, gen. ed. Robert Wauchope. Vol. 6: 333–356.

Alcoholics Anonymous
1987　*Twelve Steps and Twelve Traditions*. New York: Alcoholics Anonymous World Services, Inc.

Alkali Lake Indian Band
1985　*The Honour of All*. Williams Lake, British Columbia, Canada: Alkali Lake Indian Band, video cassette series: 1, 2, 3.

Allen, Catherine J.
1988　*The Hold Life Has: Coca and Cultural Identity in an Andean Community*. Washington, D.C.: Smithsonian Institution Press.

American Psychiatric Association
1987　*Diagnostic and Statistical Manual of Mental Disorders*. 3d ed. rev. Washington, D.C.

Arias, Jacinto
1973　The Numinous World of the Maya: Contemporary Structure and Change. Master's thesis, Catholic University, Washington, D.C.
1985　*San Pedro Chenalhó: Algo de su historia, cuentos y costumbres*. Chiapas: Publicación Bilinque de la Dirección de Fortalecimiento y Fomento a las Culturas de la Sub-Secretaría de Asuntos Indígenas.

Arriaga Alarcón, Pedro, Rodrigo González Torres, and Carlos Morfín Otero, eds.
1998　*Acteal: Una herida abierta*. Tlaquepaque, Jalisco, México: Instituto Tecnológico y de Estudios Superiores de Occidente (ITESCO).

Aubry, Andrés, and Angélica Inda
1998　"Acteal antes del 22 de diciembre." In *Acteal: Una herida abierta*, eds. Arriaga Alarcón et al., 71–83. Tlaquepaque, Jalisco, México: ITESCO.

Bateson, Gregory
1971   The Cybernetics of "Self": A Theory of Alcoholism. *Psychiatry* 34:1–18.

Beals, Ralph
1946   *Cherán: A Sierra Tarascan Village.* Washington, D.C.: Smithsonian Institution, Institute of Social Anthropology, Publication no. 2.

Behar, Ruth
1993   *Translated Woman: Crossing the Border with Esperanza's Story.* Boston: Beacon Press.

Bell, Diane
1983   *Daughters of the Dreaming.* Melbourne: McPhee Gribble Publishers.

Bennholdt-Thomsen, Veronica
1993   Comercio como arte: Las vendedores de Juchitan, Oaxaca en el decado novento. Paper presented in a pre-session of the XIII International Congress of Anthropological and Ethnological Sciences, San Cristóbal de Las Casas, Chiapas, Mexico.

Berger, John
1979   *Pig Earth.* New York: Pantheon Books.

Berryman, Phillip
1987   *Liberation Theology: The Essential Facts about the Revolutionary Movement in Latin America and Beyond.* New York: Pantheon Books.

Blaffer, S. C.
1972   *The Black-man of Zinacantán: A Central American Legend.* Austin: University of Texas Press.

Bossen, Laurel
1983   Sexual Stratification in Mesoamerica. In *Heritage of Conquest: Thirty Years Later,* ed. C. Kendall, J. Hawkins, and L. Bossen, 35–72. Albuquerque: University of New Mexico Press.
1984   *The Redivision of Labor: Women and Economic Choice in Four Guatemalan Communities.* Albany: State University of New York Press.

Breedlove, Dennis, and Robert Laughlin
1993   *The Flowering of Man: A Tzotzil Botany of Zinacantán.* Vol. 1. Smithsonian Contributions to Anthropology, no. 35. Washington, D.C.: Smithsonian Institution Press.

Bricker, Victoria R.
1973   *Ritual Humor in Highland Chiapas.* Austin: University of Texas Press.
1981   *The Indian Christ, The Indian King: The Historical Substrate of Maya Myth and Ritual.* Austin: University of Texas Press.

Bunzel, Ruth
1940   The Role of Alcoholism in Two Central American Cultures. *Psychiatry* 3:361–387.

Burkhart, Louise
1992   Las mujeres mexicas en el frente del hogar: Trabajo doméstico y religión en el México azteca. *Mesoamérica* 23:23–54.

Caetano, R.
1987 Drinking Patterns and Alcohol Problems in a National Survey of U.S. Hispanics. In *Alcohol Use among U.S. Ethnic Minorities.* ed. D. Spiegler, D. Tate, S. Aitken, and C. Christian, 147–162. NIAAA Research Monograph No. 18 DHHS Pub. No. (ADM) 89-1435. Washington, D.C.: Supt. of Docs., U.S. Govt. Printing Office.

Calderon-Narvaez, Guillermo
1968 Consideraciones acerca del alcoholism entre los pueblos prehispanicos de México. *Revista del Instituto Nacional de Neurologia* 2 (3): 5–13.

Calnek, Edward A.
1988 Highland Chiapas before the Spanish Conquest. In *Archaeology, Ethnohistory, and Ethnoarchaeology in the Maya Highlands of Chiapas, Mexico,* no. 55 Provo, Utah: New World Archaeological Foundation.

Calvo, Angelino, Anna María Garza, María Fernanda Paz, and Juan María Ruiz
1989 *Voces de la historia: Nuevo San Juana Chamula, Nuevo Huixtán, Nuevo Matzam.* San Cristóbal de Las Casas: DESMI, A.C.- CEI, UNACH.

Cancian, Frank
1965 *Economics and Prestige in a Maya Community: The Religious Cargo System in Zinacantán.* Stanford: Stanford University Press.

Carter, W. E.
1977 Ritual, the Aymara, and the Role of Alcohol in Human Society. In *Drugs, Rituals and Altered States of Consciousness,* ed. B. de Toit, 101–110. Rotterdam: A. A. Halkema.

Centro de Derechos Humanos Fray Bartolomé de Las Casas
1998 *Camino a la masacre. Informe especial sobre Chenalhó.* San Cristóbal de Las Casas, Chiapas, México: Centro de Derechos Humanos.

Chalfant, H., and B. Roper
1980 *Social and Behavioral Aspects of Female Alcoholism: An Annotated Bibliography.* Westport, Conn.: Greenwood Press.

Chanteau, Miguel
1999 *Las Andanzas de Miguel: La autobiografía del padre expulsado de Chenalhó.* San Cristóbal de Las Casas, Chiapas, México: Editorial Fray Bartolomé de Las Casas, A.C.

Chiñas, Beverly
1973 *The Isthmus Zapotecs: Women's Roles in Cultural Context.* New York: Holt, Rinehart and Winston.

Chodorow, Nancy
1974 Family Structure and Feminine Personality. In *Woman, Culture and Society,* ed. Michelle Rosaldo and Louise Lamphere, 43–67. Stanford: Stanford University Press.

Clark, W. B., and L. Midanik
1988 Alcohol Use and Alcohol Problems among U.S. Adults: Results of the 1979 National Survey. In *Alcohol Consumption and Related Problems,* 3–50.

NIAAA Alcohol and Health Monograph No. 1 DHHS Pub. No. (ADM) 82-1190. Washington, D.C.: Supt. of Docs., U.S. Govt. Printing Office.

Clifford, James, and George Marcus, eds.

1986 *Writing Culture: The Poetics and Politics of Ethnography.* Berkeley: University of California Press.

Collier, George

1990 Seeking Food and Seeking Money: Changing Productive Relations in a Highland Mexican Community. United Nations Research Institute for Development. Occasional Paper.

Collier, George, with Elizabeth Quaratiello

1999 *Basta—Land and the Zapatista Rebellion in Chiapas,* 2nd edition. Oakland, CA: Food First Books, Institute for Food and Development Policy.

Collier, Jane

1968 *Courtship and Marriage in Zinacantán, Chiapas, Mexico.* New Orleans. Middle American Research Institute. Publication 25: 149–201.

1973 *Law and Social Change in Zinacantán.* Stanford: Stanford University Press.

Collier, Jane, and Michelle Rosaldo

1981 Politics and Gender in Simple Societies. In *Sexual Meanings, the Cultural Construction of Gender,* ed. Sherry Ortner and Harriet Whitehead, 275–329. Cambridge: Cambridge University Press.

Colson, Elizabeth, and Thayer Scudder

1988 *For Prayer and Profit: The Ritual, Economic, and Social Importance of Beer in Gwembe District, Zambia, 1950–1982.* Stanford: Stanford University Press.

Cortes, Beatriz

1988 La funcionalidad contradictoria del consumo colectivo de alcohol. *Nueva Antropología* 10 (34): 157–186.

Crump, Thomas

1987 The Alternative Economy of Alcohol in the Chiapas Highlands. In *Constructive Drinking,* ed. Mary Douglas, 239–249. New York: Cambridge University Press.

Dentan, Robert K.

1988 Ambiguity, Synecdoche and Affect in Semai Medicine. *Social Science and Medicine* 27 (8): 857–877.

1992 The Rise, Maintenance and Destruction of Peaceable Polity: A Preliminary Essay in Political Ecology. In *Aggression and Peacefulness in Humans and Other Primates,* ed. James Silverberg and Patrick Gray, 214–269. New York: Oxford University Press.

Devereaux, Leslie

1987 Gender Difference and the Relations of Inequality in Zinacantán. In *Dealing with Inequality: Analysing Gender Relations in Melanesia and Beyond,* ed. M. Strathern, 89–111. Cambridge: Cambridge University Press.

di Leonardo, Micaela

1989 Malinowski's Nephews. *The Nation* (March 13): 350–352.

1991 Gender, Culture and Political Economy: Feminist Anthropology in Historical Perspective. In *Gender at the Crossroads of Knowledge: Feminist Anthropology in the Postmodern Era,* ed. Micaela di Leonardo, 1–48. Berkeley: University of California Press.

Dinnerstein, Dorothy

1975 *The Mermaid and the Minotaur: Sexual Arrangements and Human Malaise.* New York: Harper and Row.

Doble Jornada

1994 "Ley Revolucionaria de mujeres." February 7.

Dorris, Michael

1989 *The Broken Cord: A Family's Ongoing Struggle With Fetal Alcohol Syndrome.* New York: Harper and Row.

1990 Pregnancy and Alcohol. *Winds of Change* 5 (4): 36–40.

Eber, Christine E.

2000 "'That They Be in the Middle, Lord:' Women, Weaving and Cultural Survival in Highland Chiapas, Mexico." In *Artisans and Cooperatives: Developing Alternative Trade for the Global Economy,* eds. Kimberly Grimes and Lynne Milgram. Tucson: University of Arizona Press.

1999 "Seeking Our Own Food: Indigenous Women's Power and Autonomy in San Pedro Chenalhó, Chiapas (1980–1998)." *Latin American Perspectives* 26 (3): 6–36.

1998 "Seeking Justice, Valuing Community: Two Women's Paths in the Wake of the Zapatista Rebellion." East Lansing, MI: Center for Women in International Development Working Papers Series #265, Michigan State University.

n.d. "Buscando una nueva vida (Searching for a new life): Liberation through Autonomy in San Pedro Chenalhó, 1970–1998." In *Taking the Future into Our Own Hands: The Impact of the Uprising in Chiapas Four Years After,* eds. Jan Rus, Shannon Mattiace, and Rosalva Aída Hernández Castillo. *Forthcoming.*

1991 Before God's Flowering Face: Women and Drinking in a Tzotzil-Maya Community. Ph.D. diss., State University of New York at Buffalo.

Eber, Christine E., and Brenda P. Rosenbaum

1993 "That We May Serve Beneath Your Flowery Hands and Feet": Women Weavers in Highland Chiapas, Mexico. In *Crafts in the World Market: The Impact of Global Exchange on Middle American Artisans,* ed. June Nash, 154–180. Albany: State University of New York Press.

Ehlers, Tracy

1990 *Silent Looms: Women and Production in a Guatemalan Town.* Boulder: Westview Press.

1991   Debunking Marianismo: Economic Vulnerability and Survival Strategies among Guatemalan Wives. *Ethnology* 30:1–16.

Elmendorf, Mary

1976   *Nine Mayan Women.* New York: Schenkman Publishing Co.

Evans-Pritchard, E. E.

1940   *The Nuer: A Description of the Modes of Livelihood and Political Institutions of a Nilotic People.* Oxford: Clarendon Press.

Fabrega, Horacio, and Daniel Silver

1973   *Illness and Shamanistic Curing in Zinacantán: An Ethnomedical Analysis.* Stanford: Stanford University Press.

Farriss, Nancy

1984   *Maya under Colonial Rule.* Princeton, N. J.: Princeton University Press.

Foster, George M.

1944   Nagualism in Mexico and Guatemala. *Acta Americana* 2:85–103.

Freidel, David, and Linda Schele

1993   Maya Royal Women: A Lesson in Precolumbian History. In *Gender in Cross-Cultural Perspective,* ed. C. Brettell and C. Sargent, 59–63. Englewood Cliffs, N.J.: Prentice Hall.

Freyermuth Enciso, Graciela

n.d.   "Violencia y etnia en Chenalhó formas comunitarias de revolución de conflictos." Unpublished manuscript.

Freyermuth Enciso, Graciela, and Mariana Fernández Guerrero

1993   *Migration, Organization and Identity. The Women's Group Case in San Cristóbal de Las Casas.* Paper presented in a pre-session of the XIII International Congress of Anthropological and Ethnological Sciences, San Cristóbal de Las Casas, Chiapas, Mexico.

Gage, Thomas

1958   *Travels in the New World.* Edited by J. E. S. Thompson. Norman: Oklahoma University Press.

Garza Caligaris, Ana María

n.d.   "Pluralidad legal y género en la vida cotidiana de San Pedro Chenalhó." Doctoral thesis.

Garza Caligaris, Ana María, and Rosalva Aída Hernández Castillo

1998   "Encuentros y enfrentamientos de los Tzotziles Pedranos con el estado mexicano: Una perspectiva histórico-antropológica para entender la violencia en Chenalhó." In *La otra palabra: Violencia y la mujer en Chiapas, antes y despues de Acteal,* ed. Rosalva Aída Hernández Castillo. México: CIESAS, COLEM, and CIAM, 39–62.

Garza Caligaris, Ana María, and Juana María Ruiz Ortiz

1992   Madres solteras indígenas. *Mesoamérica* 23:67–77.

Gates, William

1978   Identification of Plant Names Mentioned in Landa's Text. In *Yucatán be-*

fore and after the Conquest, by Friar Diego de Landa, translated with notes by William Gates, 161. New York: Dover.

Gleason, Judith
1998 *Chiapas: Prayer for the Weavers.* Video cassette. New York: Filmmakers Library.

Global Exchange
1998 *On the Offensive: Intensified Military Occupation in Chiapas Six Months since the Massacre at Acteal, A Special Investigative Report.* San Francisco: Global Exchange. (www.globalexchange.org).

Goldin, Liliana, and Brent Metz
1991 An Expression of Cultural Change: Invisible Converts to Protestantism among Highland Guatemala Mayas. *Ethnology* 30 (4): 325–338.

Gomberg, Edith S.
1982 Historical and Political Perspectives: Women and Drug Use. *Journal of Social Issues* 38 (2): 9–24.

Gossen, Gary H.
1974 *Chamulas in the World of the Sun: Time and Space in a Maya Oral Tradition.* Prospect Heights, Ill.: Waveland Press.

1986a The Chamula Festival of Games: Native Macroanalysis and Social Commentary in a Maya Carnival. In *Symbol and Meaning Beyond the Closed Corporate Community: Essays in Mesoamerican Ideas,* ed. Gary Gossen, 227–254. Studies in Culture, vol. 1. Albany: Institute for Mesoamerican Studies, State University of New York.

1986b Mesoamerican Ideas as a Foundation for Regional Synthesis. In *Symbol and Meaning beyond the Closed Corporate Community: Essays in Mesoamerican Ideas,* ed. Gary Gossen, 1–8. Studies in Culture, vol. 1. Albany: Institute for Mesoamerican Studies, State University of New York.

1989 Life, Death, and Apotheosis of a Chamula Protestant Leader: Biography as Social History. In *Ethnographic Encounters in Southern Mesoamerica,* ed. V. Bricker and G. Gossen, 217–229. Studies on Culture and Society, vol. 3. Albany: Institute for Mesoamerican Studies, State University of New York.

Gossen, Gary H., and Richard Leventhal
1993 The Topography of Ancient Maya Religious Pluralism: A Dialogue with the Present. In *Lowland Maya Civilization in the Eighth Century A.D.,* ed. J. A. Sabloff and J. S. Henderson, 185–218. Washington, D.C.: Dumbarton Oaks.

Guiteras-Holmes, Calixta
1961 *Perils of the Soul: The World View of a Tzotzil Indian.* Chicago: University of Chicago Press.

Gutiérrez Pérez, Antonio
1998 "Testimonio de un desplazado después de la masacre." In *Acteal: Una*

herida abierta, ed. Arriaga Alarcón et al., 99–104. Tlaquepaque, Jalisco, México: ITESCO.

Haaken, Janice
1993   From Al-Anon to ACOA: Codependence and the Reconstruction of Caregiving. *Signs* 18 (2): 321–345.

Harstock, Nancy
1987   Rethinking Modernism. *Cultural Critique* 7:187–206.

Harvey, Neil
1998   *The Chiapas Rebellion: The Struggle for Land and Democracy.* Durham, NC: Duke University Press.

Harvey, Neil, and Chris Halverson
1999   "The Secret and the Promise: Women's Struggles in Chiapas." In *Discourse Theory and Political Analysis,* ed. Aletta Norval and David Howarth. Manchester, England: Manchester University Press.

Harvey, Penelope M.
1988   Drunken Speech and the Construction of Meaning: Bilingual Competence in the Southern Peruvian Andes. Paper presented at the XIV International Congress of the Latin American Studies Association, New Orleans.

Haviland, John
1977   *Gossip, Reputation and Knowledge in Zinacantán.* Chicago: University of Chicago Press.

Haviland, John, and Leslie Haviland
1979   "Inside the Fence": The Social Basis of Privacy in Nabenchauk. In *Estudios de Cultura Maya,* 323–351. Mexico City: UNAM, IIF, Centro de Estudios Maya.

Heath, Dwight B.
1981   Determining the Sociocultural Context of Alcohol Use. *Journal of Studies on Alcohol* Suppl. 9:9–17.
1988   Emerging Anthropological Theory and Models of Alcohol Use and Alcoholism. In *Theories on Alcoholism,* ed. C. Douglas Chaudron and D. Adrian Wilkinson, 353–410. Toronto: Addiction Research Foundation.
1991   Women and Alcohol: Cross-Cultural Perspectives. *Journal of Substance Abuse* 3:175–185.

Hellbom, Anna-Britta
1967   *La participación cultural de las mujeres: Indias y mestizas en el México precortesiano y postrevolucionario.* Monograph Series, no. 10. Stockholm: The Ethnographic Museum.

Hernández Castillo, Rosalva Aída, et al.
1998   "Antes y despues de Acteal: Voces, memorias y experiencias desde las mujeres de San Pedro Chenalhó." In *La otra palabra: Violencia y la mujer*

en Chiapas, antes y despues de Acteal, ed. Rosalva Aída Hernández Castillo. México: CIESAS, COLEM and CIAM, 15–36.

Hernandez Palomo, José Jesús
1974 *El aguardiente de caña en México (1724–1810).* Seville: Publicaciones de la Escuela de Estudios Hispano-Americanos de Sevilla.

Hidalgo, Onésimo
1998 "El Vuelo de Las Abejas." In *Acteal: Una herida abierta,* eds. Arriaga Alarcón et al. Tlaquepaque, Jalisco, México: ITESCO.

Holland, William
1963 *Medicina maya en los altos de Chiapas.* México: Instituto Nacional Indigenista.

Jellinek, E. M.
1977 The Symbolism of Drinking: A Cultural-Historical Approach. *Quarterly Journal of Studies on Alcohol* 38:849–866.

Jiménez López, Loxa, and Ambar Past
1987 I Am Woman My Woman. In *Ixok Amar Go: Central American Women's Poetry for Peace,* ed. Zoe Anglesey, 36–39. Penobscot, Maine: Granite Press.

Jones, B. M., and J. K. Jones
1976 Women and Alcohol: Intoxication, Metabolism, and the Menstrual Cycle. In *Alcoholism Problems in Women and Children ,* ed. M. Greenblatt and M. A. Schuckit, 103–136. New York: Grune and Stratton.

Juarez Ch'ix, Isabel, and Petrona de la Cruz Cruz
1992 La desconfiada. *Mesoamérica* 23:135–141.

Kaberry, P. M.
1939 *Aboriginal Woman, Sacred and Profane.* London: George Routledge and Sons.

Kearney, Michael
1970 Drunkenness and Religious Conversion in a Mexican Village. *Quarterly Journal of Studies on Alcohol* 31:132–152.

Kennedy, Elizabeth, and Madeline Davis
1993 *Boots of Leather, Slippers of Gold: The History of a Lesbian Community.* New York: Routledge.

Kennedy, John
1978 The Role of Beer in Tarahumara Culture. *American Anthropologist* 60:620–640.

Kilbourne, Jean
1991 The Spirit of the Czar: Selling Addictions to Women. In *Alcohol and Drugs Are Women's Issues,* vol. 1, *A Review of the Issues,* ed. P. Roth, 10–22. Metuchen, N.J.: Women's Action Alliance and Scarecrow Press.

Kintz, Ellen
1990 Planting by the Moon: The Myths and Realities of Maya Women. Paper

presented at the American Anthropological Association Meetings, New Orleans.

Komes Peres, María, with Diana Rus and Salvador Guzmán

1990   *Bordando milpas.* San Cristóbal de Las Casas: Instituto de Asesoría Antropológica para la Regíon Maya, A.C.

Kovic, Christine and Christine Eber, eds.

n.d.   "Defending Their Dignity: Women and the Struggle for Peace and Democracy in Chiapas." Unpublished manuscript.

Lacy, Sara

1976   Antel. Bachelor thesis, Department of Anthropology, Harvard University.

LaDue, Robin

1991   Coyote Returns: Survival for Native American Women. In *Alcohol and Drugs Are Women's Issues,* vol. 1, *A Review of the Issues,* ed. P. Roth, 23–31. Metuchen, N.J.: Women's Action Alliance and Scarecrow Press.

Landa, Fray Diego de

1941   *Landa's Relación de las cosas de Yucatán.* Translated and edited by Alfred M. Tozzer. Cambridge: Peabody Museum of Archaeology and Ethnology.

Larson, Brooke, and Robert Wasserstrom

1982   Consumo forzoso en Cochabamba y Chiapa durante la epoca colonial. *Historia Mexicana* 31 (3): 361–408.

Laughlin, Miriam

1991   *The Drama of Mayan Women. MS,* July/August, 88–89.

Laughlin, Robert

1963   *Through the Looking Glass: Reflections on Zinacantán Courtship and Marriage.* Ph.D. diss., Harvard University.

1975   *The Great Tzotzil Dictionary from San Lorenzo Zinacantán.* Smithsonian Contributions to Anthropology, no. 19. Washington, D.C.: Smithsonian Institution Press.

1976   *Of Wonders Wild and New: Dreams from Zinacantán.* Smithsonian Contributions to Anthropology, no. 22. Washington, D.C.: Smithsonian Institution Press.

1988   *The People of the Bat: Mayan Tales and Dreams from Zinacantán.* Washington, D.C.: Smithsonian Institution Press.

1993a For a Handful, a Fistful. In *The Flowering of Man: A Tzotzil Botany of Zinacantán,* vol. 1, ed. Dennis Breedlove and Robert Laughlin, 49–65. Smithsonian Contributions to Anthropology, no. 35. Washington, D.C.: Smithsonian Institution Press.

1993b Poetic License. In *The Flowering of Man: A Tzotzil Botany of Zinacantán,* vol. 1, ed. Dennis Breedlove and Robert Laughlin, 101–108. Smithsonian Contributions to Anthropology, no. 35. Washington, D.C.: Smithsonian Institution Press.

Leacock, Eleanor

1972   Introduction. In *The Origins of the Family, Private Property and the State*, by Frederick Engels, 7–76. New York: International Publishers.

1983   Interpreting the Origins of Gender Inequality: Conceptual and Historical Problems. *Dialectical Anthropology* 7:263–284.

Leacock, E., and June Nash

1977   Ideologies of Sex: Archetypes and Stereotypes. *New York Academy of Sciences Annals* 285:618–645.

Linn, Priscilla R.

1976   The Religious Office Holders in Chamula: A Study of Gods, Ritual and Sacrifice. Ph.D. diss., Department of Anthropology and Geography, Oxford University.

1989   Souls and Selves in Chamula: A Thought on Individualism, Fatalism, and Denial. In *Ethnographic Encounters in Southern Mesoamerica: Essays in Honor of Evon Zartman Vogt, Jr.*, ed. V. Bricker and G. Gossen. Studies on Culture and Society, vol. 3. Albany: Institute for Mesoamerican Studies, State University of New York.

Lomnitz, L.

1969   Patterns of Alcohol Consumption among the Mapuche. *Human Organization* 28 (4): 287–295.

Loyola, Luis

1988   The Use of Alcohol among Indians and Ladinos in Chiapas, Mexico. In *Drugs in Latin America*, ed. Edmundo Morales, 125–148. Studies in Third World Societies, no. 37. Williamsburg, Va.: Department of Anthropology, College of William and Mary.

MacAndrew, Craig, and Robert B. Edgerton

1969   *Drunken Comportment: A Social Explanation.* Chicago: Aldine Publishing Company.

MacCormack, C., and M. Strathern

1980   *Nature, Culture and Gender.* Cambridge: Cambridge University Press.

MacEoin, Gary

1995   *The People's Church: Bishop Samuel Ruiz of Mexico and Why He Matters.* New York: Crossroad Publishing Company.

MacLeod, Murdo

1973   *Spanish Central America: A Socioeconomic History, 1520–1720.* Berkeley: University of California Press.

1989   Dominican Explanations for Revolts and Their Suppression in Colonial Chiapas, 1545–1715. In *Indian-Religious Relations in Colonial Spanish America*, ed. Susan E. Ramírez, 39–53. Foreign and Comparative Studies/Latin American Series 9. Syracuse, N.Y.: Maxwell School of Citizenship and Public Affairs, Syracuse University.

Malinowski, Bronislaw

1961　*Argonauts of the Western Pacific.* New York: E. P. Dutton and Co.

Marcus, George, and Michael Fischer

1986　*Anthropology as Cultural Critique.* Chicago: University of Chicago Press.

Marín, Carlos

1998a　"Plan del ejército en Chiapas, desde 1994: Crear bandas paramilitares, desplazar a la población, destruir las bases de apoyo del EZLN." *Proceso* 1105 (January 4): 6–11.

1998b "Acteal, 22 de diciembre." *Proceso* 1113 (March 1): 6–11.

Marsh, Jeanne, Mary Ellen Colten, and M. Belinda Tucker

1982　Women's Use of Drugs and Alcohol: New Perspectives. *Journal of Social Issues* 38 (2): 1–8.

Marshall, Mac

1979　*Weekend Warriors: Alcohol in a Micronesian Culture.* World Ethnology Series. Palo Alto, Calif.: Mayfield Publishing Company.

1991　"Problem Deflation" and the Ethnographic Record: Interpretation and Introspection in Anthropological Studies of Alcohol. *Journal of Substance Abuse* 2:353–367.

Marshall, Mac, and Leslie B. Marshall

1990　*Silent Voices Speak: Women and Prohibition in Truk.* Belmont, Calif.: Wadsworth Publishing Co.

Mascia-Lees, Frances E., Patricia Sharpe, and Colleen Ballerino Cohen

1989　The Postmodernist Turn in Anthropology: Cautions from a Feminist Perspective. *Signs* 15 (11): 7–33.

Mathews, Holly H.

1985　"We Are Mayordomo": A Reinterpretation of Women's Roles in the Mexican Cargo System. *American Ethnologist* 17:285–301.

Maurer, Eugenio

1983　*Los Tseltales: Paganos o Cristianos? Su religion: sincretismo o síntesis?* Mexico City: Centro de Estudios Educativos, A.C.

Mauss, Marcel

1954　*The Gift.* Translated by I. Cunnison. London: Cohen and West.

Maynard, Eileen

1963　The Women of Palin: A Comparative Study of Indian and Ladino Women in a Guatemalan Village. Ph.D. diss., Cornell University.

McGreevy, Carol-Jean

1983　Discourse Styles: Tzotzil Greetings as Ethnic Markers. Paper presented at 22d Conference on American Indian Languages, American Anthropological Association Meetings, Chicago.

Mead, Margaret

1949　*Sex and Temperament in Three Primitive Societies.* New York: Dell Publishing Company.

Medicine, Beatrice A.
1983   An Ethnography of Drinking and Sobriety among the Lakota Sioux. Ph.D. diss., University of Wisconsin, Madison.

Menéndez, Eduardo, ed.
1992   Prácticas e ideologías "científicas" y "populares" respecta del "alcoholismo" en México. México: Centro de Investigaciones y Estudios Superiores en Antropología Social.

México, Viceroyalty. Laws, statutes, etc.
1736   Bebidas prohibidas, 1736–1755. In *The Ayer Collection*, Newberry Library, Chicago.
1853–1856   Bebidas prohibidas. In *Diccionario universal de historia y de geografía*. Apendice I: 354–362. Mexico: Rafael.

Modiano, Nancy
1973   Indian Education in the Chiapas Highlands. New York: Holt, Rinehart and Winston.

Mora, Juana, and M. Jean Gilbert
1991   Issues for Latinas: Mexican American Women. In *Alcohol and Drugs Are Women's Issues*, vol. 1, *A Review of the Issues*, ed. P. Roth, 43–47. Metuchen, N.J.: Women's Action Alliance and Scarecrow Press.

Morgan, Patricia
1987   Women and Alcohol: The Disinhibition Rhetoric in an Analysis of Domination. *Journal of Psychoactive Drugs* 19 (2): 129–133.

Morris, Walter F.
1987   *Symbolism of a Ceremonial Huipil of the Highland Tzotzil Maya Community of Magdalenas, Chiapas*. Notes of the New World Archaeological Foundation, no. 4. Provo, Utah: New World Archaeological Foundation, Brigham Young University.
1988   *The Living Maya*. New York: Harry N. Abrams.

Nash, June
1967   The Logic of Behavior: Curing in a Maya Indian Town. *Human Organization* 26 (3): 132.
1973   The Betrothal: A Study of Ideology and Behavior in a Maya Indian Community. In *Drinking Patterns in Highland Chiapas*, ed. H. Siverts. Bergen: The Norwegian Research Council for Science and the Humanities.
1978   The Aztecs and the Ideology of Male Dominance. *Signs* 4 (21): 349–362.
1980   Aztec Women: The Transition from Status to Class in Empire and Colony. In *Women and Colonization: Anthropological Perspectives*, ed. Eleanor Leacock and Mona Etienne, 134–148. New York: Praeger.
1985   *In the Eyes of the Ancestors: Belief and Behavior in a Maya Community*. Prospect Heights, Ill.: Waveland Press.
1993   Maya Household Production in the Modern World. In *Crafts in the World*

Market: The Impact of Global Exchange on Middle American Artisans, ed. June Nash, 1–24. Albany: State University of New York Press.

1995 "The Reassertion of Indigenous Identity: Mayan Responses to State Intervention in Chiapas." *Latin American Research Review* 30 (3): 7–41.

National Institute on Alcohol Abuse and Alcoholism (NIAAA)

1990 *Alcohol and Women.* Alcohol Alert no. 10. PH 290. Rockville, Md.: Public Health Service.

Navarette-Pellicer, Sergio

1988 *El flor de aguardiente: El aguardiente en una comunidad maya de los altos de Chiapas.* México: Instituto Nacional de Antropología e Historia, Colección Regional de México.

Nero, Karen L.

1990 The Hidden Pain: Drunkenness and Domestic Violence in Palau. *Pacific Studies* 13 (3): 63–92.

Nueva Antropología

1988 Introduction. 10 (34): 3–9.

O'Brian, Robin

1994 The Peso and the Loom: The Political Economy of Maya Women's Work in Highland Chiapas. Ph.D. diss., University of California at Los Angeles.

1997 "Maya Market Women's Sales Strategies in a Stationary Artisan Market and Response to Changing Gender Relations in Highland Chiapas, Mexico." East Lansing, MI: Center for Women in International Development Working Papers Series #261, Michigan State University.

Ontario Native Women's Association (ONWA)

1989 *Breaking Free: A Proposal to Change Aboriginal Family Violence.* Thunder Bay, Ontario: ONWA.

Ortíz, Teresa

2000 "Never again a World without Us: Testimonies from Maya Zapatista Communities in Rebellion." Unpublished manuscript.

Ortner, Sherry, and Harriet Whitehead, eds.

1981 *The Cultural Construction of Gender and Sexuality.* Cambridge: Cambridge University Press.

Paredes, Alfonso

1975 Social Control of Drinking among the Aztec Indians of Mesoamerica. *Quarterly Journal of Studies on Alcohol* 36 (9): 1139–1153.

Pérez Pérez, Elias

1991 La educacíon oficial y religiosa en una comunidad Tsotsil, Chimtic, Chiapas: Contrastes y continuidades. Master's thesis, Universidad Pedagógica Nacional, San Cristóbal de Las Casas.

Pérez Tzu, Mariáno

1995 "Los primeros meses de los zapatistas: Una crónica tzotzil en siete escenas." *Ojarasca* 40–41: 13–16.

1999 "Conversaciones interrumpidas: Las voces indigenas del mercado de San Cristóbal." In *Democracia en tierras mayas: Las elecciones de 1991–1998 en los Altos de Chiapas*, ed. J. P. Viqueira and W. Sonnleitner. Mexico, DF: Colmex. Translated by Jan Rus.

Pozas, Ricardo
1959 *Chamula: Un pueblo indio de los Altos de Chiapas*. 2 vols. Memorias del Instituto Nacional Indigenista, no. 8. Mexico City: Instituto Nacional Indigenista.
1962 *Juan, the Chamula: An Ethnological Recreation of the Life of a Mexican Indian*. Berkeley: University of California Press.

Proskouriakoff, Tatiana
1961 Portraits of Women in Maya Art. In *Essays in Precolumbian Art and Archaeology*, ed. S. K. Lothrop et al., 81–99. Cambridge: Harvard University.

Rapp, Rayna
1979 Review Essay: Anthropology. *Signs* 4 (3): 497–513.

Read, Kenneth
1965 *The High Valley*. New York: Charles Scribners and Sons.

Redfield, Robert, and Alfonso Villa Rojas
1941 *Chan Kom: A Maya Village*. Publication 488 of the Carnegie Institute of Washington. Washington, D.C.

Research Institute on Alcoholism
1991 Getting the Word Out. *Research Institute on Alcoholism Report* 5 (1): 1.

Rogers, Julia Ellen
1905 *The Tree Book: A Popular Guide to a Knowledge of the Trees of North America and to Their Uses and Cultivation*. New York: Doubleday, Page & Co.

Rojas, Rosa, ed.
1996 *Chiapas: Y las mujeres qué?* Mexico City: Ediciones La Correa Feminista.

Room, Robin
1984 Alcohol and Ethnography: A Case of Problem Deflation? *Current Anthropology* 25 (2): 169–191.

Rosaldo, Michelle
1974 Woman, Culture and Society: A Theoretical Overview. In *Woman, Culture and Society*, ed. Michelle Rosaldo and Louise Lamphere, 17–43. Stanford: Stanford University Press.
1980 The Use and Abuse of Anthropology: Reflections on Feminism and Cross-Cultural Understanding. *Signs* 8: 389–417.

Rosaldo, Michelle, and Louise Lamphere, eds.
1974 *Woman, Culture and Society*. Stanford: Stanford University Press.

Rosenbaum, Brenda P.
1993 *With Our Heads Bowed: The Dynamics of Gender in a Maya Community*. Albany: Institute for Mesoamerican Studies, State University of New York.

1996 Women and Gender. In *The Legacy of Mesoamerica,* ed. Robert Carmack, Janine Gasco, and Gary Gossen, 321–352. Englewood Cliffs, N.J.: Prentice Hall.

Rosenbaum, Brenda P., and Christine Eber
1992 Trayendo el margen al centro: Mujer y género en Mesoamérica. *Mesoamérica* 23:xv–xxv.

Rothstein, Frances
1983 Women and Men in the Family Economy. *Anthropological Quarterly* 5:10–23.

Rovira, Guiomar
1997 *Mujeres de maíz: La voz de las indígenas de Chiapas y la rebelión Zapatista.* Barcelona: Ediciones La Lletra SCCL.

Roys, Ralph L.
1931 *The Ethno-Botany of the Maya.* New Orleans: Middle American Research Institute, Tulane University.

Ruby, Jay, and Barbara Myerhoff, eds.
1982 *A Crack in the Mirror: Reflexive Perspectives in Anthropology.* Philadelphia: University of Pennsylvania Press.

Rus, Diane
1990 *La crisis económica y la mujer indígena: El caso de Chamula, Chiapas.* San Cristóbal de Las Casas: Instituto de Asesoría Antropológica para la Región Maya, A.C.

Rus, Jan
1989 The "Caste War" of 1869 from the Indian's Perspective: A Challenge for Ethnohistory. In *Memorias del Segundo Coloquio Internacional de Mayistas,* vol. 2, 1033–1047. Mexico City: Universidad Nacional Autónoma de México.
1994 The "Comunidad Revolucionaria Institucional": The Subversion of Native Government in Highland Chiapas, 1936–1968. In *Everyday Forms of State Formation: Revolution and the Negotiation of Rule in Modern Mexico,* ed. Gilbert Joseph and Daniel Nugent, 19–40. Chapel Hill: Duke University Press, forthcoming.
1995 "Local Adaptation to Global Change: The Reordering of Native Society in Highland Chiapas, Mexico, 1974–1994." *European Review of Latin American and Caribbean Studies* 58 (June): 71–89.

Rus, Jan, Rosalva Aída Hernández Castillo, and Shannan Mattiace
n.d. *Taking the Future into Our Own Hands: The Impact of the Uprising in Chiapas Four Years After.* Unpublished manuscript.

Rus, Jan, and Robert Wasserstrom
1980 Civil-Religious Hierarchies in Central Chiapas: A Critical Perspective. *American Ethnologist* 7 (3): 466–478.

Safa, Helen
1988 Gender and Social Science Concepts in Latin America. Paper prepared

for XIV International Congress of the Latin American Studies Association, New Orleans.

Sahagún, Bernardino de

1982 *Florentine Codex: General History of the Things of New Spain.* Translated by Arthur J. O. Anderson and Charles E. Dibble. Salt Lake City: University of Utah Press.

San Cristóbal, Asuntos Civiles

1796–1811 Archivo histórico de la catedral de San Cristóbal de Las Casas. San Cristóbal de Las Casas, Chiapas, Mexico.

Schaef, Anne Wilson

1987 *When Society Becomes an Addict.* San Francisco: Harper and Row.

Schele, Linda, and Mary Ellen Miller

1986 *The Blood of Kings: Dynasty and Ritual in Maya Art.* New York: George Braziller.

Scott, James

1990 *Domination and the Arts of Resistance: Hidden Transcripts.* New Haven: Yale University Press.

Shkilnyk, Anastasia

1985 *A Poison Stronger than Love: The Destruction of an Ojibwa Community.* New Haven: Yale University Press.

Silverblatt, Irene

1987 *Sun, Moon and Witches: Gender Ideologies and Class in Inca and Colonial Peru.* Princeton, N.J.: Princeton University Press.

Siskel, Suzanne E.

1974 With the Spirit of a Jaguar: A Study of Shamanism in 'Incinton, Chamula. A.B. honors thesis, Radcliffe College.

Siverts, Henning, ed.

1973 *Drinking Patterns in Highland Chiapas.* Bergen: Universitetsforlaget.

Solache-Alcaraz, Graciela, R. Tapia-Conyer, G. Leon, F. Lazcano, V. Borja, and J. Sepulveda

1990 Encuesta Nacional de Salud: El consumo de bebidas alcohólicas. *Salud Mental* 13 (3): 13–19.

Speed, Shannon

n.d. "Actions Speak Louder than Words: Indigenous Women and Gendered Resistance in the Wake of Acteal." Unpublished manuscript.

Stephen, Lynn

1991 *Zapotec Women.* Austin: University of Texas Press.

1996 "Democracy for Whom? Women's Grassroots Political Activism in the 1990s, Mexico City and Chiapas." In *Neoliberalism Revisited: Economic Restructuring and Mexico's Political Future,* ed. Gerardo Otero, 167–186. Boulder: Westview Press.

Stross, Brian

1977 *Love in the Armpit, Tzeltal Tales of Love, Murder and Cannibalism: Modern*

Folk Tales from a Tzeltal Maya Town of Tenejapa, Chiapas. Columbia, Mo.: Museum of Anthropology, University of Missouri.

Sullivan, Kathleen
1992 Protagonists of Change. *Cultural Survival* 16 (4): 38–40.

Tanski, Janet, and Christine Eber
n.d.a "Confronting Globalization in Mexico: Insights from Feminist Theory and Indigenous Women's Experiences." Unpublished manuscript.
n.d.b "Obstacles to Women's Grassroots Economic Initiatives in Highland Chiapas." Forthcoming in *The Review of Radical Political Economics.*

Taylor, William B.
1979 *Drinking, Homicide and Rebellion in Colonial Mexican Villages.* Stanford: Stanford University Press.

Tedlock, Barbara
1986 A Phenomenological Approach to Religious Change in Highland Guatemala. In *Heritage of Conquest: Thirty Years Later,* ed. C. Kendall, J. Hawkins, and L. Bossen, 235–246. Albuquerque: University of New Mexico Press.
1987 An Interpretive Solution to the Problem of Humoral Medicine in Latin America. *Social Science and Medicine* 24 (12): 1069–1083.

Tedlock, Dennis, trans.
1985 *Popul Vuh: A Mayan Book of the Dawn of Life.* New York: Simon and Schuster.

Thompson, Donald E.
1954 Maya Paganism and Christianity: A History of the Fusion of Two Religions. In *Nativism and Syncretism,* 5–35. Tulane University, Middle American Research Institute. Publication no. 19. New Orleans.

Thompson, J. Eric S.
1954 *The Rise and Fall of Maya Civilization.* Norman: University of Oklahoma Press.
1970 *Maya History and Religion.* Norman: University of Oklahoma Press.
1972 *A Commentary on the Dresden Codex: A Maya Hieroglyphic Book.* Memoirs of the American Philosophical Society, no. 93. Philadelphia: American Philosophical Society.

Tozzer, Alfred M.
1907 *A Comparative Study of the Mayas and the Lacandones.* New York: Published for the Archaeological Institute of America by the Macmillan Co.

Traven, Bruno
1971 *The March to the Montería.* New York: Hill and Wang.

Trens, Manuel B.
1957 *Historia de Chiapas.* Vol. 1, *Chiapas Precolonial.* México: Talleres Gráficos de la Nación.

Underhill, Ruth
1936 *The Autobiography of a Papago Woman.* American Anthropological Association, Memoir no. 46.

Van Den Berg, Nan
1991   Having Bitten the Apple: A Feminist Perspective on Addictions. In *Feminist Perspectives on Addictions,* ed. Nan Van Den Berg, 3–30. New York: Springer Publishing Company.

Vogt, Evon Z.
1969   *Zinacantán: A Maya Community in the Highlands of Chiapas.* Cambridge: Harvard University Press, Belknap Press.
1985   The Chiapas Writers' Cooperative. *Cultural Survival* 9 (3): 46–48.

Wali, Alaka
1974   Dependence and Dominance: The Status of Women in Zinacantán. A.B. honors thesis, Radcliffe College.

Wasserstrom, Robert
1983   *Class and Society in Central Chiapas.* Berkeley: University of California Press.

Watanabe, John
1992   *Maya Saints and Souls in a Changing World.* Austin: University of Texas Press.

Weber, Max
1958   *The Protestant Ethic and the Spirit of Capitalism.* New York: Charles Scribner's Sons.

Weiner, Annette B.
1976   *Women of Value, Men of Renown: New Perspectives on Trobriand Exchange.* Austin: University of Texas Press.

Wilsnack, R., S. Wilsnack, and A. D. Klassen
1984   Women's Drinking and Drinking Problems: Patterns from a 1981 National Survey. *American Journal of Public Health* 74 (11): 1231–1238.

Wilsnack, Sharon C.
1984   *Alcohol Problems in Women: Antecedents, Consequences and Intervention.* New York: Guilford Press.

Wilsnack, S. C., R. W. Wilsnack, and A. D. Klassen
1986   Epidemiological Research on Women's Drinking, 1978–1989. In *Women and Alcohol: Health Related Issues,* 1–68. NIAAA Research Monograph No. 16, DHHS Pub. No. (ADM) 86–1139. Washington, D.C.: Superintendent of Documents, U.S. Government Printing Office.

Wilson, Carter
1966   *Crazy February.* New York: J. B. Lippincott Co.
1973   Expressions of Personal Relations through Drinking. In *Drinking Patterns in Highland Chiapas,* ed. H. Siverts, 121–146. Bergen: Universitetsforlaget.

Wolin, Steven, and Linda Bennett
1984   Family Rituals. *Family Process* 23:401–420.

Young, Kate
1982   Creation of a Relative Surplus Population: A Case Study from Mexico.

In *Women and Development: The Sexual Division of Labor in Rural Societies,* ed. L. Benería, 149–178. New York: Praeger.

Zorita, Alonzo de
1971   *The Brief Summary Relation of the Lords of New Spain.* Translated and with an introduction by Benjamin Keen. New Brunswick: Rutgers University Press.

Index

abstinence (see also *la acción*), 34, 93, 94–95, 257–258

abuse (*see also* drinking, and violence; sexual abuse; violence; violence, toward Indigenous women): as cause of illness, 112, 113, 120, 175, 202; toward children, 112, 113, 120, 202; toward single women, 199, 242; support for victims of, 77, 206, 238; toward women, xxi, xxii, 120–122, 125, 126, 127, 130, 135, 175, 196, 197, 200–205, 279n.6

la acción (the action): defined, 272n.7; in ritual drinking, 93, 94, 96, 272n.7, 274n.10; as strategy to limit drinking, 54, 94, 118, 159, 257

Acción Católica. *See* Catholic Action

Acteal, 250, 256, 280n.8

Adams, Abigail E., 277n.15

Adams, R. H., 275n.1

addiction (*see also* alcoholism; compulsive drinking; problem drinking), 172

age: and heat, 191; respect for, 67, 75, 78, 139; and women's drinking, 93, 94, 191

aging and women, 77, 78, 139

aguardiente. *See* rum

aire, 62

ak'bil ch'ulelal, 160, 161

Alanon, 13; mentioned, 138, 181

alcohol: gender differences in production of, 7, 8; societal functions of, 7

Alcoholics Anonymous (AA), 9, 13, 58, 124, 138, 148, 259, 264–265

alcoholism (*see also* problem drinking), 7, 9, 148, 238, 275n.7; treatment of, 6, 9, 10, 269n.5

alcohol sales. *See* rum sales

alcohol use (*see also* chicha; drinking; problem drinking; ritual drinking; rum): gender differences in, 7–9, 23, 139; laws controlling, 21, 23, 30, 31

Alkali Lake Band, 269n.5

Amatenango, 34, 37 (map), 239, 270n.3, 272n.4, 267n.5

anger: and problem drinking, 147, 167, 188; and envy, 188; and heat, 275n.3; and illness, 167, 275n.3; "letting go of," 274n.6; Pedrano and AA ideas of, 274n.6; vented in song-prayers, 48, 144

animals: in dreams, 62, 71, 159, 178, 181; and ideas about illness, 62, 152, 157, 182; as spirit companions of drunkards, 275n.2; as spirit companions of people, (*vayhel*), 156, 157; as spirit companions of shamans, 155, 275n.2; as spirit companions of witches (*nagual*), 152, 157, 182–183

anjel (male force in Earth), 105

Arias, Jacinto, xii, 7, 65, 73, 202, 271n.2, 272n.1

Arias, Manuel, xii, 29, 33, 36, 60, 275n.3, 276n.12

Arias, Tomás, 28–29

atole, xxiii; economic benefits of selling, 196; mentioned, 102, 162, 183, 199, 204, 216

authority: and heat, 191

ance of, in form of lakes, 209–212; appearance of, to Juan Diego, 25; as comforter of Indigenous women, 26, 115–117, 123, 143; as defender of traditions, 123, 143, 211; in dreams to control or quit drinking, 115–117, 207, 211–212; and ethnic identity, 186; as female aspect of *totil me'il*, 210; and gifts of rum in dreams, 143; invoked in prayers and song-prayers, 131, 156, 164, 166, 170, 174, 176, 179, 180; and Moon, 23, 24, 66, 263; and mother/daughter relationship, 143; and revitalization movements, 26–27, 207, 236; and thirst for rum, 123; and Tonantzin, 25; and women's relegation to domestic sphere, 240; and water, 23–24, 236
Vogt, Evon Z., 7
vokaroil (gift of rum), 92

Wali, Alaka, 8
Wasserstrom, Robert, 19, 217
Watanabe, John, 277–278n.4
water (*see also* Moon; Virgin Mary), 23–25, 236; and being a Zapatista, 257
weaning, 74–75
Weathers, Kenneth, 266, 267
weaving, 5, 69–70, 78, 80, 237–238, 243, 259, 260, 273n.8
Weber, Max, 277n.4
Weiner, Annette, 10, 105
Whitehead, Harriet, 5
Wilson, Carter, 7, 8, 274n.1
witchcraft, 152, 155, 183, 275n.1; and antisocial behavior, 35; and heavy drinking, 152, 190; and Holy Cross, 184; and illness, 156, 275n.1; and rum, 34, 35, 129, 190; relation of, to shamanic healing, 184, 190; techniques of, 275n.1; mentioned, 183, 184, 190, 191
witches, 152, 157, 178, 181, 275nn.1,4
Wolin, Steven, 273n.8

women, symbolic associations with: and authority to speak out in public, 235–237
women's experiences, diversity of conceptual frameworks on, 3–4
women's genitals as threat to men's power, 84, 273n.1
women's ritual service, ethnographers' analyses of, 10, 105, 274n.11
women's temperance movements, 278n.3
"word of God," xvii, 215, 220, 253
work: as burden to Pedranas, 68, 253–255; and cash economy, 69–70, 251, 253, 255, 260; and children, 72–73, 253; colonial Mexicans' ideas of, 22; gendered division of, 67–70; and interdependence between kinswomen, xxiii, 55, 64, 193; on plantations, 55, 69, 78, 79, 80, 122, 169, 272n.2; as source of women's self-esteem, xxiii, 67, 68, 104–105, 136–137; traditional Pedrano ideas about, xxiii, 67–68; and value of women's, 67, 251, 260; and women's cargo service, xxiii, 104, 254
World Tree, 23–25, 66, 257, 263

xob, 105
xiel (fright), 74
xpak'in te, 271n.4
xtabai, 270n.4

Yav Teklum, 231, 233
Yucatec Maya, 19

Zapatista National Liberation Army, 252, 271n.11, 278n.1; and alcohol use, 252, 257–260 passim; and autonomy, 256; and support bases, 254–256 passim; and Women's Law, 254, 280n.5
Zinacantán, 13, 36, 37 (map), 69, 230, 271n.1, 272n.5; mentioned, 42, 237
Zorita, Alonzo de, 19, 270n.1

Index of Major Characters

CPSIA information can be obtained at www.ICGtesting.com
Printed in the USA
BVOW070916090712

294607BV00002B/3/P